T0074987

Cybercrime Investigations

Cybercrime Investigations

A Comprehensive Resource for Everyone

John Bandler
Antonia Merzon

CRC Press
Taylor & Francis Group
Boca Raton London New York

CRC Press is an imprint of the
Taylor & Francis Group, an **informa** business

First edition published 2020
by CRC Press
6000 Broken Sound Parkway NW, Suite 300, Boca Raton, FL 33487-2742

and by CRC Press
2 Park Square, Milton Park, Abingdon, Oxon, OX14 4RN

First issued in paperback 2022

ISBN 13: 978-1-03-239998-0 (pbk)
ISBN 13: 978-0-367-19623-3 (hbk)
ISBN 13: 978-1-003-03352-3 (ebk)

DOI: 10.1201/9781003033523

Library of Congress Cataloging-in-Publication Data

Library of Congress Cataloging-in-Publication Data

Names: Bandler, John, author. | Merzon, Antonia, author.
Title: Cybercrime investigations : the comprehensive resource for everyone / by John Bandler
and Antonia Merzon.
Description: First edition. | Boca Raton, FL : CRC Press/ Taylor & Francis Group, 2020. | Includes bibliographical references and index. | Summary: "Cybercrime continues to skyrocket but we are not combatting it effectively yet. We need more cybercrime investigators from all backgrounds and working in every sector to conduct effective investigations. This book is a comprehensive resource for everyone who encounters and investigates cybercrime, no matter their title, including those working on behalf of law enforcement, private organizations, regulatory agencies, or individual victims. It provides helpful background material about cybercrime's technological and legal underpinnings, plus in-depth detail about the legal and practical aspects of conducting cybercrime investigations. Key features of this book include : Understanding cybercrime, computers, forensics, and cybersecurity, law for the cybercrime investigator, including cybercrime offenses ; cyber evidence-gathering ; criminal, private and regulatory law, and nation-state implications ; cybercrime investigation from three key perspectives : law enforcement, private sector, and regulatory ; financial investigation ; identification (attribution) of cyber-conduct ; apprehension ; litigation in the criminal and civil arenas. This far-reaching book is an essential reference for prosecutors and law enforcement officers, agents and analysts ; as well as for private sector lawyers, consultants, information security professionals, digital forensic examiners, and more. It also functions as an excellent course book for educators and trainers. We need more investigators who know how to fight cybercrime, and this book was written to achieve that goal. Authored by two former cybercrime prosecutors with a diverse array of expertise in criminal justice and the private sector, this book is informative, practical, and readable, with innovative methods and fascinating anecdotes throughout"— Provided by publisher.
Identifiers: LCCN 2020000272 | ISBN 9780367196233 (hardback) | ISBN 9781003033523 (ebook)
Subjects: LCSH: Computer crimes–Investigation.
Classification: LCC HV8079.C65 B36 2020 | DDC 363.25/968–dc23
LC record available at https://lccn.loc.gov/2020000272

Visit the Taylor & Francis Web site at
http://www.taylorandfrancis.com

and the CRC Press Web site at
http://www.crcpress.com

Dedication

To all cybercrime investigators, past, present, and future, whose diligent and professional work keeps us safe.
J.B. and A.M.

To my wife, children, and parents.
J.B.

To my wonderful family.
A.M.

Contents

PART II   Law for the Cybercrime Investigator   63

PART IV   *Litigation*   293

About the Authors

John Bandler and **Antonia Merzon** served together as Assistant District Attorneys at the New York County District Attorney's Office (DANY), hired by the legendary Robert Morgenthau. They investigated and prosecuted a wide variety of criminal offenses, ranging from those that garnered headlines to the many that received little attention but were equally essential for the administration of justice and protection of the public. Antonia founded and led the Identity Theft Unit (since renamed the Cybercrime and Identity Theft Bureau), recruiting John as an early member. The unit's work quickly revealed the close connection between identity theft and cybercrime, and brought amazing cases, including the Western Express case, which you will read about. As Unit Chief, Antonia supervised the work of hundreds of prosecutors and thousands of investigations, guiding and developing both people and cases. This fledgling unit with scarce resources did terrific work in a new and evolving area of crime. Eventually, their service at DANY came to an end, and they share their expertise now as lawyers and consultants in a variety of areas.

Their experiences during and after DANY are what convinced them to write this book together.

John Bandler runs a law firm and a consulting practice that helps organizations and individuals with cybersecurity, cybercrime investigations, and anti-money laundering efforts among other areas. Before becoming a prosecutor, he served as a State Trooper in the New York State Police for eight years, assigned to one of the state's busiest stations that provided full police services to the local community. While serving in the State Police he attended law school at night at Pace University School of Law, and upon graduating he went to work for Mr. Morgenthau. Since leaving government service he has represented a range of clients, from individuals to banks, on many issues ranging from cybersecurity, privacy, anti-fraud, and threats. John is admitted to the bars of New York, Connecticut, and Washington D.C., holds a number of certifications, and writes, lectures, and teaches on law, cybersecurity, cybercrime, and more.

Antonia Merzon provides legal and consulting expertise related to security, investigations, and law enforcement, especially as they intersect with the worlds of law, technology, privacy, and fraud. She graduated from Fordham University School of Law and then was hired by Mr. Morgenthau. During her time at DANY, she built the new Identity Theft Unit that investigated and prosecuted cybercrime and virtual currency money laundering – before these areas were in the public awareness – and developed the unit's digital forensic and investigative capacity. Cybercrime and traditional investigations are among her specialties, including developing best practices. She also is an expert on a diverse array of investigation and litigation best practices for law enforcement, including the use of body-worn cameras, eyewitness identification, and the electronic recording of custodial interrogations.

John and Antonia can be contacted through their book website:
CybercrimeInvestigationsBook.com

Mail can be directed to:
John Bandler
Antonia Merzon
c/o Bandler Law Firm PLLC
Bandler Group LLC
48 Wall Street, 11th Floor
New York, NY, 10005

Acknowledgments

There are many people who made this book possible and contributed to it.

Tracy Suhr provided invaluable and detailed assistance in all the areas of the book, including cybercrime, law, investigations, and editing and grammar. This book is vastly improved thanks to her. We had the privilege to work with her at DANY, where she rose to become Deputy Bureau Chief of the Cybercrime and Identity Theft Bureau.

Rob Bandler, John's cousin, former Deputy Director of IT Security at Cornell University and career IT professional, made the book better from start to finish, providing valuable assistance throughout on both subject matter and editing.

Christopher Jones gave extensive help throughout as well.

Many others also helped with this book, reading chapters, providing valuable feedback, and bringing diverse expertise in areas that included cybersecurity, cybercrime, law, business, and editing. They include: William Darrow, Robert Barnsby, Preston Miller, J-Michael Roberts, Bret Rubin, Stephen Hines, Joshua Larocca, Elizabeth Roper, Nicolette Endara-Popovitch, and Stephen Moccia.

We have worked a lot of great investigations and cybercrime cases, including one you will read about in this book, and we learned a lot along the way. None of that – and none of this book – could have been possible without the many dedicated professionals with whom we worked. Thank you to the paralegals, analysts, police officers, detectives, investigators, special agents, prosecutors, victims, private sector investigators, and corporations who helped us become better investigators.

Special thanks to Charles D. Tansey whose magnificent cartoon characters grace our diagrams. Art is but one of his many talents, and we are grateful for the chance to use his work in this book.

Finally, none of this would be possible or worthwhile without the support of our families, and our deepest thanks go to them.

John Bandler
New York, NY

Antonia Merzon,
Boulder, Colorado
April, 2020

Part I

Understanding Cybercrime, Computers, and Cybersecurity

1 Introduction
The Need for Good Cybercrime Investigators

This chapter (and book) is for:

- You
- Law enforcement of all types: police, investigators, agents, prosecutors, analysts
- Those in the private sector investigating or dealing with cybercrime
- Regulators
- The technically skilled and those who are not
- Beginning cyber investigators, intermediate, and even experienced looking for a comprehensive view
- Lawyers and non-lawyers.

At the start of each chapter, we will identify the type of cybercrime investigator for whom that chapter is primarily intended. Cybercrime investigators do not just have the title of "investigator". They come from many jobs and backgrounds – lawyers and non-lawyers; technical experts and technical beginners; experienced traditional investigators who are learning about cybercrime, and investigators whose only experience is with cybercrime; law enforcement agents, industry regulators, and members of the private sector; and students and trainees just starting out. Given this diversity of backgrounds, we recognize that some readers might read the book straight through, and some might skip chapters because they are working on a time-sensitive matter, or because existing skill sets make certain chapters less critical. That said, we think you will get something out of every chapter.

1.1 WHY THIS BOOK

Let us start with three fundamental truths about investigating cybercrime:

1. *We all can investigate cybercrime.* Cybercriminals are running amok online partly because of the misconception that only specialized investigators with vast technological resources can work these cases. Tech skills and gadgets are great to have, but they are, by no means, a requirement for handling a cyber investigation.

2. *Cybercrime can be solved*. Just because it is a cybercrime, doesn't mean it is hard to solve. Cybercriminals – like every type of criminal – run the gamut, from low-level scammers to highly sophisticated organizations. They are not all tech-wizards. They are not all hard to find.
3. *Even the most sophisticated cybercriminals can be caught*.

Bottom line: the common preconception that cybercrime is too difficult to investigate is wrong. Every case can and should be investigated. Every investigator can take positive steps to solve a case. Instead of looking at a cyber incident and assuming there is not much that can be done, we can use these core truths about cybercrime to frame a plan of action.

Cybercrime is a relatively new phenomenon. Malicious actors no longer need to be in the immediate vicinity of their victims, but can attack and steal remotely, even from abroad. The reach of the Internet means cybercrime is a safety and security problem for every community, industry, business, and law enforcement agency – large or small.

Investigating cybercrime is an even newer endeavor than cybercrime itself, and because it involves technology, it can seem daunting to many investigators and victims. How do you start investigating when one of these incidents happens? How do you figure out who did it when the perpetrator is hiding online? What do you do with a crime that seems to lead across the country, let alone around the world?

When we first started working on cybercrime cases as prosecutors, we had the same questions. We did not come to this work from a tech background, and we often had minimal resources available. But through time, effort, and creativity we learned how to find the answers. We learned that cybercrime can be investigated, offenders can be found, and cases can be successfully prosecuted.

We wrote this book to share this knowledge with you, and to inspire more people to become cybercrime investigators – especially those who might think cybercrime is too challenging to take on.

We understand that, in some places, law enforcement and private security lack experience, training, and resources when it comes to cybercrime. That is another reason we wrote this book. We want to give any interested investigator the knowledge and tools to handle these cases. As cybercrime continues to grow, we need more investigators on the frontlines ready, willing and able to take it on. There are concrete steps that every investigator can take to tackle cybercrime. This book is designed to make these steps understandable and doable for investigators everywhere.

Why is it so important to bolster the investigative response to cybercrime? Let's look at some of the major repercussions of cybercrime in today's world.

- *Profit and Losses*. Cybercrime is immensely profitable for cybercriminals, but immensely costly to the rest of us. Each year, U.S. businesses and consumers lose billions of dollars through cybercrime while the criminal and private investigation of these events remains completely inadequate. It is astonishing to consider that billions of dollars can be stolen annually without proper investigation or redress.
- *Terrorism and Espionage*. The profitable and disruptive nature of cybercrime means it is an activity of interest for terrorists and nation-states seeking income, intelligence, or simply a new way to inflict harm. The Internet provides a gateway and a network for all manner of nefarious activity at the local, national, and international levels. Our will to investigate this activity must measure up to the threat it presents.
- *New Ways to Move Money*. Cybercriminals have developed innovative money laundering techniques to pay each other and disguise their illicit income. Virtual currencies and cryptocurrencies, international wire transfer schemes, money held and

moved in stored-value cards (like gift cards), criminal proceeds funneled through multiplayer video games – these are some of the methods cybercriminals use, along with more traditional money laundering mechanisms. Once proven successful, these techniques are adopted not just by cyber thieves, but by other criminals looking to conduct illicit transactions, such as child pornographers, narcotics dealers, and terrorists.

- *Stalking, Revenge, and Harassment.* Stealing is not the only form of cybercrime – the Internet is used to commit a wide variety of crimes meant to harass, stalk, menace, or otherwise target specific individuals. The increasingly sophisticated methods used to conduct these crimes are capable of inflicting tremendous, ongoing harm to victims. The scenarios range from teen sexting to cyber-revenge acts directed at employers, intimate partners, and political figures – and often require a response from a combination of law enforcement and private sector investigators.
- *Civil Liability and Regulation.* The scourge of cybercrime has an enormous impact on both our civil law and regulatory systems. When cybercriminals steal funds or data, injured victims may use the civil legal system to seek redress, including for cybersecurity negligence. Government regulators create and enforce rules that deal with the real threats that cybercrime presents to sensitive data and online commerce.

This book discusses all of these topics, and many other pressing issues around cybercrime, in a manner designed to help every kind of investigator find useful information.

1.2   WHO INVESTIGATES CYBERCRIME?

Cybercrime creates many types of victims, and its ripple effects have led to an intense focus on cybersecurity, information security, and privacy. As a result, cybercrime is investigated for a variety of reasons. To provide information in the most effective way throughout this book, we considered the needs and concerns of investigators representing these three important groups:

- *Law Enforcement*

Law enforcement, including police, federal law enforcement, and prosecutors, receive thousands of cybercrime reports every year from individual and corporate victims. When state and local police investigate cybercrimes, along with prosecutors, it is usually because they get the first calls when local residents are victimized. Traditionally, more complex cases are tackled by federal law enforcement agencies (such as the FBI, U.S. Secret Service, and Department of Homeland Security) and federal prosecutors. These agencies use monetary thresholds and other criteria to take on a select number of investigations. Some state Attorney General's offices also handle "bigger" cybercrime cases. A few local District Attorneys' (DA) offices handle significant cybercrime cases, as we did while working at the Manhattan DA's office. But the truth is, the vast majority of cybercrimes go uninvestigated.

One of this book's goals is to change the way investigators look at cyber cases. Historically, investigators have categorized cases too quickly as being "local" or "small", only realizing, after some investigation, that they are really one piece of a larger scheme. Nowadays, all police agencies, whether an enormous department like the New York City Police Department, or a small-town force with fewer than 20 sworn officers, will be called upon to take a cybercrime complaint and conduct an initial investigation – actions that may lead to uncovering larger, additional crimes. Since these investigations normally require prosecutorial assistance, it is essential that prosecutors in local DAs' offices also know how to investigate cybercrime. As we explain in this book, when a "small" case turns out to be part of a big scheme, there are many choices investigators can make about how to proceed – including identifying and collaborating with agencies that have the resources to assist with or take on a broader investigation. Of course, the objective is always to better investigate, identify, and prosecute those responsible for cybercrime.

- *Regulators and State Attorneys General*

Not all investigations of cybercrime are conducted for the purpose of criminal prosecution. Federal regulators and state Attorneys General investigate cybercrime to determine whether consumer protection laws have been violated, or to ensure compliance with industry regulations. These regulatory investigations often focus on specific aspects of cybercrime that fall under the agencies' authority – such as ensuring private sector compliance with cybersecurity, privacy, and data breach notification laws, or taking legal action when companies fail to comply with laws or regulations.

- *Private Sector*

Many cybercrime investigations are undertaken by individuals and businesses who fall victim to cybercrime, then want to know how it happened, who was responsible, and what has to be done to prevent further harm. An increasing number of these investigations are prompted by laws and regulations that require victimized businesses to investigate and report cybercrime, including financial institutions, health care services, and businesses of all sizes.

The goals of a private sector investigation may diverge from those of law enforcement and government regulators. For example, businesses damaged by cybercrime may be concerned about how to apportion legal responsibility among themselves for settlement or insurance purposes. Even when law enforcement conducts an investigation, private entities may investigate as well. At times, private sector resources and access to information can greatly assist law enforcement, providing benefits to both groups.

Private sector investigations might be conducted in-house or might require the hiring of specialized firms or individuals. The decision about who should investigate within the private sector depends upon the size of the organization, circumstances, and resources.

1.3   HOW THIS BOOK IS ORGANIZED

This book is organized into four parts.

Part I: Understanding Cybercrime, Computers, and Cybersecurity
Part II: Law for the Cybercrime Investigator
Part III: The Cybercrime Investigation
Part IV: Litigation: Cybercrime Investigations in Court

In Part I, we present chapters with essential background knowledge for understanding cybercrime. We cover criminal activities that can be called a "cybercrime" – including the most prevalent types of online schemes and who commits them. We also introduce computers, networks, digital forensics, and information security. For those who are concerned they are unqualified to investigate cybercrime because of a lack of such expertise, these chapters are a primer that will help you get up to speed on some of the technological terms and actions that might come up in a cyber investigation.

In Part II, we review the laws and rules about cybercrime and gathering evidence. It is hard to conduct an investigation if you do not know what facts might be relevant and how the legal process might play out. First, we provide an introduction to criminal and civil law. Our intention here is to demystify central legal concepts and explain them in straightforward terms. Next, we look at the criminal statutes defining cybercrime. There is no "crime" in cybercrime unless there is a statute prohibiting an act; thus, an important part of a successful criminal investigation is focusing on the correct criminal charges to pursue. Then, we examine the tools used by law enforcement to find and collect evidence of cybercrimes, while describing the restrictions our legal system imposes to protect privacy and regulate government action. We also discuss the civil and regulatory implications of cybercrime, as government and business face increasing regulatory and security standards for handling cyber threats. Part II includes an overview of cyber actions committed by nation-states or terrorists, recognizing that some investigations may reveal these national cyber threats.

Part III focuses on conducting a cyber investigation. After first looking at the broader objectives and strategies of any cyber investigation, we devote individual chapters to investigations performed within the private sector, by law enforcement, and by regulators. This part also provides in-depth discussion of some of the key investigative methods and stages in a cyber investigation – including the cyclical investigative process, open-source investigation, obtaining records and analyzing them, investigations into financial activity and money laundering, uncovering cybercriminals' true identities, and locating and apprehending suspects once they are identified (within the United States and internationally).

Part IV explains how a cyber investigation plays out in the context of litigation. From the perspectives of both criminal and civil cases, we look at how an investigator's methods and results are presented and dissected in court. Knowing how an investigation might eventually be used in litigation can enable better investigative decision-making.

1.4   KEEPING IT FUN: ANECDOTES, CASES, DIAGRAMS, AND CARTOONS

Throughout the book, we work to keep the material lively and interesting, by using:

A thread case. We give real-life examples of the many investigative topics covered in the book by weaving through the chapters our "thread case", the Western Express case we both prosecuted. The phases and events from this investigation provide real-world examples of how some of these legal and investigative concepts can be applied.

Western Express Example Text Box

The Western Express case involved the indictment, arrest and prosecution of 17 defendants from all around the United States and four other countries. It centered on a vast cyber money-laundering operation used to hide the proceeds from the theft, sale, and use of tens of thousands of stolen credit and debit card account profiles.

Anecdotes. We also include interesting anecdotes throughout the text, including several from our years spent as Manhattan prosecutors.

Cartoons and diagrams. The text of the book is illustrated by numerous diagrams and cartoons. We offer these visual aids in order to present complex concepts in a digestible format and to make the material easier to remember. As they say, a picture is worth a thousand words, as depicted in Figure 1.1.

FIGURE 1.1   Cartoon Example.

1.5   ONWARD AND UPWARD

Most importantly, we hope you have as much fun reading this book as we had writing it!

2 What Is Cybercrime and Why Is It Committed?

This chapter is primarily for:

- Those new to cybercrime and the various cyber offenses
- Those wanting to understand motives and schemes.

2.1 INTRODUCTION

Before we can dive into learning how to investigate "cybercrime", and all the underlying law and technology, we need to understand the term itself. What activities are considered a cybercrime? Who is committing these offenses? And what about the Internet has allowed a criminal ecosystem to flourish? This chapter gives an overview of these fundamental questions.

Very few cybercrimes consist of a single illegal act, even though a single act is all a particular investigator may encounter.[1] This chapter provides the context for individual cybercrimes so that investigators can begin to see how a single event often fits into a larger picture. While this world of cybercrime is relatively new, it is still just another form of crime that needs to be investigated. It is important for investigators to realize that traditional investigative skills are essential in cybercrime cases. This chapter also will discuss comparisons between "street crimes" and "cybercrimes", including traditional investigation concepts that translate well to the investigation of cybercrime and some that need to be adapted.

2.2 WHAT MAKES A "CYBER" ACTIVITY A CRIME? A QUICK INTRODUCTION TO CYBERCRIME OFFENSES

Let's start by looking at the most common kinds of illegal activity that fall under the heading of "cybercrime". These offenses can be grouped into general categories, although individual cybercriminals might undertake many of these different types of crime.

As a general concept, crimes in so-called "cyberspace" can be analogized to traditional crimes. Trespass is not allowed on real property or in a residence, and it is not allowed in a computer system or network. Theft of someone's notebook or day planner is not permitted, nor is theft of their electronic data. Stealing funds, harassing another person and extortion are illegal, and when they are conducted through the Internet, they are still illegal.

---

[1] As we mentioned in the introduction, we use the term "investigator" not just for those with specific job titles, but for all of those involved with investigating a cybercrime.

Damaging someone's property is unlawful, whether it is with a rock through the window, or by tampering with their computer system.

When learning about various cybercrimes, and when investigating a new incident, it can be helpful to think about what the same situation would look like in the physical world. Was something stolen? Was someone hurt or something damaged? Was there an illegal sale or purchase of stolen property or contraband? Framing your analysis in these terms can make it easier to see past the technicalities of how the crime was committed, to what actually occurred. In addition, although a crime is "cyber" in nature, it inevitably has components in the physical world (people, money, locations). Identifying those connections can be helpful in understanding the nature of a cyber incident.

Here is a list of Internet-related activities that generally fall under the umbrella of cybercrime. In Chapter 6, we will cover the statutes outlawing this conduct.

- Computer intrusions, network intrusions, and data breaches
- Transmission and use of malware
- Tampering with or damaging someone's network or system
- Theft of data and data trafficking
- Identity theft and impersonation
- Theft of funds and fraud schemes
- Blackmail and extortion
- Forging identification, credit/debit cards, and other documents/devices
- Money laundering
- Harassment, threats, stalking, and revenge porn
- Possessing, selling, or sharing child pornography
- Trafficking of brick-and-mortar contraband (drugs, guns, endangered species, etc.)
- Gambling.

We will describe these categories briefly to give you an overall sense of what actions each one entails.

2.2.1 COMPUTER AND NETWORK INTRUSIONS

Computer intrusions and network intrusions involve a person breaking into someone else's computer system without permission. It's like entering someone's home or place of business without permission, when you have no business being there. There is a temptation to call all of this conduct "hacking" because that term is frequently used in the media. But "hacking" is a word with multiple meanings, one of which is the use of computer expertise to overcome a problem, not necessarily for criminal purposes. Early computer hackers often broke into systems for the thrill of it rather than to commit additional crimes.

While there are still some thrill-seekers out there, most intrusions are committed by cybercriminals to further other crimes, and are accomplished using a host of mechanisms. There are many ways a cybercriminal might unlawfully enter another's computer system, gain a foothold, then work to increase control of the system. These methods might include the use of stolen or guessed usernames and passwords, taking advantage of vulnerabilities in software or firmware,[2] using malware, and tricking users into clicking on links or downloading attachments. Whatever mechanism is used, the goal is to assert unauthorized control over computers and systems.

---

[2] Firmware is a form of software that provides a basic operating system for computing components such as routers and printers.

2.2.2 DATA BREACHES, THEFT OF DATA, AND DATA TRAFFICKING

Frequently, computer and network intrusions are conducted for the sole purpose of breaching databases and stealing data. Data trafficking is the sale or transfer of stolen data, including financial account information, Internet account login credentials, and personal identifying information that can be used to impersonate victims. Certain data is targeted because it can be sold on the cyber black market. An early (and ongoing) type of cybercrime is called "carding". Criminals steal credit card and debit card account information from retailers and businesses – often through unauthorized intrusion into their computer systems and breaching their customer databases. The data is then sold to numerous other criminals who use it to commit a variety of thefts and frauds.

Any cyber theft and sale of stolen data can be equated to similar situations in the physical world. For example, if burglars break into a jewelry store, steal a bunch of rings and watches, and then sell them to shady jewelers or pawn them for cash, they are committing the same types of criminal acts as cybercriminals who break into a system and sell the data they steal.

Cybertheft sometimes targets intellectual property, including trade secrets. Other cyberthefts involve copyright violations, where certain protected text, images, or other content are copied without authorization.

2.2.3 TRANSMISSION AND USE OF MALWARE

Malware is malicious software that cybercriminals seek to introduce into victim computers in order to commit various crimes, including unauthorized access. There are many ways that a computer can be infected with malware – including through email as an attachment or by visiting a malicious website. Malware includes viruses, trojan horses, and ransomware.

Malware can allow criminals to control a computer or network. Cybercriminals use malware to bypass or disable security controls, direct the computers to perform actions, and record user activity, including keystrokes and the entering of personal or financial information. Some malware allows criminals to control millions of computers at a time, turning each unsuspecting computer into a "bot". The "bots" may be part of a bot network – or "botnet" – which can be used to conduct powerful malicious computing activity (such as sending millions of spam emails, or allowing cybercriminals to hide their online traffic behind shields of dummy computers).

2.2.4 TAMPERING WITH OR DAMAGING A NETWORK OR SYSTEM

Some cybercrimes are intended to damage or impair the victim's computer system. These attacks are analogous to criminal mischief and vandalism, and include deliberately destroying data, encrypting data using malware to demand ransom, and attacking a website to make it unavailable to customers. The street crime equivalents would be smashing a storefront window, sabotaging delivery trucks, or changing the combination on a safe so the victim cannot access documents or funds inside.

Sometimes criminal tampering or damage is only visible to the victim. In these cases, a victim may discover that some internal component of a system is malfunctioning, data is missing or damaged, or employees are receiving strange communications from the company. Other attacks have very public consequences. For example, in a denial-of-service (DOS) attack, criminals take action to disable an information system, and make it unavailable to users. A common DOS attack uses many computers to bombard a website with traffic, to the point where the system overloads and the website shuts down. Now, real customers cannot access the website's products or services, and the functioning of the business or organization is impaired. When many attacking computers are involved, such an effort usually relies upon malware-infected botnets and is called a distributed denial-of-service (DDOS) attack. In some instances, criminals simply threaten these attacks to extort payments from a business' worried owner. And as discussed in Chapter 8, there have been DOS attacks for political reasons, such as the 2007 cyberattacks on the government of Estonia.

2.2.5   IDENTITY THEFT AND IMPERSONATION

Identity theft and impersonation are hallmarks of cybercrime. Assuming the identity of another person is both a crime in and of itself, and a tool used to commit numerous other cybercrimes. Identity theft usually involves the use of another person's identity and identifying information to accomplish some criminal purpose, such as to gain use of the victim's Internet accounts, financial accounts, or medical insurance. In addition, cybercriminals often use stolen identities to create new Internet and financial accounts unbeknownst to the victim. The ultimate goals are to steal money, goods, or services, and to operate online under another person's name and identifiers.

Identity theft operates on the same principles in the cyber realm as in the physical world. Whether a criminal obtains a victim's identifiers by illegally accessing his computer or by stealing his wallet, the general steps to assume his identity and commit frauds are the same.

Identity theft schemes are many and diverse and include credit card fraud, check fraud, and account takeovers. Synthetic identity fraud is a close relative, but instead of assuming an actual person's identity, the criminal creates a fictitious identity using a combination of fake and stolen information.

Much like cybercrime, identity theft presents investigative challenges. Prosecutors and governments hoping to crack down on cybercrime must address identity theft, because it so often is the gateway to cyber schemes. Seemingly low-level crimes (like credit card fraud and check fraud) are tied to cybercrime. These identity theft crimes can be lucrative with much lower risk of apprehension than street crimes. If caught, the punishment is usually less, making identity theft an attractive area of criminality for street criminals. It was through attention to identity theft cases during our time with Mr. Morgenthau's office that our unit successfully brought many local cases, and also groundbreaking international cybercrime cases.[3]

2.2.6   THEFT OF FUNDS AND FRAUD SCHEMES

Most cybercrime is focused on theft, and criminals have come up with a seemingly endless number of creative online schemes to steal. Many of these schemes use the Internet with the objective of stealing physical money or goods from victim businesses and individuals through several layers of virtual and real-world fraud, often involving identity theft. Other schemes, however, are conducted entirely online. With varying levels of sophistication, these frauds are designed to get people and businesses to part with their funds electronically.

One common scheme involves the online compromise of financial and email accounts, which are then used to bring about a fraudulent funds transfer. In one version, the criminal hijacks Victim A's email account and impersonates him in order to trick Victim B (a business associate) to wire funds to a certain location. This scheme is known as "business email compromise" or "CEO Fraud", because it often is perpetrated by taking advantage of a victim's business contacts or position in a large organization.[4] In other versions, criminals impersonate businesses or

---

[3] Robert Morgenthau was District Attorney of New York County from 1974 until his retirement in 2009. He built a renowned office that brought a number of landmark cases.

[4] John Bandler, The Cybercrime Scheme that Attacks Email Accounts and Your Bank Accounts, *Huffington Post* (August 3, 2017), www.huffingtonpost.com/entry/the-cybercrime-scheme-that-attacks-email-accounts-and_us_59834649e4b03d0624b0aca6.

employees and induce others to purchase services that will never be provided. All of these scams, like similar frauds conducted face-to-face or over the phone, are a form of theft. Many cybercrime scams involve related activity which is known as "social engineering", where con artistry is employed and the victim is tricked into performing some type of action, whether it is transferring funds, clicking on a link, or downloading an attachment.

2.2.7 BLACKMAIL AND EXTORTION

Another category of cybertheft is the use of online blackmail and extortion techniques. Extorting "voluntary" payments is a growing form of cybercrime. It often is less work for cybercriminals than stealing the funds through fraud and identity theft schemes, but still highly lucrative. Of course, it is still theft, but of a different flavor.

Internet extortion methods include the use of "ransomware", a form of malware that maliciously encrypts data, rendering it unavailable to the owner. The criminal then demands a ransom, in return for which he says he will provide the victim with the key to unlock the data. Another method is "sextortion", where criminals claim to have compromising photos or information about a victim and threaten to publicly release it if the victim does not pay. Criminals also may claim they implanted malware in the victim's computer and monitored the victim's visits to pornographic websites and other personal activities. Another cyber extortion scheme involves criminals claiming to have kidnapped a family member, with threats to harm this person unless payment is immediately made. With ransomware, the threats are real; with the others the threats are almost always a con, but many victims panic and pay.

Extortion schemes can be coupled with threats to impair the victim's information systems (such as data, networks, or websites). This cybercrime extortion is analogous to traditional organized crime methods – demand payment in exchange for "protection" from broken windows and arson. To be clear, extortion is not a new crime, but the Internet provides new ways to extort and deceive.

2.2.8 MONEY LAUNDERING

Since cybercrime is mostly a "for profit" enterprise, it is essential to consider what criminals do with the money they steal. Where does all this money go? How do criminals hide the trail of money from the theft to their pockets? We devote Chapter 15 to exploring these questions.

Criminals "launder money" to disguise the fact that funds were earned through crime. When a criminal sells drugs, for example, he doesn't want the trail of money leading directly to him. By transferring the money through various forms of currency and different accounts, he can make the trail much harder to follow.

Cybercriminals use many methods to move funds to facilitate their schemes and launder the profits, including credit cards, checks, bank wires, and money remittances. Stolen identities and fictitious identities are important tools for moving funds and avoiding detection.

Cybercriminals also have been laundering funds through virtual currency for over two decades now. "Virtual currency" is digital money created and issued by private individuals or companies. People (and criminals) can buy units of the currency using real money and can do so anonymously, making it an excellent way to hide criminal profits. Many incorrectly believe that virtual currency began when Bitcoin came on the scene in 2009, but there have been many virtual currencies in use for far longer. Only a handful of virtual currency money laundering cases have been successfully pursued around the world. This aspect of cybercrime is an area for increased investigative action and is discussed in more depth in Chapter 15.

Cyber money laundering also involves moving funds or goods back and forth between the Internet and the physical world (through banks, money transfer services, virtual currency, or carrying it from place to place). Since cybercriminals frequently work internationally and want to insulate themselves from their crimes, they often need to recruit someone in the victim's country to act as a "money mule". These mules receive illicit funds stolen from victims and then forward them to accounts (or other mules) set up by the criminal participants. Money mules may have varying degrees of culpability, from unsophisticated participants caught up in a scam, to street criminals looking for a more lucrative fraud. When questioned or arrested, some mules may provide a full statement, explaining their involvement in the scheme. Investigators should always follow the money, even when a low-level participant is arrested or a small cyber incident occurs, since these cases provide far more leads into the money trail of larger cyber schemes than many realize.

Two Myths about Cybercrime

If you have seen the media headlines about cybercrime over the last few years, two names probably have popped out at you: "the Dark Web" and "Bitcoin". While these terms have garnered a lot of attention, there are two important points to remember:

1. The "Dark Web" is mentioned often in reference to an emerging cyber black market, where cybercrime tools, stolen data, and contraband are bought and sold using technical safeguards to escape detection. But many may not realize (and the media rarely mentions) that the cybercrime underground existed long before the "Dark Web" that we hear about now. Cybercriminals have been using a wide array of Internet technologies to create secret meeting places, conduct business, and exchange information for many years. The "Dark Web" is a recent chapter of this story, and there will be new ones to follow as technology evolves. For more on the Dark Web, and the technology surrounding it, see the discussion of Tor, also known as The Onion Router, in Chapter 3.
2. Bitcoin has become synonymous with virtual currency in the popular media, but the fact is that virtual currencies have existed for decades. Bitcoin is one of hundreds, if not thousands, of different forms of virtual currency in use today. Cybercriminals' use of virtual currency began long before Bitcoin. In fact, cybercriminals have been some of the innovators in the use of virtual currency, employing virtual currencies in many novel ways to facilitate their schemes and launder their proceeds.

2.2.9   HARASSMENT, THREATS, STALKING, AND REVENGE PORN

There is a significant segment of cybercrime that is not related to stealing, but rather to harassing, stalking, or threatening another person. The Internet provides harassers and stalkers with abundant opportunities to intrude into their targets' lives. Personal information might be publicly posted, either to harass the victim or to prompt other criminals to commit identity theft. False information about the victims might be sent to friends, families, or employers. In a growing form of crime called "revenge porn", criminals post explicit photos of a victim without his or her consent. Harassment and stalking also can include other types of cybercrime, including account takeovers, computer intrusions, data destruction, and impersonation.

Sometimes, it may not be clear where the line is between illegal harassment and legal free speech. Certain statements have protections under the First Amendment. Statements that injure a personal reputation, but that do not rise to the level of harassment, might merit only a civil remedy such as an action for defamation, rather than a criminal prosecution.

2.2.10 Possessing, Selling, or Sharing Child Pornography

Many criminal activities are easier to conduct and get away with thanks to computers and the Internet. Sadly, crimes related to the possession and distribution of child pornography fall into this category. Cellphones, tablets, and computers allow criminals to create and store child pornography without fear of detection. Before this technology, photographs or videos were made on film that required developing – either by unwitting photo stores that might notice and report the content, or by criminal associates who had to maintain a dark room and necessary chemicals (which might be noticed, as well).

The Internet and its many anonymizing features also enable the dissemination of child pornography. Photos and videos are no longer sold or shared via the mail or during personal encounters. Instead, they are sent online in countless different manners that are more difficult to detect. Similarly, the Internet allows people selling child pornography to collect payment using anonymous methods including virtual currencies. Investigations into cyber money laundering operations often reveal a portion of the criminal clientele that is earning money through child pornography.

2.2.11 Trafficking of Physical Contraband

The Internet also creates avenues for the sale and purchase of physical contraband, such as narcotics, weapons, stolen property, and endangered species. To avoid the face-to-face contact or layers of middlemen that traditionally characterize the physical trafficking of these items, criminal buyers and sellers can communicate and transact online with far less likelihood of detection. Of course, the physical goods must be transported and delivered at some stage of the process, and investigators may learn of a cyber trafficking operation by happening upon this phase. As discussed earlier, any crime involving online transactions is ripe for a money laundering investigation. The trail of money will lead to more evidence, suspects, and a fuller understanding of the criminal scheme.

2.2.12 Gambling

Gambling that crosses state lines is illegal under federal law, and since Internet traffic routinely bounces across state and international boundaries, this rule means that online gambling through a website based in the United States is prohibited. Placing bets using websites established in other countries may be legal. Some states allow gambling within the state, including sports betting. In addition, certain online "betting" activities generally are not considered "gambling", such as fantasy sports leagues.

Online gambling closely mirrors traditional gambling, and the same laws apply to both. Gambling websites may offer new betting options, including the ability to bet against others around the world, but many may escape the regulation that casinos are accustomed to following.

2.3 CYBERCRIME VS. TRADITIONAL STREET CRIME: THE DIFFERENCES

Now that we have reviewed the main categories of cybercrime, and how they parallel crimes in the physical world, let us look at the differences between street and cybercrime. There are a number of factors that make cybercrime different, and greatly affect how it should be investigated. Some of these factors are:

- Technology, the Internet, and networks
- Distance: the national and international nexus
- Investigation rate and solve rate
- Connection to a broad criminal ecosystem
- Potential nation-state involvement.

2.3.1   TECHNOLOGY, INTERNET AND NETWORKS

A cybercrime, by definition, involves technology. An offense is considered a cybercrime because it is committed using the Internet, computers, networks, and other forms of technology. As a result, cybercrime investigations always involve the gathering of digital evidence from devices, service providers, and other sources. This dependence on assembling digital evidence means that a simple cybercrime case can involve more complex investigative steps than a comparable street crime.

The presence of technology is ever-growing in the field of investigation. From the recording and management of police body-camera video to advanced case management and analytical software, investigators are using more and more technology in every facet of their work. Cybercrime investigations, by their nature, are focused on Internet and computing technology, but the facts and evidence of these crimes typically are within the working knowledge of most investigators.

Certain investigative steps in cyber cases require input from professionals with experience and knowledge about specific technology, as well as equipment and resources not necessarily available to the average investigator. For example, recovering evidence from a computer device (including cellphones) should be performed by individuals with specialized skills and training in the field of digital forensics. That said, although technical expertise is important at particular stages, it takes all types of backgrounds and experience to conduct cybercrime investigations. Victims, witnesses, and suspects need to be interviewed, logical connections and deductions need to be made from the evidence (digital or otherwise), and facts need to be articulated. When digital evidence is recovered, it needs to be analyzed for clues by those who know the case best.

2.3.2   DISTANCE: THE NATIONAL AND INTERNATIONAL NEXUS

The second major difference between cyber and street crime is that cybercrime can be committed from a distance. This criminal reach represents a monumental change and creates steep challenges for law enforcement and governments, as well as private sector interests that are victimized from afar.

Traditional crime requires the criminal to get physically close to the victim, to enter the bank or dwelling, to get near victims or their possessions in order to steal them. Before the Internet, individuals did not fear being harmed by countless criminals all over the world. Street crimes have a narrow list of suspects, since the perpetrator has to be nearby, or to have gotten away on foot or by vehicle. As a result, apprehension is much more likely. Conveniently for law enforcement and the legal system, the victim and suspect in a street crime usually are in the same jurisdiction.

Cybercrime changes that dynamic. Cybercriminals victimize from a distance with anonymity, often from another state or another country. They do not leave physical clues behind. The pool of suspects cannot be narrowed by proximity, and investigation and apprehension are made difficult due to distance and geographic boundaries.

From the cybercriminal's perspective, the pool of victims is larger. They do not need to focus on one potential victim; they can target thousands, or millions, of potential victims. Though they might choose to target a specific individual or company, they also can play the odds, netting occasional successes among thousands of failed attempts.

2.3.3 Investigation Rate and Solve Rate

Another important difference is that law enforcement's solve rate for traditional street crime is much higher than for cybercrime. Consider burglary – one of the harder street crimes to solve. Burglars break into homes or stores, steal things, and leave. If they are not caught in the act, or if they don't leave a physical clue behind (like a fingerprint or DNA), law enforcement may have a difficult time determining the burglar's identity and arresting him. For these reasons, less than 15% of reported burglaries are solved.[5] But the fact that police are out there investigating each case, some burglars do get caught, and we are reasonably safe in our offices and homes, suggests this solve rate is high enough to keep the crime in check.

With cybercrime, the solve rate has been so low that criminals can keep trying and improving until they are successful at stealing money or data. A cybercriminal can send millions of spam emails to victimize recipients, can attempt hundreds of network intrusions, and can experiment for years until his technique is successful and profitable, with limited fear of apprehension. In other words, unlike street criminals, cybercriminals operate under the reasonable assumption that they will never be caught.

The main reason we wrote this book is to change this dynamic by encouraging a far more aggressive investigative response to cybercrime. A crime that is not investigated cannot be solved. When cybercrimes are consistently investigated, investigators will get better at it, and more cybercriminals will be apprehended and prosecuted.

2.3.4 Connection to a Broad Criminal Ecosystem

Most street crimes are singular events that automatically become the primary focus of an investigation. If a victim is robbed or stabbed, or if a suspect drives drunk or sells drugs, each crime is a distinct situation that investigators can quickly assess and begin to investigate.

Cybercrimes, on the other hand, often are not discrete criminal events that are well-suited for investigation in isolation. A victim might report a cyber incident that, standing alone, appears to be small, or nearly impossible to solve, given the individual facts pertaining to that single victim. But frequently that small cybercrime is one of many – hundreds, thousands, or even millions – being perpetrated by a particular criminal or group. Together, these crimes may be part of an ongoing criminal effort reaping significant profits. If that is the case, the reported crime is related to the larger cybercrime economy, and has been aided and enabled by the criminal tools and resources shared among criminals who operate online. Individual cybercrimes, in other words, should be evaluated in the context of the broader picture. Generally, only a small portion of street crimes have this interconnected aspect – like those that are part of organized crime rings such as the Mafia or narcotics traffickers.

---

[5] FBI: Uniform Crime Reporting – 2018 Crime in the United States: Offenses Cleared, https://ucr.fbi.gov/crime-in-the-u.s/2018/crime-in-the-u.s.-2018/topic-pages/clearances.

2.4 MOTIVES AND ACTORS

A diverse array of individuals and organizations commit cybercrime. If Willie Sutton robbed banks because that's where the money was, there are thousands of @WillieSuttons committing cybercrime for the same reason. However, as we discussed when looking at the categories of cybercrime, money is not the only motive. Some people commit crimes online to stalk or harass, to buy and sell contraband, even to gamble. When evaluating a cyber incident, it is tempting to pigeonhole a certain type of criminal or crime as having a particular motive, but people are complex and it can turn out that a combination of motives and factors are at work. Since cybercrime is committed with anonymity, it may take considerable investigation before the identity and motive of the perpetrator is revealed, but here are some broad common motivations to look for:

- Profit and greed
- Personal attack
- Thrill and bragging rights
- Activism
- Corporate espionage
- Nation-state objectives
- Terrorism.

2.4.1 Profit and Greed

Profit and greed motivate most cybercriminals. Many cybercrimes involve theft, with criminals looking for ways to steal funds, or make money from stolen data. With so many different individuals and groups trying to steal, and with potential victims adjusting their defenses, these diverse criminals must employ considerable innovation, entrepreneurship, and evolution to develop their many fraud schemes. We will discuss this cybercrime-for-profit economy shortly.

Greed-motivated crimes also include blackmail and extortion, such as by encrypting data and demanding a ransom ("ransomware"), or threatening to expose a secret if the ransom is not paid.

2.4.2 Personal Attack

Some cybercrimes are committed by individuals in order to attack a specific person or organization. Unlike most other cybercrimes, these crimes are not directed at random victims. Rather, the target is chosen because of a direct connection to the criminal. Romantic rivals, former intimate partners, business competitors, disgruntled employees, academic adversaries, and personal enemies are the types of individuals who engage in cyber campaigns to damage others or their reputations. The motivation can arise from a deep personal animus, a general maliciousness towards a person or group, or even from a sense of boredom that leads some to inflict discomfort or misery upon others.

The personal attack motive leads to crimes like harassment, stalking, and sometimes computer tampering or identity theft. Revenge porn fits within this category as well.

2.4.3 Thrill and Bragging Rights

There always will be people committing illegal acts just for the thrill of it. Some cybercriminals simply get satisfaction from showing off their technical prowess. They break into a victim's cloud account or computer, just like some people might feel a thrill to trespass on someone else's property or break into a house.

Many of the earliest cybercriminals committed data breaches not for profit or espionage, but for fun, thrills, bragging rights, or to expose security weaknesses. They were brilliant technologists, understanding systems better than the creators, and manipulating them in unintended ways. That is the origin of the term "hacker", though the word has been coopted by many who believe it means anyone who illegally breaks into computer systems. Some famous early cybercriminals who were arrested for their conduct have moved on to legitimate pursuits, including security research, consulting, and journalism.

2.4.4 ACTIVISM

Some cybercriminals engage in crime as a form of activism, or so-called "hacktivism". They feel passionate about a cause, or passionately disagree with the words or actions of others and commit cybercrimes to disrupt and make their voices heard. Hacktivists often feel they have altruistic motives, or that the end justifies the means. Of course, in many instances, their victims, and the government, would beg to differ.

Hacktivist crimes include tampering with websites to change what the public sees, denial-of-service attacks that shut websites down, and data theft. Hacktivists' stated goals sometimes include providing the world with access to information, revealing the secrets of governments and corporations, exposing greed or misconduct, exposing organizations with poor security, or simply weakening organizations or governments with which they disagree.

2.4.5 CORPORATE ESPIONAGE

Theft of intellectual property is a significant category of cybercrime. This type of activity generally is known as corporate espionage. It involves stealing secrets from competing companies to benefit from their work and investment, and gain a business advantage. Corporate espionage commonly is undertaken through intrusions and malware, including spyware – a variety of malware that gives criminals the ability to view and copy the activities of computer and network users.

Some governments, especially those that exert significant control over their own economies, also engage in corporate espionage. These governments are able to direct vast nation-state resources towards attacking corporations in their own and other countries to steal information that can benefit their economies.

2.4.6 NATION-STATE OBJECTIVES

Nation-states have turned to cybercrime – sometimes for profit or for corporate espionage, and sometimes for "traditional" espionage or to effect tactical or strategic goals. Espionage has been a facet of international relations for millennia; the Internet gives it a new dimension.

Nation-state objectives may include any of the other motives already discussed. Nation-states may try to earn illicit profits to build coffers. Cybercrime also can be used to damage and harm the infrastructure of other countries, and to serve other tactical or strategic aims. Nation-states have used cybercrime in attempts to disrupt elections, damage infrastructure facilities, and harm international alliances. Propaganda and influence operations can be conducted with greater precision in today's Internet age, and in doing so, cybercrimes might be committed. An in-depth discussion of the role of nation-states (and terrorists) in cybercrime can be found in Chapter 8.

2.4.7 TERRORISM

Terrorists' main goal is to instill fear by attacking noncombatants. Some criminals commit cybercrimes to serve these ends. Cybercrime frauds are a source of funding for terrorist groups and have low risk of detection. In addition, through intrusions and other methods of obtaining unauthorized access to computer systems, cybercriminals can steal or research information about potential terrorist targets. As with many criminal organizations, individual members have specific roles. Those involved in committing cybercrime for terrorist purposes may not be directly involved in physical attacks.

Cyberterrorism is an extension of terrorist activities that occur in the physical world. This term generally refers to terror-motivated cyberattacks on critical infrastructure systems, which could have devastating consequences for large populations.

2.5 THE CYBERCRIME-FOR-PROFIT ECONOMY

Capitalism and the free market are highly successful economic systems that spur innovation, competition, experimentation, and efficiency. In the interest of earning money and market power, individuals and businesses look for opportunities to do things better than the competition, or to move into areas no one has thought to go.

The cybercrime-for-profit economy is black market capitalism, without regulation and with little law enforcement. It attracts participants looking to make money from theft and fraud, as well as from the sale and purchase of illicit goods or services that facilitate other crimes. Just like the regular economy, the cybercrime economy allows for segmentation and specialization. Cybercriminals develop expertise in particular criminal areas – like forging identification documents, stealing data, and creating malware – and sell their specialized products or assistance to other criminals. There are hundreds of theft schemes, and each scheme may require the services of different specialists. As in regular life, a cybervendor's business success is based upon his reputation for reliably supplying quality merchandise and good customer service.

But the cybercrime-for-profit economy is entirely different than the regular economy in one critical way: the participants can do business anonymously.

How is anonymous cyber business possible? First off, the Internet makes it easy to communicate anonymously. There are any number of email and online messaging services that require no identifying information from users, making them very difficult to trace. In addition, many black marketplaces are set up on Internet networks that use various forms of technology to hide the users' identities and locations (these methods are discussed in Chapter 3). Cybercriminals typically do business in the black market using online nicknames ("handles") they make up for themselves. Business reputations are built around these nicknames, and criminals protect them like a brand name would be protected in the regular economy. By communicating using anonymous, hard-to-trace methods, and referring to one another by made-up nicknames, cybercriminals work out business transactions without ever knowing the real identities of the people with whom they are interacting.

The Internet also has generated anonymous methods of payment. As we will discuss more in Chapter 15, anonymous (or pseudonymous) payment mechanisms were invented with the first virtual currency in 1996. Today, there are numerous online options available for sending and receiving payments without either party having to supply identifying information. These payment options also hide users' locations and are hard to trace. So, once a deal is made between cybercriminals in the black market cybereconomy, money can change hands without risk of exposure.

In this free, anonymous market, successful criminals can reap vast profits. Of course, not all criminals are successful. That is why we might laugh at some of the less sophisticated fraud attempts we receive and disregard. But don't laugh too hard. The anonymity of the Internet means that an unsuccessful criminal can keep trying and experimenting until he hits upon a scheme that works, and even those unsophisticated fraud attempts might find a victim.

In many respects, the cybercrime economy is more than a decade ahead of the legitimate economy. Since the turn of the millennium, underground cybercrime websites and networks have allowed cybercriminals to work together on a project-by-project basis – transacting for services, merchandise, and data in furtherance of a particular scam. Until recently, it was hard to find a similar forum for legitimate services, such as programming, website design, and graphic design. The "gig" economy, however, has existed for cybercriminals for a long time.

Even those criminals with motivations other than reaping profits – including stalkers, hacktivists, nation-states, and terrorists – utilize the cybercrime economy to find items and services that facilitate their operations. The underground cyber economy is the grease to the wheels of much of the world's cybercrime, no matter the nature of the crime or its motive.

2.5.1 THE CONNECTION BETWEEN IDENTITY THEFT AND CYBERCRIME

Identity theft is one thread that continuously interconnects various forms of cybercrime and the cybercrime economy. Enormous spikes in identity theft and cybercrime have been

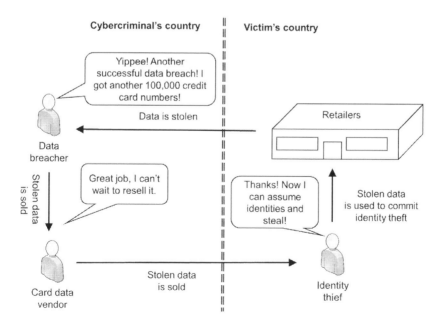

FIGURE 2.1 Cybercrime and Identity Theft with Credit and Debit Cards.

occurring together even if reported statistics, press coverage, and government action have not always highlighted this link. One of the clearest examples can be found in the massive data breaches of customer databases we repeatedly hear about in the media. When cyber-criminals strike to steal victims' personal information, they usually do so for one purpose: to use the data to commit cybercrimes. The data stolen has value. It typically is sold and resold to other cybercriminals who commit a variety of new crimes with it, all hinging on assuming the victims' identities.

Consider the data breaches we hear about in the news, when thousands or millions of credit card account numbers and other personal identifiers are stolen. If international cyber-criminals are stealing this personal information from U.S. victims, the best place to monet-ize this information is back in the U.S. Cybercriminals usually sell this stolen data to other cybercriminals and identity thieves in the U.S., who then use it to impersonate the victims for financial benefit, as depicted in Figure 2.1.

Addressing these crimes fully means addressing criminals on all sides of the cybercrime economy, not simply focusing on the immediate breach and the actors who may have caused it. Investigators should consider the following questions. What cyber tools were used by the intruders to steal the data? Where did they get them? Where did the stolen data end up? What other crimes were committed using the data?

2.5.2 THE CYBERCRIME ECONOMY EARNS MONEY AND REQUIRES PAYMENTS

Crime done for profit provides investigators with powerful investigative leads and proof. Individual criminals working for profit are stealing, as depicted in Figure 2.2. If the

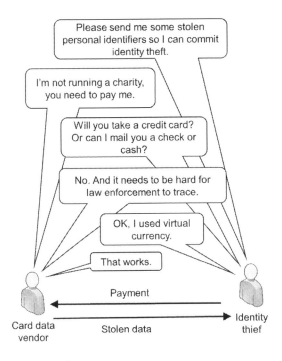

FIGURE 2.2 Payments in a For-Profit Economy.

criminal is smart, he will take steps to transmit, layer, and launder the funds before they reach him. Where profit is the motive or funds are transmitted, investigators should endeavor to "follow the money". This portion of the investigation not only provides leads about potential suspects, but could provide proof at trial about suspects' identities and the scope of their crimes. Investigators also might uncover third parties who are facilitating the flow of illicit funds.

2.6   DIGITAL EVIDENCE: THE BACKBONE OF ANY CYBER INVESTIGATION (AND TRADITIONAL INVESTIGATIONS, TOO)

As we discussed earlier in this chapter, a cybercrime by its very nature utilizes computer technology. Digital evidence, therefore, will be a part of every cybercrime investigation. In Chapter 7 we will develop a thorough understanding of the legal tools available to investigators to obtain this crucial digital evidence. But as we wrap up our overview of cybercrime and who commits it, it is worth a moment to take stock of the wealth of digital evidence an investigator can uncover in connection with these cases. Many of these forms of evidence relate to traditional investigations, as well.

Almost everyone has a smartphone now, with dozens of apps and multiple email and social media accounts. That is on top of the laptop and desktop computers we use at home or at work, and all the functions they perform. Consider how these omnipresent devices constantly are creating and storing digital evidence of our activities. Consider how often we use them to communicate with each other and to the world about what we are doing. This constant production of digital evidence means there are few criminal investigations today that cannot be enhanced with the expertise of cybercrime investigators.

Some of the common forms of digital evidence are:

- Records of digital communication (email, messaging, social media posts)
- Records of digital storage (such as the use of cloud accounts)
- Records showing how and when all these accounts were opened
- Records showing payment for these accounts
- Location related data showing a device's physical location at the time it was accessing the Internet or cell-site towers
- Data regarding a user's online searches and other Internet usage
- Data created by the user and stored on computers or devices (like documents or spreadsheets)
- Photos, videos, and music
- Financial account information (virtual and real-world)
- Contacts and calendar information
- Downloaded applications and related records of how they were used.

In Chapter 7, we will talk about how to gather this evidence, and also some of the obstacles that will arise. For example, investigators may encounter a device that is strongly encrypted that they would like to decode. Without the key or password to decrypt the device (a process explained in Chapter 3), it may not be possible to see the evidence stored inside.

Since technology is now involved in nearly all crimes, law enforcement, prosecutors, analysts, and those in the private sector need to be prepared to find and use digital

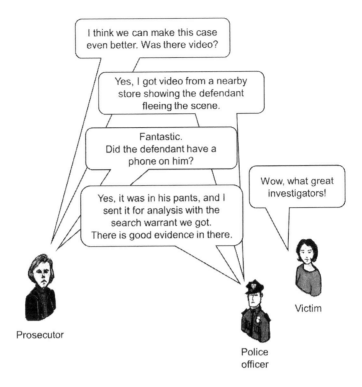

FIGURE 2.3   Using Digital Evidence to Prove Brick-and-Mortar Crimes.

evidence to investigate and prove their cases (as depicted in Figure 2.3). Some government agencies may task individuals or units with a focus on cybercrime or digital forensics, and it is wonderful to have those resources. However, traditional investigators should not abdicate their roles to the digital forensic experts and specialists. No one knows the case like the investigators assigned to it, and the best results come when investigators or team members with different backgrounds work together to further the investigation.

2.7   CONCLUSION

Having a general understanding of cybercrime, the for-profit cybercrime economy, and the many criminal participants will help investigators, lawyers, and analysts work individual cases, whether from the public or private side. With cybercrime, investigators see the tip of the iceberg but should know that under the surface are vast networks of criminal participants, methods, payments, and schemes.

As these cases are worked, the investigating team, whether from the private or public side may want to consider:

- How does this crime analogize to traditional brick-and-mortar crime? What is the basic type of crime being committed (e.g. larceny, vandalism)?
- What is the motive of the criminal?

- How does this incident fit into the broader "cybercrime economy"?
- Is this activity something the criminals did once, or part of a continuing course of conduct (e.g. their occupation)?
- How important will digital evidence be in proving this cybercrime?

As we evaluate our individual cases, it is helpful to understand the fuller cyber ecosystem, so we can comprehensively fight and reduce cybercrime.

3 Introduction to Computers, Networks, and Forensics

This chapter is primarily for:

- Those unfamiliar with, or needing a refresher in, computer technology, networks, and digital evidence gathering
- Those who want to have informed conversations with technical experts and forensics personnel.

3.1 INTRODUCTION

This chapter provides a primer on how computers and networks work, the digital forensics process, and how digital evidence is created and stored when cybercriminals use computers to commit their crimes.

In providing this overview, we recognize that cybercrime investigators come from a variety of backgrounds and with a variety of skills, and are not exclusively technical experts.

Given the nature of cybercrime, technical facts and concepts need to be communicated throughout the investigation, from the initial observers and fact-gatherers to the ultimate decision-maker. Conveying technical concepts and events properly, and using the right terminology, can be critical to the outcome of a case. If the case winds up in civil or criminal court, it will be a lawyer presenting these technical facts to a judge to obtain court orders, and perhaps to a jury to get a rightful verdict. If a company needs to make an internal or legal determination on how to proceed, ultimately it is the CEO, Executive Director, or Managing Partner who will decide, hopefully after being properly apprised of the facts and their significance. With so many types of professionals potentially involved in the investigation, things can get lost in translation.

To put these technical aspects in context, imagine Grand Central Station at rush hour, with dozens of commuter trains coming and going each hour, pedestrians streaming in and out of various entrances, the many subway lines that connect there, taxis outside, and all the places, shops and workers inside. If a complicated crime happened in such an environment, the investigator would need a general understanding of how the station functions, the layout of the station, and some of the lexicology and naming conventions used to describe where and how certain events took place.

A computer, and the data it handles, present a similar investigative environment. Cybercrime investigators need to have a basic understanding of the computer, how it functions, how data is stored, and how data comes in and out. This fundamental knowledge will help investigators find, recover, and evaluate every type of computer-related evidence, then properly present and explain this evidence to others.

3.2 HOW COMPUTERS WORK

The abacus was an early computer, developed thousands of years ago. It was used to keep track of numbers, and to add or subtract them. Each bead on an abacus can be in one of two positions, left or right, in what is called a binary system. If you haven't used an abacus lately, Figure 3.1 shows how a typical abacus looks. The bottom wire represents the ones column, next up is the tens, hundreds, etc. Beads moved to the right indicate the value of that column.

Abacus-type tools are still used today. For example, infantry soldiers use a very basic abacus when navigating by foot. To keep track of their steps, and thereby determine the distance traveled, they frequently use an abacus-type pace counter.

Computers use a binary system as well. Data is stored in binary digits ("bits"), a unit of data that can have only one of two values. Those values are represented as 1 or 0, "on" or "off". Data values cannot be stored as beads on a string, but the same binary value system is used to store the zero and one data as a specific magnetic charge (positive or negative), or a specific voltage (such as 0 volts or 5 volts). Bits are commonly stored in chips, drives, and other magnetic storage media. Scientists and engineers are always looking at new ways to store data bits, so the storage process can become more complex, but the binary principle holds.

Using these zeros and ones, computers can store enormous amounts of information, combining the bits of data into larger units. There are eight bits in a "byte" of storage, and then bytes of storage are commonly quantified in multiples of ten, such as kilobytes, megabytes, and gigabytes. Using multiples of ten for this purpose makes it more convenient for the average person to conceptualize, although the actual data storage is in multiples of two.

Binary (also called "base 2") counting is an uncomfortable numbering system for most people to use. We are accustomed to using the decimal system (base 10) for counting, and binary does not convert easily to decimal. But in the world of computers, everything is built around the number 2. For example, base 2 converts neatly into another counting system used by computers called "hexadecimal", which is base 16 (with 16 being a multiple of 2). One hexadecimal character can represent four bits (counting up to 15 and requiring the use of letters A through F), and so two characters can represent a byte (or 8 bits). See Table 3.1 for a look at how these three counting systems compare.

The concepts of binary and hexadecimal counting are good to know, especially as we later learn about Internet addressing. These counting methods help explain why certain computer-related numbers are displayed in what seems to be an unusual format. Using these systems, the number of data values that can be stored in a computer can be expressed

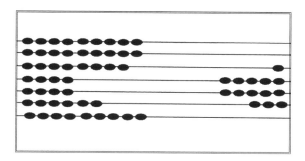

FIGURE 3.1   Abacus Showing Value of 15,530.

TABLE 3.1
Binary to Hexadecimal to Decimal

Binary – 8 bits								Hexadecimal	Decimal
0	0	0	0	0	0	0	0	0 0	0
0	0	0	0	0	0	0	1	0 1	1
0	0	0	0	0	0	1	0	0 2	2
0	0	0	0	0	0	1	1	0 3	3
0	0	0	0	0	1	0	0	0 4	4
0	0	0	0	0	1	0	1	0 5	5
0	0	0	0	0	1	1	0	0 6	6
0	0	0	0	0	1	1	1	0 7	7
0	0	0	0	1	0	0	0	0 8	8
0	0	0	0	1	0	0	1	0 9	9
0	0	0	0	1	0	1	0	0 A	10
0	0	0	0	1	0	1	1	0 B	11
0	0	0	0	1	1	0	0	0 C	12
0	0	0	0	1	1	0	1	0 D	13
0	0	0	0	1	1	1	0	0 E	14
0	0	0	0	1	1	1	1	0 F	15
0	0	0	1	0	0	0	0	1 0	16
0	0	0	1	0	0	0	1	1 1	17
↓	↓	↓	↓	↓	↓	↓	↓	↓	↓
1	1	1	1	1	1	1	1	F F	255

TABLE 3.2
Number of Bits vs. Number of Combinations

Number of bits	Expressed as	Number of combinations (can count up to)
1	2^1	2
2	2^2	4
3	2^3	8
4	2^4	16
5	2^5	32
6	2^6	64
7	2^7	128
8	2^8	256
9	2^9	512
10	2^{10}	1024
11	2^{11}	2048
12	2^{12}	4096

as the number of bits to the power of 2. All of these bytes represent the ability to store information in multiple combinations of data values. See Table 3.2.

When we are using computers, we prefer to see and use the letters of our language, rather than a binary number scheme. There are a variety of schemes to convert letters and regular digits to binary numbers for the purpose of storing them as bits of data, including ASCII (short for American Standard Code for Information Interchange). In ASCII, a byte of data stores a number, and each number corresponds to a single character, digit, or symbol. Of course, the storage process for an entire Word document, Excel Spreadsheet, or JPG image involves a much more complex conversion of information into bits and bytes – storing not just the letters, but also formatting information. A single document or video may take up many megabytes of storage. The storage device in a computer or a server, however, has the capacity to store many gigabytes or terabytes of data, in order to hold all the data the user creates, stores, and accesses, as well as applications and operating systems.

3.3   BASIC HARDWARE PARTS OF COMPUTERS

As our computing devices get sleeker and more compressed to save space, it gets harder for most users to conceptualize all the different parts that make it perform so many functions. But knowing about these separate functions is important for gathering evidence and explaining how the evidence was created and obtained. Places where data is stored, either permanently or temporarily, are of particular importance for obtaining evidence.

Let's go through a brief summary of the parts of a computer, including the:

- Case
- Power source
- Processors (CPU)
- Memory (RAM)
- Persistent storage (HDD/SSD)
- Interfaces for input and output with user
- Network interface controller (NIC)
- Physical ports
- External storage, servers, and more.

3.3.1   CASE

Computers would not last long without a case because it protects the internal components from damage, dirt, and moisture. But beyond holding the guts of the computer, the case is an important facet of the device as a whole. The case provides the interface between the device, the user, and the outside world. For example, a case might include a view-only screen, touch screen, keyboard, microphone, as well as physical ports for a keyboard, monitor, mouse, power supply, and data exchange.

From an evidence perspective, a case is what can be seen by the recovering investigator and the jury, as indicated by Figure 3.2. It can be a piece of physical evidence like any other, and may carry physical characteristics or evidence (like unique markings or fingerprints) that might be useful to the investigation. Once the case itself is assessed, the work begins to figure out what evidence is contained inside. There also may be evidence contained on the outside of the case, such as sticky notes or other markings, that may prove to be important as you begin your analysis.

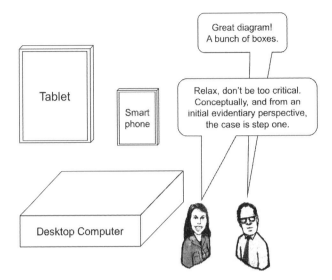

FIGURE 3.2   Computer Cases.

3.3.2   Power Source

Computers need electricity to operate, and that means they need power from an internal battery, from an electrical outlet, or both. Portable devices like laptops, tablets, and smartphones rely upon battery power, with periodic charging. Desktop computers need to be plugged into an electrical outlet, but also have a small battery in order to retain a tiny amount of data, such as the time and date, and to keep the internal clock running.

Generally, when the power source is removed, certain data (called "volatile" data) is lost forever. This data includes information about what programs are running and what is stored in volatile RAM memory. Volatile data is discussed in more detail below.

3.3.3   Processors (CPUs)

The work of a computer is done through computer processors, also known as central processing units (CPUs). These are computer chips, or groups of chips, that do the thinking (the massive number of binary calculations) of the computer necessary to run all programs. The CPU is attached to the computer's motherboard, the central piece of circuitry that connects the device's many chips and electronic components.

From a cybercrime perspective, the importance of processors was underscored in 2017, when the world learned that these components had vulnerabilities that could be attacked. These processor flaws, known as the Spectre and Meltdown vulnerabilities, allowed cybercriminals to read data stored in memory. The security weakness had to be fixed (or "patched") by updating the processor firmware (a type of mini-operating system for hardware). Firmware updates such as these typically are more difficult to deliver and are rarely automated, making vulnerabilities in their design more dangerous to users.

3.3.4 MEMORY (VOLATILE STORAGE – RAM)

A computer relies on a type of memory – known as temporary or volatile storage – to perform most functions. This volatile storage is also called random access memory (RAM). Typically, RAM is found within computer chips that store the data as electrical charges. RAM chips are connected to the motherboard of the computer, along with the CPU. RAM is volatile and temporary because, when the power is turned off, RAM is discharged and the contents are lost. RAM is fast, and is used by computers to load both the programs the user runs, as well as the data those programs access.

For example, when you start a computer, the operating system is loaded into RAM from the device's long-term storage. When you start Microsoft Word, the application is loaded into RAM, and then when you open your Word document, that document gets loaded into RAM as well. Malware that is running also would be loaded into RAM, along with information about when and how the malware started running.

RAM can store valuable evidence about a crime, but it is difficult to capture. Copying and analyzing RAM is known as live memory forensics, which we will discuss later in this chapter.

RAM has space limitations, so to increase RAM capacity and optimize performance, computers also have "virtual RAM", which acts like RAM, except the data is stored temporarily in the computer's persistent (long-term) memory. Data that might traditionally be stored in volatile RAM may also be written temporarily to the computer's persistent storage to make more room available in the RAM, or when the computer is set to "sleep" or "hibernate". The existence of "virtual RAM", or "swap-space", means some RAM data might be recoverable through digital forensics of a computer's persistent storage, as discussed later in this chapter.

3.3.5 PERSISTENT STORAGE (HDD/SSD)

Persistent (long-term) storage holds data stored in the computer even after the power is disconnected. Persistent storage mechanisms include hard disk drives (HDD) and solid state drives (SSD).

HDDs were the standard method for persistent data storage for many years. These drives have spinning disks or platters (as depicted in Figure 3.3) divided into smaller sectors, then ultimately into bit-sized storage units, each of which holds a magnetic charge holding the bit value. SSDs are a newer type of storage drive. These drives do not have any moving parts, but rather are computer chips that store the data as electrical charges. Due to massive speed and reliability improvements, SSDs are fast becoming the standard for commercial use.

Magnetic charges (used by HDDs) are relatively stable, but electrical charges (used by SSDs) tend to move towards a discharged state. Consider that batteries, which carry an electric charge, do not last forever; even if they are not being used, they tend to discharge themselves little by little, and the same is true of SSD storage devices. This difference means that HDDs can be readable after a decade or more in storage, but the jury is still out on how long SSDs will store data without electrical power.

3.3.6 COMMUNICATING WITH THE USER: INTERFACES FOR INPUT AND OUTPUT

Users (whether a victim, evidence gatherer, or cybercriminal) must be able to communicate with computers. Users send and receive information to computers through mechanisms like the keyboard, mouse, monitor, microphone, and speakers.

The user also needs methods to put stored data into the computer, or get data out of the computer. The user might use removable storage media (such as CD-ROMs, DVDs, USB drives) as well as networking mechanisms to communicate with other computers through wired and wireless technology.

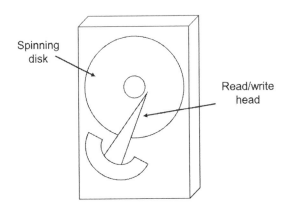

FIGURE 3.3   Hard Disk Drive (HDD).

3.3.7   COMMUNICATING WITH OTHER COMPUTERS (NIC)

Computers also need to be able to communicate with one another, and this communication is principally accomplished through a network interface controller (NIC). This controller used to be called a network interface card, because it was a separate card plugged into the computer's motherboard, but today this function typically is integrated with the computer motherboard.

The NIC can be connected to a physical port (into which a cable would be inserted), or to an antenna to receive wireless signals. If the NIC is connected through a port to a cable (typically an Ethernet cable), the other end of the cable attaches to a router or switch, which connects the device to a network. If the NIC is connected to a wireless antenna – like a Wi-Fi (wireless fidelity) antenna that receives certain wireless signals – the network connection does not require any physical cables. Bluetooth wireless antennas are a different type of wireless technology that enables users to connect to Bluetooth-enabled devices, such as a mouse, keyboard, and wireless headphones.

3.3.8   PHYSICAL PORTS

A computer uses ports to connect with the outside world, just like ships use ports to load and offload cargo. A NIC may have a port for connecting to a wired network through an Ethernet network cable, and a computer's video card has a port to connect to the computer monitor. Today's computers use a variety of universal serial bus (USB) ports for connecting to peripheral devices, including a keyboard, mouse, external storage device, video camera, and more. Mac computers use Thunderbolt ports (USB-C), while PCs often use USB-A.

3.3.9   PUTTING THE PARTS TOGETHER

We now have covered the basic computer parts. When we put them all together, our computer looks like Figure 3.4.

3.3.10   EXTERNAL STORAGE, SERVERS AND MORE

Beyond a computer's internal storage, a user might store data by connecting to external storage devices and other computers. Some common external storage devices are external hard drives, flash drives (thumb drives), or more complicated storage devices, such as network-attached storage, servers, and more.

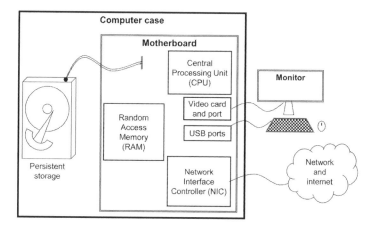

FIGURE 3.4 Motherboard and Computer Components.

Servers are computers that serve the needs of many other computers, and they are generally more powerful in terms of processing and storage capacity. Servers might be on the same local network as a computer, or might be located in the "cloud". Basically, cloud storage means the user is storing data on the servers and other computer storage resources of another entity (such as Google, Microsoft, Amazon, or a data center) as depicted in Figure 3.5. Most of us now store data in the "cloud" in one form or another. Cloud providers are able to leverage deep engineering knowledge and efficiencies of scale which can be beneficial for consumers.

External storage devices and servers can be important sources of evidence in cyber cases, since if they are used by a criminal, they likely contain evidence of crimes. Cyber-criminals might keep and use external storage and servers in places far from their devices and homes. As a result, in some cases, it is possible for investigators to find

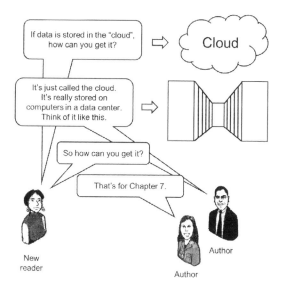

FIGURE 3.5 Cloud Data Storage.

these devices and storage services long before they have pinpointed the suspects' geographical locations. In Chapter 7, we discuss the legal process to obtain data from cloud data providers.

3.4 BASIC COMPUTER SOFTWARE CATEGORIES

Hardware is "hard", and so the term refers to the parts of a computer you can physically touch. Software is an application, a piece of computer code that is programmed to perform a function, and to tell the hardware what to do. In this section, we will summarize different software such as:

- BIOS/UEFI
- Operating systems
- Applications.

Software matters because when the computer is on, software is constantly running, checking the system, waiting for and reacting to user input, and making changes to the data. This process results in the creation and recording of potential evidence. The mere act of turning on a computer makes changes to certain data within it, since the computer will read from and write to certain files as part of the startup process.

3.4.1 BIOS/UEFI

The most basic level of software is the code the computer runs first when it is powered on. Imagine if, every time you woke up in the morning, you had forgotten how to open your eyelids, move your limbs, and speak; your memory was gone and you had to learn everything anew. That phenomenon is essentially what it is like to be a computer. The initial power-on software tells the computer how to perform its basic operations, talk to itself, and communicate with the world. The job of this software is simply to load the minimum amount of code needed to detect an operating system and "boot" it.

For decades, computers used the Basic Input-Output System (BIOS) to start up when powered on. The BIOS name is apt, because this software tells the computer how to conduct basic operations for receiving and sending data. Until the computer is instructed about how to do these essential steps, it cannot hear, see, or communicate.

Now computers are transitioning to a new program called the Unified Extended Firmware Interface (UEFI). UEFI avoids some of the limitations of BIOS, and can start up on larger drives. It is standardized for different computers and operating systems, is faster, more secure, and allows for better troubleshooting. For all these reasons, it is better suited to today's larger, faster computing environment.

3.4.2 Operating Systems

After the BIOS or UEFI completes the steps to get the computer up and running the computer operating system loads. The operating system is the software platform upon which applications run, and it connects those applications to the hardware.

The main operating systems in use for desktop and laptop computers are:

- Microsoft: Windows 10, Windows 8, Windows 7, Windows Server 2019 (etc.)
- Apple: MacOS (Mojave, Catalina, etc.)
- Google's Chrome OS for Chromebooks
- Linux.

The main operating systems in use for mobile devices such as smartphones and tablets are:

- Android (used on Google, Samsung, and other devices)
- Apple iOS
- Windows 10 Mobile.

Operating systems are continually being changed and updated by the companies that produce them.

3.4.3 APPLICATIONS

Applications are software packages that perform specific tasks. Some commonly used applications (or "apps") are Microsoft's Outlook, Word, PowerPoint, and Excel, and Apple's Mail, Pages, and Numbers. Many service and retail companies offer software apps to facilitate using or accessing their products on mobile devices. An essential application we all use is a web browser, such as Internet Explorer, Chrome, Safari, and Firefox. These applications are used not only to surf the web, but to access and work with other browser-based applications.

Applications also include software we might take for granted, or think are part of the operating system, such as the calculator application or clock. Though they come bundled with the operating system, these basic features are actually separate software applications.

3.5 BASIC NETWORKING AND INTERNET USAGE

Networking is the process of allowing two or more computers to communicate with one another. Computer networks can be small or large. In the home, many people use Wi-Fi routers to establish a Wi-Fi network for our many family devices. Large corporations have major networks of computing and storage devices. And the Internet is an enormous network, consisting of millions of connected computers and servers, providing information to the world.

To gain a general understanding of how networks operate, and what evidence they might potentially hold for an investigation, we will look at some basic information about networking hardware, communication protocols, and Internet Protocol (IP) addresses.

3.5.1 NETWORKING HARDWARE

Hardware relevant to networking and Internet usage includes:

- Network Interface Controller (NIC)
- Cables, wireless, and network switches
- Modem
- Router.

3.5.1.1 NIC and MAC Addresses

The Network Interface Controller (NIC) in a computer has a unique identifier assigned by the manufacturer, called a Media Access Control (MAC) address. The MAC address helps identify a particular device, especially on a local network. A tech-savvy cybercriminal can change the MAC address of his NIC to disguise his device, conduct attacks, and impersonate other computers.

3.5.1.2   Cables, Wireless, and Network Switches

One of the main functions of a computer is to send and receive all kinds of data, so it is important to consider how the data travels between computers, routers, and switches. The data has to get from Point A to Point B, and often that transmission is through a cable. Traditional cables are made of copper, transmitting electrical signals that are converted to and from bits as they enter or exit a computer. Newer cables are fiber-optic, transmitting the data as bursts of light through specialized fibers. Whatever the type of cable, the signals sent through them degrade over distance, and periodic boosting through devices such as switches helps to relay, or repeat, the signal.

Data also can be transmitted wirelessly. Wireless transmission uses radio signals that travel through the air as radio waves. All wireless technology relies on some form of hardware to transmit and relay the radio signals. For example, our cell phones connect to cell towers that send and receive wireless data, including phone conversations, Internet surfing, email, and text messages. Our computers and other devices connect to Wi-Fi networks to send and receive wireless signals. Wireless earbuds, mice, and keyboards also send and receive data through the air.

As data travels, it can be intercepted. If the data goes through a cable, securing the cable itself and endpoints from physical access is important to ensure data security. If the data goes through the air, it is potentially accessible to anyone in the vicinity, unless it is secured by encryption.

A switch is a network hardware device that forwards data, but does so automatically, without thinking or processing anything as a router would. Switches are important to relay data over long distances, because otherwise the data signal degrades over the length of the cable and would not reach the destination. Switches also can be a point of compromise for criminals seeking unauthorized access to data.

3.5.1.3   Modem

The modem is a piece of external hardware that sits between the computer and the Internet service provider. Typically, Internet service comes into a home or business through a cable and connects to a modem. The modem acts as a translator. In the early days of the Internet, data was transmitted using telephone lines and analog sounds, and the modem did the translating into computer data protocols. Today, the modem is still needed to translate between different data transmission protocols – those inside your network, and those controlled by the Internet provider.

3.5.1.4   Router

Routers "route" data and information. Routers are needed in the business and home environment to move data among the many computing devices on a network. In the home, the modem and router might be housed within a single hardware unit.

In the common home set-up, the modem connects to the router, which then connects to computing devices either by cable or wirelessly. The router establishes a network and routes data along it, allowing multiple devices to communicate with one another and share resources, especially Internet access. A typical home Wi-Fi router can allow a dozen devices to connect wirelessly, all accessing the Internet simultaneously through a single modem. The router keeps track of every conversation that every device in the home is having with every website or other Internet location, and ensures each conversation can proceed without any of the data getting mixed up. Consider it like a mailroom that sends and receives mail on behalf of many building occupants. The networks of an organization are more complex, so more sophisticated routers are used to keep that data moving properly.

Routers create routing tables to keep track of the various devices in the network, and to keep track of their communications. This function makes routers a potential source of evidence in an investigation, since the tables may contain valuable information about who was using a particular network and what communication occurred. Routers are also susceptible to compromise by cybercriminals. Routers have firmware (an operating system) and, like every application, vulnerabilities are periodically discovered. If this firmware is not updated regularly, an attacker may be able to compromise the router. Routers have administrator portals that are secured with a password, and weak or default passwords also can make routers vulnerable to attack.

Since Wi-Fi networks move data through the air, the data is subject to interception. Well-secured Wi-Fi networks use strong encryption to transmit data, and require a strong password to join the network. An open, or public, Wi-Fi network allows anyone to join it. Data transmitted on these unsecured networks is available for anyone to see.

3.5.2 NETWORKING COMMUNICATION AND INTERNET PROTOCOL (IP) ADDRESSES

The Internet is an enormous network of computers that relay data to, from, and on behalf of other computers. Often, two computers using the network will connect with each other to send and receive data, such as when you visit a website. Each portal to the Internet has a unique Internet Protocol (IP) address. These addresses enable Internet communication by specifying the destination and return address of each device online. For communication through the Internet to work, a device needs to know its own IP address, and the IP address of the other computer with which it is communicating, as depicted in Figure 3.6.

Data sent between two computers must be broken up into smaller pieces, or "packets", to allow transmission through the Internet to the ultimate destination. Data moving to and from destinations around the world through the Internet passes through a series of computers along the way. Each packet might take a different route from sender to recipient, where it is then reassembled into the original large chunk. To envision this process, imagine you are at a crowded baseball game and want to buy a hotdog from the roaming vendor, but you are stuck ten seats into the row. To pay the vendor standing in the aisle, you might need to pass your money through the crowd, until it gets to the vendor, he gets the hot dog ready and then sends your hotdog back to you with the change. On the Internet, there is a similar dynamic that relies on intermediary computers to send along the data. Unlike

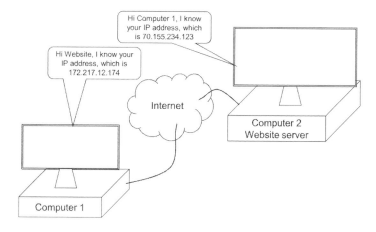

FIGURE 3.6 Computer to Website Connection.

passing money and hotdogs straight along the row, however, data travels through the Internet using many different routes, depending upon which Internet servers are available.

There are two kinds of IP addresses: public and private. Public IP addresses are used on the Internet, and private IP addresses are used for private networks in homes or offices, sometimes known as local area networks (LANs). A computer that communicates with the Internet uses both a private IP address on its local network and a public IP address as identification online. This process of translating between a public IP and a private IP is known as network address translation (NAT), and is done by the router. Multiple computers can share the same public IP address. The router gives each computer a private IP address on the local network and routes their traffic through the public IP address to the Internet.

Public IP addresses are set up by the Internet Assigned Numbers Authority (IANA), a multinational organization that helps administer IP addresses and other Internet-related systems. IANA allocates address ranges to each country (while some addresses are reserved for private use). Each country then distributes its set of public IP addresses to the nation's Internet Service Providers (ISPs), the entities through which users access the Internet. When users go online, they use IP addresses from their ISP (e.g. from Comcast, Verizon, etc.).

On a local network, such as the network established by your home Wi-Fi router, the router assigns a *private* IP address for each device on the local network, including itself. The router uses these private IP addresses to keep track of all the devices on the network, and the data being transmitted into and out of each one. The routing table tracks the MAC address and IP address of each device on the network, and assigns virtual ports (virtual mailboxes) to keep track of each computing device's conversations with the outside world.

IP addresses traditionally use the IPv4 format, which uses four sets of numbers separated by periods. The entire address is stored in four bytes, and each byte can store a number from 0 to 255. These four numbers are displayed with decimals in between, allowing for IP addresses ranging from:

    0.0.0.0   to   255.255.255.255

In establishing the IPv4 protocol, some IP address ranges were reserved exclusively for private use. Any address within these ranges cannot be a public IP, but is reserved for private companies and individuals to use in their local internal or home networks. When a local network is established, the administrator decides what IP addresses within the private ranges to use. You don't need permission from anyone, and different companies and individuals can use the same private IP addresses in their respective private networks.

The private IP address ranges are:

    10.0.0.0   to   10.255.255.255
    172.16.0.0   to   172.31.255.255
    192.168.0.0   to   192.168.255.255 (most home networks are in this range)

IP addresses are a common clue regarding network and Internet activity, and investigators should be knowledgeable about whether an IP address is private or public. If it is a private IP address, you look within its local network to identify the device, including by looking at the routing tables. If it is a public IP address, you need to look to see what ISP is assigned that IP address. There are a number of reputable and free online services to look up IP addresses.

Thanks to network address translation, a public IP address is often shared by more than one device. If a cybercrime investigator learns that a public IP address was used to commit a crime, investigation may reveal that the public IP address was shared by many computers on the local area network. The investigator would then examine local network records showing which device (and which private IP address) was used to commit the crime. Other investigation avenues would also be followed to identify the specific computer and user involved.

The Internet is outgrowing IPv4, as there are too many people and devices needing an IP address. A new addressing system, called IPv6, was developed to allow for more addresses. IPv6 is a 16-byte system, allowing millions of additional address combinations to be generated. The IPv6 addresses are written in hexadecimal form, separated by colons, and might look something like this:

2001:4860:4860:0000:0000:0000:0000:8888

Because IPv6 addresses are so much longer, there are some conventions for shortening how they are written where the value of certain bytes is zero (0000). One way to do this is simply to delete the four zeroes, resulting in two back-to-back colons.

Thus, the above address could be shortened to this:

2001:4860:4860::8888

Investigators may encounter both IPv4 and IPv6 addresses when looking at records of Internet activity.

3.5.3   TCP versus UDP

While IP addresses are the addressing system on the Internet that allow computers to find one another, computers still need a common language to talk to each other. In network speak, that language is known as a protocol, and there are two main protocols for Internet communication – Transmission Control Protocol (TCP) and User Datagram Protocol (UDP). TCP is a controlled form of communication that reliably delivers data exactly as it is sent and checks regularly to make sure nothing is missing or got misrouted through the Internet as the packets were separated and then reassembled. TCP is used for many of the Internet's core functions, such as email and websites. TCP's accurate process takes time, however, and slows down the transfer of data.

UDP, on the other hand, is faster but less accurate. It is used for transferring large amounts of data quickly, such as for streaming music or video, or for multi-player video games. UDP does not check to ensure all the data is received exactly as sent, because that level of precision is not needed for these purposes. A small loss or error in packet delivery will not have a noticeable effect upon your movie viewing, but waiting for 100% packet delivery would be a noticeable interruption.

3.5.4   Domain Name System (DNS)

As we mentioned, computers communicate with one another on the Internet by specifying both a destination and origination IP address. For computers, IP addresses are easy to remember, but for us humans, IP addresses are inconvenient. Imagine if you had to remember an IPv4 address to go to a website? You would have to type something like "72.167.241.180" into your web browser address bar to visit it. But thanks to the domain name system (DNS), we do not have to do that. Instead, we can type the domain name of our website (such as cybercrimeinvestigationsbook.com or cnn.com) into the address bar. The domain name system will look up that domain name in a database and direct the computer to the IP address where the website is hosted.

To rent a domain name, you first have to go to a domain name registrar and check to see if the domain name is available. If it is available, you can rent it for a chosen period of time. The domain name includes a specific top-level domain suffix (such as .com, .org, or .net). CNN.com, for example, is a completely different domain name from CNN.net. When renting (registering) a domain name, you are asked to provide contact information. This registration information might be made public, but domain registrars usually offer the option of keeping it private for an extra fee.

Cybercriminals may register domain names that sound similar to legitimate businesses or services to trick unsuspecting users (such as domain names similar to the websites of banks and credit card companies). They also can manipulate the domain name system to misdirect website traffic to the wrong website server, so that a user trying to reach a legitimate company's website is directed to the criminals' fake website instead. There are many open source tools to investigate domain name registration. In a law enforcement investigation, subpoenas to domain name registrars and website hosting companies for customer registration and usage details also can yield helpful information.

3.5.5 Website Hosting

After a domain name is registered (rented), the registrant may decide to host a website at that domain. Web hosting services – which are companies that provide server space for the websites of many customers – make this easy. The domain name system is notified that the website's domain is hosted at the particular IP address of the server, so that website visitors can be routed there. Using a hosting service is not required; anyone could host a website from his or her personal or business computer.

Often, multiple websites will share the same IP address – a practice known as shared website hosting. This sharing system is for websites that do not have a lot of traffic, allowing the data for many websites to share the IP address and server. Some websites need a dedicated IP address because the amount of traffic they receive requires the entire capacity of a server and the IP address' entire bandwidth. Some websites even use multiple IP addresses and multiple servers to handle the volume of their business. A global website like Google.com or CNN.com will need multiple IP addresses and servers all over the world, so that users are routed to an IP address and server closer to them. Sophisticated load balancing may take place when some servers or regions are overloaded – or attacked – so that extra traffic can be transferred to other sites.

Websites are often attacked by cybercriminals, including through distributed denial-of-service (DDOS) attacks designed to exceed the capacity of a site and make it unavailable to legitimate users. Some load-balancing services also help mitigate these attacks, rerouting attackers to where they will do less damage, and routing legitimate users so that they can access the site. Cybercriminals also attempt to gain control of websites to deface them, use them to send spam, or for other malicious purposes.

Importantly, when a website visitor sees text and images displayed on the same page, those might come from many different sources and not just from the server where the website is hosted. For example, a website may display a Twitter feed (with content obtained from Twitter), videos (with content obtained from YouTube or Vimeo), and advertising (also from third parties). Investigators should consider whether the data they seek is located on the website at the domain in question, from another source, or both, to determine the entity or entities they should approach to obtain evidence.

3.6   PROXIES, VPNS, AND TOR

We mentioned how Internet communication conceptually goes from point to point, with each party to the communication knowing the IP address of the counterparty's device. The parties intentionally send and receive data between devices at these identified IP addresses.

Cybercriminals conducting an attack or implementing a scheme do not want to expose their true IP addresses because that would make it too easy to find and catch them. It would be like a criminal burglarizing a home, and then leaving a trail of footprints right back to his own front door.

Instead, many cybercriminals take steps to mask their IP addresses. One way to mask an IP address is by using a proxy – in other words, a criminal can send his Internet traffic through a second "proxy" computer, so that it is the second computer's IP address that is recorded by websites, email services, and other Internet locations visited or used by the criminal. The criminal's actual IP address is disguised.

A proxy could simply be another computer, somewhere in the world, connected to the Internet with its own IP address. Sometimes a proxy belongs to an unwitting participant, whose computer is infected with malware and is surreptitiously being used by criminals. Criminals might use chains of proxies, to make it even harder to trace online activity back to them.

A virtual private network (VPN) also works as a proxy, though it also has the feature of encrypting the data in transit between the user and the VPN. Figure 3.7 depicts the use of a proxy or VPN to disguise one's true IP address.

A VPN is a service provided by a company for free or as a paid subscription, that routes a customer's Internet traffic through the company's own computers. VPNs can be a useful tool for protecting the privacy and security of law-abiding people, assuming they use a reliable VPN provider. Aside from disguising the customer's IP address, the VPN encrypts communications between the user and the VPN provider adding a layer of confidentiality. Anyone trying to secretly monitor Internet communication between the user and the VPN can see only encrypted traffic, and cannot see the ultimate destinations or the content of the data.

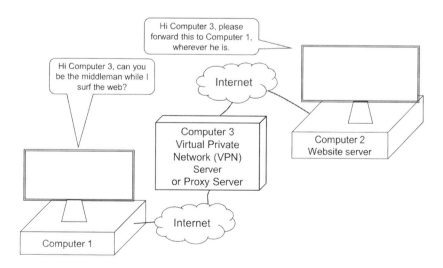

FIGURE 3.7   Computer Using VPN or Proxy to Connect to Website.

Western Express and Proxies

In the Western Express case, many cybercriminals and identity thieves used proxies to conduct all their online business. Eskalibur – a major vendor of stolen credit and debit card account information – was even in the business of renting out proxies for use by other cybercriminals early in his cybercrime career. Another unidentified cybercriminal used a variety of proxy computers all over the country to place online orders paid with stolen credit card information. And one identity thief shielded his true location and IP information by "borrowing" the unsecured Wi-Fi networks of his neighbors to do his business online.

Cybercrime investigators need to be familiar with how proxying occurs to pierce through criminals' anonymity attempts. If an IP address is discovered in connection with a crime, investigators need to consider whether that IP address is merely a proxy.

When a criminal is ultimately caught, he may falsely claim his own computer was used as a proxy by someone else, and he was just an unwitting party. A thorough investigation can defeat such false defenses.

When a user visits a website through a VPN, the website can only see that the user is coming from the IP address of the VPN provider, and cannot see the user's true IP address. Using a VPN, however, does not prevent websites from learning certain information about the device connecting to it. For example, a website still might be able to detect the visiting device's operating system, computer monitor, language, time zone, and other information. Websites that collect detailed information about visiting devices are said to "fingerprint" the computer devices.

If an investigation reveals a suspect is using a VPN to navigate online, in addition to looking for information from websites the suspect visited, the investigator might consider requesting or compelling records from the VPN provider itself. Many VPN services advertise that they do not keep logs, implying they retain no data that would be responsive to a subpoena or request. But some service providers, in fact, do keep records and logs, or may have relevant payment information.

The Onion Router (Tor) is another method used to mask IP addresses. We introduced Tor in Chapter 2, and it is associated with untraceable criminal activity online and the "Dark Web". In sum, Tor is a privacy tool that is being misused by cybercriminals. It began as a research project of the U.S. military in the 1990s, and later was further developed by the Electronic Frontier Foundation (EFF). It now is administered for public use by a non-profit organization called The Tor Project.[1] By 2013, Tor gained media notoriety in connection with the "Silk Road" online criminal marketplace.

Tor essentially is an Internet proxy system on steroids. Instead of using one computer as a proxy, it uses multiple computers, known as Tor nodes, as a series of proxies. Each computer in the process can see no further than the computers with which they are directly interacting.

A computer user might use the Tor system to connect to a website on the traditional web. In that case, the website would only see that the traffic was coming from a Tor exit node (server) and respond to that node, as depicted in Figure 3.8.

Websites also can be hosted on Tor, meaning a user would not know where exactly a Tor website server is located, and the website would not know where exactly the Tor user is located. Figure 3.9 depicts how this website traffic is routed.

Tor encrypts the addressing information of the Tor nodes and the path communications take, thereby protecting the location of the sender and recipient from each other, and concealing the location of Tor nodes beyond the direct hop. It also encrypts the data en route

---

[1] *See* The Tor Project, www.torproject.org.

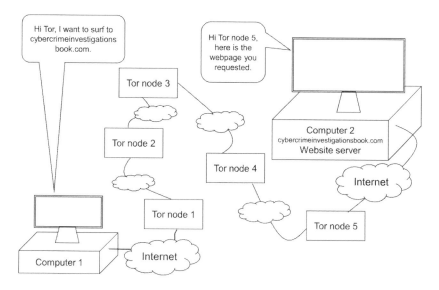

FIGURE 3.8 Computer Using Tor to Visit a Traditional Website.

between the Tor nodes. End-to-end encryption is achieved separately through encryption in transit as discussed next.

While there are many legitimate privacy purposes for Tor, including to enable freer Internet use within repressive countries, cybercriminals are naturally drawn to this tool.

3.7 ENCRYPTION

Encryption is the process by which data is encoded so that only authorized people can access it. When data is encrypted, it is passed through an algorithm that essentially scrambles the data into gibberish. A user needs a special "key" in order to decode – or "decrypt" – the data. Encryption relies upon the mathematical science and art of cryptography.

Encryption is an important way to keep data confidential, and is even recommended or required for some kinds of sensitive data by certain laws, regulations, and information security frameworks, as we cover in Chapter 4.

3.7.1 ENCRYPTION IN TRANSIT

Data can be encrypted for its ride through a local network or across the Internet. This type of encryption is known as encryption in transit or in motion. Encrypting transmitted information is an important concept because traffic on the Internet gets routed through many computers as it is forwarded along to its ultimate destination. While the data is en route, it is vulnerable to unauthorized viewing or even tampering. Encrypting data in transit protects it from these risks by encoding the data, so that it cannot be deciphered without the secret key. If you visit a website and the connection is "HTTPS", the communication with the website is encrypted, whereas a website communication through "HTTP" is not encrypted.

3.7.2 ENCRYPTION AT REST

Data also can be encrypted while it is stored on a computing device. Data in storage is called data "at rest". Data breaches often compromise stored data, making encryption an

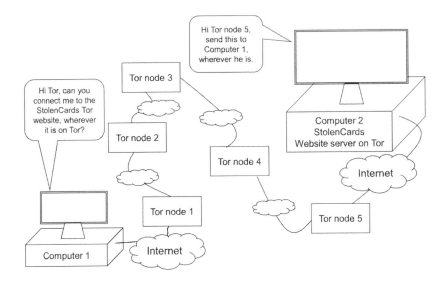

FIGURE 3.9   Computer Using Tor to Visit a Tor Website.

important form of protection. Even if encrypted data is accessed and stolen, the information cannot be deciphered without the decryption key. As we will discuss in Chapter 13, cybercrime investigations can be hampered by encryption at rest, as more and more devices use operating systems with automatic full-disk encryption. Law enforcement may have a search warrant based upon probable cause that the device contains evidence of a crime, yet the data within these devices is encrypted and cannot be revealed without the password, or perhaps significant effort to decode it. For investigators, encryption may mean that other avenues need to be pursued to find digital evidence.

3.8   DIGITAL FORENSICS AND EVIDENCE GATHERING

Not surprisingly, the digital evidence in cybercrime cases typically includes data from three sources

- Computers, other electronic devices, and networks
- Email, text messages, and other electronic communication
- Websites.

Now that we have a general understanding of how computers and the Internet work, we can use this knowledge to better understand the technological methods that thoroughly and properly capture evidence of this nature.

In this section, we will look at techniques for extracting data from computers and other devices, and introduce concepts for documenting information on websites and analyzing email evidence. Gathering evidence from a computer or other electronic device involves a specialized "forensic" examination of all of the hardware and software components we have reviewed in this chapter. We also will introduce the fundamental principles relating to digital forensics in this section.

3.8.1   ENSURING INTEGRITY OF STORED DATA: HASHING

Whenever investigators are handling data that might be evidence in a case – such as from a website, email, or device – it is important to keep a secure copy that remains in the exact condition in which it was received. This practice keeps a clean data set available for use as evidence in any future legal proceedings. A separate copy of the data set can then be used for examination and analysis, with less fear of potential changes that might occur.

An important method for maintaining data integrity is called hashing, which is a cryptographic technique that helps ensure data has not been changed or corrupted. Think of it as a point-by-point scan of a set of data that is then recorded and protected by a one-way encryption algorithm. Data is put through the algorithm, and a result is returned. That result is called a hash value. Hash values are long alphanumerical (hexadecimal) numbers unique to a particular set of data. If any of the data is changed and the scan is performed again, the algorithm will return a different hash value result. In other words, if the hash algorithm returns an identical result for a set of data at two points in time, we can be confident that the data was not changed in the interim. Similarly, if two sets of data return the same hash value, we know the data sets are exactly the same.

Hashing is used by computer forensic examiners to ensure they are making an accurate copy of data seized in the course of investigations, and to ensure the data they have examined has not been altered or corrupted. Hashing is also used in many other settings to verify the integrity of data or transactions.

Figure 3.10 shows how a forensic examiner uses hash values to verify her work, ensure the evidence was not tampered with, and rebut future defense allegations about the integrity of the evidence.

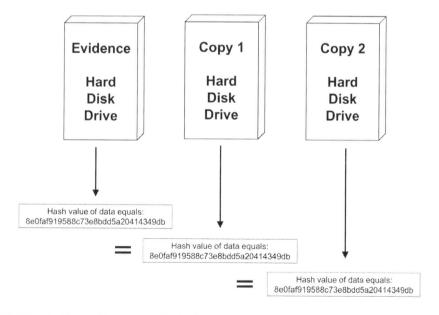

FIGURE 3.10   Hashing to Ensure Data is the Same.

3.8.2   Stored Data (Persistent Storage) in Devices: Forensically Obtaining Evidence through Imaging and Analysis

When devices are obtained as evidence in an investigation – such as by consent or a search warrant – the data stored in them must be preserved and analyzed for potential evidence. Whether it is a smartphone, tablet, laptop, or desktop computer, that device has persistent storage, meaning it has data that can be recovered.

A cybercrime investigation might focus on a particular device because:

- The cybercriminal attacked that computer or device
- The cybercriminal used a victim's computer or device as a tool to commit a crime
- That was the cybercriminal's computer or device, used to carry out criminal activities.

To obtain and preserve data in persistent storage in a sound forensic manner requires cybercrime investigators to follow certain practices. The key principles of forensics are not to alter the digital evidence in any way (unless it is necessary to conduct the analysis, and is properly documented), and to recover data in a manner that preserves the integrity of the evidence at every step in the process. Stored data recovered in this manner will be accurate, admissible in court, and withstand future defense attacks about its integrity.

3.8.2.1   Preview/Triage

Under certain circumstances, investigators might determine that some data should be obtained from a device at the site where it is found, before removing it to a laboratory or other facility for fuller forensic analysis. This process is known as a preview or triage.

For example, if a search warrant is executed at a home or other location, and investigators discover a device that might shut down or encrypt if they unplug it to remove for analysis, they might elect to conduct an on-site triage. The triage consists of an initial review of the devices in a forensically sound manner. Trained investigators at the location where the device is found might copy out data that appears relevant, then seize the device for later imaging and analysis. Investigators also sometimes opt for on-site triage when they know their agency lacks the resources to promptly image and analyze the seized computers. The on-site triage may be their best option to get information and evidence to further the investigation. Like all forensic examination, on-site triage requires specialized training and software tools.

3.8.2.2   Imaging

When a device is removed to a laboratory for forensic analysis, the first step forensic examiners take is to "image" the stored data within it. Imaging is the process of making an exact copy of the data stored on a device. This copying ensures that the entirety of the data is captured – not only files and images the user can access, but also deleted documents and other vestiges of computer usage that the ordinary user of the device would not be able to access.

Imaging is usually conducted using a "write blocker", which ensures the forensic examiner only has "read only" access to the data, and cannot alter it in any way during the copying process. There are both hardware and software write blockers, though the hardware write blocker is preferred, and is a device which is attached to the hard drive or other data storage device that will be imaged.

Using software, the data is then copied to new, blank external hard drives. Typically, two copies of the data are made – one copy is a working copy, and the other copy is stored for safe keeping. Both before imaging and after the copies are made, hash values are obtained and compared to ensure that the copies are identical to the original.

3.8.2.3 Analysis

If digital evidence is obtained through a preview/triage process, it will likely have been obtained in a format that is convenient for the average computer user to review. In other words, the data will consist of common file types such as word processing documents, spreadsheets, images, and emails, which can be viewed and searched by ordinary computer users. Investigators who know the case are best equipped to perform this analysis. Their familiarity with the facts and circumstances of the investigation will enable them to understand the potential relevance of facts and details within the recovered digital evidence.

When digital evidence is obtained through imaging, it is of no use to the average user because a forensic software tool is needed to review the data. This specialized software analyzes the data and recognizes common file types (like documents, spreadsheets, and graphic images), finds deleted files, and obtains details about computer usage (such as the Internet browser history). Today's computer devices contain enormous amounts of data, so reviewing a forensic image with this software can be a lengthy process.

Typically, an investigator with computer forensic expertise conducts the review, but this investigator may have no direct knowledge about the case. Therefore, it is important that an investigator with a detailed understanding of the case assist with the forensic review. The more these two investigators can work together, and are informed and trained about what the other is looking for and can do, the better the results from this analysis. Finding evidence to prove the case, or leads that might further the investigation, depends upon this collaboration.

"Data about data" is also important, and is known as metadata. In the forensic context, investigators might look for helpful metadata such as the time and date that certain data was created or received, as well as the source, file name, size, and author of the data. It is not enough to show that a suspect's computer contained a photo or a Word document; it is also necessary to show how it got there. Metadata can provide this information by showing when the document was created, modified, accessed, and more.

Western Express Forensics

One of our favorite success stories involved a search warrant conducted by Ukrainian authorities at the residence of Egor Shevelev in Kiev. A Secret Service agent who was fluent in Russian was present as an observer. Perhaps the best evidence had been concealed or destroyed by the suspect's associates, but other computer evidence was found, including older hard drives. The hard drives were imaged, and another Secret Service agent conducted the computer forensic analysis. This agent, like the first was fluent in Russian, and was a fantastic forensic examiner. He took the time to learn the case, including the facts, names, dates, and events that combined to cement the proof that Egor Shevelev was, in fact, Eskalibur – a major cybercriminal laundering money through Western Express in New York.

The examining agent found clues throughout the computer, often in hidden places that helped prove those devices were used by Eskalibur, and that tied Shevelev to Eskalibur's cybercrime activity and criminal profits. Before and at trial, the testimony of both agents, coupled with clear and logical trial exhibits, helped get this essential evidence to the jury in a compelling fashion. It was memorable when one of the defense attorneys attempted to undermine an agent's testimony and Russian language abilities, and how the agent was able to explain the fine points of Russian and Ukrainian pronunciation. The courtroom was impressed and the attorney moved on. Defense attacks on other government witnesses fared no better, thanks to their integrity, expertise, and good preparation.

Many people may not fully appreciate how much data is created and stored in their digital devices. Consider the typical smartphone that we carry constantly. It stores or accesses emails, contacts, calendar items, and a record of all phone calls. It contains information about all of the places we have been, perhaps tracking our whereabouts within a matter of yards or feet. It records the Internet searches we have done, websites we have visited and apps we have downloaded. And depending on the apps we have installed and our settings, it might be creating, transmitting, and storing troves of additional data. All of this information is potential evidence in a cybercrime investigation.

Of course, if the storage device is encrypted, it needs to be decoded for analysis to occur, either by using the password or by breaking the code. Left encrypted, the data extracted from the device will be gibberish. Sometimes, rather than full-disk encryption, only individual files are encrypted. Regardless of the type of encryption, there are tools that forensic examiners can use to try to break the encryption or guess the password.

3.8.3   Volatile Memory: Conducting Memory Forensics

Volatile memory, stored in RAM and which would be lost if the computer was turned off, also can be captured and analyzed. This type of forensic work requires a higher degree of skill and effort, involving special techniques and software tools that can copy, analyze, and document a device's volatile memory (including all programs running). This forensic approach may be used only in specialized cases. For example, if a company is attacked by malware or a data breach, it may decide to isolate an affected computer from the network and Internet and conduct memory forensics. The examination might identify the malware or method of breach.

3.8.4   Website Evidence: Viewing and Preserving

Websites contain evidence of many types of information and activity that can offer leads and intelligence for an investigation. In Chapter 11, we will provide some tips on how investigators can gather, store, and analyze website evidence. Here, we will briefly mention some of the digital evidence that should be recovered, which includes:

* Date and time of the preservation
* Website address, meaning universal resource locator (URL), including domain and webpage
* What is displayed to the website visitor (text, images, or videos)
* Data that may not be displayed, including links to other websites
* Follow-on research regarding domain name registration and website hosting.

Since the content of webpages is temporary and can be altered or removed at any time by the website administrators, it may be important to preserve a website for the evidence it contains at a particular date and time. Much of the Internet is open for us to search, and cybercrime investigators can find valuable evidence by becoming adept at open source investigation, as we cover in Chapter 11. Obtaining website data through legal process, such as using a subpoena, may be another option for private sector and law enforcement investigation, as discussed in Chapters 7 and 9.

3.8.5   Emails and Email Headers

Emails contain hidden information stored in the email "header" that is helpful for investigative purposes. We are accustomed to seeing our personal and business emails displayed in a friendly format that shows the sender, recipient, the names of other people copied on the email, the date and time, and the subject line.

Headers contain much more information beyond the basic display we see in normal use. A full header contains details such as the IP address from which the email was sent and the route it took through the Internet to its destination, sort of like a postage cancellation stamp indicates where a letter was mailed. As email messages are processed by mail gateways, header information is added to annotate actions taken. Some email technologies can make it more difficult for criminals to manipulate the information captured in a full email header.

Chapter 11 has more information for investigators on reading headers and analyzing them for evidence.

3.8.6 FORENSIC EXAMINATION TOOLS

As you can see, forensic examination involves several steps and tasks, and there are many software tools available to perform them. Some of these software packages are complex and require training to use properly. Many are proprietary tools requiring annual licensing fees. There are, however, some free and open source tools available.

Change occurs rapidly, and there are many forensic software products on the market. Some forensic steps for which software tools may be needed include:

- Hashing to calculate and verify hashes of data sets
- Preview/triage of laptop and desktop computers
- Imaging of laptop and desktop computers
- Imaging of mobile devices (smartphones, tablets)
- Analysis of laptop and desktop computers
- Analysis of mobile devices
- Capturing (imaging) volatile memory
- Analysis of volatile memory
- Malware analysis
- Preserving websites
- Analyzing email records
- Parsing and presentation of various software activity logs.

3.9 CONCLUSION

Improving one's basic technical knowledge helps any investigator better understand how cyber-crime is committed and how to investigate it, and this chapter provides that foundation. Data may be stored in many places. When found, it must be properly handled and analyzed to ensure it is authentic, and to defeat false claims that it has been altered. Searching for digital evidence, understanding it and presenting it to others requires some knowledge about how devices create and store data, and how they communicate with other devices.

Often, it is not enough to show the data was there. Investigators must find proof of who was using the device or caused the action in question. This type of evidence is found through detailed analysis of the data and surrounding circumstances. By understanding computers and the technology used to extract and analyze data, investigators can successfully demonstrate when cyber-criminals have "ownership and control" of a device used to commit criminal activity.

4 Introduction to Information Security and Cybersecurity

This chapter is primarily for:

- Those who are not information security professionals
- Those seeking a better understanding of how information systems are secured
- Those interested in the intersection between cybercrime and information security.

4.1 INTRODUCTION

In the last chapter, we summarized how computers, networks, and technology work, with an eye towards understanding how cybercrimes are committed and investigated, and the technical aspects of obtaining digital evidence.

In this chapter, we focus on information security basics, the controls and defenses that private and government organizations put in place to prevent cybercrime, and how cybercriminals might circumvent those controls. These basic principles apply to organizations of all sizes, and can be tailored to an organization's needs and resources. Again, this discussion is geared towards the investigator who needs to figure out how the cybercrime happened, who did it, what security measures were in place, how they were avoided, and how to prevent the crime in the future. To find the answers to these questions, an investigator needs to be able to intelligently communicate with information technology, information security, and digital forensics professionals, who are well situated to find and preserve evidence relating to a criminal attack.

The topic of information security also encompasses incident response. We will look at the process of detecting and responding to a potential cybercrime. This chapter also lays a foundation regarding the civil and regulatory aspects of information security, which often come down to an analysis of whether cyber defenses were "reasonable" and "adequate" under the circumstances. Chapter 9 covers civil and regulatory issues in more detail, including compliance with information security regulations and evolving norms.

4.2 BASIC INFORMATION SECURITY AND CYBERSECURITY PRINCIPLES

The field of information security centers on protecting an organization's information assets from a broad range of threats, including cybercrime, natural disaster, brick-and-mortar burglary, and social engineering. Information security is an established profession that was around long before we started putting "cyber" in front of all manner of dictionary words. In other words, the broader discipline of information security encompasses the newer world of cybersecurity, a term used to describe measures specifically designed to protect data and networks from Internet threats.

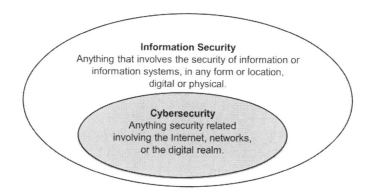

FIGURE 4.1   Information Security vs. Cybersecurity.

The bigger picture of "information security" is demonstrated in Figure 4.1.

Cybercrime often represents a compromise of cybersecurity defenses – such as unauthorized access to data or systems. Cybercrime investigation and cybersecurity, therefore, are two disciplines that go together. The information security professionals can help further the investigation, and the investigators can help improve security. This potential symbiotic relationship is greatly enhanced when cybercrime investigators understand information security concepts and can communicate well with "infosec" experts and personnel.

Many private sector and regulatory cyber investigations stem from incidents related to information security. The law surrounding cybersecurity negligence is developing, with an increasing focus on whether security was reasonable in light of the circumstances, and whether it complied with security principles, norms, and frameworks. Evolving laws, regulations, and court decisions provide guidance that the private sector must incorporate, while simultaneously working to keep up with new and different information security threats.

Now that we know the relevance of information security, let's look at its principles and various standards.

4.2.1   CIA: The Three Information Security Objectives

Information security centers around three basic objectives for protecting information assets: confidentiality, integrity, and availability. Configuring information systems often requires compromises among these three objectives. When investigating a cybercrime, or defending against a cyberattack, distinguishing which objective is implicated can be a useful place to start.

Confidentiality means ensuring the secrecy of information that is meant to remain private, and ensuring that only authorized individuals can access it. A cybercriminal who breaches a company's network and steals data has violated the confidentiality that it was supposed to have. Similarly, an individual who steals a victim's password and accesses her email has violated the confidentiality of her account.

Integrity means ensuring that information cannot be altered or tampered with by unauthorized parties. An employee who changes the company's financial data to give himself a bonus or hide a theft has violated the integrity of the data. Integrity compromises also might include a cyber intruder breaching a website and defacing it, or breaching an email system and sending emails as if he were the rightful account owner.

Availability means ensuring that systems and information are available for use by those who need them and are authorized to use them, such as employees, customers, and account holders. Long before cybercrime, businesses worked to anticipate the effects of floods and fires to ensure they would not shut down information systems for too long or cause paper records to be destroyed. With cybercrime, malicious actors might impair the availability of information by attacking websites to render them inaccessible for users, or by using ransomware to encrypt a victim's data.

4.2.2 Controls to Protect Information Systems

In order to ensure these three objectives, various control measures need to be applied to systems, data, and people. These controls usually are broken into three different types: administrative, technical, and physical. In a cyberattack, investigators might consider which controls were circumvented, or should have been in place but were not.

An *administrative control* is a management tool, such as a policy, procedure, governance structure, or training. For example, a company may require employees to attend trainings on securing their devices and accounts, or may have a written policy that states only select employees can access sensitive data. If a cybercrime occurs, the investigation may review governance documents setting forth these controls to determine whether they are reasonable, and whether the company ensured compliance with them. Organizations of larger sizes require a more mature security posture, including greater documentation. Inaccurate or inadequate documentation by the organization can play a role in determining root causes of a successful cyberattack and who is liable for any damage.

A *technical control* is a rule in software or hardware that works to protect information and prevent unauthorized access. For example, there may be a technical control that requires passwords to be at least ten characters long, and of sufficient complexity, and will not allow a user to create a simpler or shorter password. Firewalls (software or hardware barriers that monitor and regulate contact with the Internet and other networks), intrusion detection systems, encryption, and access control software are also examples of technical controls.

Physical controls protect the physical locations where information and systems are accessible. Such controls include doors, locks, fencing, lighting, security alarms, and security guards. Physical security is essential for information security. If you lose or damage your laptop or smartphone, you create opportunities for unauthorized access to your data and information systems. If an attacker gains physical access to a computing device, router, switch, or cabling, the attacker may be able to obtain data contained within or passing through these forms of hardware.

Administrative, technical, and physical controls can protect one or more of the "CIA" objectives.

4.2.3 Authentication to Guard Access (*Who Are You Anyway?*)

Authentication is a technical control that enforces administrative rules about access to data. It is one of the most widely used information security methods and a familiar one to most users. An authentication process verifies that a user of a computer system is who she purports to be, and is authorized to access certain resources. Every time we log into a computer system, or into our email or other cloud accounts, we go through an authentication process.

There are three main "factors" used to authenticate users of information systems:

- Something you *know*, such as a password
- Something you *have*, such as a smartphone, key fob, or other token
- Something you *are*, such as a fingerprint pattern, retinal pattern, or facial features.

Some information security systems rely on just one of these factors, while others use a combination of factors for authentication.

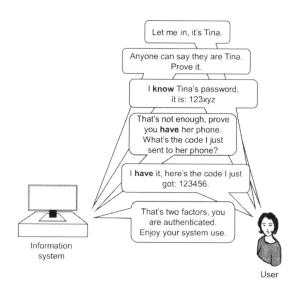

FIGURE 4.2 Prove Who You Are: Multi-Factor Authentication.

Passwords, although the most common authentication factor, have many vulnerabilities, and can be compromised through a number of techniques. Where information systems are available through the Internet – to anyone with an Internet connection – a password alone may be inadequate to provide reasonable security. A second factor of authentication may be required. When a system requires two or more factors of authentication to authenticate a user, this method is called two-factor authentication or multi-factor authentication (2FA, MFA as depicted in Figure 4.2). Of course, no security measure is impenetrable and cybercrime techniques continually evolve to beat enhanced authentication security.

Two-Factor Authentication Lawsuit

Two-factor authentication is not foolproof. Consider the example of Michael Terpin, a cryptocurrency enthusiast who secured his virtual currency account using two-factor authentication (a password plus a SMS text message to his cellular phone). His cellular service was supplied by AT&T.

Cybercriminals targeted Terpin, learned his cell phone number, and – with the help of a low-level AT&T employee – gained control of his cellphone account. The criminals then were able to take over Terpin's cryptocurrency account by changing its password. When the cryptocurrency sought to verify the change by sending a text to Terpin's cellphone, the criminals were able to confirm the change as if they were Terpin. Within a short time, they stole nearly $24 million in cryptocurrency funds from the account.

Terpin sued AT&T in the U.S. District Court for the District of California in Los Angeles for $224 million, a figure representing his lost funds plus $200 million in punitive damages for failing to safeguard his cellphone account.[1] Terpin also sued Nicholas Truglia, a 21-year-old New York resident who was arrested by federal authorities for

---

[1] Ian Demartino, A Complete Explanation of the Michael Terpin, AT&T Lawsuit, *CoinJournal* (August 24, 2018), https://coinjournal.net/a-complete-explanation-of-the-michael-terpin-att-lawsuit/.

conducting the fraud against Terpin and other wealthy targets. In May 2019, Terpin won a $75.8 million judgment against Truglia in a California court.[2] Whether he will collect any of that judgement remains to be seen.

4.2.4 PRINCIPLE OF LEAST PRIVILEGE (YOU DON'T NEED TO KNOW THAT OR DO THAT, SO I'M NOT LETTING YOU)

The principle of "least privilege" is an information security principle along the lines of "need to know". If you do not need access to information or systems, then you should not have it. If you do not need the ability to perform certain functions, you should not have it, as depicted in Figure 4.3.

"Least privilege" is a doctrine that limits users to the access and abilities they need to do their jobs, but no more than that. A person in human resources does not need access to analyst data, and an analyst does not need to know people's salaries or performance reviews. Most users do not need the ability to install programs onto their computers, or make other overarching changes, so they do not need administrator rights.

This principle yields important security benefits. It limits the harm an authorized user can do intentionally or unintentionally. It also limits the harm that can be inflicted if the user's account is compromised. The attacker only gets the user's limited access, no more. It is like having watertight compartments in a ship that limit the damage if one compartment is breached.

The concept of least privilege often arises during cybercrime investigations involving employees suspected of compromising their companies' data or systems. Note that a user's intentional wrongful act that exceeds their authority on a computer system might violate criminal statutes, as we cover in Chapter 6.

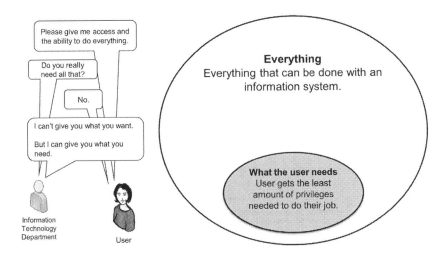

FIGURE 4.3   Principle of Least Privilege.

[2] Adrian Zmudzinski, *US Blockchain Investor Terpin Awarded over $75 Million in SIM Swapping Case*, CoinTelegraph (May 11, 2019), https://cointelegraph.com/news/us-blockchain-investor-terpin-awarded-over-75-million-in-sim-swapping-case.

4.2.5 INCIDENT RESPONSE

A strong information security program typically includes a plan for responding to incidents and attacks. The incident response cycle generally consists of these phases:

- Preparation for an incident
- Identification and detection of an incident
- Containment of a threat or attack
- Eradication of a threat or attack
- Recovery and resumption of normal operations
- Aftermath and lessons learned.[3]

Preparation for an incident. The premise for incident response planning is that organizations are constantly under attack. Good preparation for an incident in this environment relies on three basic ideas:

- Awareness. Develop awareness of ongoing cyber threats and prudent cyber safety practices, and educate individuals in the organization about these topics.
- Prevention. Take steps to prevent attacks through strong administrative, technical, and physical controls, and regular data back-ups.
- Planning. Formulate an incident response plan with a set of reactive steps, and designate people to perform them.

Preparation is important for organizations of any size, and starts with written policies and procedures that contemplate what steps will be taken for various scenarios. Someone will have to determine whether a cybercrime-related incident has occurred, and then respond to the incident appropriately. Often, the response will involve enlisting the help of the right personnel, and making the appropriate notifications and disclosures.

Designating an incident response team in advance is important. Members might come from a broad array of backgrounds, and may be internal or external to the organization. The people and tasks involved with incident preparation might include an assigned incident handler, legal counsel, IT personnel, information security personnel, forensics investigators, insurance companies, public relations professionals, and liaisons with law enforcement. Of course, in smaller organizations, the response will be proportional and one person might fulfill multiple roles.

Detection and identification of an incident. Detection of an incident means identifying abnormal events and distinguishing a cyberattack from a technical glitch. Knowing that an incident could happen at any time, and in an unexpected way, groups of any size with sensitive data or systems need to continuously monitor for unusual activity.

Once an incident is detected, the investigation begins. Responders work to determine what happened and how, what data was affected, and to document what occurred. We will talk more about how organizations initiate the investigation into a cyberattack in Chapter 12. Certain types of incidents may trigger legally mandated steps to initiate notifications to affected people (whose data was compromised), and to law enforcement, regulators, and other government entities.

These legal requirements underscore the need to identify promptly and correctly the nature of the event and whether it potentially affects the security of sensitive or regulated information.

---

[3] *See* NIST SP 800–61 rev 2, Computer Security Incident Handling Guide (August 2012), https://nvlpubs.nist.gov/nistpubs/specialpublications/nist.sp.800-61r2.pdf.
  See also, John Bandler, Prepare for and Plan against a Cyberattack, *American Bar Association Journal* (July 2018), www.abajournal.com/magazine/article/prepare_plan_against_cyberattack;
  John Bandler, *Cybersecurity for the Home and Office*, American Bar Association (August 2017).

Containment of a threat or attack. Containment means stopping the spread of a cyberattack and reducing the amount of damage it causes. When a potential threat is detected, an important part of incident response is to secure the organization's information systems, thereby protecting them from further compromise and preserving the integrity of the data.

Eradication of a threat or attack. Eradicating a threat or attack involves removing the cyber attackers from a network, as well as any malware and other software or hardware used to improperly access devices, information systems, and data. Ensuring a threat is eradicated also requires the identification and rectification of any vulnerabilities that could be used to reenter the system. For a compromise on an individual's cloud account, eradication might be as simple as changing a password, switching to two-factor authentication, and ensuring any sessions are logged out. With more sophisticated attacks, eradication might involve complex information technology efforts to restructure and secure a large network.

Recovery and resumption of normal operations. As threats are contained and eradicated, and the investigation into the incident proceeds, the affected organization still needs to do business. An important phase of incident response is recovering data and getting information systems running normally, which may include restoring backed-up data (if it exists).

Aftermath and lessons learned. When the threat is contained, the investigation completed, and normal operations have resumed, organizations can benefit by reviewing their incident response. This review might include an evaluation of the entity's preparation, the information security measures that were in place, as well as the other response phases. A review also helps ensure that information security practices are improved and aligned with best practices, laws, and regulations. Related criminal, regulatory, or civil investigations or litigation may continue for months or years.

4.3   INFORMATION SECURITY FRAMEWORKS

There are a number of information security frameworks that organizations can choose to follow when implementing an information security program to apply the principles we mentioned above. These frameworks are designed to help an entity organize and manage their risks and employ security measures in a systematic way. In a sense, many of these frameworks compete with each other and cover the same territory, although they might organize content differently and use different terminology. It can be a challenge for an organization to condense the disparate security requirements of different frameworks into the organization's information security program. Some organizations seek certification of compliance with certain frameworks, which provides some assurance to business partners and customers about their level of security.

No framework provides a magic answer or template dictating what an organization should do, nor what is "reasonable" and what is not. While frameworks (and regulations) indicate general safeguards, they rarely specify exact measures that should be implemented. Every organization has different needs, data, IT systems, and culture, and faces different threats, so information security is not "one size fits all."

It is helpful for investigators to learn something about these frameworks so that they gain an understanding of the basic norms for cybersecurity, and can intelligently discuss them with information security professionals. When an organization is affected by cybercrime, its policies, standards, and procedures may be aligned to a particular framework, which could prove relevant.

These frameworks all vary to some extent which can be cause for some confusion. In addition, the growing body of law and regulation surrounding information security has its own layers of security requirements, as we will discuss in Chapter 9. Organizations must navigate the implementation of a security framework that both protects its assets and helps to comply with laws and regulations. With civil lawsuits and regulatory actions related to information security on the rise, evidence of compliance with a framework is becoming increasingly significant as it may be evidence of reasonable information security measures.

Conversely, lack of compliance, or discrepancies between policy and practice, may make allegations of inadequate security more credible.

Let's take a look at some basic framework principles and well-known security frameworks.

4.3.1   The Four Pillars: Knowledge, Devices, Data, and Networks

If we could create the world's simplest information security framework, it might be built around four pillars of security – user knowledge, devices, data, and networks/Internet-usage, as depicted in Figure 4.4.[4] For someone not familiar with information security frameworks, these pillars offer a simple and conceptual way to understand them, as well as a helpful method to secure smaller information systems in the home or small office.

Knowledge about computers, information security, and threats is the first step towards information security, because without it, organizations and individuals do not know how to configure their IT systems or how to protect themselves from cybercrime threats. Next comes *devices*, keeping track of them, keeping possession of them and configuring them securely. Then comes *data*, ensuring you know where it is, and how to use it efficiently, back it up securely, and secure it from being breached. Finally comes the most complicated step, securely configuring *networks and Internet usage*, ensuring networks are not compromised, and that we use secure methods of communicating with others and accessing data through the Internet.

These four pillars are a simplified version of most information security frameworks. You will see that these pillars are the primary areas of focus of the frameworks we will now review.

4.3.2   CIS Critical Security Controls

The Center for Internet Security (CIS), a non-profit organization dedicated to developing and promoting best practice solutions for cyber defense, maintains the Critical Security Controls (CSCs), 20 actions (or "controls") that enable organizations to holistically address information security. The nice thing about these controls is that they are prioritized and start with the basics, which are readily understood – such as making an inventory of computing devices and securely configuring them. Then, the controls move on to more complicated tasks, such as regulating email usage, data, and networks, and finally engaging in penetration testing.

In Table 4.1, we have summarized the 20 controls in terms that are friendly for the layperson. The official name for each control is listed in the second column.[5]

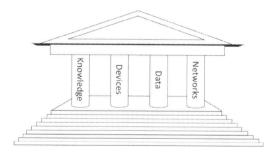

FIGURE 4.4   The Four Pillars of Security.

[4] This simplified framework is set forth in John's book: *Cybersecurity for the Home and Office*, published by the American Bar Association in 2017. The book also contains additional helpful information about information security, especially as it applies to individuals and small organizations.

[5] The Critical Security Controls are found at the Center for Internet Security, www.cisecurity.org/. The understandable and "friendly" name is adapted from Bandler, *Cybersecurity for the Home and Office*.

TABLE 4.1

CIS Critical Security Controls

CSC #	Friendly name	Official name
CSC 1	Inventory devices (both authorized and unauthorized)	Inventory of Authorized and Unauthorized Devices
CSC 2	Inventory software (both authorized and unauthorized)	Inventory of Authorized and Unauthorized Software
CSC 3	Configure devices and software securely	Secure Configurations for Hardware and Software on Mobile Devices, Laptops, Work-stations, and Servers
CSC 4	Review vulnerabilities continually	Continuous Vulnerability Assessment and Remediation
CSC 5	Don't use administrator accounts for normal computer usage	Controlled Use of Administrative Privileges
CSC 6	Enable automatic logging of system activity (and review the logs)	Maintenance, Monitoring, and Analysis of Audit Logs
CSC 7	Secure e-mail and web browser use	E-mail and Web Browser Protections
CSC 8	Use anti-malware software and protections	Malware Defenses
CSC 9	Disable (or "lock down") services and features you don't need (least privilege)	Limitation and Control of Network Ports, Protocols, and Services
CSC 10	Back up your data in a way you can recover it	Data Recovery Capability
CSC 11	Secure your router (and hardware firewall)	Secure Configurations for Network Devices such as Firewalls, Routers, and Switches
CSC 12	Implement firewalls and controls to defend your system boundaries	Boundary Defense
CSC 13	Protect your data	Data Protection
CSC 14	Don't give a user more access than is needed	Controlled Access Based on the Need to Know
CSC 15	Secure wireless networks	Wireless Access Control
CSC 16	Monitor accounts for suspicious activity	Account Monitoring and Control
CSC 17	Continual training	Security Skills Assessment and Appropriate Training to Fill Gaps
CSC 18	Secure company applications and web applications	Application Software Security
CSC 19	Have a plan for cyber incidents	Incident Response and Management
CSC 20	Test your defenses with penetration testers ("ethical hackers")	Penetration Tests and Red Team Exercises

This is just a list of the control categories. The framework provides detailed specifications on how to secure an information system within each of these twenty categories.

4.3.3   NIST Cybersecurity Framework (CSF)

The National Institute of Standards and Technology (NIST), a Department of Commerce agency, has developed some of the most widely used frameworks and guidance for many types of organizations.

The NIST cybersecurity framework (or "CSF", and officially titled the "Framework for Improving Critical Infrastructure Cybersecurity") provides direction on how organizations can protect themselves from cybercrime.[6] The five main actions are:

- Identify
- Protect
- Detect
- Respond
- Recover.

These actions are meant to be used in a cyclical, continuing process of identifying critical assets, protecting them, detecting threats, responding, and recovering from them. Within each of these five functions, there are more detailed areas of focus ("categories"), as indicated in Table 4.2:

4.3.4   NIST SP 800-53

NIST also provides a more detailed and comprehensive standard that predates their CSF, but remains widely used. This security framework is issued under NIST Special Publication 800-53, titled "Security and Privacy Controls for Federal Information Systems and Organizations".[7] Though the framework is a standard and catalog of security controls for U.S. government information systems, it is suitable for any organization with a large IT system. NIST SP 800-53 requires more controls than the CSF framework, and the categories are different as indicated below:

- Access Control (AC)
- Awareness and Training (AT)
- Audit and Accountability (AU)
- Security Assessment and Authorization (CA)
- Configuration Management (CM)
- Contingency Planning (CP)
- Identification and Authentication (IA)
- Incident Response (IR)
- Maintenance (MA)
- Media Protection (MP)
- Physical and Environmental Protection (PE)
- Planning (PL)
- Program Management (PM)
- Personnel Security (PS)
- Risk Assessment (RA)

---

[6] NIST, *Cybersecurity Framework*, www.nist.gov/cyberframework; NIST, *Framework for Improving Critical Infrastructure Cybersecurity* (April 16, 2018), ver. 1.1, https://nvlpubs.nist.gov/nistpubs/CSWP/NIST.CSWP.04162018.pdf.

[7] NIST SP 800–53 rev 4, *Security and Privacy Controls for Federal Information Systems and Organizations*, https://nvlpubs.nist.gov/nistpubs/SpecialPublications/NIST.SP.800-53r4.pdf.

   NIST also puts forth a guide on how to assess compliance with this standard. NIST SP 800-53A rev 4, *Assessing Security and Privacy Controls in Federal Information Systems and Organizations*, https://nvlpubs.nist.gov/nistpubs/SpecialPublications/NIST.SP.800-53Ar4.pdf.

TABLE 4.2
NIST Cybersecurity Framework Functions and Categories

Identify	• Asset Management (ID.AM) • Business Environment (ID.BE) • Governance (ID.GV) • Risk Assessment (ID.RA) • Risk Management Strategy (ID.RM) • Supply Chain Risk Management (ID.SC)
Protect	• Identity Management, Authentication and Access Control (PR.AC) • Awareness and Training (PR.AT) • Data Security (PR.DS) • Information Protection Processes and Procedures (PR.IP) • Maintenance (PR.MA) • Protective Technology (PR.PT)
Detect	• Anomalies and Events (DE.AE) • Security Continuous Monitoring (DE.CM) • Detection Processes (DE.DP)
Respond	• Response Planning (RS.RP) • Communications (RS.CO) • Analysis (RS.AN) • Mitigation (RS.MI) • Improvements (RS.IM)
Recover	• Recovery Planning (RC.RP) • Improvements (RC.IM) • Communications (RC.CO)

- System and Services Acquisition (SA)
- System and Communications Protection (SC)
- System and Information Integrity (SI).

4.3.5 ISO/IEC 27000 Series

The International Organization for Standardization (ISO) and International Electrotechnical Commission (IEC) – two organizations working to create international standards for various forms of technology – collaborated to develop the ISO/IEC 27000 series. The series is a group of publications that includes ISO 27001, a set of standards addressing information security management.[8] Organizations may seek certification of compliance with these standards, which provides some assurance about the security of the organization. This framework has a main text and an annex that divides the control categories as follows:

[8] ISO, www.iso.org/iso/home.html.
See International Organization for Standardization, *ISO/IEC 27001 Information Security Management*, www.iso.org/iso/home/standards/management-standards/iso27001.htm. The remainder of the standards are available for sale at www.iso.org/obp/ui/#iso:std:iso-iec:27001:ed-2:v1:en.

A.5: Information security policies

A.6: Organization of information security

A.7: Human resource security

A.8: Asset management

A.9: Access control

A.10: Cryptography

A.11: Physical and environmental security

A.12: Operations security

A.13: Communications security

A.14: System acquisition, development and maintenance

A.15: Supplier relationships

A.16: Information security incident management

A.17: Information security aspects of business continuity management

A.18: Compliance; with internal requirements, such as policies, and with external requirements, such as laws.

4.3.6 AICPA SSAE 18

The American Institute of Certified Public Accountants (AICPA) has issued the Statement of Standards for Attestation Engagement (SSAE). SSAE 18 became effective in 2017, and sets forth standards for companies who desire independent attestation to their compliance with information security principles known as Service and Organization Controls (SOC).[9]

Using these standards, companies can be audited for compliance in three different areas. SOC 1 concerns internal control over financial reporting. SOC 2 relates to entities providing services in which data is entrusted to them, and has an information security component addressing five principles for managing customer data. The five principles addressed are security, availability, processing integrity, confidentiality, and privacy. SOC 3 covers the SOC 2 areas but is presented in a format that can be freely distributed to customers to provide assurance of the company's internal processes.

4.3.7 OTHER INFORMATION SECURITY FRAMEWORKS

There are many other information security frameworks used by organizations of various kinds, including:

- PCI-DSS
- COBIT from ISACA
- ISA/IEC 62443
- OWASP Top Ten Project.

The Payment Card Industry Data Security Standard (PCI-DSS) is an industry-specific standard for businesses that accept or process credit and debit card payments.[10] It was developed by major credit card processors such as Visa, MasterCard, American Express, and Discover.

---

[9] American Institute of CPAs (AICPA), www.aicpa.org. For a comparison of SOC 1, SOC 2 and SOC 3 reports, see AICPA, SOC for Service Organizations ..., www.aicpa.org/interestareas/frc/assuranceadvisoryservices/cpas.html.

[10] PCI Security Standards Council, www.pcisecuritystandards.org.
  The Prioritized Approach to Pursue PCI DSS Compliance, PCI (June 2018), www.pcisecuritystandards.org/documents/Prioritized-Approach-for-PCI-DSS-v3_2_1.pdf.

COBIT (Control Objectives for Information and Related Technologies) is a framework from ISACA, an information systems security, assurance, and auditing organization.[11]

The International Society of Automation (ISA) also provides a cybersecurity framework geared towards industrial automation and control systems, which is known as ISA/IEC 62443.[12]

The Open Web Application Security Project (OWASP) is a non-profit organization that has developed information security standards relating to web-based applications, and lists ten vulnerabilities that should be addressed.[13] The OWASP Top 10 list as of 2017 includes:

A1:2017-Injection
A2:2017-Broken Authentication
A3:2017-Sensitive Data Exposure
A4:2017-XML External Entities (XXE)
A5:2017-Broken Access Control [Merged]
A6:2017-Security Misconfiguration
A7:2017-Cross-Site Scripting (XSS)
A8:2017-Insecure Deserialization
A9:2017-Using Components with Known Vulnerabilities
A10:2017-Insufficient Logging & Monitoring.

Since web-based applications are so popular, they are a lucrative vector for cybercrime attack. Standards that help protect these applications are an important step in cybersecurity.

4.4   CONCLUSION

With this quick primer on information security, investigators gain a different perspective on cybercrime attacks. When an attack occurs, its success often hinges on the level of information security maintained around the targeted data or networks. Good information security – including strong administrative, technical, and physical protections – can thwart many cyberattacks. If an attack does get through security defenses, a well-informed incident response plan can greatly limit the damage caused and assist the investigation. Investigators with an understanding of the security principles used to protect data and systems can more quickly assess an incident and initiate an effective investigative response.

It is good to know about all of the various information security frameworks, but unnecessary to master them all. The key idea is that security frameworks, coupled with an increasing number of laws and regulations, are an important basis for determining whether an organization's security was reasonable. The question of "reasonableness" plays a large role in civil litigation and regulatory review. Plaintiffs or government regulators may allege inadequate information security or incident response, and organizations may be put in a position of defending the security posture in place at the time of the incident. Response and improvement from past incidents might also be a factor. In this context, cybercrime investigators can be called upon to uncover the facts of an incident. With knowledge of information security principles, investigators can put those facts into the proper information security perspective.

[11] ISACA, www.isaca.org. For information about COBIT, see www.isaca.org/COBIT/Pages/FAQs.aspx.
[12] International Society of Automation (ISA), www.isa.org, and www.isasecure.org.
[13] OWASP, www.owasp.org. *The Ten Most Critical Web Application Security Risks*, www.owasp.org/images/7/72/OWASP_Top_10-2017_%28en%29.pdf.pdf.

Part II

Law for the Cybercrime Investigator

5 Fundamental Principles of Criminal and Civil Law

This chapter is for:

- Non-lawyers and anyone looking to brush up on essential elements of our criminal and civil justice systems
- Investigators on either the civil side or criminal side.

5.1 INTRODUCTION

This chapter continues building the foundation for cybercrime investigation by discussing some of the basic principles of criminal and civil law. The law is continually evolving, and often new legal issues arising from technology need to be analyzed in the context of established legal principles.

First, we explore some fundamental areas of criminal law. The criminal system involves our government investigating and prosecuting what we consider to be wrongs against society. We will discuss who investigates and prosecutes crime, and the process we use to hold people accountable for their criminal actions while preserving their rights.

Next, we explore key components of our civil laws. The civil system involves private individuals, organizations, or the government seeking redress for more specific harm or loss, or to shape future behavior. Cybercrime, more than any other criminal activity, usually has civil law implications as well, since it often includes massive thefts of data and funds, leaving victims to seek redress civilly from third parties. Companies that are negligent in how they secure systems or data, or that breach contracts promising cybersecurity, may be sued civilly by cybercrime victims.

Regulations and laws that require certain standards for cybersecurity are another method federal and state governments are using to reduce cybercrime, so it is important to introduce these concepts. Government agencies enforcing cybersecurity and other regulations may use civil litigation to drive compliance.

5.2 CRIMINAL LAW AND PROCEDURE

We will begin our discussion with an overview of criminal procedure and some key principles of criminal law. Any investigator unraveling a cybercrime will benefit from a general knowledge of how a case proceeds when criminal charges are pursued.

More specific detail about criminal statutes and criminal procedure law can be found in Chapters 6 and 7. We will discuss the criminal litigation process in Chapter 18.

5.2.1 THE PARTICIPANTS

There are several participants in the U.S. criminal justice process, including:

- *Suspects/offenders* (known as "defendants", once criminally charged)
- *Law enforcement officials* (officers and agents with the power to investigate crimes and arrest suspects)
- *Prosecutors* (attorneys for the government with the authority to file and litigate criminal charges against suspects in court)
- *Defense attorneys* (lawyers advocating on behalf of suspects or defendants; defendants who cannot afford to pay for a defense attorney will be assigned an attorney by the court paid through public funding)
- *Judges and magistrates* (neutral arbiters who oversee the investigative and prosecutorial process).

Investigation into criminal wrongdoing and arrests of suspected offenders are conducted by various law enforcement agencies on behalf of local, state, or federal government. Cities, towns, and villages may have their own local police departments. Counties generally have sheriffs' departments, and states have state police and other statewide law enforcement agencies. All of these officers are sworn to enforce the laws of the state or U.S. territory where they serve. The federal government also has many law enforcement agencies such as the Federal Bureau of Investigation (FBI), the United States Secret Service (USSS), and the Department of Homeland Security (DHS), who work across the nation to investigate and arrest those who violate federal laws.

Prosecutors are government attorneys who similarly work on behalf of different bodies of government. Each county within a state has a District Attorney (sometimes called a State's or Commonwealth Attorney), who initiates prosecutions for violations of that state's laws. At the statewide level, the Attorney General for each state also conducts prosecutions under state law, usually with a focus on more complex crimes. Federal prosecutions are conducted by federal prosecutors based on violations of federal law. Federal prosecutors work in United States Attorneys' Offices, which are branches of the U.S. Department of Justice (DOJ) located in each state, as well as in specialized DOJ divisions located in Washington D.C., such as the Computer Crime and Intellectual Property Section (CCIPS). There is at least one federal district in each state, and each federal district has a head prosecutor (the U.S. Attorney) who is appointed by the President and confirmed by the U.S. Senate.

We will talk more about which of these agencies might take on a particular criminal case in Section 5.3.

5.2.2 THE CRIMINAL JUSTICE PROCESS

Here is a brief summary of the general stages of a felony investigation and prosecution:

- *Pre-arrest investigation by law enforcement.* This may be minimal, such as responding to a 911 call and speaking with witnesses, or extensive, as in a long-term cybercrime investigation.[1]

---

[1] As discussed later, there are circumstances in which the pre-arrest investigation is extensive, and charges are initiated by Grand Jury indictment. In that scenario, an arrest warrant is issued, the defendant is arrested, and the process skips right to "Arraignment on Indictment".

- *Arrest.* Law enforcement takes the defendant into custody (with or without an arrest warrant) based upon probable cause he committed a crime. Probable cause means that there are reasonable grounds to believe the defendant committed the crime.
- *Arraignment on initial charges.* The defendant is informed in court of the charges against him. The prosecution can ask the court to hold the defendant in custody on bail or bond if there is a risk he will flee to avoid the charges. At arraignment, the defendant may be informed of some of the evidence obtained by law enforcement. The defendant is represented by his attorney at this and all future court proceedings.[2]
- *Grand Jury or preliminary hearing review.* The Grand Jury or a court reviews evidence gathered through investigation and decides if there is probable cause to charge the defendant with felony crimes.
- *Arraignment on indictment/judicially-approved felony charges.* The defendant is informed of felony charges approved by the Grand Jury or the preliminary hearing judge. The prosecution can make a renewed bail or bond application based on the fact that the defendant is now definitively facing a felony case, and any other new factors.
- *Discovery.* The prosecution must provide the defense with copies of certain investigative documents and reports related to the defendant's case, as well as access to view or test physical evidence. The defense must supply reports of expert witnesses and other limited defense evidence.
- *Defense and prosecution motions (pre-trial motions).* The defense submits legal arguments or "motions", usually in writing. These motions can raise any legal issue, including the appropriateness of the charged counts. Many defense motions challenge the admissibility of evidence, alleging it was obtained unlawfully or other reasons the evidence should not be used against the defendant. The prosecution responds and may make its own motions. The court makes a decision on these motions, and if there are factual issues that need to be addressed, will order a pre-trial hearing.
- *Pre-trial hearings.* The motions may raise issues of fact that require a hearing and testimony from witnesses, including to determine whether law enforcement acted properly when recovering evidence. Typically, the prosecution calls law enforcement witnesses to establish how evidence was recovered, then the defense cross-examines them. After the hearing, both sides present arguments, and the judge decides whether the witnesses were credible, makes findings of fact, and decides the ultimate hearing issue, which is often whether certain evidence is admissible at trial or whether it must be excluded (suppressed). We will discuss exclusion of evidence in more depth shortly.
- *Pleas and plea negotiations.* The defendant is presumed innocent at all times but also has a right to plead guilty to the charges. The defense and prosecution may also enter into plea negotiations at any time, including what is commonly referred to as a "plea bargain". This process recognizes that the criminal justice system lacks the capacity to bring every criminal case to trial and that not every defendant wants to go to trial. In fact, only a small percentage of prosecutions proceed to trial. When the defendant seeks to plea bargain, an agreement must be reached

---

[2] For defendants charged with misdemeanors and petty offenses, this initial arraignment is the only arraignment. There is no Grand Jury proceeding, preliminary hearing or subsequent arraignment.

with the prosecution about the crimes to which he will plead guilty and the punishment. The negotiated agreement must be reviewed and approved by the judge presiding over the case.[3]

- *Trial.* At trial, the prosecution calls witnesses and presents evidence gathered during the investigation. It is the prosecution's burden to demonstrate the defendant's guilt beyond a reasonable doubt by proving each element of any crime charged, and to disprove any defenses. The defendant may present evidence but has no burden to do so. The judge is the gatekeeper to ensure that the jury sees only evidence that was lawfully obtained, is authentic, relevant, and not unfairly prejudicial to the defendant. After all the witnesses and evidence have been presented, each side argues to the jury about why they should prevail, and then the jury deliberates in secret. To find the defendant guilty of a crime, they typically must agree unanimously on a guilty verdict.

- *Sentencing.* If a defendant is convicted, either after a guilty plea or guilty verdict, the judge will sentence a defendant within the available range of penalties set forth in the relevant criminal statutes. Before the judge issues the sentence, the prosecution and defense each make arguments about why a particular sentence is appropriate. Under some laws, victims are allowed to make statements to the court about the impact of the defendant's crimes. The judge then determines the sentence and informs the parties. A criminal conviction can also have civil consequences.[4]

- *Appeals and other post-conviction proceedings.* After sentencing, the defendant can appeal the conviction (and the sentence imposed) by asking a higher (appellate) court to overturn the actions of the trial court judge. A defendant can also make post-conviction motions in the trial court, including for a new trial if there are newly discovered facts. If the defendant loses on appeal, he can try to appeal that decision to an even higher appellate court. When a defendant is convicted in state court, he also can bring a challenge to that conviction in federal court on the basis that his federal constitutional rights were violated.

For more in-depth information on the entire criminal litigation process, go to Chapter 18.

5.2.3 CRIMINAL JUSTICE PROTECTIONS

One of the hallmarks of our criminal justice process is the protection of a defendant's rights throughout the stages of investigation, arrest, charging, prosecution, and sentencing. The rights and protections afforded defendants derive from several sources, including:

- *The U.S. Constitution and Bill of Rights.* Our founding documents set forth numerous protections for individuals facing criminal charges. These protections limit the power of the government and include the search warrant requirement, the Grand Jury, the right to due process, and the right against self-incrimination. These rights are also applicable to state governments. Federal and state statutes reflect these protections.

---

[3] Forfeiture of a defendant's criminally-gained assets may be a part of plea negotiations, or may be conducted through proceedings that either accompany the criminal litigation or are initiated through a parallel civil suit. We will discuss asset forfeiture more in Chapters 9 and 19.

[4] Among other things, a convicted individual could lose the ability to vote, possess a firearm or rifle, or hold certain licenses, and non-citizens could be subject to deportation. A regulated corporation might lose its license, effectively putting it out of business.

- *State constitutions.* Each state has its own constitution establishing protections for defendants, with some states extending protections beyond what the federal government provides.
- *Court decisions.* Centuries of judicial interpretation of constitutional and statutory protections by the U.S. Supreme Court and state appellate courts have created a body of law dictating what law enforcement and prosecutors can and cannot do during the different phases of a case.
- *Prosecutorial ethics.* The rules of ethics emphasize the prosecutor's duty to fairness and justice, not just to win convictions or maximize punishment. These duties require a prosecutor to dismiss a case if evidence shows the defendant is innocent, and to turn over evidence favorable to the defendant even when guilt is clear.
- *Defense bar and the adversarial system.* Our criminal justice system is premised on an adversarial system in which the government and defense argue their positions before the court. Attorneys representing criminal defendants have a principal duty to safeguard the legal rights of their clients. Even if he or she perceives a defendant to be guilty, a defense attorney must zealously advocate for the client, which may mean putting the prosecution to its burden of proof.
- *Neutral magistrate.* Criminal justice matters are overseen by a neutral judge, who is part of a separate branch of government (the judicial branch) than the prosecution (the executive branch). This constitutional structure is designed to ensure the government does not have overwhelming power over a criminal defendant.
- *Fair and impartial jury.* Our system provides defendants with the right to have average citizens serve on a jury to determine whether to charge them with serious crimes (Grand Jury) and to determine whether the prosecution has proven them guilty at trial (Petit Jury).
- *Rules and policies.* Most law enforcement and prosecution agencies have policies, rules, and internal procedures that officers and attorneys must follow in performing their jobs, including procedures intended to protect the rights of suspects.

5.2.4 How Investigations and Prosecutions are Started

There are two general phases in the criminal justice process: investigation/arrest and prosecution in court. The first phase is usually conducted by law enforcement officers and agents, often in close collaboration with prosecutors. Law enforcement responds to crimes, investigates, and makes arrests, with prosecutors providing guidance about legal issues and helping to obtain subpoenas, search warrants, and other "legal process". The second phase – the prosecution – usually begins when a criminal offender is arrested, although some prosecutions officially commence with the filing of an accusatory instrument before the offender is in custody.

The most common way for a criminal investigation and prosecution to start is when police make a summary arrest based upon probable cause. Consider the police officer on patrol who responds to a robbery in progress and makes an arrest. He and other officers gather evidence at the robbery scene (stolen property, weapons, and other relevant items), interview any witnesses, and note any statements made by the suspect. The officers then bring the defendant to the police station, where routine procedures are undertaken (paperwork, fingerprinting, etc.). The officers notify the local prosecutor's office or court (depending on the jurisdiction) of the arrest and crimes charged, and the defendant is brought to court. This process is depicted in Figure 5.1.

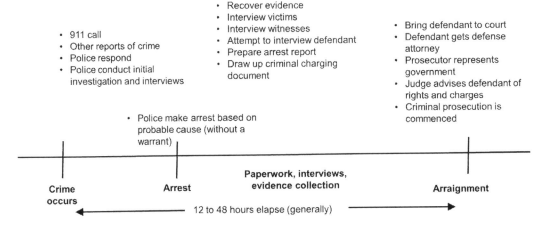

FIGURE 5.1   Police Officer Summary Arrest Based on Probable Cause.

Sometimes extensive investigations are conducted before an arrest. Under this approach, evidence is gathered, and investigators and prosecutors consider whom to charge with what crimes before anyone is arrested. Prosecutors present evidence to a Grand Jury or judge (as discussed shortly), who decides whether to officially charge the suspects. If charges are approved, the court issues an arrest warrant for the suspects, and officers then apprehend them. Cybercrime investigations frequently fall within this category, since it often takes a longer investigation to identify cybercriminals and their criminal acts. This process is depicted in Figure 5.2.

5.2.5   CATEGORIES OF CRIMINAL CHARGES

Both federal and state laws categorize every crime according to the seriousness of the misconduct. The major classifications are:

*   Felonies (typically provide for maximum punishment in excess of one year in prison)
*   Misdemeanors (typically provide for a maximum punishment of one year in jail or less)
*   Petty offenses (often called violations, infractions, or similar names).

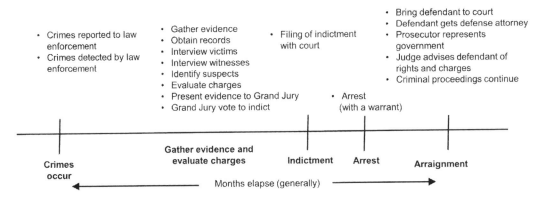

FIGURE 5.2   Diagram Long-Term Investigation: Arrest Following Indictment.

The procedures for filing felony charges typically are more rigorous than those for lesser crimes, requiring the approval of a Grand Jury or judge (a process discussed further in the next section).

A major distinction between statutory offenses is the range of penalties that could be imposed upon conviction. Felonies are the most serious offenses, and there typically are different levels of felonies. Federal and state laws contain extensive provisions describing the sentencing options that judges may impose for a particular offense, ranging from probation, fines, community service, treatment programs, to prison sentences. The sentence could include restitution for financial losses. When deciding upon which sentence to impose within the range of options, the sentencing judge normally considers aggravating and mitigating factors surrounding a defendant's conduct, criminal history, and background.

5.2.6 CHARGING THE DEFENDANT AND JUDICIAL REVIEW: COMPLAINTS, INDICTMENTS, GRAND JURY, PRELIMINARY HEARINGS

There are two legal mechanisms typically used to charge defendants with a crime:

- *Law enforcement affidavit*. The most common charging method is through an "affidavit", which is a written allegation of criminal charges based on probable cause, signed and sworn to by a law enforcement officer. Officers usually file such an affidavit, often called a "complaint" or "information", following the summary arrest of an individual. An affidavit/complaint also can be filed pre-arrest to obtain an arrest warrant for a suspect.
- *Indictment issued by a Grand Jury.* The Grand Jury is a legal body established in the Fifth Amendment to the U.S. Constitution and within state constitutions, and consists of local citizens who are summoned to jury duty. Prosecutors present evidence about a suspect's criminal acts to the Grand Jury through witnesses, documents, and other evidence and the jurors vote whether to charge him or her. If charges are approved, the Grand Jury issues a "true bill" and prosecutors create the indictment, the document through which a Grand Jury officially files the criminal charges. Many long-term investigations utilize this procedure since extensive facts and evidence are needed to support the charges.

For misdemeanors, a sworn complaint is typically the only charging document required to bring the defendant to trial. But for felonies, an extra step is required because our criminal justice process recognizes the burdens a felony prosecution puts upon a defendant. Our laws require felony charges to be reviewed by a neutral authority and there are two possible processes for this review:[5]

- *Grand Jury review.* Prosecutors present evidence to a Grand Jury regarding a defendant's conduct. If the Grand Jury finds probable cause that the defendant committed crimes, it will approve criminal charges by voting a true bill, after which an indictment is filed with the court. In the federal system and in some states, this Grand Jury review of felony charges is the standard procedure. After the indictment is filed, a judge typically reviews a transcript of the Grand Jury proceedings as an additional safeguard to ensure the evidence was sufficient and prosecutors conducted the proceeding properly.

---

[5] Some states (like New York) may require a Grand Jury indictment before proceeding to trial, but also allow for a preliminary hearing in certain circumstances, such as to keep a defendant in custody pending Grand Jury proceedings.

- *Preliminary hearing.* Prosecutors present evidence to a judge, subject to cross-examination and challenge by the defense. The judge then makes a determination about probable cause and, if found, the case can proceed towards trial. In some states, preliminary hearings are the standard method of reviewing felony complaint charges.

If pre-arrest charges were brought via indictment, no additional Grand Jury review or preliminary hearing is necessary when the defendant is apprehended (since the Grand Jury already has decided the initial sufficiency of the charges). All Grand Jury proceedings are secret, and jurors are under a duty not to discuss the information they learn with anyone outside the Grand Jury.

5.2.7 THE INVESTIGATIVE ROLE OF THE GRAND JURY

Along with its power to charge defendants and review felony complaint charges for probable cause, the Grand Jury serves a crucial investigative function in the criminal justice system. Prosecutors may request that a Grand Jury initiate an investigation into suspected criminal activity and issue subpoenas to compel the production of evidence and testimony that would further the inquiry.

As we will discuss further in Chapter 13, opening a Grand Jury investigation is a critical step in cybercrime investigations, since subpoenas are required to obtain many forms of evidence (such as records of Internet communications and activity, financial records, and security video). As a result of the evidence obtained through Grand Jury investigations, prosecutors often are able to present cybercrime cases to the Grand Jury and seek criminal charges against the offenders.

5.3 WHO INVESTIGATES AND PROSECUTES CRIMES?

With this legal overview of arrests, charging and prosecutions, the next question is: who does these jobs within the criminal justice system? What is the difference between a federal and a state case, and why would a crime be investigated by one type of agency over another?

Here we will take a look at some of the factors that go into the determination of who might investigate and prosecute a particular crime.

5.3.1 STATE/LOCAL ENFORCEMENT AND FEDERAL ENFORCEMENT

State and federal criminal statutes usually address similar conduct, so the determination of who will investigate and prosecute is often not related to the statutes, but rather the different priorities and focus of state and federal law enforcement.

By overwhelming majority, most arrests and prosecutions are conducted by local and state law enforcement and prosecutors. These agencies are responsible for responding to the daily flow of criminal activity within their physical jurisdictions, handling everything from jaywalking to identity theft to murder. The typical arrest is made by local police officers who submit the case to the local county prosecutor's office. The prosecutors then charge the offender in a state court. Local prosecutors mostly prosecute violations of state laws, but might also prosecute violations of city, town, or village laws. The size and investigative capacities of state and local agencies vary greatly.

Federal investigations and arrests come about quite differently. While the FBI and other federal law enforcement agencies respond reactively to some violations of federal law (like an act of terrorism, or criminal activity on land or facilities owned by the federal government), much of their work focuses on long-term investigations within particular subject areas (like securities fraud, human trafficking, and cyber-crime), as well as other crimes of a certain complexity or financial magnitude. The resources available to federal agencies are much greater than what most state-level law enforcement agencies enjoy but the number of federal agents and prosecutors is rela-tively small. As a result, federal agencies may choose not to expend resources on a particular investigation.

Federal prosecutors exercise "prosecutorial discretion" in deciding whether to start an investigation or prosecution. In other words, the FBI or USSS may inform an Assistant United States Attorney (AUSA) about cybercrime acts, but the prosecutor may choose not to prosecute the case after considering likely outcomes and the resources required.[6] In making this decision, prosecutors (and federal law enforcement agents that bring them cases) may use monetary thresholds. For example, if the crime resulted in a theft of less than a hundred thousand dollars, or even a million dollars, they might not investigate or prosecute it. Often, this decision means the case is dead and will not be referred to a state or local agency, and so significant crimes detected by federal law enforcement may fall into an investigative "black hole". One of our goals in this book is to help investigators at all levels work together, so that more people and resources are available to investigate cybercrimes of any size.

5.3.2 JURISDICTION AND VENUE

Jurisdiction and venue are separate but related concepts. Jurisdiction is the legal authority of a court, including the authority to preside over a criminal investigation or prosecution. Venue is the court where a case is heard. In local and state cases, venue and jurisdiction are usually the same, tied together by geography. However, in federal cases they are separate concepts.

At the state level, jurisdiction usually is determined simply by virtue of a crime hap-pening within the borders of a geographical boundary. Federal courts have nationwide jurisdiction over federal crimes. Whether state or federal, law enforcement agencies and prosecutor's offices must have authority over a crime to investigate and prosecute it, meaning they must do so in accordance with the jurisdiction of the court that will over-see the case. For example, if a robbery, burglary, or murder is committed within a county, the county's police agencies and prosecutor's office will investigate and file charges under the auspices of the court with jurisdiction over that county. Courts also might have jurisdiction over a crime that directed a particular effect or harm into that county or federal district, such as if a faraway cybercriminal victimizes a resident in that locality. Jurisdiction also may be established if communications occur to or from the physical boundary, such as by mailing a package, having a phone call, sending an email, or committing a data breach into a computer in that area. Jurisdiction rules vary state by state.

The federal government by contrast, must meet special criteria to establish jurisdiction over an offense, but this is easily done. To investigate and prosecute, federal authorities must establish a potential crime occurred involving federal property, a federal victim, or

---

[6] Federal prosecutors handle significantly fewer cases per year. For example, in 2018, the Manhattan District Attor-ney's (DANY) office handled about 55,000 new cases, including about 10,000 felonies. DANY, www.manhattanda.org/data/. The U.S. Attorney's Office for the Southern District of New York, which includes Manhattan, the Bronx and six other counties, handled about 2,000 new cases, including about 1,600 felonies. USAO SDNY, www.justice.gov/usao/page/file/1199336/download.

that affects interstate or foreign commerce (something most cybercrime affects because of its reliance on the Internet). For some offenses, there may be additional factors that establish federal jurisdiction.

Venue is a related legal concept that concerns the geographical location, within the proper jurisdiction, where the charges should be filed and the case prosecuted. A court must be the correct legal venue to hear a case. In state cases, the correct venue is almost always the same courthouse or court system that has jurisdiction over the case.

Venue in federal cases works differently because of the national scope of federal jurisdiction. It is an important legal concept because it determines which federal prosecutor handles a case. The federal government may have jurisdiction over an offense, but in which of the nearly 100 federal districts should the case be heard? Venue protections ensure a defendant does not have to defend charges in an inappropriate location.

When crimes are conducted via the Internet, multiple law enforcement agencies might have authority to investigate, including federal authorities and various states. Agencies may dispute who should take on a particular investigation or prosecution.

5.3.3   RESOURCES, EXPERTISE, AND COLLABORATION

Many cybercrime cases require considerable time, specialized resources, and expert assistance to investigate and prosecute. Today, some departments lack the personnel or funding to properly investigate many cybercrimes to which their residents fall victim. On the other hand, there are a number of agencies in the criminal justice system, such as federal agencies and state Attorney General's offices, with the necessary resources and expertise for complex cybercrime investigations and prosecutions. Police departments and prosecutor's offices in some major cities also have developed the tools and training for cybercrime cases, like our former office in Manhattan.

The disparity in investigative resources often becomes an issue when a cyber-related case starts out as a routine police report to a smaller agency, but initial investigative steps reveal the incident is difficult to solve or connected to a large criminal enterprise. Collaboration is the bridge to the divide between "large" and "small" law enforcement agencies that encounter cybercrime. When a case mushrooms or overlaps another investigation, agencies without the capacity to investigate fully can refer a case to an appropriate law enforcement agency so that leads can be pursued. In many parts of the country, task forces of law enforcement agencies (large and small) meet regularly to learn about crime trends, offer assistance, and uncover connections within their work. Efforts like these are essential to increasing the number of cybercrimes investigated. Crime that is not investigated cannot be solved.

5.4   WHAT CONSTITUTES A CRIME AND ITS ELEMENTS

Improper conduct constitutes a crime only if there is a specific criminal statute prohibiting it. Though statutes specify what acts are criminal, judges play an important role in interpreting these statutes through decisions that become part of the relevant case law. Each state and the federal government has its own set of criminal statutes, but the following principles are universal.

Every criminal statute has elements that must be satisfied, including:

- An act (or occasionally a failure to act),
- A culpable mental state (or guilty mind), and
- Other elements of the offense (for example, value, damage, or injury).

To charge someone with a crime, or to prove it at trial, each element must be established to the applicable burden – either probable cause (for charging) or beyond a reasonable doubt (at trial). Understanding that criminal statutes are written in this manner can spur investigators to gather evidence in support of all of the elements of the crime.

For example, the crime of theft usually has the general elements of (1) intentionally (the mental state), (2) taking unlawfully (the act), (3) property (4) from an owner (other elements). Each of these elements has its own legal definition. Investigators and prosecutors with a theft case will check the facts and evidence to make sure there is proof of each element as defined in the statute.

With this idea in mind, let's learn more about some of the most common elements.

5.4.1   ACT OR OMISSION (*ACTUS REUS*)

Most crimes require that the defendant perform some type of unlawful act, meaning a bodily movement such as a punch, squeeze of a trigger, taking of an item, or click of a mouse. Historically, this element of a crime is known by the Latin term *actus reus*, or "guilty act". In certain circumstances, an omission, or failure to act, can be criminal if the person had a duty to act but failed to do so. An example is a case of child neglect, where the defendant had a duty to care for a child, to feed, clean, or clothe him, but did nothing.

5.4.2   CULPABLE MENTAL STATES (*MENS REA*)

Most crimes require that the defendant commit the unlawful act or omission with a "guilty mind", a culpable mental state known as *mens rea*. Different jurisdictions may have slightly different names for them, but the primary mental states include:

* Intent
* Knowledge
* Criminal negligence
* Recklessness.

Intent and knowledge are the most common *mens rea* elements. Determining, or proving, what someone was thinking is a difficult but common task in criminal law. The proof often relies on applying common sense, while considering the defendant's actions in the circumstances of the case.

The following is a brief description of the common mental states.

Intent. Intent means a person's conscious objective or purpose. Proof of an offender's intent may come from his own statements after a crime, where he might admit to some or all of the criminal conduct. Without an admission, proof of intent can be found by examining all the circumstances of the case.

Here are some scenarios demonstrating how intent might be determined.

* Susan hides store merchandise in her underwear and walks out of the store without paying. She probably intended to steal that merchandise.
* Robert is in the store with his unruly six-year-old, who secretly puts merchandise in Robert's jacket pocket. Without realizing it is there, Robert walks out of the store without paying for it. Robert lacked the intent to steal it.

Remember that motive is different from intent. Motive – or the reason why someone did something – is never an element of a crime, and some crimes are truly senseless.

Investigators and prosecutors are not required to prove motive, though sometimes they may decide to prove it in order to strengthen the proof of other elements of the crime. Understanding the various motives of cybercriminals (discussed in Chapter 2), such as the need to hide their identities and criminal profits, can be very helpful in both investigating and proving particular criminal acts.

Knowingly. Knowledge, in the criminal context, means that a person is aware of what he or she is doing or possessing. Statutes criminalizing possession of weapons or drugs generally include the mental state element of "knowing". It is not enough to simply possess the banned item. To be guilty of the crime, the offender must know that he possessed the illegal item. Consider what a suspect might say if found in possession of contraband.

- "This isn't my car. I didn't know the drugs/guns were in there," is a common refrain when officers find controlled substances or weapons during encounters with motorists. If true, the element of knowledge would be lacking. Investigators and prosecutors often rely upon other facts to determine whether the driver's statements are true – for example, checking vehicle records, or looking at what other items were in the car. With some possession crimes, the statutes include a legal presumption the driver knows what he has with him, aiding the prosecution.

Criminal negligence. Criminal negligence is different and more pronounced than ordinary civil negligence. Ordinary civil negligence involves a deviation from the standard of care a reasonable person would exercise in a given situation. It might be civilly negligent, for example, to drive around in a car with broken taillights or drive through a stop sign. Criminal negligence, on the other hand, is a significant deviation from that standard of care, while failing to perceive a substantial and unjustifiable risk. Driving a car when you know the brakes do not work might be criminally negligent, or a bus driver who is watching a movie while driving might be criminally negligent. Criminal law generally only punishes criminal negligence when serious consequences result.

Recklessly. Recklessness is more extreme than criminal negligence and means that the actor was aware of and consciously disregarded a substantial and unjustifiable risk. Reckless conduct also greatly departs from the "reasonable person" standard of care (sometimes called a "gross deviation"). Someone who throws heavy objects from a bridge or building, knowing there are people or vehicles below, would surely be acting recklessly even though he may not have intended to injure or kill anyone. Driving drunk, or driving at exorbitant speeds in a residential area while violating other traffic laws might also be reckless.

Crimes with no mental state element. Some crimes and most petty offenses have no mental state element. These crimes are called strict liability crimes, which means the mental state of the offender is irrelevant to his or her guilt. Defective taillights, driving through stop signs and speeding offenses, for example, do not require the prosecution to establish any mental state. It does not matter what the driver knew or intended, only that the act was committed.

5.4.3   ANTICIPATORY OFFENSES (SUCH AS ATTEMPT AND CONSPIRACY)

It is easy to conceptualize a completed criminal act, such as a theft, assault, or murder, but sometimes criminals do not complete the criminal acts they set out to accomplish. Though unfinished, these actions might still be a crime, such as an attempt, conspiracy, facilitation, and solicitation, which are known as anticipatory offenses.

An *attempt* to commit a crime occurs when someone intentionally tried to complete the crime but was unable to do so. He had the intent to commit the crime, and he engaged in conduct tending to make it happen, but for some reason the act was not completed.

Someone who shoots another probably intends to kill, but if the victim does not die, the act might constitute an attempted murder.

A *conspiracy* to commit a crime occurs when two or more people agree to intentionally commit a crime, and then an act is committed to further that agreement. An act to further a conspiracy is sometimes described as an "overt act". For example, if three individuals plot to shoot a victim, and they buy the gun and research the victim's travels, they may have conspired to murder the victim (even if the murder is never attempted or committed). The plotting, gun purchase, and research would constitute overt acts in furtherance of the murder conspiracy.

Solicitation occurs when one person asks another to commit a crime, and *facilitation* occurs when one person helps another to commit a crime. In both of these scenarios, the crime may not be accomplished. The criminal act is simply the asking or the assistance with the potential crime.

5.5 DEFENSES (SUCH AS SELF-DEFENSE AND ENTRAPMENT)

There are a number of legal defenses to committing a crime that a defendant can raise after being criminally charged, including these common claims:

- *Justification.* The individual is not guilty of the crime if the conduct was necessary as an emergency measure to avoid an imminent public or personal harm (often raised in the context of self-defense).
- *Entrapment.* The individual would not have committed the crime, except for the actions or enticement of law enforcement.
- *Infancy.* The individual was under the age of criminal liability at the time of the conduct (and should be charged in a juvenile court).
- *Duress.* The individual was forced to commit the crime.
- *Renunciation.* The individual voluntarily withdrew from participation in the crime.
- *Mental disease or defect.* The individual did not know what he was doing or that it was wrong, due to mental disease or defect.

Investigators who anticipate the defenses that suspects might raise can build stronger cases by gathering evidence that might disprove them. However unlikely a defense, it is law enforcement's responsibility to disprove it beyond a reasonable doubt if the case goes to trial.

The defense of justification, sometimes called necessity, bears deeper discussion in the context of cybercrime and cybersecurity, as some have advocated that cybercrime victims should fight back against their perceived attackers with electronic countermeasures that normally would be illegal ("hack back"). This idea is not supported by the law and may put the victim in legal jeopardy, as we will discuss in Chapter 9.

5.6 THE FOURTH AMENDMENT: CONSTITUTIONAL RULES FOR SEARCH AND SEIZURE

Law enforcement searches of homes, offices, electronic devices, and other personal locations and property, as well as the seizure of evidence, are both critical investigative steps and the frequent subject of legal dispute. In this section, we review the basic constitutional principles that guide law enforcement search and seizure procedures.

The law regarding search and seizure stems from the Fourth Amendment to the U.S. Constitution, where legal protections were created to safeguard individuals from government intrusion.

The Fourth Amendment states:

> The right of the people to be secure in their persons, houses, papers, and effects, against unreasonable searches and seizures, shall not be violated, and no Warrants shall issue, but upon probable cause, supported by Oath or affirmation, and particularly describing the place to be searched, and the persons or things to be seized.[7]

These precepts have been interpreted and reinterpreted since the founding of the country, and a body of law has evolved directing law enforcement on constitutionally permissible search and seizure methods. Some of the central legal concepts include:

- Expectation of privacy
- Consent
- The search warrant requirement
- Exceptions to the search warrant requirement
- Workplace searching and monitoring
- Private searches versus public searches.

5.6.1 EXPECTATION OF PRIVACY

At its core, the Fourth Amendment is a recognition that certain spaces and property are private to the owner and should be free from unwarranted government intrusion.[8] The threshold question, then, is what locations and things are private under the law? Much of the law related to search and seizure focuses on answering this question.

Some items or spaces are inherently public. Imagine you put a sign on your front lawn saying you support the New York Yankees, or a public post in your Twitter feed saying: "Go Yankees! I know you're gonna beat the Red Sox tonight!" In this example, you are purposely presenting information about yourself in publicly viewable spaces, and in a manner visible to any passerby.

Some items or spaces, on the other hand, are inherently private. To give an easy example, if you keep a diary in your bedroom, the information inside is private – both because it is a diary (an object normally created to hold sensitive personal information), and because you have it in your bedroom (a very private location). The same would be true if you created the diary on your personal laptop and stored it on the laptop's hard drive.

Not every situation is as clear-cut, however, and the law has developed a standard to help determine whether a thing or place is public or private. This standard is known as the "reasonable expectation of privacy". Under this standard, when an item, location or activity is something you expect to be private, and it was reasonable for you to expect it, given our usual social customs and beliefs, that privacy will be protected from wanton intrusion by law enforcement or other government agents.[9] You would have a reasonable expectation of privacy in your diary, either the paper or the electronic version. You would not have a reasonable expectation if you posted the contents of your diary on your public blog.

---

[7] U.S. CONST. amend. IV. Our country's founders did not like British soldiers forcing their way into colonial homes, and wanted to ensure their new government could not do this.

[8] The Amendment addresses government conduct and does not address conduct of private parties, which is regulated by other laws.

[9] This privacy standard was articulated in *Katz v. United States*, 389 U.S. 347 (1967), a foundational United States Supreme Court case regarding the expectation of privacy in telephone communications.

This right to privacy from government intrusion directly impacts law enforcement investigations. When a reasonable expectation of privacy exists, law enforcement must follow strict rules and obtain authorization from a judge to access that private space or material. For example, a person's home is the most commonly recognized location in which he or she has a reasonable expectation of privacy. To search a home for evidence, law enforcement must convince a judge that there are facts providing probable cause to believe evidence of a crime is inside. A judge must agree and issue a search warrant, or else a search would be illegal (absent unusual circumstances that are exceptions to the search warrant requirement, such as a life-or-death emergency).

As the law evolves to encompass the virtual world, the reasonable expectation of privacy is extending to places and actions on the Internet, and how it will be applied is still uncertain. Some of these places include password-protected accounts, storage sites, and non-public communications platforms. The actions include communicating by email, text messages, and other forms of communication. People also reasonably expect privacy in their devices, hard drives, portable storage media, and other forms of hardware.

The law recognizes there might be a higher or lower expectation of privacy depending on the nature of the item, activity, or location. Sometimes access or information may be shared with others, yet a level of privacy is retained. As we will learn, the proper procedures for law enforcement investigation include a range of options, reflecting the level of privacy expected for the item or location in question.

5.6.2   CONSENT

Whenever privacy is a factor, so is the concept of consent. Individuals and entities that have an expectation of privacy in spaces, things, or communications also have the power to consent to law enforcement entering or viewing those spaces or items. If the owner or holder consents to an investigator accessing a private account, data repository or communication – knowing what consent entails and intentionally providing it – then he or she essentially is waiving the expectation of privacy. For the consent exception to be valid, police must reasonably believe the person authorizing consent for a search or seizure has the authority to do so (for example, that the consenter lives in the home to be searched).[10]

To be legally effective, consent must be given knowingly and voluntarily. In other words, the consenter must be acting of free will and fully understand what he or she is agreeing to. If a court is asked to review this issue and comes to believe the consent was obtained by trickery or coercion, then it will be considered invalid. Law enforcement and prosecutors will not be able to use evidence acquired through unknowing or involuntary consent.

Consent plays a role when it comes to information available through open source online investigation. When someone "exposes information to the public", such as photos, videos, or other data, they are forgoing any right to privacy.[11] The person or entity publicizing this data has, in effect, consented to its viewing by whomever comes across it. Ironically, the malicious acts of a wrongdoer to expose other people's private information can negate their lack of consent.[12]

---

[10] *Illinois v. Rodriguez*, 497 U.S. 177 (1990).

[11] *See e.g., Katz v. United States*, 389 U.S. 347 (1967), at 351.

[12] When one person maliciously places compromising photos or other private items online in order to threaten or harass another person, a new consent issue arises. This new issue is not whether the person who posted the photos consented to public viewing but whether the victim consented, and the suspect's intent in exposing the materials. For more on this subject, see Chapter 6 regarding the laws against cyber stalking and cyber harassment.

Consent is an area that may be litigated after the fact, so we will look at methods for obtaining authorized, lawful consent from an owner or account holder in Chapters 12 and 13.

5.6.3 THE SEARCH WARRANT REQUIREMENT

When there is a reasonable expectation of privacy in a location or item, and the owner has not consented to law enforcement action, the law requires officers to obtain a search warrant to enter the premises or open the item (such as a safe or file cabinet), search inside, and seize evidence.

A search warrant is an order from a court with jurisdiction over the investigation permitting law enforcement officials to search a location (physical or virtual) and seize specified items found within. A court may authorize a search warrant only when law enforcement has demonstrated probable cause to believe criminal evidence will be present in the target location. Here, probable cause means that there are reasonable grounds to believe the evidence will be found, or that it "probably" will be found there.

The procedures and requirements for obtaining search warrants for physical locations/ items and digital accounts are described in Chapter 7.

5.6.4 EXCEPTIONS TO THE SEARCH WARRANT REQUIREMENT

While a search warrant is presumptively required to search a private space, item, device, or account, there are also many exceptions to this rule. Some of the main exceptions to the search warrant requirement are:

- *Consent.* As we learned earlier, individuals can consent to a search of their person, property, vehicle, device, account, or any other space or item. The consent must be voluntary and the person must have the authority to consent.
- *Plain view.* If contraband is viewable to police who are in a lawful vantage point, the officers may seize it without obtaining a search warrant. This exception is based on the understanding that the time needed to obtain a warrant might allow the contraband to be moved, hidden, or destroyed.[13] The plain view doctrine has been applied to searches of data. For example, if police execute a search warrant on a computer looking for evidence of one crime but happen to come across evidence of a different crime, they may seize what is in plain view. In order to actively look for evidence pertaining to the second crime they would need an amended search warrant.[14]
- *Automobiles.* Because cars are mobile and can quickly move out of investigative reach, a search warrant is not required to search them if there is probable cause to believe the car contains evidence of a crime or contraband.[15]
- *Search incident to lawful arrest.* After lawfully arresting an individual, police may search the individual and any area within his reach. This exception exists as a protective measure to enhance officer safety and prevent evidence destruction.[16]

---

[13] The U.S. Supreme Court addressed the plain view doctrine in *Horton v. California*, 496 U.S. 128 (1990), and expanded the concept to plain smell, feel, and hearing in *Minnesota v. Dickerson*, 508 U.S. 366 (1993).

[14] *See e.g.*, *United States v. Wong*, 334 F.3d 831 (9th Cir. 2003); *United States v. Carey*, 172 F.3d 1268 (10th Cir. 1999).

[15] The automobile exception was first stated in the Prohibition Era case of *Carroll v. United States*, 267 U.S. 132 (1925). A long series of cases since then has clarified the use of the exception.

[16] *Chimel v. California*, 395 U.S. 752 (1969). In a more recent case, the U.S. Supreme Court held that police may conduct a warrantless search of the passenger area of a vehicle under this exception if they reasonably believe an arrestee may have access to weapons in that area. *Arizona v. Gant*, 556 U.S. 332 (2009).

- *Frisk/pat down*. Police may temporarily detain a person if they reasonably suspect he is involved in a crime, and police may then conduct a pat down frisk of his outer clothing if they reasonably suspect he is armed.[17] Reasonable suspicion is a lower standard of proof than probable cause.
- *Emergencies and hot pursuit*. Under emergency or "exigent" circumstances, such as a threat to life, health, or property, police are allowed to search without stopping to get authorization from a judge. Similarly, if a suspect flees officers investigating a crime, the officers may follow him into a home or other space in "hot pursuit" of the suspect. For example, police can follow a fleeing robber into a house to apprehend him.[18]
- *Inventory*. Police are generally allowed to inventory property they must safeguard, such as the contents of an automobile when it is impounded, or the personal property of someone taken into custody. Inventories are done for safety, and to reduce theft or false claims of theft. Contraband encountered during an inventory may be seized as evidence, even though no search warrant was obtained.

5.6.5 WORKPLACE SEARCHES AND MONITORING

Privacy in the workplace is a complex legal issue that impacts both law enforcement and private sector investigations. To what extent does an organization have the ability to monitor or search its own property, data, networks, and physical space, and what privacy rights do employees or customers have? The answer to this question may depend upon the organization's policies and notice provided to employees. When employees are given notice that they have no expectation of privacy in the workplace or its computer systems, the results of these private searches usually will be admissible as evidence if the employee is ever prosecuted for a crime.

Privacy in the workplace is discussed further in Chapter 7.

5.6.6 PRIVATE SEARCHES VERSUS PUBLIC SEARCHES

The Constitution contains prohibitions on government intrusion, not restrictions upon private action. In other words, the Fourth Amendment says what government agents cannot do, but does not address the actions of private investigators. In the 1921 case of *Burdeau v. McDowell*, the Supreme Court made this distinction clear, holding that searches by private parties do not implicate the Fourth Amendment and, therefore, suppression of evidence is not a remedy to a questionable private search.[19]

Still, this principle is not absolute, because sometimes the Constitution *does* apply to private action. If a private search was done at the request of government officials, or the private party is deemed an agent of the government, it would be deemed a government search. Evidence recovered unlawfully would be subject to suppression. Further, even when suppression under the Fourth Amendment might not be a remedy, private investigators must follow the many other laws that prohibit intrusive private conduct (such as trespass and eavesdropping laws) or they could be subject to civil or even criminal liability.

---

[17] *Terry v. Ohio*, 392 U.S. 1 (1968).

[18] *Kentucky v. King*, 563 U.S. 452 (2011). In this case, the court found a warrantless search of a home acceptable when officers followed a suspect in a drug case, knocked on the door and announced themselves, and then heard the suspect flushing the toilet.

[19] *Burdeau v. McDowell*, 256 U.S. 465 (1921). See also *United States v. Jacobsen*, 466 U.S. 109, 113 (1984).

5.7   THE EXCLUSIONARY RULE: PROTECTIONS AND CONSEQUENCES FOR IMPROPER INVESTIGATIVE ACTION

The exclusionary rule holds that when law enforcement obtains evidence unlawfully it will be suppressed – meaning excluded from all criminal proceedings. Criminal charges cannot be based on the suppressed evidence and if the case goes to trial, the jury will never hear about it. This rule evolved from U.S. Supreme Court rulings over the last hundred years to ensure law enforcement complies with constitutional requirements and defendants have an adequate remedy for improper evidence gathering. The rule applies to physical evidence, suspect confessions, and other types of evidence, as we will discuss.

5.7.1   Physical Evidence

If physical evidence is obtained by law enforcement in a manner that violates the Fourth Amendment, a court must suppress, or exclude, that evidence from being used against a criminal defendant.[20] In other words, if drugs were seized unlawfully, without a search warrant or a valid exception to the search warrant requirement, then the remedy is to suppress it. The evidence cannot be used by the prosecution to prove the defendant's guilt and a jury will never hear about it. Similarly, if a defendant was arrested illegally and evidence obtained as a result, the evidence will be excluded from the case. These rules on physical evidence extend to digital evidence, as we discuss in Chapter 7.

5.7.2   Other Forms of Evidence: Unlawful Arrests, Statements, and Witness Identifications

The exclusionary rule applies not only to search and seizure evidence under the Fourth Amendment, but also to other forms of evidence, including:

- *Anything resulting from an unlawful arrest or temporary detention.* If a defendant is stopped or arrested unlawfully, that could be grounds for suppression of evidence that was later recovered, including physical evidence and statements from the defendant, or identification of the defendant by a witness.[21]
- *Statements by a defendant.* Statements need to be obtained lawfully by police and other law enforcement. Of primary concern is the defendant's constitutional right to remain silent if questioned by law enforcement, so a confession can be suppressed if it was coerced. "Miranda warnings" are one important protection for defendants being interrogated. Prior to interrogation, officers must advise defendants in custody that they have the right to remain silent, that their statements to law enforcement could be used as evidence against them, and that they have the right to have an attorney present during questioning.[22] Despite popular media's depictions, Miranda warnings are required only if the defendant is both in custody *and* being interrogated.

---

[20] *See, Weeks v. United States*, 232 U.S. 383 (1914) (creating the exclusionary rule for actions by federal law enforcement), and *Mapp v. Ohio*, 367 U.S. 643 (1961) (making the exclusionary rule binding on state and local law enforcement).

[21] *Dunaway v. New York*, 442 U.S. 200 (1979).

[22] *Miranda v. Arizona*, 384 U.S. 436 (1966), *Jackson v. Denno*, 378 U.S. 368 (1964).

* *A witness identification of a defendant.* Identification procedures are used by law enforcement to determine if an eyewitness can pick out the perpetrator. A line-up is a classic example, where the suspect and fillers sit for viewing by an eyewitness to a crime. Other procedures include a "show-up", where a suspect is apprehended shortly after the commission of a crime, and the witness is given an opportunity to view him and tell the police whether it is the perpetrator. Another identification procedure is the photo array, where the witness is shown a group of pictures, and tells law enforcement if he sees the perpetrator. These procedures must comply with a number of legal rules to avoid suggesting the identification of a suspect to the witness. Improper procedures can lead to the suppression of identification evidence.[23]

5.7.3   FRUIT OF THE POISONOUS TREE DOCTRINE

The exclusionary rule is taken one step further with the "fruit of the poisonous tree" doctrine. To ensure that investigations do not benefit from illegal conduct by law enforcement, a court will suppress not just the evidence directly obtained by illegal law enforcement conduct, but any evidence indirectly obtained afterwards based on that illegal conduct.[24]

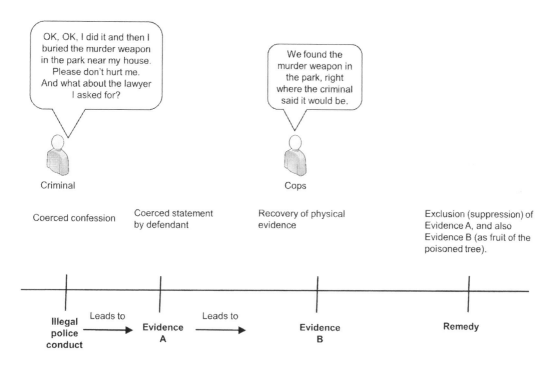

FIGURE 5.3   Exclusionary Rule: Suppression of Evidence – Fruit of Poisonous Tree.

---

[23] *United States v. Wade*, 388 U.S. 218 (1967).

[24] *Nardone v. United States*, 308 U.S. 338 (1939). Prosecutors can attempt to convince the court that the additional evidence should not be suppressed because it would have been discovered anyway ("inevitable discovery"), or obtained from an independent source, *Murray v. United States*, 487 U.S. 533 (1988), *Nix v. Williams*, 467 U.S. 431 (1984).

The terminology refers to the idea that an illegally seized fruit, planted in the ground, yields only a poisoned tree, from which nothing is admissible. Figure 5.3 illustrates how evidence obtained following a coerced confession would be suppressed.

Under this rule, an illegal action early in an investigation could contaminate every investigative step that comes after it. For example, if an illegal search for drugs uncovers evidence of a murder, the murder evidence may be suppressed. Similar scenarios arise in cybercrime investigations. If officers improperly search a phone, laptop, or email account for evidence of a fraud scheme without proper legal authority (a warrant or valid consent), and stumble upon evidence of unrelated crimes (like child pornography or drug trafficking), all the evidence from the resulting investigation may be excluded as the product of an unlawful search. When a warrant is obtained to search for evidence of certain crimes and new crimes are discovered, law enforcement should stop their search and ask the court to amend the search warrant to include the newly discovered crimes. Without an amended warrant (or an exception to the warrant requirement), further searching for newly discovered crimes is illegal.

These rules magnify the responsibility of investigators to continuously evaluate their conduct to ensure it is proper. If arguably improper conduct somehow occurs, the taint of this action must be removed and isolated from the ensuing investigation.

5.8   CIVIL LAW AND PROCEDURE

Civil lawsuits are brought by organizations or private individuals seeking to hold others accountable for harming them intentionally or negligently, or for breaking contractual promises. Remedies in civil law include money damages (restitution and punitive damages) as well as court orders prohibiting conduct or requiring certain actions. In this section, we will survey some of the primary areas of civil law. Because cybercrime often targets the data and funds held by organizations and individuals, it plays a significant role in private sector investigations and civil lawsuits.

5.8.1   THE CIVIL LITIGATION PROCESS

The civil litigation process may include these phases:[25]

- *Pre-litigation investigation.* The private sector investigation into a disputed event to determine the nature of the incident, the acts or omissions that caused it, the potential responsibility of various parties, and the resulting financial and other damage.
- *Pre-litigation settlement negotiations.* Some civil disputes are settled by the parties before formal legal action is taken, as both sides recognize the financial and reputational costs of filing a lawsuit. In these negotiations, the results of prior investigation can be crucial to persuading the other party to agree to settle.
- *Complaint and answer.* The complaint is the legal document used to file an official lawsuit in civil court. The filing party is the "plaintiff", who seeks damages or restrictions against the "defendant". The complaint may include multiple counts, or causes of action. The complaint must be filed with a court that has proper subject matter jurisdiction over the dispute, and that is the proper venue.[26]

---

[25] The Federal Rules of Civil Procedure can be found at www.law.cornell.edu/rules/frcp. Each state has its own rules for commencing and litigating civil suits. Some state procedures closely follow the federal rules, while others are unique to that state. For links to many state rules, see www.law.cornell.edu/wex/table_civil_procedure.

[26] As discussed in the context of criminal cases, proper subject matter jurisdiction and venue are requirements for civil lawsuits. Jurisdiction and venue may be found in the area where a party resides or has a place of business, or where the conduct at issue occurred. We discuss these concepts, and personal jurisdiction, in more detail in Chapter 19.

The defendant is typically personally served with a copy of the complaint and a summons, which gives the court personal jurisdiction over the defendant. The defendant usually files a response to the complaint in a document called an "answer". In civil cases, defendants may countersue, filing their own complaints against the plaintiffs.

- *Motion to dismiss.* In most civil actions, the defendant files written motions asking the court to dismiss the plaintiff's lawsuit (or portions of it) on various legal grounds. The court decisions on these motions (and others) are important factors for settlement negotiations.
- *Discovery.* During this pre-trial phase, the parties are required to share the documents and other evidence they plan to use to prove their arguments at trial. Civil litigation often involves an enormous volume of document production and review.
- *Summary judgment motion.* Among other motions, each side typically files a summary judgment motion when discovery is complete, on the grounds that the discovered facts do not establish any factual dispute requiring a jury trial for some or all causes of action. If the court agrees, it can enter judgment on those causes of action.
- *Trial.* Should all attempts to settle the case prior to trial fail, it will proceed to trial before a judge and often a jury. Both sides present witnesses and evidence. In most states, civil juries are comprised of fewer jurors than criminal juries, and sometimes a unanimous verdict is not required.
- *Appeal.* Parties may appeal court decisions to appellate courts regarding motions, trial decisions, and whether the jury verdict was in accordance with the law. Some cases may go through several levels of appeals.

Very few civil cases proceed all the way through trial, as the process is expensive and lengthy. Whereas a criminal case involves highly personal decisions by the defendant about whether to plead guilty or not, civil litigants are typically in a position to make business decisions about potential costs and outcomes and whether to settle or continue litigating a case. Settlement is a possibility at all stages of civil litigation.

For a deeper look at the civil litigation process, read Chapter 19.

5.8.2   Causes of Action

Civil litigation involving cybercrime may be based upon these general categories of causes of action:

- Intentional torts
- Negligence torts
- Breach of contract
- Cybercrime-specific causes of action
- Regulatory action.

We will cover each in turn.

5.8.2.1   Intentional Torts

A "tort" is a "wrong", so intentional torts are intentional actions that harm someone. Civil laws classify some criminal activity as intentional torts, so an act potentially could be the subject of both a civil suit and criminal prosecution.

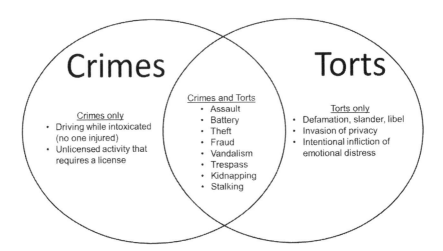

FIGURE 5.4   Crimes and Torts Compared.

Some common intentional torts are:

- *Assault.* Intentional threats or attempts to inflict harm
- *Battery.* Intentional touching of another in an offensive way
- *Theft (conversion).* Stealing or improperly exercising control over another's property
- *Fraud.* Committing a deceptive action to damage another or gain a personal benefit
- *Trespass to personal property.* Interfering with another's personal property
- *Trespass to land and buildings.* Wrongful interference with another's real property
- *Intentional infliction of mental or emotional distress.* Extreme and outrageous actions that cause mental distress
- *Defamation, slander and libel.* Stating or publishing false information about someone that damages his or her reputation and/or causes financial harm
- *Invasion of privacy.* Violating a person's privacy rights
- *Malicious prosecution.* Subjecting someone to a baseless criminal prosecution or civil action
- *False imprisonment.* Wrongfully detaining someone or impeding his movement.

The distinction and overlap among torts and crimes is depicted in Figure 5.4. A single act might be both a tort and a crime, but civil and criminal courts are separate forums with different laws and legal standards.

5.8.2.2 Negligence Torts

Negligence torts occur when an actor fails to exercise the standard of care of a reasonable person and this negligence causes harm to another person (or his property). The elements of a negligence case are:

- The actor owed a *duty of care* to the harmed person
- There was a *breach* of that duty
- *Causation* – the breach of the duty caused harm to the other person.

Automobile accidents are traditional negligence torts. The plaintiff alleges the defendant was negligent in his operation of the car leading to a collision, and thereby caused defendant's injuries.

In the context of cybercrime and cybersecurity, a negligence claim might arise when a plaintiff is injured by cybercrime and the cybercrime was caused by the negligence of the defendant. Perhaps a bank failed to implement reasonable cybersecurity or anti-fraud measures, enabling a cybercriminal to access customer accounts, and the plaintiff suffered financial losses of millions of dollars. The cybercriminal committed an intentional crime and tort, but the bank may have committed a negligent tort by failing to employ adequate information security. There might be little hope of identifying or recovering money from the cybercriminal, but recovery of damages against the bank might be possible.

5.8.2.3   Breach of Contract

Breach of contract is another common civil law action. Contracts are legal agreements between two or more parties regarding commercial transactions, employment, provision of services, and other business dealings.[27] When one party believes another has breached the promises made in a contract, she has grounds to sue in civil court.

More than ever, breach of contract suits involve cybercrime and cybersecurity. Today, contracts between organizations frequently describe measures relating to security against cybercrime or other disruption. Entities providing services like email hosting and cloud computing and storage outline their security and potential liability in contracts with their customers. And when merchants contract with third parties to process credit and debit card payments, these contracts include requirements about data and network security. When cybercrimes occur, losses can be substantial, and one party may allege that the other party did not to live up to the contract by failing to provide security or processes at the promised standard. The resulting dispute and potential lawsuit would include a claim for breach of contract.

Insurance companies sell "cyber insurance" to cover expenses and damages that result from cybercrime. To obtain a policy, an organization completes an application that may require promises about its internal data practices, as well as its level of security and anti-fraud protection. The insurer issues a policy that defines terms and describes what losses will be covered. If a cybercrime occurs and the losses are considerable, inevitably, some organizations will have their claims denied on the grounds that the loss is not covered, or that the organization misrepresented its security posture. In this scenario, the insured may sue the insurer alleging breach of contract.

Privacy policies and terms of service created by companies that collect and store personal information are a contract between an organization and its clients or customers. As Internet users, we regularly agree to these contracts. If a company violates its privacy policy, such as by misrepresenting a poor cybersecurity posture and allowing customer data to be stolen, it could be sued by customers (or by the government for failure to comply with relevant regulations).

5.8.2.4   Cybercrime-Specific Causes of Action

There are some federal and state statutes specifically relating to cybercrime that create a civil cause of action. These statutory causes of action generally are enacted in tandem with criminal laws prohibiting cybercrime, enabling victims to recover money damages from cybercriminals and to seek court orders restraining their activities. Cybercrime-specific

---

[27] A contract is formed after mutual understanding of the terms, offer, and acceptance by the parties, and (generally) the exchange of something of value. Many contracts are in writing, but they can be made orally.

causes of action may relate to Internet impersonation, harassment/stalking, phishing activity, transmission of malware, and spam communications. We cover this topic in greater detail in Chapters 6 and 9.

5.8.2.5 Regulatory Actions

Regulatory actions are worthy of a separate cause of action category. Some industries are licensed and regulated by government agencies, and these regulators can take action to hold an organization accountable for compliance deficiencies. A regulatory action might be administrative (internal to the regulator) laying out alleged deficiencies and giving the organization an opportunity to respond in a quasi-judicial forum. After these proceedings, the regulator's adjudicatory body may issue a decision and penalties, such as a fine or loss of license. After this decision, the matter might continue to be litigated in civil court. A regulator might pursue a court order against a business to enforce regulatory requirements or penalties, or a business might challenge the decisions of a regulator in court.

5.9 LICENSING AND REGULATORY LAW

Knowing regulatory actions are a type of civil suit, let us explore further this area of licensing and regulatory law. This topic includes "regulatory-type" law where non-regulated companies are now facing requirements for cybersecurity that traditionally were applied only to regulated industries.

Federal and state governments pass laws that require individuals and entities involved in certain lines of business to follow a regulatory framework. Regulated industries include banks, hospitals, and utilities. Under these laws, a government agency is assigned to perform the regulation. That regulator may set forth its own rules and requirements, including that regulated organizations obtain licenses, report events, create policies, maintain documentation, and submit to inspection. Regulatory agencies also may establish a quasi-judicial body to resolve disputes, as we covered earlier. In the context of cybercrime and cybersecurity, regulators increasingly require regulated organizations to maintain cybersecurity, privacy, anti-fraud, and anti-money laundering (AML) programs.

A regulator may investigate and decide that a particular entity is not complying with the required standards. The law empowers regulatory agencies to take action against non-compliant entities, including by issuing fines or revoking licenses. Some entities might try to negotiate with the regulators to arrive at a favorable outcome, minimize the fine and negative publicity, and bring themselves into compliance. Others might decide to fight the finding through the regulatory body's adjudication process, an administrative hearing, and then through the courts.

Cybercrime investigators may encounter crimes that call into question whether a business complied with regulatory cybersecurity rules. Regulated sectors might include:

- Financial industry
- Healthcare industry
- Utilities and other service providers
- Generalized consumer protection and privacy.

For example, financial institutions and money service businesses are licensed and regulated by both state and federal regulating bodies, and these regulations include both cybersecurity and anti-money laundering (AML) requirements. AML and financial investigation are covered in greater depth in Chapter 15.

Some businesses and organizations are not regulated or licensed, but face regulatory-type cybersecurity requirements, often enforced by state Attorneys General, the Federal Trade Commission (FTC), or other agencies. These government entities investigate alleged violations of laws regarding data breach notification, security standards, and fair trade practices. The ultimate result of such an investigation could be a civil lawsuit seeking monetary penalties and a court order prohibiting future violations. As more regulations and laws are imposed relating to Internet commerce and information security, more of this regulatory-type litigation is likely (discussed further in Chapter 9).

5.10   CONCLUSION

This chapter provided the fundamentals of criminal and civil law that serve as the foundation of any cybercrime investigation. Cybercrime investigators may be called upon to investigate cybercrime from different perspectives, looking for violations of criminal law, civil torts, and breaches of contract, or potential regulatory violations. Many cybercrime cases involve a combination of these issues. Knowledge of the basic legal principles underlying both criminal and civil law and procedure is essential to achieving an investigative outcome that can support litigation.

When litigation occurs, the methods investigators used to gather evidence will face legal scrutiny. Investigative steps must respect the constitutional protections afforded criminal suspects and the rights of other parties. If evidence is obtained unlawfully, it may be inadmissible in a courtroom, resulting in the unraveling of criminal or civil cases. Working on cybercrime cases means applying legal principles in an arena where many issues are complex and evolving. This environment requires investigators to understand these fundamentals in order to adapt to new situations and conform with the law. When this responsibility is met, investigators protect their cases and clients, their own reputations, and the strength of their investigations.

6 Cybercrime Defined
The Criminal Statutes Outlawing Criminal Conduct Online

This chapter is for:

- Law enforcement and the public sector to learn about criminal statutes applicable to cybercrime
- Those in the private sector who want to learn how law enforcement evaluates a crime.

6.1 INTRODUCTION

To do the best job we can as investigators, we need a clear grasp of how the law defines cybercrime. Our federal and state governments have a multitude of criminal codes and statutes setting forth the types of misconduct involving computers and the Internet that constitute chargeable offenses. By understanding the requirements and definitions of these criminal statutes, investigators can determine whether a crime occurred, and direct their cyber investigations towards the evidence necessary to support an arrest and prove charges in court.

In this chapter, we will focus first on crimes that pertain directly to cyber activity. These are offenses specifically addressing criminal conduct that involves computers and the Internet. Several federal statutes prohibit cybercrime activity, and we will review the key portions of these laws. Equally important, we will discuss the body of state law directly prohibiting computer and Internet crimes.

Along with these "computer crimes", cybercrimes almost always violate traditional criminal laws, such as theft and forgery. In this chapter, we also will review the traditional criminal offenses that commonly apply to cybercrime. Both traditional and cyber-specific charges are powerful tools in bringing a cybercriminal to justice.

6.2 FEDERAL AND STATE LAW

As we covered in Chapter 5, there are two separate bodies of criminal law – federal and state – that prohibit activity such as cybercrime. Federal law, drafted and passed by Congress and signed by the President, is contained within the United States Code. The U.S. Code includes criminal statutes that are enforceable throughout the country. These federal offenses address crimes that present a national concern – either because they are committed against U.S. governmental agencies or property, or because they affect national interests, like the free flow of interstate commerce.

States (and territories) each have their own set of criminal laws prohibiting criminal conduct, including statutes applicable to cybercrime. States generally have jurisdiction over crimes committed within the state, and often over crimes that occurred outside the state but caused harm within the state or involved communications to or from the state.

Federal and state laws often overlap, which means many cybercrimes could be investigated by both state and federal authorities, and prosecution could occur in state or federal court. In some instances, however, one body of law has a more applicable or powerful statute addressing the criminal conduct, or one agency has better resources to handle the case.

All criminal laws specify potential penalties for each offense. If a defendant is convicted of a crime, generally the judge decides what sentence, within that range, the defendant will receive.

6.3 FEDERAL CYBERCRIME LAW

There are several federal laws that specifically prohibit cyber-related crime, such as computer intrusions, denial-of-service attacks, and the use of malware or spyware. This section provides an overview of these fundamental federal cybercrime laws.[1]

6.3.1 THE COMPUTER FRAUD AND ABUSE ACT (CFAA)

Federal law began directly addressing cybercrime in 1986, with the enactment of the Computer Fraud and Abuse Act (CFAA).[2] The CFAA has been updated several times since its inception, adding new provisions to correspond with changes in technology and criminal activity.

Some key terms within the CFAA to be aware of are:

*   *Protected computer*, as defined within 18 U.S.C. § 1030(e)(2). A protected computer is any computer used in or affecting interstate commerce, or used exclusively by a financial institution or the U.S. government. Because of the Internet's innate interstate capacity, courts have determined that any computer connected to the Internet is a protected computer.
*   *Without authorization*. This term is not defined in the statute, but its natural and court-interpreted meaning refers to having no authority or permission of any kind for access to a particular computer or network. In other words, someone acting "without authorization" is an outsider who has illicitly gained access to a protected computer or network.
*   *Exceeds authorized access*, as defined within 18 U.S.C. § 1030(e)(6). If a user has authorization to perform certain functions or to access certain data within a computer or system, but goes beyond those boundaries to obtain or alter other data or functions, then the user has "exceeded authorized access".

The CFAA has numerous subsections that criminalize specific types of misconduct related to computers, including:

---

[1] For a detailed analysis of federal computer and cybercrime laws, see *Prosecuting Computer Crimes*, U.S. Department of Justice Computer Crime and Intellectual Property Section (2010). www.justice.gov/sites/default/files/criminal-ccips/legacy/2015/01/14/ccmanual.pdf.

[2] The Computer Fraud and Abuse Act is part of the United States Code, at 18 U.S.C. § 1030.

- *Intrusions into computers to obtain information, 18 U.S.C. § 1030(a)(2).* Individuals violate this statute by intentionally accessing a computer (without authorization or by exceeding authorized access) to obtain financial records from a financial institution, data from an agency of the U.S. government, or any information from a protected computer.
- *Intrusions into computers to commit fraud, 18 U.S.C. § 1030(a)(4).* A violation of this statute occurs when someone knowingly, and with an intent to defraud accesses a protected computer (either without authorization or by exceeding authorized access), and then uses this access to further- a fraud and obtain anything of value.
- *Damaging a computer through transmission of a program, information, code or command, 18 U.S.C. § 1030(a)(5)(A).* When a person intentionally sends malware, viruses, worms, vandalizing code, or other malicious programs or commands to a protected computer, and causes damage to it without authorization, he has violated this subsection.
- *Damaging a computer through unauthorized access, 18 U.S.C. §§ 1030(a)(5)(B) and (C).* These subsections focus on an outsider who intentionally accesses a protected computer without authorization and, as a result, causes damage or loss. If the offender recklessly caused the damage, higher penalties may result.
- *Trafficking in computer passwords, 18 U.S.C. § 1030(a)(6).* A person is guilty of this crime if he buys, sells, or transfers passwords (or similar information) through which computers can be accessed without authorization. The trafficking must be done knowingly and with intent to defraud. It also must affect either interstate or foreign commerce (which can be established if the passwords affected computer usage linked to the Internet), or computers used by or for the U.S. government.
- *Extortion involving computers, 18 U.S.C. § 1030(a)(7).* When someone threatens to damage a protected computer, or to expose or obtain information from a protected computer, he commits a violation of this statute. Similarly, if a person demands money or another item of value in connection to causing computer damage to facilitate an extortion, he has violated this statute. "Damage" means any impairment to the integrity or availability of data or information (such as encryption of a victim's data by ransomware).
- *Intrusions into computers used by the U.S. government and theft of national security information, 18 U.S.C. §§ 1030(a)(1), (2)(B), (3), and (6)(B).* Several sections of the CFAA describe offenses for accessing computers or data belonging to or used on behalf of the U.S. government. When the data is related to national security or foreign relations, particularly harsh penalties are imposed.
- *Attempt or conspiracy to commit any of these offenses, 18 U.S.C. § 1030(b).*

The CFAA creates both misdemeanor and felony-level crimes. Whether a charge is a felony generally hinges upon: (a) the amount of loss or damage caused by the criminal activity, (b) whether actual (or threats to commit) personal injury occurred, (c) whether public safety or property damage were a factor, (d) whether the activity was undertaken with fraudulent intent, or (e) whether threatened or actual theft or damage to national security and/or government computers was involved. The Act also creates a basis for civil lawsuits seeking monetary or other compensation for loss, injury, or damage resulting from CFAA violations. Table 6.1 summarizes various CFAA provisions.

6.3.2   THE WIRETAP ACT

The Wiretap Act is another set of federal statutes that specifically target cybercrime.[3] Originally developed to regulate private and government wiretaps in the era of telephones, the

---

[3] The Wiretap Act is found at 18 U.S.C. §§ 2510–2522. Criminal interception offenses can be in found in § 2511(1).

TABLE 6.1

Summary of CFAA provisions

Type of cybercrime conduct	Title	CFAA subsection
Intrusion	Obtaining National Security Information	18 USC §1030 (a)(1)
Intrusion	Accessing a Computer and Obtaining Information	18 USC §1030 (a)(2)
Intrusion	Trespassing in a Government Computer	18 USC §1030 (a)(3)
Intrusion & Fraud	Accessing a Computer to Defraud & Obtain Value	18 USC §1030 (a)(4)
Damage	Intentionally Damaging by Knowing Transmission of Programs, Code	18 USC §1030 (a)(5)(A)
Damage	Recklessly Damaging by Intentional Access	18 USC §1030 (a)(5)(B)
Damage	Negligently Causing Damage & Loss by Intentional Access	18 USC §1030 (a)(5)(C)
Trafficking	Trafficking in Passwords	18 USC §1030 (a)(6)
Ransomware and other extortion	Extortion Involving Computers	18 USC §1030 (a)(7)

Wiretap Act was amended with the creation of the CFAA specifically to cover "electronic communications". As a result, the Wiretap Act criminalizes the use of technology that surreptitiously intercepts email, texts, and other forms of digital communication. These methods include spyware, network "sniffing", and cloning techniques. All violations of the Wiretap Act are felony-level crimes.

Some key terms within the Wiretap Act are:

- *Intercept*, as defined by 18 U.S.C. § 2510(4). A person "intercepts" an oral, wire, or electronic communication when he acquires the contents of the communication using an electronic, mechanical, or other device.
- *Oral, wire, and electronic communication* as defined by 18 U.S.C. § 2510(1), (2) and (12). These terms have long technical descriptions, but they essentially refer to verbal communication (oral), telephonic communication (wire), and digital communications (electronic). The vast majority of everyday conversations, phone calls, emails, text messages, and online postings fall under these definitions.
- *Electronic, mechanical, or other device*, as defined by 18 U.S.C. § 2510(5). This language refers to any equipment or apparatus that can be used to intercept an oral, wire, or electronic communication.

The Wiretap Act establishes several different interception-related crimes covering a range of conduct including:

- *Intercepting a communication*, 18 U.S.C. § 2511(1)(a). It is a criminal offense to intercept, try to intercept or get another person to intercept, without authorization, any oral, wire, or electronic communication.
- *Disclosing intercepted communications*, 18 U.S.C. § 2511(1)(c). A person violates this section if he knows an oral, wire, or electronic communication was unlawfully intercepted, and he discloses or tries to disclose the contents of the communication to another person.

- *Using intercepted communications*, 18 U.S.C. § 2511(1)(d). A person violates this section if he knows an oral, wire, or electronic communication was unlawfully intercepted, and he uses or tries to use the contents of the communication.

The Wiretap Act also sets forth the rules that law enforcement must follow to lawfully intercept communications in furtherance of a criminal investigation. This aspect of the Wiretap Act is discussed in Chapter 7.

6.3.3 UNLAWFUL ACCESS TO STORED COMMUNICATIONS

Another federal law against cybercrime prohibits Unlawful Access to Stored Communications, making it a crime to obtain, alter, or prevent access to email, texts or other digital communications that are stored with service providers. If there is a fraudulent, damaging or other criminal purpose to illegally accessing the stored communications, the conduct is chargeable as a felony.

The basic elements of this charge as laid out in 18 U.S.C. § 2701 are:

- Intentional access,
- Without authorization or exceeding authorization (same definition as in the CFAA above),
- To a facility providing electronic communication services, and
- Obtaining or altering data, or preventing authorized access by others.
- (Felony – additional element) For commercial advantage, malicious destruction, private gain, or to further another wrongful act.

This criminal offense contemplates that online communications (like email and text messages) may be retained with email or other service providers for extended periods of time and might contain troves of personal information of interest to data thieves.

Unlawful Access to Stored Communications is part of the Electronic Communications Privacy Act (ECPA), a significant federal law governing Internet communications. As discussed in Chapter 7, ECPA also establishes the rules law enforcement must follow to obtain information about the users of electronic communications accounts, as well as the content of their communications.

6.3.4 THE CONTROLLING THE ASSAULT OF NON-SOLICITED PORNOGRAPHY AND MARKETING ACT (CAN-SPAM ACT)

Federal law prohibits sending unsolicited emails that advertise commercial products or services. The Controlling the Assault of Non-Solicited Pornography and Marketing (CAN-SPAM) Act went into effect in 2004 and makes it a crime to send large quantities of commercial email or electronic messages while hiding one's identity or location (18 U.S.C. § 1037). Some of the forbidden spamming methods covered by the statute include:

- Using unauthorized computer access to send commercial email
- Using a computer to send commercial email with the intent to deceive or mislead the recipients as to the origin of the email
- Falsifying the header information in commercial emails
- Falsifying the registration information for multiple email accounts or Internet Protocol addresses that are then used to send commercial email.

Criminal spamming is elevated to a CAN-SPAM felony by exceeding a threshold number of communications or false "sender" accounts. Causing loss, damage, or theft of over $5,000 in one year, or organizing three or more people to commit these spamming offenses, also can lead to felony charges.

6.3.5 COMMUNICATION INTERFERENCE

Not surprisingly, federal law also protects the nation's communications infrastructure, including the physical components of the Internet. The crime of Communication Interference makes it a felony to cause willful or malicious damage or interference to radio, telephone, and other means of communication (including electronic) that are controlled by the United States, or used by the military or for civil defense (18 U.S.C. § 1362). Since the Internet is such a system, almost any criminal activity designed to damage or interfere with the equipment or property that enables online communications will fall under the purview of this statute.

6.4 STATE CYBERCRIME LAW

Over the past three decades, as computers and the Internet have evolved into universal tools for people and organizations, state legislatures have created laws designed both to protect the cyber-safety of residents and to outlaw harmful cyber conduct. For many types of criminal offenses, a model law is drafted by an independent organization – like the American Law Institute or the Uniform Laws Commission – to provide guidance to state legislatures seeking to enact comprehensive statutes in their criminal codes.[4] But in the area of cybercrimes, no such model exists. As a result, each state has charted its own course, crafting and amending laws as technology and criminal exploits change.

Like the federal government, most states began drafting computer crime laws in the 1980s, when business computers, and then home computers, became commonplace. Today, all 50 states have some criminal statutes aimed at combatting computer-related offenses.

Every state currently has a section of criminal code making it a crime to obtain unauthorized access to a computer or computer system.[5] Beyond this common basic prohibition, however, the states' approaches to outlawing cybercrime vary widely.

Some states (such as California and Washington) have been proactive by enacting statutes that address a wide range of cyber offenses, while using statutory language that anticipates the potential for evolving forms of cyber malfeasance. In these states, criminal laws target the full array of computer and online crime – unauthorized access, data theft, and tampering, the dissemination of malware and spyware, the use of ransomware and other extortion techniques, spam, and attacks directed at critical government and utility functions. In doing so, some states have chosen to mirror the federal statutory approach. Others have created their own frameworks. In some instances, such as in California, state law goes further than the federal law, criminalizing conduct that is not included in the comparable federal statutes.

---

[4] The American Law Institute's (ALI) model codes can be found at: www.ali.org/publications/#publication-type-model-codes. The Uniform Laws Commission's (ULC) uniform and model acts can be found at: www.uniformlaws.org/home. The ULC has created a uniform code for regulating virtual currency and is drafting a code for collection and use of personal data.

[5] Links to the cybercrime statutes of all 50 states can be found on the website of the National Conference of State Legislatures, at www.ncsl.org/research/telecommunications-and-information-technology/computer-hacking-and-unauthorized-access-laws.aspx. The NCSL is a bipartisan group that provides research, training and advocacy on behalf of state legislatures across the country.

Most states have not created a comprehensive set of laws against cybercrime. Instead, most have added cybercrime offenses to their criminal codes in piecemeal fashion, as the pressing need for statutes outlawing specific conduct has become clear (often through public outcry). As a result of this irregular updating of cybercrime offenses, these states tend to address an unpredictable assortment of cybercrimes.

State cybercrimes typically are codified at both the misdemeanor and felony levels. Typically, certain aggravating factors raise the level of criminal conduct to a felony. Some of the common factors are:

- Threshold amounts of monetary value for stolen, altered or damaged data, programs, computers, networks, systems, or other property
- The fraudulent or repeated nature of the crime
- The offender has prior convictions for the same or similar criminal conduct
- The crimes targeted sensitive data (such as medical information)
- The crimes targeted systems or data of government agencies, public transportation entities, or public utilities.

In a small number of states, such as Massachusetts and Idaho, the body of statutes prohibiting cybercrime is minimal. Legislatures in these states have not enacted many laws directed at cyber offenses, requiring investigators and prosecutors to rely upon existing statutes (like theft or forgery) to prosecute cyber cases.

Many state cybercrime laws also create causes of action for civil lawsuits against individuals or entities involved in transmitting spam emails, phishing emails, malware, spyware, and other cyber offenses.

6.5 "TRADITIONAL" FEDERAL AND STATE LAWS THAT APPLY TO CYBERCRIME

Although specific laws have been created to combat cybercrimes, cybercrime conduct often falls within the definitions of other longstanding criminal offenses. In other words, numerous "traditional" crimes can and should be charged when a cybercrime occurs, even though the Internet and computers have changed some of the ways the crimes are perpetrated.

In this section, we will look at some of the traditional offenses that commonly apply to cybercrimes. When evaluating what traditional crimes might be pertinent, investigators should consider the motives of the criminal actors (like greed or revenge) and the methods they are employing to achieve those ends (like identity theft, fraud, or stalking). With this analysis in mind, investigators might find that one or more of the following traditional crimes should be charged:

- Theft/Larceny
- Possession/Receiving of Stolen Property
- Identity Theft
- Impersonation
- Credit/Debit Card Fraud
- Bank Fraud
- Wire Fraud
- Forgery
- Money Laundering
- Harassment, Stalking, Menacing
- Extortion
- Vandalism/Criminal Mischief
- Child Pornography
- Organized Crime
- Attempt and Conspiracy.

6.5.1 Theft/Larceny

Cybercrime routinely involves the theft of money, goods, services, data, and other property that has value. As a result, theft (sometimes called larceny) is often one of the easiest charges to prove against high-tech criminals. The Internet adds a new wrinkle to theft by allowing cybercriminals to steal from victims remotely, and within different jurisdictions, but the nature of the offense remains the same as illustrated in Figure 6.1.

All jurisdictions have statutes prohibiting theft. Federal theft crimes require federal jurisdiction, which can be found if the theft crime involves activity affecting interstate commerce. Theft involving Internet use affects interstate commerce, as does stealing packages or merchandise from delivery and transportation services, a type of theft which is a component of some cyber frauds. In addition, certain federal statutes cover theft from industries regulated by the federal government, such as banks and healthcare providers.

Most theft, however, is investigated and prosecuted at the state level. While each state uses its own language to define theft or larceny, the crime has a basic, essential definition: the taking of property that belongs to another. Most theft statutes use a framework that elevates the level of crime (felony or misdemeanor, as well as seriousness of the felony) based upon threshold dollar values of the items stolen. In New York, for example, the Penal Code has sections for Grand Larceny in the First

FIGURE 6.1 Cybercrime and Theft.

through Fourth Degrees. A Fourth Degree Grand Larceny means a theft of property valued at more than $1,000. The degrees of larceny rise to First Degree, which requires a theft of greater than $1 million.[6]

States also typically associate different types of theft with different levels of crime. Thefts of certain property – such as motor vehicles, livestock, scientific material, or firearms – often merit more serious felony treatment. Some methods of theft, such as embezzlement, extortion and fraud, often receive specific focus within state criminal codes, including particular definitions and felony status.[7] And some states increase the punishment for theft that victimizes certain vulnerable groups, like the elderly and dependent adults. All of these aggravating factors apply equally to online theft.

State theft statutes often encompass criminal conduct related to con artistry, social engineering, and other forms of trickery (such as Theft by Deception, Theft by False Pretenses, or Larceny by Trick). These forms of larceny prohibit theft accomplished by deceiving victims in a manner that persuades them to part with their property. Offenses such as these can be directly applicable to certain cyber frauds, where criminals falsely represent themselves as individuals, financial institutions, government agencies, or charitable entities, and work to convince victims to make payments, give access to accounts, or send money for seemingly legitimate purposes.

6.5.2 Possession/Receiving of Stolen Property

When cybercrime involves stealing, investigators and prosecutors often consider charges for "possession of stolen property", since criminal actors will seek to possess, control, and use these stolen items. Stolen property in this context might include physical items purchased or obtained through cyber fraud. Stolen property also might include electronic items such as stolen data.

All states and the federal government have laws criminalizing the possession or receipt of stolen property. The primary federal law in this area prohibits the knowing receipt or sale of stolen goods that have crossed state or national borders.[8] Because cybercrime regularly involves the movement and shipment of property around the country and the globe, this element often can be proven easily.

State laws generally criminalize the knowing possession of a stolen item. Under these charges, a person need not have participated in the theft to be guilty of criminally possessing the stolen property. In some jurisdictions, although knowledge that the property is stolen is an element of the crime, charges might still be brought if a defendant should have known based on the facts and circumstances. The value or nature of the property in question often determines the felony or misdemeanor level of the crime.

6.5.2.1 Property: A Changing Concept in the Cyber Age

Many criminal statutes include the element of taking or possessing property that rightfully belongs to someone else. From the cyber perspective, it is important to note that a number of states have expanded their definition of "property" to include computers, computer

---

[6] New York Penal Code, Article 155 (Larceny).
[7] Many states and the federal government have separate offenses for embezzlement, extortion, and other types of specialized theft. These statutes often are applicable to cybercrimes, and can be charged along with "computer crimes" offenses. For example, two federal laws – the Hobbs Act (Interference with Commerce by Threats or Violence, 18 U.S.C. § 1951) and Receiving the Proceeds of Extortion (18 U.S.C. § 880) prohibit obtaining or possessing property taken from another by extortion. The CFAA (18 U.S.C. § 1030) prohibits extortion involving computers. Charges under all three statutes might be appropriate in a cyber case.
[8] Sale or Receipt of Stolen Goods, Securities, Moneys, or Fraudulent State Tax Stamps, 18 U.S. Code § 2315.

systems and networks, data, code, computer software, and computer programs. Therefore, stealing or appropriating in the cyber realm can be equivalent to the theft of tangible items. These computer-centered additions are sometimes found in the general definition of "property" within the state's criminal statutes, or sometimes within amended sections related to computer crimes laws.

6.5.3   IDENTITY THEFT

Identity theft is both a treasure and a tool in the world of cybercrime. Identity thieves use stolen identifying information to commit numerous forms of cyber fraud, like exploiting stolen identities to steal from victims' financial accounts. To fuel these frauds, many cybercrimes are directed entirely at stealing identifying information. Cybercriminals also use stolen identities to shield themselves from discovery in the virtual world of the Internet. For these reasons, investigations into cybercrime incidents regularly turn up information and evidence linked to identity theft.

The federal government, all 50 states, Washington D.C., and the U.S. territories have laws penalizing identity theft.[9] These crimes universally focus on the theft or misuse of personal identifying information. In each jurisdiction, this term – sometimes called "means of identification" or "identification information" – is defined using a list of identifiers that typically includes:

- Name, address, and telephone number
- Date of birth
- Social security number
- Mother's maiden name
- Driver's license number
- Financial account numbers, PIN numbers, or other access codes
- Computer passwords
- Signature
- Unique biometric data (like a fingerprint, voiceprint, or retinal image).

Each law contains its own list of identifiers, and many statutes also include language noting that any name, number, or feature that can be used to identify a specific individual qualifies as "identifying information".

The federal identity theft law, found at 18 U.S.C. § 1028, covers many aspects of identity theft and related activity. The statute includes offenses related to the misuse of identity documents, including prohibitions against the production, possession, or transfer of:

- Another person's identification documents
- False identification documents
- Implements for making false identification documents. Computers, software, and other code are considered potential implements.

Federal law also addresses most identity theft schemes and frauds by outlawing the knowing transfer, possession, or use of another person's identifying information with the intent to commit or aid any unlawful activity under federal or state law.

---

[9] For a compendium of state and territorial identity theft statutes, see the NCSL website, www.ncsl.org/research/financial-services-and-commerce/identity-theft-state-statutes.aspx.

Most state laws have similar provisions, although not always within one statute. Some criminal codes have distinct crimes for simply stealing, possessing, or trafficking in identity information, and separate offenses that bar the criminal use of stolen identity information. In many states, the felony level for an identity theft charge increases based upon certain thresholds of monetary damage. Also, many states elevate the felony level for repeat identity theft offenders.

6.5.4   IMPERSONATION

Along with prohibiting identity theft, some criminal codes prohibit conduct related to impersonating another individual or representatives of an organization. When online activity involves this type of impersonation, criminal charges can be sought under these laws.

Impersonation statutes – sometimes titled "Criminal Impersonation" or "False Personation" – often focus on impersonating people in trusted roles, such as law enforcement officials, public servants, representatives of charitable organizations, or members of licensed professions (like doctors or lawyers). Impersonation of this type is a form of fraud, usually intended to induce another person to give money, pay for services, or submit to authority, based on false pretenses.

The federal False Personation law targets conduct that negatively affects national and government functions, such as impersonating a U.S. citizen, an officer, or employee of the U.S. government, a foreign diplomat or members of the Red Cross.[10] Some state impersonation statutes take a broader view, targeting individuals who assume any false identity for the purpose of defrauding others.[11]

A few states have crafted laws specific to online impersonation. In 2007, New York added a section to Criminal Impersonation in the Second Degree, creating a misdemeanor crime for impersonating another by communicating via an Internet website or electronic means, with the intent to obtain a benefit, injure another, or pretend to be a public servant.[12] Although the new law did not make much of a change from the existing impersonation statute, it did recognize that impersonation can be conducted online. In 2011, Texas added the crime of Online Impersonation, making it a felony to use another person's name or persona to create a website or social network presence – or post messages on those platforms – in order to harm, defraud, intimidate, or threaten another person. Under this law, it is a misdemeanor to send an email, text message, or similar communication that references the identifying information of another person without his or her consent, with the intent to cause the recipient to believe the message is from the real person in order to harm or defraud.[13]

California, Hawaii, Mississippi, New Jersey, and Rhode Island also have enacted similar criminal statutes or amendments prohibiting online impersonation.[14] Washington has a civil cause of action for "electronic impersonation".[15]

---

[10] False Personation, 18 U.S.C. §§ 911–917.
[11] *See, e.g.*, the State of Washington's Criminal Impersonation in the First Degree, Revised Code of Washington, § 9A.60.040, or Colorado's Criminal Impersonation, Colorado Revised Statutes, § 18-5-113 (2016).
[12] New York State Penal Law, § 190.25(4).
[13] Texas Penal Code, Title 7, Chapter 33, § 33.07.
[14] California Penal Code, § 528.5; Hawaii Revised Statutes, § 711–1106.6; Mississippi Code, § 97-45-33; New Jersey Revised Statutes, § 2C:21–17; Rhode Island General Laws, § 11-52-7.1.
[15] Revised Code of Washington, § 4.24.790.

6.5.5   CREDIT/DEBIT CARD FRAUD

Criminals worldwide steal millions of dollars every year conducting cyber frauds involving credit, debit, and other payment cards. The pervasiveness and variety of these frauds has spurred the federal government and all 50 states to establish criminal offenses for this conduct.

Card crimes can be broken down into general categories:

- *Stolen physical cards.* Theft, possession, or use of physical cards belonging to another person
- *Forged cards.* Producing, selling, distributing, or using forged cards created with stolen account information
- *Theft and use of account information.* "Skimming" the magnetic strips of real cards, breaching retailers' databases or merchant accounting systems, abusing inside access to customer account information, and other means of theft; plus use of this stolen account information to conduct frauds
- *Fraudulent applications.* Obtaining cards from a bank or credit card issuer by applying with personal identifying information belonging to another person.

Credit and debit card fraud may be categorized as either "in store" or "online" activity, a useful distinction for investigators. Some card crimes, or stages of them, are conducted by a human being in a physical location. For example, retail purchases made with stolen or forged cards, or the skimming of cards by salespeople or restaurant servers, are "in store" frauds. Other crimes or stages are conducted online, such as using stolen account information to make purchases via websites or through fraudulent applications for credit accounts. Another important category is whether the physical card is present at the time of transaction or not. "Card not present" transactions include both online transactions and in-store payments using services such as Apple Pay, where the card is not physically used but is part of the payment process. Knowing how the transaction occurred is the first step towards tracking down the evidence of that crime.

The primary federal law in this area – Fraud and Related Activity in Connection with Access Devices (18 U.S.C. § 1029) – covers most types of credit/debit card fraud. Like many state laws, the statute uses the term "access device" to describe any card, plate, account number, PIN, service, or any other means of obtaining or transferring money, goods, or services. Anyone who uses, produces, or traffics counterfeit access devices, or simply possesses 15 or more counterfeit access devices, violates this statute. The law also prohibits producing or possessing equipment used to make counterfeit devices, equipment that intercepts Internet or other telecommunications services, as well as obtaining or selling information needed to apply for credit cards and other access devices.

State laws follow a number of different approaches. Some are comprehensive, using language and definitions similar to federal law and addressing most methods of conducting access device fraud.[16] Other states have very basic provisions about card-related crimes, and rely on other offenses (like theft, fraud, and forgery) to bring fraud charges.[17]

---

[16] *See, e.g.*, California Penal Code, §§ 484(d)-(j), and Illinois Statutes, Chapter 720, §§ 5/17-31 through 5/17-48.

[17] *See, e.g.*, New York Penal Law, §§ 155.30(4) (theft of a credit or debit card) and 165.45 (possession of a stolen credit or debit card). New York also has two misdemeanor crimes for using a stolen credit or debit card, or possessing a skimming device. Credit card and other access device fraud generally is prosecuted using a combination of other offenses, such as Identity Theft, Forgery, and Grand Larceny.

6.5.6   BANK FRAUD

Along with laws against access device fraud, the federal government and all states have laws against frauds targeting banks and financial institutions. Because so many cybercrimes result in theft from financial institutions, bank fraud charges are often suitable. For example, in schemes involving phishing emails that induce people to wire money under false pretenses, or phony online applications for loans, a bank is the direct or indirect target. And many types of identity theft cybercrimes seek illicit access to individual victims' bank account information in order to withdraw or transfer funds. All of these criminal activities potentially merit charges of bank fraud. Many banks are also access-device issuers (credit and debit cards), so a financial institution also may be defrauded through carding crimes. All of these criminal activities potentially merit charges of bank fraud.

Under the federal Bank Fraud statute (18 U.S.C. § 1344), anyone who knowingly takes steps to defraud a financial institution, or to get money or assets from a financial institution under fraudulent pretense, has committed an offense.

As with the laws against credit card and other access device crimes, the states have used varied approaches in crafting charges for bank fraud. Most do not have a separate "bank fraud" crime. Instead, the various types of bank fraud are charged using a combination of other offenses – such as laws prohibiting check fraud, forgery, larceny, identity theft, and credit/debit card fraud. Some states also have other applicable fraud charges, like "Scheme to Defraud" or "Fraudulent Practices", that can be used to address fraud against financial institutions.[18]

6.5.7   WIRE FRAUD

Federal law contains another powerful fraud statute that can be used to combat cybercrime. Fraud by Radio, Wire, or Television (18 U.S.C. § 1343), a statute commonly known as Wire Fraud, states that someone commits this offense if he or she devises a scheme or artifice (trick) to defraud, or obtains money or property by fraudulent pretenses, and then transmits any writing or picture across state or national borders by wire for the purpose of executing the fraud. Internet transmissions fall within the statute's definition of "wire" communications.

Wire Fraud is similar to the section of the federal CFAA devoted to "accessing a computer to defraud and obtain value".[19] Under the CFAA, it is a crime to access a computer or network without authorization to further an intended fraud, and obtain something of value (like money, services, goods, or data). Since accessing a computer or network without authorization typically requires use of the Internet, and since the Internet inherently relies upon interstate and international transmissions to function, actions that violate this section of the CFAA will also violate the Wire Fraud statute. An important difference is that the sentences for Wire Fraud are much higher.

6.5.8   FORGERY

Forgery, one of the oldest offenses in the law books, is still a powerful tool against today's cybercriminals. In earlier times, the crime mostly referred to the painstaking process of manually creating false documents, or copying someone's signature by hand, in order to

---

[18] *See, e.g.*, New York Penal Law, §§ 190.60 and 190.65 (Scheme to Defraud); 2018 Florida Statutes, Section 817.034 (Florida Communications Fraud Act).
[19] 18 U.S.C. § 1030(a)(4).

gain some benefit. Computers, however, have made forgery a simpler process that greatly facilitates a number of cybercrimes. Forgery statutes originally were intended for paper documents but now may be applied to electronic documents, potentially even emails.

All jurisdictions – state and federal – have laws against forgery. The primary federal forgery statutes focus on counterfeit currency, securities, postage stamps, contracts, deeds, and similar items.[20] However, as discussed earlier, the federal identity theft law establishes several offenses involving the forging of identification documents.[21]

At the state level, forgery is typically described as the making, altering, use, or possession of a false "instrument" or "writing" with an intent to defraud. If the document has legal power then the forgery charge may be elevated – such as with a will, deed, power of attorney, driver's license or other identification, currency, check, bill, or other record of a transaction. State forgery laws vary in language, but all criminalize the creation of false documents and the fraudulent alteration of real documents.[22]

In the cyber context, forging documents is essential to criminal success. For example, forged identification documents (especially driver's licenses) are needed for many identity theft, credit/debit card and banking frauds, since a form of identification is required for many transactions to proceed. Forged checks, credit/debit cards, applications, and other documents are also key to many cyber scams.

6.5.9 Money Laundering

Whenever a criminal or criminal organization generates profits, the money or value has to make its way into the pocket of the criminal. If one man robs another of his wallet, the process is simple. The robber gets the wallet with the money and credit cards directly. With more complex crimes involving high profits, smart criminals try to insulate themselves from detection by hiding the source of the stolen profits they are generating. The most common method is to move stolen money through a series of transactions before it gets to the criminals or to leaders of crime rings. That is because the flow of illicit profits – unless disguised – can help prove connection to the original crime. Further, criminals will want to feign innocence about any connection to criminal activity if law enforcement starts looking at the funds.

This distancing process is sometimes referred to as "layering" and the criminal statute prohibiting this activity is called "money laundering". In Chapter 15, we will examine the ins-and-outs of money laundering in detail.

In general, a person commits the crime of money laundering when he:

- Knows that funds or property are proceeds of criminal activity, and
- Engages in financial transactions with, or transports, those proceeds with the intent to:
  - Further criminal activity, or
  - Disguise the true source, ownership, location or destination of the funds or property, or
  - Avoid laws that require financial institutions to report certain transactions to the government.

---

[20] Counterfeiting and Forgery, 18 U.S.C. §§ 470–514.

[21] Fraud and Related Activity in Connection with Identification Documents, Authentication Features, and Information, 18 U.S.C. § 1028.

[22] For a listing of state forgery laws, see https://statelaws.findlaw.com/criminal-laws/forgery.html.

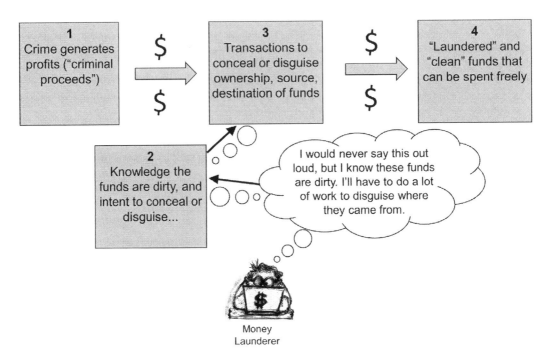

FIGURE 6.2   General Money Laundering Elements.

These general elements are depicted in Figure 6.2.

Federal money laundering statutes criminalize methods of laundering the proceeds of "unlawful activity". It is also a federal crime to transport or transfer money or property in or out of the United States in order to further "unlawful activity", disguise the source of criminal proceeds, or to violate an Internal Revenue Service (IRS) or other reporting requirement.[23] "Unlawful activity" under the federal statute includes most felonies, including the CFAA, and so the federal money laundering statute would apply to cybercrimes.

More than half the states have money laundering offenses in their criminal codes. In these states, the statutes are similar to the federal model. Most states have degrees or levels of money laundering crimes, with a range of potential sentences based on the amount of money or property at issue, or the type of underlying crime involved.[24]

Because of the importance to criminals of moving their illicit funds, federal and state laws require "money transmitters" to obtain a state license and register with the federal government as a money service business (MSB). Engaging in money transmitting activity without a license is a crime.[25] A money transmitter is a business that provides money transfer services, such as Western Union. Like money transmitters, banks also must be licensed,

---

[23] Laundering of Monetary Instruments, 18 U.S.C. § 1956; Engaging in Monetary Transactions in Property Derived from Specified Unlawful Activity, 18 U.S.C. § 1957.

[24] For a listing of state money laundering statutes, see https://statelaws.findlaw.com/criminal-laws/money-laundering.html.

[25] Prohibition of Unlicensed Money Transmitting Businesses, 18 U.S.C. § 1960. For a helpful summary of state money transmitter laws, see Thomas Brown, 50 State Survey: Money Transmitter Licensing Requirements, https://abnk.assembly.ca.gov/sites/abnk.assembly.ca.gov/files/50%20State%20Survey%20-%20MTL%20Licensing%20Requirements(72986803_4).pdf.

bringing them under the state and federal regulatory umbrella as well.[26] One purpose of this regulation is to reduce dirty money flowing through the financial system.

6.5.10 HARASSMENT, STALKING, AND SEXTORTION

The Internet has become an all-too-common vehicle for harassment, bullying, and stalking behavior, as well as extortion using explicit images of a victim. In response to the rapid growth of this disturbing phenomenon, both federal and state governments have enacted laws directly criminalizing this type of conduct.

Several federal offenses can be charged for online threats, harassment, or stalking. Under the Stalking statute (18 U.S.C. § 2216(A)), it is a crime to use the Internet with the intent to harm, harass, or intimidate a victim, and engage in a course of conduct that either makes the victim fear harm or causes substantial emotional distress. These protections apply to both victims and their families. Another statute makes it a crime to send communications that are obscene or contain child pornography.[27]

In addition, some of the general federal cybercrime offenses also can be charged for harassment or stalking behavior. For example, when email accounts or hard drives are compromised to obtain photos or information about a victim, the CFAA's sections prohibiting intrusion and extortion are available, as are charges under the overarching federal extortion law.[28]

At the state level, all 50 states have laws barring harassment and stalking, with each utilizing its own definitions and statutory scheme.[29] Some states have created specific statutes targeting cyber activity of this nature. For example, Illinois, Louisiana, Mississippi, and Washington have designated cyberstalking as a distinct crime.[30] Other states have amended existing laws to encompass harassment, bullying, stalking, and sextortion using computers and the Internet.[31]

In addition, at least 14 states allow victims of harassment and stalking to sue for damages in civil court, a topic we covered in Chapter 5 and will revisit in Chapter 9 (Civil and Regulatory).

6.5.10.1 First Amendment Considerations

When evaluating emails, texts, online posts, or other forms of communications to determine whether they constitute threats or harassment, investigators must consider whether the content is the type of speech protected by the First Amendment to the U.S. Constitution. The First Amendment preserves the right to "free speech", which generally means that the government cannot criminalize most things people say, including political commentary, satire, and artistic expression, even when such statements are offensive.[32] A few types of speech are not protected under the First Amendment, however, including speech intended to threaten, blackmail, or defame another person, and speech that contains obscenity or child pornography.

---

[26] Since these financial institutions and money service businesses are regulated, they may need to comply with a host of information security requirements (as we will discuss in Chapter 9), as well as anti-money laundering requirements (as we will mention in Chapter 15).

[27] Obscene or Harassing Telephone Calls in the District of Columbia or in Interstate or Foreign Communications. 47 U.S.C. § 223.

[28] CFAA, 18 U.S.C. § 1030, and Interstate Communications, 18 U.S.C § 875.

[29] For a listing of criminal harassment and stalking laws in all states, see http://victimsofcrime.org/our-programs/stalking-resource-center/stalking-laws/criminal-stalking-laws-by-state.

[30] 720 Illinois Criminal Statutes, § 5/12-7.5; Louisiana Revised Statutes, § 14:40.3; Mississippi Code Annotated, § 97-3-107; Revised Code of Washington, § 9.61.260.

[31] Sextortion generally means blackmailing a victim to provide money or engage in certain conduct through threats to expose intimate pictures or videos online.

[32] *See, e.g., United States v. Popa*, 187 F.3d 672 (D.C. Cir. 1999).

There is some cyber conduct where the line between harassment and protected speech is blurry. For example, if someone sends repeated emails to another person expressing a political viewpoint that the recipient finds offensive, the case would have to be analyzed carefully to determine whether this is an example of protected speech or a course of conduct intended to cause emotional distress. The full content of the communications, along with other actions by the sender, would be important evidence in this determination. Consider that speech may fall somewhere along a continuum. At one end is speech that is absolutely protected and cannot be infringed upon through criminal charges or civil lawsuits. Then there is speech that cannot be the basis of criminal charges but might be the proper subject of a civil lawsuit for slander or libel. And then there is speech, such as blackmail, that can be both the subject of criminal charges (for extortion) and a civil action.

6.5.11   Child Exploitation and Pornography

Another category of cyber offenses concerns the production, possession, and distribution of child pornography. Some offenders use the Internet to meet and groom children for sexually explicit conduct; others collect and share photographic and video images of victimized children. Computer devices and the Internet are instruments for this illicit activity, which is deeply harmful to victims. As a result, laws criminalize the production, possession, sale, purchase, transfer, or other distribution of child pornography, including possession on computer storage devices and dissemination through the Internet.

Even investigators who do not specialize in child pornography or human trafficking cases should be fully aware of the applicable statutes. Investigators sometimes discover child pornography on computers being searched for evidence of other cybercrimes. In addition, federal and state laws mandate that certain professionals – including law enforcement officers – report incidents involving the sexual abuse of children to the appropriate government agencies. If child pornography is detected during an investigation, special steps must be taken to prevent its further dissemination.

Federal law prohibits all activity related to child pornography that affects interstate or foreign commerce – from inducing a child to engage in sexually explicit conduct, to the production and transmission of visual images of such conduct (18 U.S.C. §§ 2251 and 2252).[33] The federal statutes set forth that using a computer to send, receive, ship, sell, purchase, or possess pornographic images of a child is a criminal offense. Moreover, any use of the Internet with regard to these images is considered to affect interstate commerce.

All 50 states and the U.S. territories have laws banning child pornography, with each criminal code defining its own offenses and penalties.[34] Some state laws mirror the federal law closely, while others use different terms and elements. However, all laws encompass sexually explicit conduct involving children that is facilitated by use of the Internet.

6.5.12   Vandalism

Some forms of cybercrime involve intentionally causing damage to property, and so fall under the definition of vandalism (sometimes called "mischief" or "criminal damage"). These criminal offenses prohibit activity intended to deface, harm, or destroy property belonging to another person or entity. Traditional acts of vandalism include graffiti,

---

[33] *See,* U.S. Department of Justice guidance about federal child pornography laws at: www.justice.gov/criminal-ceos/citizens-guide-us-federal-law-child-pornography.
[34] For a list of all states' child pornography laws, see https://statelaws.findlaw.com/criminal-laws/child-pornography.html.

slashing tires, or defacing public property. In the cyber context, damage may be directed at a physical device, network or data, or at the code behind website content and graphics.

Under federal law, the crime of Malicious Mischief (18 U.S.C. § 1361) bans the physical damage or destruction of buildings, facilities, or personal property belonging to the U.S. government. Other federal statutes criminalize vandalism to specific federal property, such as national parks and railroads.[35]

Every state has vandalism crimes, as well. The level and type of offense often is dictated by the value of the damaged property or the cost of repairing the damage. If the acts are directed at religious or minority groups, some states have separate vandalism offenses that are treated as hate crimes.

As mentioned earlier, some states have modified their definition of "property" to include computers, software, data, code, and other forms of technology. Where such definitions exist, cyber vandalism is even more readily encompassed within traditional vandalism laws.

6.5.13   ORGANIZED CRIME

State and federal statutes targeting organized crime are another set of laws that can be used against cybercrime. For both technological and logistical reasons, the attacks and frauds perpetrated in the cyber sphere often involve numerous actors, each of whom plays a certain role or contributes a certain skill. This type of criminal network or organization, which enables rampant criminal activity while insulating the criminal leaders, is what laws prohibiting organized crime are intended to combat.

The principal law on this topic in the federal code is the Racketeer Influenced and Corrupt Organizations Act (RICO).[36] Although the statute and its interpretation are complex, RICO essentially outlaws a person or group from engaging in a pattern of racketeering activity, or from having an interest in a seemingly legitimate business that is funded or controlled by racketeering activity. "Racketeering activity" includes a long list of criminal offenses, such as murder and narcotics trafficking. Offenses salient to cybercrime are included as well, like extortion, forgery, counterfeiting, identity theft, access device fraud, wire fraud, money laundering, and financial institution fraud. Civil remedies also are available under RICO for both the government and individuals to enjoin racketeering conduct and collect monetary damages.

At least 20 states have their own criminal and civil laws outlawing racketeering activity and corrupt organizations. Many of these laws mirror the federal RICO language, although some states utilize their own concepts and definitions within their statutes.[37] Additional states include similar prohibitions in criminal statutes focused on gang activity.

6.5.14   ATTEMPT AND CONSPIRACY

Up until now, we have talked about "completed" crimes, meaning offenses the criminal intended to do and actually carried out. As we outlined in Chapter 5, unsuccessful criminal

---

[35] National Parks, 33 C.F.R. § 2.31; Railroads, 49 U.S.C. §20151.

[36] Racketeer Influenced and Corrupt Organizations Act,18 U.S.C. §§ 1961–1968.

[37] *See, e.g.*, New York Penal Law, Article 460 (Organized Crime Control Act). In the Western Express case, New York's highest court was hesitant to apply this law to cybercrime, essentially finding that this cybercrime ring did not meet the statute's definition of organized crime. The judge writing the dissenting opinion argued that in a changing technological world, the nature of criminal organizations changes as well, and the courts and law must be ready to extend the application of criminal statutes to online crime. *See, People v. Western Express, Inc.*, 19 N. Y.3d 652 (2012).

efforts also may constitute an offense. If a criminal takes enough steps towards a crime, but does not get the job done, his conduct still may be chargeable as an attempt or conspiracy to commit the crime. Attempt and conspiracy are called "anticipatory" or "uncompleted" offenses under federal and state law.

Attempt

With most criminal laws, both federal and state, an attempt to commit the crime is also an offense. Under federal law, there typically is no separate crime or code section for "attempting" a crime.[38] When an attempt to commit a crime is an offense, federal statutes – such as the federal CFAA – specifically indicate that fact. For example, the CFAA states that a person guilty of attempting or conspiring to commit the crime will be treated as if he or she successfully completed the offense.[39]

In most states, however, an "attempt" to commit a crime has an umbrella definition that can be applied to most, if not all, offenses in the criminal code. Usually, a conviction for an attempted crime carries a sentence that is one level lower than a conviction for successful completion of the crime.

Conspiracy

At both the state and federal levels, a conspiracy to commit a crime is a separate punishable offense.[40] Conspiracy is generally defined as an agreement among two or more people to do something unlawful. Some conspiracy laws require proof that a member of the conspiracy took an affirmative action (an "overt act") to further the plan. Because conspiracy is considered a separate offense from the crime the group agreed to commit, if three people were found to have conspired to steal data, and they were successful, they could be convicted of both computer intrusion crimes and a conspiracy to commit them.

Within the federal code, the mechanism for charging a conspiracy to commit a crime sometimes is contained within the definition of the underlying offense (such as with the CFAA). In other instances, the federal code has a separate statute outlining conspiracy charges (such as Conspiracy to Commit an Offense Against or to Defraud the United States).[41] Each statute describes the penalty for these conspiracy crimes. Some, like the CFAA, punish a conspiracy to commit the crime at the same level as a conviction for the underlying crime itself.

All states have laws against a conspiracy to commit a criminal offense. In some, a conspiracy conviction garners the same sentence as a conviction for the underlying offense, while in others it is a lower level offense.

6.6   CONCLUSION

In this chapter, we have reviewed the types of criminal offenses – both cyber and traditional – that can apply in cyber cases.

Federal and state criminal codes have evolved to include many criminal offenses directly related to malfeasance involving computers and the Internet, such as unauthorized access, fraud and theft of data. New statutes and amendments are added regularly as technology and crime advance.

---

[38]   Charles Doyle, *Attempt: An Overview of Federal Law*, Congressional Research Service (2015).
[39]   18 U.S.C. § 1030(b).
[40]   Charles Doyle, *Federal Conspiracy Law: A Brief Overview*, Congressional Research Service (2016).
[41]   Conspiracy to Commit Offense or to Defraud United States, 18 U.S.C. § 371.

Investigators should not limit their analysis to "cyber" offenses. Many "traditional" offenses also are applicable to cybercrimes, including identity theft – a frequent component of cyber frauds. Other offenses include larceny, possession of stolen property, forgery, bank and credit/debit card fraud, extortion, money laundering, and organized crime. When a cybercriminal's motive is to harass and alarm, investigators should also look to traditional harassment and stalking statutes.

An understanding of these offenses provides the lens through which investigators and prosecutors can evaluate the facts of a case to see if a crime occurred. Making this determination is one of the significant roles an investigator plays. Also, by knowing what possible crimes to consider, investigators can decide how best to gather evidence that will prove that each element of the particular offense was committed.

7 The Law Enforcement Legal Toolkit for Investigating Cybercrime

Laws for Gathering Criminal Cyber Evidence

This chapter is for:

- Law enforcement cybercrime investigators and prosecutors who want to learn about legal tools to investigate
- All readers who want to learn more about what the government does.

7.1 INTRODUCTION

In a cyber case, much of the evidence comes from the suspects' online activity or electronic footprint – their electronic communications, stored data, websites, and other Internet usage. The law has been evolving to keep up with this new realm of evidence, creating rules for evidence gathering that balance the Internet's complex mix of public information, privacy interests, corporate policies, and government regulation. This chapter explores nine tools available to law enforcement investigators who are following the digital trail that cybercrime leaves behind, including how to use legal tools to obtain evidence of electronic communications under the Electronic Communications Privacy Act (ECPA).[1]

Not all evidence in a cybercrime case comes from online sources. Additional evidence can be recovered by searching the devices, physical spaces, vehicles, and other items or areas used by victims or suspects. Many of the legal tools discussed in this chapter can be used by law enforcement to acquire more "traditional" forms of evidence.

The reach of the Internet means that records of online activity, computing devices, and other physical items linked to a criminal event might be located in multiple states, as well as in foreign countries. This chapter will review law enforcement's tools for obtaining interstate and international evidence of cybercrimes.

By the end of this chapter, readers should have a good understanding of the toolkit law enforcement uses to investigate a cybercrime. In Chapter 13, we will return to these tools again, with hands-on information about how to apply them during an investigation.

---

[1] For an excellent summary of the law surrounding electronic evidence, see *Searching and Seizing Computers and Obtaining Electronic Evidence in Criminal Investigations*, U.S. DOJ CCIPS (2009), www.justice.gov/sites/default/files/criminal-ccips/legacy/2015/01/14/ssmanual2009.pdf.

7.2 PRIVACY AND CONSENT: APPLYING THESE PRINCIPLES TO COMMUNICATIONS

When law enforcement investigators identify a potential piece of evidence, and want to take the correct steps to obtain it, they start with a threshold question:

> *Is this item, information, account, or location publicly accessible, or is it within the private authority of the owner or creator?*

Making this determination is essential, because the expectation of privacy attached to a piece of evidence (and its location) dictates which investigative tool must be used for acquiring it.[2] This privacy analysis applies both to evidence created through the Internet (like communications, stored data, and account records), as well as to physical items and locations.

To get started, we will quickly review the legal principles from Chapter 5 that define privacy and the related concept of consent.

- *Reasonable expectation of privacy.* The reasonable expectation of privacy is the legal standard that helps law enforcement determine whether a thing or a place is public or private. If someone reasonably expects privacy in an item or location, the law provides some protections from government intrusion. Those protections include the requirement to use certain legally authorized tools to investigate in those areas.
- *Consent.* When a person has a reasonable expectation of privacy in a place or thing, he or she also has the authority to consent to a government search or seizure. Effective consent must be given knowingly and voluntarily. Once consent is given, no additional legal documents or judicial approval are needed to gather evidence. The information and items recovered are now valid evidence in any investigation or prosecution. Methods for obtaining authorized, lawful consent from an owner or account holder are discussed in Chapter 13.

7.2.1 COMMUNICATIONS AND PRIVACY

Court decisions and statutes have determined that there is a reasonable expectation of privacy in our electronic, telephonic, mail, and other forms of communication. In other words, a conversation between two or more people is presumed to be private and free from government intrusion.

This expectation exists for all forms of communication – face-to-face conversations, letters, phone calls, emails, text messages, video-enabled calls, or any other electronic or wire format. Based on the foundational privacy protections from government intrusion created in our Constitution and related laws, a police officer cannot open our mail or put a bug in our house to hear us talking unless these actions are needed for a criminal investigation and the officer has obtained judicial permission.

When landline telephones became the primary method of communication, a complex set of rules arose to regulate when and how law enforcement could intercept private calls to

---

[2] This chapter focuses on privacy from the perspective of government intrusion, the legality of government actions, and whether seized evidence is legally admissible in a criminal case. This subject is different from the growing field of Internet and data privacy, with burgeoning laws and regulations about the civil privacy responsibilities of individuals and entities online.

investigate crime. Laws also were passed by the federal government and the individual states making it a crime for private citizens to eavesdrop on phone calls.[3]

With the introduction of computers, and then the Internet, these laws and regulations have been expanded to encompass the many forms of electronic communication available. A cyber investigator must be well-versed in the methods for legally obtaining both the records generated by online communication platforms and the content of the communications themselves, as covered later.

7.2.2 Communications and Consent

Consent is a significant consideration when it comes to obtaining evidence of communications, both electronic and traditional.

First, although there is a reasonable expectation that the government is not listening to our communications, parties generally can record their own conversations and share them with law enforcement. Self-recordings are not considered unlawful eavesdropping under federal law and under the laws of most states. In other words, in those "one party" jurisdictions, if you are talking to someone on the phone, you can record the conversation and share it with whomever you choose, including the police. Eleven states follow the "all party" rule and require the agreement of all parties to the communication for the recording to be considered consensual.[4]

Second, there is no reasonable expectation of privacy in information that is publicly exposed, and people can make the choice to go public with their communications. For example, if you make a phone call to a friend, the law says you have a reasonable expectation that law enforcement is not listening. Law enforcement can only eavesdrop with judicial authorization to do so, based on proven reasons to believe you will be discussing a crime. However, if you decide to live-stream the conversation on social media, that privacy expectation has changed. You have consented to giving everyone, including law enforcement officials, public access to the contents of what is said. Whoever listens to you on social media is not eavesdropping; the conversation is open for anyone to hear and any privacy expectation about the government is irrelevant.

The same analysis would hold true if you emailed a friend or colleague who then posted the message publicly. As a party to the email, your friend has the authority to reveal its contents, and anyone (including law enforcement) can lawfully view and preserve a copy of the email.

In cyber investigations, communications between suspects and victims, or suspects and associates, are often a key form of evidence. If any party to those communications consents to share them – with another person, by posting them online, or directly with an investigator – the expectation of privacy is removed, and the communications are viable evidence.

Sometimes, such sharing might seem like appropriate behavior to expose criminal conduct or assist law enforcement; sometimes it might seem impolite, unethical, or even constitute a civil tort. But for the purposes of this chapter, the issue is whether this consensual public exposure permits lawful use of the evidence by law enforcement.

---

[3] Wire and Electronic Communications Interception and Interception of Oral Communications,18 U.S.C. §§ 2510–2522.

[4] One-party consent is the law in 39 states and the District of Columbia. All party consent is the law in 11 states, where the consent of all parties to a communication is required for it no longer to be treated as private. These states are California, Delaware, Florida, Illinois, Maryland, Massachusetts, Montana, New Hampshire, Oregon, Pennsylvania and Washington. Some states, like Connecticut, Michigan, and Nevada, apply different consent requirements for in-person or electronic conversations, or for criminal or civil liability. *See* Justia, www.justia.com/50-state-surveys/recording-phone-calls-and-conversations/, and Conflicts Among Federal and State Wiretap Statutes Present Practical Challenges for Businesses, *National Law Review* (September 26, 2018), www.natlawreview.com/article/conflicts-among-federal-and-state-wiretap-statutes-present-practical-challenges.

7.2.3 REASONABLE EXPECTATION OF PRIVACY IN THE WORKPLACE

A significant percentage of stored and transmitted data originates from the workplace, so it is important that we understand how the law views the concept of privacy at work. Workplace Internet usage can take many forms, including emails, messages, posts, data creation, data storage, website design and use, data management, and commercial transactions. In many criminal investigations, including when an employee is a potential suspect or witness, the data and records kept by organizations can be central to unraveling the cybercrime.

Employees often have a different expectation of privacy in the workplace than they would have in their personal lives. Since companies control their computers, networks, email systems, websites, and other Internet-enabled components, they have the ability to set rules and policies about their usage. One common workplace policy found in many employment agreements and personnel handbooks gives the company authority to view, monitor, and search all company devices, accounts, and networks. In other words, an employee would be using the company's computers, tablets, phones, email accounts, websites, and networks every day with no privacy protections. The company also has the authority to consent to entry or search by law enforcement or other investigators and employee consent is not needed. Businesses implement these policies for a number of reasons, including training purposes, customer service support, cybersecurity monitoring, and investigative access if wrongdoing is suspected.

If a company establishes this type of policy and properly informs its employees, its access to records and data regarding employee activity on company computer systems can greatly aid law enforcement – particularly when a cyber investigation involves a business that has been targeted by cybercrime or an employee suspected of criminal activity.

We will cover more about the legal issues private organizations face when conducting a cybercrime investigation in Chapter 12.

7.3 THE NINE TOOLS FOR GATHERING EVIDENCE

Now that we have an understanding of the reasonable expectation of privacy, the potential for consent, and the special privacy considerations for communications, we can look at how law enforcement gathers evidence of a crime.

There are nine legal tools that government investigators primarily use to get evidence – both digital and physical – and each tool reflects the level of privacy associated with the evidence sought.

- Open-source investigation (covered in Chapter 11)
- Obtaining consent
- Subpoenas duces tecum
- Judicial orders obtained under Section 2703(d) of the federal Stored Communications Act (only used for certain records of electronic communications)
- Search warrants
- Pen registers and trap-and-trace devices
- Wiretaps.

In addition to these methods for obtaining evidence, there are two additional tools that law enforcement can use to protect evidence and its disclosure during the investigative process. These are:

- Letters of Preservation
- Non-disclosure requests and orders.

There are also emergency procedures for expedited information requests when the normal legal process would take too much time and speeding up the process might prevent injury or death. Often, when these procedures are used, law enforcement must follow up later using the normal legal tool to seek the information.

Together, these methods form law enforcement's evidence-gathering toolkit and most of them are a form of "legal process".[5] As we know, an investigator's first step is to assess the public or private nature of the sought-after evidence. The result of that analysis will tell the investigator which legal tool to use. Later in this chapter, we discuss how these tools fit into the framework of the ECPA, a complex statute detailing how to obtain evidence of electronic communications. The investigative use of each of these tools is covered in more depth in Chapter 13.

7.3.1 Open-Source Investigation

The simplest tool at law enforcement's disposal is a search for publicly accessible evidence. When individuals or entities place information in the public domain, they are consenting to, if not seeking, public access. As a result, there are no privacy expectations to consider, and no legal barriers to gathering this evidence.[6] Individuals, private-sector investigators, and law enforcement officials have full access to the evidence contained within open Internet locations, and any personal, business, or government records made available to the public. The same open-source analysis applies to physical documents and other tangible items in the public domain.

The investigative methods and benefits of open-source investigation are discussed in Chapter 11.

7.3.2 Obtaining Consent

When evidence is not publicly available through open-source investigation, but rather is in the control of some entity or individual, an investigator's next potential tool is obtaining the evidence through consent. With the consent of the owner of a device or location (physical or virtual), or the business that controls the desired records or data, an investigator can acquire evidence without any further legal procedures. We introduced consent in Chapter 5 and will cover it in the investigative context in later chapters, including the preference for obtaining consent in writing.

7.3.3 Subpoena Duces Tecum

The *subpoena duces tecum* is the simplest legal mechanism used to compel individuals, businesses, and organizations to produce evidence for a law enforcement investigation or prosecution. A subpoena duces tecum is a court summons that orders the recipient to supply specified records, books, documents or other physical items to the court in connection with a criminal or civil matter.[7] Often, the prosecutor receives and stores these items on behalf of the court.

---

[5] "Legal process" is a general term for various types of legal demands. In the toolkit, a subpoena, 2703(d) Order, search warrant, pen/trap order and wiretap order are forms of legal process.

[6] Notable examples (such as Wikileaks and the Panama Papers) have demonstrated that when a third party, acting independently and with no connection to the government, improperly accesses data and posts it publicly, law enforcement may review that information.

[7] *Duces tecum* is a Latin phrase that means "bring with you", so a *subpoena duces tecum* orders the recipient to bring certain items with him or her to court. A subpoena to appear and testify before a court or Grand Jury is called a *subpoena ad testificandum*.

Subpoenas are used to obtain evidence that is not publicly available, but in which no reasonable expectation of privacy exists. In the federal system and in most states, the government generally does not have to demonstrate reasons to support the issuing of a subpoena or supply a court with information about the underlying investigation (unlike with other evidence-gathering tools, such as search warrants). The subpoena simply must seek specific evidence with some relevance to the investigation.[8]

Subpoenas are issued in three ways:

- *Grand Jury subpoena.* This is a subpoena authorized by a Grand Jury for the purposes of an ongoing Grand Jury investigation. Grand Jury subpoenas typically are drafted and signed by a prosecutor's office on behalf of the Grand Jury.
- *Administrative subpoena.* Some government agencies are authorized by federal, state or local laws to issue "administrative" subpoenas, often for specific investigative purposes.[9] These agencies draft and issue the subpoenas themselves pursuant to internal approval procedures.
- *Trial subpoena.* Once a defendant has been criminally charged in an indictment or complaint, subpoenas for evidence are issued by the trial court overseeing the criminal case at the request of a party.

Once a subpoena is obtained, it must be served on the person or entity holding the records or other items. Federal and state statutes describe authorized ways to serve subpoenas. They typically include electronic methods (like email), certified mail, or personal delivery. Most Internet service providers and financial institutions receive so many legal requests that they have offices and personnel to receive subpoenas and court orders. Many providers publish law enforcement guides to help investigators navigate this process.

If businesses or individuals served with a subpoena believe it would be "unreasonable or oppressive" to respond, they can move to quash (terminate) the subpoena, or to modify its demands.[10] In other words, if the recipient thinks there is an expectation of privacy in the items demanded by the subpoena, or some other reason not to comply, she can go before a judge and make her arguments. The judge then rules on whether or not to enforce the subpoena, or to make changes to its scope.

As we will cover later in this chapter, some companies will inform account holders if they receive a subpoena about their accounts, so law enforcement desiring to keep its investigation confidential needs to obtain a Non-Disclosure Order.

7.3.4 SECTION 2703(d) ORDER

The next tool in the law enforcement toolkit is commonly called a "2703(d) Order". These are judicial orders obtained under the federal Stored Communications Act (SCA), 18 U.S.C. § 2703(d). This order is an intermediate step of legal process between a subpoena and a search warrant in terms of what data it can obtain and the evidentiary burden it needs to meet.

---

[8] Federal and state statutes sometimes require additional steps when subpoenas are used for certain types of records. Under some circumstances, for example, subpoenas for financial records, medical records, and other records containing personal identifying information may require judicial approval or notification to customers or patients.

[9] Charles Doyle, *Administrative Subpoenas in Criminal Investigations: A Brief Legal Analysis*, Congressional Research Service (2006), https://fas.org/sgp/crs/intel/RL33321.pdf.

[10] Federal Rules of Criminal Procedure (FRCrP), Rule 17. State laws governing subpoena practice also contain procedures to quash or modify the demands.

A 2703(d) Order allows law enforcement investigators to gather very specific types of account information from electronic communications and storage companies. As we will learn, basic account-holder information can be acquired using a subpoena. Certain other types of user information – such as contact lists, or details about the accounts with which a user is corresponding – can be obtained using a 2703(d) Order (or a search warrant) obtained from a judge.

This statutory tool recognizes that some user data is more private than the basic sub-scriber information a user supplies to set up and pay for an account. Section 2703(d) requires investigators who want more sensitive user details to submit an affidavit to a court with jurisdiction over the case that sets forth "specific and articulable facts showing that there are reasonable grounds to believe that … the records or other information sought, are relevant and material to an ongoing criminal investigation." This process ensures judicial oversight when law enforcement seeks this more-private information.

2703(d) Orders are served in the same manner as subpoenas. Since these orders are always directed to an Internet service provider, the best method of service is found in the law enforcement guidelines provided by the company. We will learn more about 2703(d) Orders later in this chapter.

7.3.5 SEARCH WARRANT

As we covered in Chapter 5, a search warrant is a court order authorizing law enforcement agents to search an account, device, vehicle, container, or physical premises for specific evidence of a crime, and to seize evidence found. The law acknowledges that owners of such items and locations have a reasonable expectation of privacy, and the procedures for getting a search warrant are designed to limit law enforcement intrusion.

The Federal Rules of Criminal Procedure set forth the procedures for obtaining and executing federal search warrants.[11] Each state also has a similar law.[12] Search warrant applications are made by law enforcement officials either through a sworn written affida-vit or sworn testimony. Along with offering factual proof of probable cause to conduct the search, the application must specifically describe the location (real or virtual) to be searched, and the items to be seized. These requirements limit the government's privacy intrusion to only those exact places and items authorized by the court and are laid out in Figure 7.1

Requirements for a Search Warrant:

- ❑ Probable cause
- ❑ Specific description of place or item to be searched
- ❑ Specific description of evidence to be seized
- ❑ Application to appropriate court (jurisdiction/venue)
- ❑ Execution within statutory window of time
- ❑ Receipts and copy of warrant given to property owners
- ❑ Return to the court (with inventory of items seized)

FIGURE 7.1   Requirements for a Search Warrant.

---

[11] FRCrP Rule 41.
[12] For a listing of the search warrant laws of all 50 states, see: https://resources.lawinfo.com/criminal-defense/search-seizure-laws-by-state.html.

In addition, federal and state laws designate which courts can hear search warrant applications. In most situations, the court must have physical jurisdiction over the location where the search will occur, though this is not the case for certain electronic evidence stored by third parties (as we cover next). The court also must be a proper "venue", meaning it has authority to issue search warrants. Search warrant procedures indicate the window of time in which the warrant must be executed (for example, within ten days or two weeks of the warrant being issued). They also instruct law enforcement to provide the court with an inventory of items seized (often called "returning the warrant").[13] Law enforcement must give a copy of the warrant to the owners of the searched location, as well as official receipts for any property seized.

Federal and state laws allow a search warrant based on probable cause to be issued for electronic storage media or the seizure or copying of electronically stored information. In the federal system under ECPA, a warrant for stored data can be obtained from any court with jurisdiction over the investigation, and does not have to be obtained from a court where the data is located. Law enforcement agents do not have to physically conduct the search when a warrant is issued for electronic data kept by an Internet service company or other third-party provider. Rather, the provider can search its systems and give the relevant data to law enforcement. Many state laws follow a similar approach to search warrants directed to third-party service providers.

More to come in this chapter on using a search warrant for Internet communications.

7.3.6   Pen Register and Trap-and-Trace Device

Sometimes, investigators want to monitor a suspect's communications as they are happening, to conduct ground surveillance or to identify and locate suspects. To get real-time dialing, routing, addressing, and signaling information about the communications coming into and out of a phone or Internet account, law enforcement investigators use two combined mechanisms – a pen register and a trap-and-trace device.

Pen registers record live information about outgoing communications made from a targeted account or device. A trap-and-trace device records information about incoming communications to a targeted account or device. Both mechanisms often are incorporated within a single software application.[14]

Because a pen/trap monitors only these usage details (and not the content of any communications), statutes and related court decisions have found a low expectation of privacy in the records captured by a pen/trap.[15]

Federal and state codes direct law enforcement to obtain a court order for installation of a pen register/trap-and-trace device. Agents must demonstrate to the court that the requested pen/trap will gather information "relevant to an ongoing criminal investigation."[16] This

---

[13] The phrase "search warrant return" is derived from the concept of physically returning all seized items to the court, where they would be kept for the duration of the case. In practice, courts permit the physical evidence to be kept in a secure law enforcement facility, and the return is accomplished through the inventory listing each seized item.

[14] It is a federal crime for someone to install a pen register or trap-and-trace device on another person's phone or communications account without court authorization. General Prohibition on Pen Register and Trap and Trace Device Use; Exception,18 U.S.C. § 3121. Many states have analogous statutes.

[15] 18 U.S.C. §§ 3121–3127; *Smith v. Maryland*, 442 U.S. 735 (1979), in which the U.S. Supreme Court found that the user of a telephone service has no reasonable expectation of privacy in the numbers he or she dials to make calls. By voluntarily disclosing this information to the phone company, the user has divulged this information to a third party, and so no expectation of privacy can exist.

[16] 18 U.S.C. § 3122(b)(1)(2).

standard is relatively low, requiring less factual proof than the probable cause needed for a search warrant. Law enforcement simply must show how pen/trap evidence will assist the criminal case. A pen/trap order typically authorizes data collection for 60 days and applications for extensions of that time period are allowed.

If location data is needed (cell site, GPS, etc.), additional legal requirements are implicated, and the investigator's affidavit or testimony seeking location data should contain facts indicating probable cause to believe the location data will provide evidence of criminal activity. This is the same probable cause standard used for search warrants. Later in this chapter, we will look more closely at the different standard for location data.

7.3.7   WIRETAP

The final investigative method available to law enforcement is the real-time interception of the content of a target's communications. Live monitoring and collection of oral, wire, and electronic communications is accomplished using a wiretap.

A wiretap order, by definition, gives law enforcement permission to "eavesdrop" on a target's ongoing conversations, messages, and other communications. Courts have long held that we have a reasonable expectation of privacy in our communications, as we reasonably expect that our private phone calls, emails or Skype conferences are private and are not being overheard or intercepted.

In the days before cellphones and the Internet, a wiretap was a physical device used to intercept phone calls. When intercepting electronic communications today, software usually is used, either by the third-party company providing the communications service or by law enforcement agents. Software wiretapping can be a technically complex process during which communications are diverted to a law-enforcement monitoring center in a manner that does not alert the user of the targeted account.

Wiretap orders are obtained through an extensive, painstaking application process before a court with jurisdiction over the investigation.[17] Under federal and state statutes, a wiretap can be used to investigate only certain "predicate felony" crimes. Most wiretap statutes contain a long list of serious felony crimes that qualify as predicate felonies. At the federal level, several felonies on the list are especially pertinent to cybercrime, including violations of the Computer Fraud and Abuse Act (CFAA), identity theft, larceny/theft, money laundering, bank fraud, and wire fraud. These crimes are covered in depth in Chapter 6.

7.3.8   LETTER OF PRESERVATION

Letters of Preservation are a way of informing third-party providers, or other entities in control of potential evidence, that a law enforcement investigation will be seeking certain items through future legal process. These letters simply request that the sought-after evidence be kept intact until the necessary legal documents are generated, authorized, and served. Letters of Preservation are extremely useful with regard to electronic evidence, since many providers and storage applications routinely purge or modify data through an automated process after a certain time threshold has passed. Some providers have a legal obligation to comply with a Letter of Preservation, while others do not.

---

[17] 18 U.S.C. §§ 2510–2522.

7.3.9 NON-DISCLOSURE REQUEST AND ORDER

A non-disclosure request or order can be used in some circumstances to prevent the target from learning about the existence of the investigation. Some targets who become aware that law enforcement is investigating their activity might flee, destroy evidence, or intimidate witnesses. Non-disclosure requests and orders are used by law enforcement to safeguard the secrecy of an investigation when such consequences are likely.

Some businesses may have a policy to inform customers or users about legal requests for information, unless they have a legal duty not to make such a disclosure. ECPA and some state statutes envision that, as a general rule, targets of legal process should be informed so they have an opportunity to challenge the demand.[18]

To mitigate the likelihood of disclosure about the investigation, investigators can include a Non-Disclosure Request with the legal process, asking the recipient to keep the existence of the legal demand confidential because of the potential detrimental effects on the investigation. Of course, this is merely a request, and prosecutors and law enforcement officials drafting such requests must be careful not to imply a legal duty where none exists. Since the recipient is free to ignore such a request, investigators should first inquire whether the request will be honored, and then make an informed decision about whether to risk the disclosure or get a court order.

A second, safer, option is to seek a Non-Disclosure Order from a court. To do so, a prosecutor or investigator sets forth the reasons why the non-disclosure order is necessary, such as the risk disclosure poses to an ongoing investigation or to someone's safety. Since most forms of legal process in the toolkit require a judge's authorization anyway, obtaining a non-disclosure order simply adds a small burden. If granted, the legal process issued by the court also will contain a lawful order prohibiting its disclosure.

For some types of legal process (such as a wiretap or pen register order), a non-disclosure order is required to be included by statute. For others (such as a subpoena or 2703(d) Order), law enforcement must demonstrate why the normal rules favoring disclosure should be disregarded. As some federal courts have put it, law enforcement must offer facts and circumstances showing a "compelling necessity" for secrecy.[19]

7.4 THE ELECTRONIC COMMUNICATIONS PRIVACY ACT (ECPA): APPLYING THE TOOLS TO ONLINE COMMUNICATIONS

Electronic communications are a major source of evidence in cybercrime cases. When cyber-criminals conduct their crimes and interact with victims and associates using methods like email, messaging, and text messages, they leave a potential trail of information behind. These services are available through hundreds of private companies that provide an array of free and for-pay services. Of course, mobile and cellular phone services are inextricably intertwined with Internet functionality.

From an investigative perspective, gathering evidence related to electronic communications presents tricky privacy questions. Does the reasonable expectation of privacy apply to all types of electronic communications? What about the information associated with an online communication – such as the routing or addressing details? Does it matter that all these communications are transmitted through private companies? What about messages and data that users store online?

---

[18] *See, e.g.*, California Electronic Communications Privacy Act (CalECPA), Cal. Penal Code § 1546.2(a).
[19] *See, e.g.*, *In re Grand Jury Subpoena Duces Tecum*, 797 F.2d 676 (8th Cir.), *cert. dismissed*, 479 U.S. 1013 (1986).

Since 1986, with the passage of the Electronic Communications Privacy Act (ECPA), federal statutes have answered these questions with a complex set of rules that instruct law enforcement on how to obtain evidence of Internet communications. ECPA contains three major provisions:[20]

- The Stored Communications Act (SCA) covers records of past communications, meaning communications received by a user and stored in the service provider's system.
- The Pen Register and Trap and Trace Statute (Pen/Trap Statute) deals with monitoring the dialing and addressing information from live communications.
- Wiretap Act amendments cover the live interception of the content of a target's electronic communications.

In passing ECPA, Congress attempted to align the reasonable expectation of privacy in various types of records associated with online communications with the appropriate legal tools for law enforcement to gather this information as criminal evidence.[21] Subsequent amendments to ECPA and a body of court decisions have refined these rules.

These federal laws provide the framework for law enforcement efforts to obtain evidence related to electronic communications. State investigators and prosecutors are guided by this federal framework when seeking communications evidence. Some states have their own laws on these topics, particularly in the areas of wiretapping and pen/traps, and many of these statutes follow the federal model. Some state statutes do not comprehensively address law enforcement procedures to obtain electronic evidence.

In Chapter 6 we covered the criminal offenses created by ECPA; this chapter discusses ECPA's procedural provisions to obtain evidence.

7.4.1   The Stored Communications Act: Records of Past Communications

The rules for law enforcement investigators seeking records of past electronic communications, including user messages stored by service providers, are found in the SCA. The SCA applies to most electronic communication and data storage providers. If a company does not offer services specified in the SCA, however, this statute does not regulate law enforcement access to its records.

---

[20] This table summarizes the organization and statutory sections:
   The Electronic Communications Privacy Act (ECPA)

   Title I: Wiretap Act. 18 U.S.C. §§ 2510–2522
   (also known as Title III of the Omnibus Crime Control and Safe Streets Act of 1968)
   Title II: The Stored Communications Act (SCA), 18 U.S.C. §§ 2701–2712
   Title III: Pen Registers and Trap and Trace Devices 18 U.S.C. §§ 3121–3127

[21] As alluded to earlier, ECPA anticipates that law enforcement might need immediate access to a target's electronic communications because of an imminent danger of death or serious physical injury. In these cases, this evidence can be requested and turned over without following the normal legal process. 18 U.S.C. § 2702(b) and (c). The Pen/Trap Statute and Wiretap Act have procedures for emergency law enforcement monitoring of communications in cases involving conspiratorial conduct characteristic of organized crime or immediate threats to national security. The government must obtain a pen/trap or wiretap order within 48 hours of the emergency installation. 18 U.S.C. §§ 2518(7), 3125. The Pen/Trap Statute allows emergency monitoring in some instances where there is an ongoing attack on a protected computer.

In this section, we will look at the SCA's key definitions, rules, and privacy factors, including:

- The Role of Third-Party Providers
- Services Covered by the SCA (ECS and RCS)
- The Four Categories of Stored Communications Evidence
  - Subscriber Information
  - Sensitive Non-Content Information
  - Location Information
  - Content Information
- SCA Rules for Letters of Preservation and Non-Disclosure Orders.

7.4.1.1   The Role of Third-Party Providers

Unless we are having a face-to-face conversation, we depend on communication services to do the work of transmitting our written, oral, and video messages to the intended recipients. Our email and other Internet communications travel from one account to another thanks to the data systems of online service providers. In other words, we rely upon "third parties" – companies that are not participants in our communications – to deliver them on our behalf.

Along with sending and receiving communications, the providers of Internet and cellphone services perform an additional function. They store their customers' messages. In the pre-Internet days, when letters came in the mail or messages were left on an answering machine, the recipient stored the document or recording somewhere in his or her possession. With Internet and cellphone communications, however, third-party providers perform the storage function, allowing customers to keep the contents of their email, text, voice, and video messages within the provider's servers, often indefinitely. As a result, third-party providers hold communications records that may be needed as evidence in criminal investigations.

As discussed in the section on consent, there is no reasonable expectation of privacy for information that is publicly exposed. A related legal doctrine, called "the third-party doctrine", generally means there is no expectation of privacy in information that a user voluntarily makes available to a third party, including to communications providers, banks, and other companies. It is called the third-party doctrine because the third party is given access to this information.

Traditionally, the third-party doctrine meant a subpoena was all that was needed to obtain any records held by a company about a customer or user. As we will see, ECPA changed how the doctrine is applied to electronic communications and implements statutory protections for customers of certain services.

7.4.1.2   Services Covered by the SCA (ECS and RCS)

The SCA governs records held by two classes of service providers.

- Electronic Communication Services (ECS) offer users the ability to send or receive electronic or wire communications – such as an ISP, a social media platform, a telephone company, or a web or cloud-based email provider.[22] An ECS keeps communications in temporary electronic storage as it sends and delivers them.

---

[22] 18 U.S.C. § 2510(15).

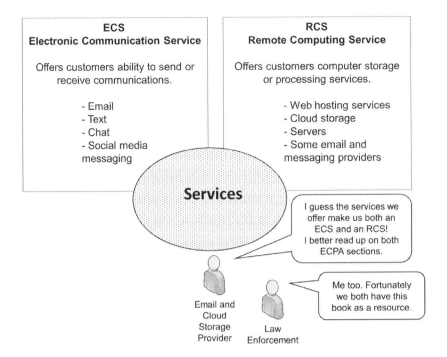

FIGURE 7.2   ECS vs. RCS: Electronic Communication Service vs. Remote Computing Service.

- Remote Computing Services (RCS) provide long-term computer storage or process-ing services to users by means of an electronic communications system.[23] An RCS stores data and communications a user has decided to keep. Cloud-based storage providers, email providers, and web hosting companies are often considered an RCS.

As you can see in Figure 7.2, a provider can be both an ECS and an RCS if it provides both communication and storage services. If a company does not fall into either class, the SCA does not apply, and law enforcement can obtain evidence using normal procedures for obtaining evidence, such as a subpoena or search warrant.

As with other parts of the SCA, these service categories are outdated and no longer reflect the landscape of Internet service and use. As technology has advanced, the ability of providers to send and store communications has both expanded and consolidated, so that it is quite common for one company to offer services within both the ECS and RCS defin-itions. It also is increasingly common for major communication providers – such as social media platforms – to provide services that can be categorized as those of an ECS or RCS, along with services that do not coincide with either definition. As a result, determining how to classify a provider can be tricky. Many providers publicly state their own interpretations of their status under the SCA.

---

[23] 18 U.S.C § 2711(2). Though the statute defines an RCS as offering these services "to the public", that term simply means the service is publicly available, even if for a cost.

7.4.1.3 "Content" vs. "Non-Content" Information

The SCA divides providers' records of electronic communications and stored data into two groups – "non-content" and "content". For many types of communication, such as email or text messages, providers keep a combination of non-content and content records. But the distinction between the two categories is important because different investigative rules apply to each.

"Non-content" information means details about an email, text message, voicemail, or other form of electronic communication related to its addressing and transmission. Non-content information is sometimes described as "envelope information", because it consists of addressing formalities similar to those on the outside of a traditional envelope (which ensure a letter gets to its destination), but not what is contained within the letter inside.[24]

There are two categories of "non-content" information under the SCA. The first is subscriber and session information, the second covers more sensitive information.

7.4.1.4 Subscriber and Session Information

Subscriber and session information encompasses the details supplied by the user to open an online account, and to send and receive communications. These details include:

- User's name, address, telephone number, and other identifiers (although the providers of many free services do not collect or verify identifiers, allowing people to sign up using fake or stolen names)
- Payment details for the account (for fee-based services)
- Date when the user signed up with the provider
- Types of services utilized
- Number, username, or other identifier assigned to the user on the network
- Dates and times the account was used
- Duration of each log-in or account usage
- Internet Protocol address(es) from which an account was accessed.[25]

Depending on what data is collected by the provider, and how long the provider stores that data, providers may not maintain records of all of this information for every account.

The SCA allows providers to disclose subscriber information to law enforcement when the provider is served a subpoena duces tecum (in line with traditional application of the third-party doctrine and no expectation of privacy in this material).

7.4.1.5 Sensitive Non-Content Information

The second category of non-content information refers to any non-content communication details beyond subscriber information. It generally includes:

- Email or other account addresses with which a user corresponds,
- A user's contact or friend list,
- Full message headers for communications sent to and from the user's account (but not the subject lines, which are considered to be part of the content of the message).

---

[24] Orin S Kerr, *Internet Surveillance Law after the USA PATRIOT Act: The Big Brother that Isn't*, George Washington University Law School, Public Law and Legal Theory Working Paper No. 043 (originally published 2003, last revised March 25, 2015).

[25] The categories of subscriber and session information can be found at 18 U.S.C. 2703(c)(2).

The SCA treats non-content information that goes beyond basic subscriber facts as more privacy-sensitive. Even though this second category does not divulge the content of messages or calls, it has the potential to reveal a target's associates and other intrusive facts. Because there is a heightened personal sensitivity for this kind of information, the SCA requires law enforcement to obtain a 2703(d) Order (or search warrant) from a court to obtain it. A 2703(d) Order application must present "specific and articulable facts" showing how the sensitive non-content information will be material and relevant to the investigation.

7.4.1.6 Location Information

In 2018, the U.S. Supreme Court created a third category of non-content information that was not contemplated within the SCA – "location data" – and gave it heightened protection. Now, an order based on probable cause is required to get records about a user's location associated with stored emails, voicemails, and other communications, including:

- Cell-site records showing where communications were transmitted
- E911 records
- GPS tracking data
- Other location tracking records.[26]

Third-party providers (including cellular telephone service providers) use these technologies to pinpoint the location of users at the time they send or receive communications and for billing purposes. These records documenting a target's location can be critical evidence in an investigation.

The Supreme Court determined that the SCA erred by including location data within the category of Sensitive Non-Content Information, finding that a 2703(d) Order provided insufficient privacy protections for the user's historical cell-site location information.[27] The Court assessed the Fourth Amendment privacy concerns relating to location-tracking technology and decided that location information about wire and electronic communications is as private as the actual contents of the communications.

The Court also rejected the "third-party doctrine" for these location records, deciding that the intrusive nature of location data overrides the consent-based theory surrounding third-party providers' records. What is more, the Court reasoned, users do not affirmatively agree to allow their phone-service providers to keep cell-site records, including when they are not actively using their phone.

7.4.1.7 Content Information

Content information means the portion of the communication that carries its meaning or purpose. In practical terms, "content" refers to the actual message contained in an email, a text message, posting, voice recording, and includes photos, videos, and attachments. The subject line of an email is considered part of the message's meaningful content.

---

[26] Cell-site data provides geographical information by pinpointing the cell tower through which individual cellular calls are transmitted. Enhanced 911 (E911) data shows the physical location of callers to the 911 emergency system, used throughout North America. Global Positioning System (GPS) tracking is a general term for data tools that track user location through the Global Navigation Satellite System.

[27] *Carpenter v. United States*, 585 U.S. ___ (2018). This case concerned a multi-state robbery spree and cell-site records that helped tie the defendants to the crime scenes.

A search warrant is law enforcement's safest tool for obtaining the content of email and other communications from third-party providers.[28] Any SCA provisions that authorize a lesser legal tool reflect an outdated analysis of the privacy expectations of today's Internet user, as follows:

- *The SCA's original guidelines and changing norms.* When the SCA was enacted in the 1980s, its rules about obtaining content evidence made distinctions based upon whether a user had opened a communication and how long a communication had been stored. At the time, users periodically dialed in to their providers to download or open email. As Internet use has evolved, these time-based rules and distinctions between opened and unopened messages no longer reflect the average user's experience or expectation of privacy. Users regularly store communications in accounts indefinitely (whether open or unopened) and expect them to remain private for as long as they are stored. Further, the distinction between "open" and "unopened" content has become meaningless since many messaging systems no longer require a user to "open" communications to view them.
- *Court decisions and third-party policies align with the changing landscape.* As the Internet evolves and the SCA's rules become more disconnected from today's practice, some federal courts have concluded there is a reasonable expectation of privacy in all of our stored messages, and that law enforcement should use a search warrant to obtain any stored content.[29] Given these legal developments, many third-party providers will not supply records containing content to law enforcement without the issuance of a search warrant. As a result, the U.S. Department of Justice generally treats all content as having a reasonable expectation of privacy, obtaining search warrants for stored content, no matter how long the communications have been stored with a provider.[30]

Bills have been introduced in the U.S. Congress to modify ECPA and extend the search warrant requirement to all stored communications. As of this writing, however, no amendment has been enacted.[31] In 2019, Utah became the first state in the nation to require a search warrant for all stored communications and other data.[32]

The SCA's rules for obtaining evidence of stored electronic communications are summarized in Table 7.1.

---

[28] As discussed, getting a search warrant for content is always the safest investigative option. The SCA, as written, offers the alternative to use a subpoena or 2703(d) Order to obtain certain content records when the government gives notice to the subscriber. As explained above, there is a strong argument that a search warrant is legally required to protect privacy rights.

[29] *See, e.g., United States v. Warshak*, 631 F.3d 266 (6th Cir. 2010).

[30] Mysti Degani and Louisa Marion, Making the Most of Your Statutory Electronic Evidence Toolbox, *United States Attorneys' Bulletin*, Vol. 64, No. 3 (May 2016), www.justice.gov/usao/file/851856/download.

[31] *See, e.g.,* the ECPA Modernization Act of 2017, S. 1657, 115th Cong (2017), and the Email Privacy Act of 2017, H.R. 387, 115th Cong (2017).

[32] The bill passed by the Utah legislature can be found at: https://le.utah.gov/~2019/bills/static/HB0057.html.

TABLE 7.1

Stored Communications Evidence

	Description of Data	Tool Needed
Subscriber and Session Information (non-content)	Subscriber name; address; records of session times and durations; local and long-distance telephone connection records; length of customer's service (including start date); types of service utilized by customer; subscriber number or identifier; means and source of payment for service (including any credit card or bank account number)	**Subpoena duces tecum** *Can also use:* • 2703(d) Order • Search Warrant
Sensitive Non-Content Information (non-content)	Numbers/addresses of accounts corresponding with target; full email header (except for subject line): contact or friend lists;	**2703(d) Order** *Can also use:* • Search Warrant
Location data (non-content)	Cell-site transmission data E911 data GPS tracking data Other location tracking records	**Search warrant**
Content	Content (words, images, attachments) of email, email subject lines, social media messaging, text messages, voicemail, etc.	**Search warrant** *Be aware:* Statutory language may appear to permit lesser legal process in certain circumstances, but use a search warrant!

7.4.1.8 SCA Rules for Letters of Preservation, Non-Disclosure, and Delayed Disclosure Orders

The SCA has rules for using Letters of Preservation related to electronic communications. Under the SCA, when an investigation identifies an account of interest, law enforcement can make a preservation request to the relevant electronic records provider (ECS or RCS).[33] Once such a request is made, the provider is required to preserve the records and data for that account for a period of 90 days, while the investigation obtains the necessary legal process for accessing the evidence. Supplemental requests can extend the 90-day period when needed.[34]

The SCA also permits investigators to seek a Non-Disclosure Order for third-party service providers from whom evidence will be obtained using a subpoena, 2703(d) Order, or search warrant.[35] A Non-Disclosure Order commands the entity not to inform its customer or subscriber that law enforcement is gathering evidence about his or her accounts. Under the SCA, a court may authorize a non-disclosure order when there are facts indicating that disclosure presents a risk that:

• Someone's life or physical safety will be put in jeopardy
• A target might flee from prosecution
• Evidence might be tampered with or destroyed

---

[33] Though ECPA provisions on Letters of Preservation apply only to ECS and RCS providers, this 90-day timeline is commonly used for letters requesting preservation from any type of entity.
[34] 18 U.S.C. § 2703(f).
[35] 18 U.S.C. § 2705(b).

- Witnesses might be intimidated
- Some other serious threat or delay to the investigation might ensue.

A Non-Disclosure Order can be issued for such period as the court deems appropriate. Extensions of the order can be obtained with a showing of the need for continued non-disclosure.

7.4.2 The Pen/Trap Statute: Live Monitoring of Non-Content Information

The Pen/Trap statute codifies law enforcement procedures for federal and state investigators to obtain most non-content information about wire and electronic communications in real-time.[36] As we learned earlier in the chapter, a pen/trap enables live monitoring of dialing, addressing, routing, and signaling information.

The Pen/Trap statute lays out the application process for obtaining a pen/trap order. The application must include the account number or identifier of the targeted account, the identity of the account's subscriber (if known), the identity of the target of the investigation (if known), and a factual certification from the law enforcement applicant that the pen/trap will likely obtain information "relevant to an ongoing criminal investigation".[37] The statute also instructs that pen/trap orders will include a non-disclosure provision directing the third-party provider not to disclose the pen/trap's existence.[38] Pen/traps can be authorized for up to 60 days, with the option to seek extensions for additional 60-day periods.[39]

Under the terms of a related law, the Communications Assistance for Law Enforcement Act (CALEA), a pen/trap cannot be used to obtain live cell-site tower or other location data.[40] CALEA requires certain types of providers to incorporate technology that enables law enforcement to conduct wiretaps and pen/traps. When enacted in 1994, CALEA applied only to telephone companies. In 2005, CALEA was expanded to include all "telecommunications carriers". This group includes online communications services, like email, voicemail, text messaging, and Voice-over-Internet-Protocol (VoIP) service providers (like Skype).

The Pen/Trap statute and CALEA do not address location data. Given the new protections on location information instituted by the Supreme Court, law enforcement agents who want to obtain real-time location data along with a pen/trap order must establish probable cause for this monitoring in their application.

7.4.3 The Wiretap Act: Live Monitoring of Content Information

The third major component of ECPA is a set of amendments to the Wiretap Act that created interception rules and procedures applicable to all wire and electronic communications. Before ECPA, the Wiretap Act was focused primarily on telephone communications.

A wiretap allows investigators to hear or see communications coming to and from a targeted account live, in real-time. Given a wiretap's intensely invasive nature, the Wiretap Act (together with related court decisions) creates onerous requirements for law enforcement to intercept communications.[41] Analogous state statutes have similar requirements.[42]

---

[36] 18 U.S.C. §§ 3121–3127.
[37] 18 U.S.C. § 3122(b)(2).
[38] 18 U.S.C. § 3123(d)(2).
[39] 18 U.S.C. § 3123(c).
[40] 47 U.S.C. § 1002(a)(2)(B). CALEA is codified at 47 U.S.C. §§ 1001–1010.
[41] The Wiretap Act is found at 18 U.SC. §§ 2510–2522. The application process is detailed in Section 2518.
[42] For a listing of the wiretap laws in the 50 states, see, Appendix D of Charles Doyle, *Privacy: An Overview of the Electronic Privacy Act*, Congressional Research Service (2012).

TABLE 7.2

Live Communications Evidence

	Description	Tool Needed
Subscriber Information and Sensitive Non-Content Information	Dialing, addressing, routing, and signaling data; IP addresses; contact addresses, header information	**Pen Register with Trap-and-Trace Device**
Location Data	Cell-site transmission data E911 data GPS tracking data	**Pen Register with Trap-and-Trace Device, plus** **Order based on probable cause** ("prospective location information order")
Content	Content of email, email subject lines, social media messaging, text messages, voicemail, etc.	**Wiretap**

The process is designed to ensure interceptions occur only when necessary and follow a strict, judicially supervised procedure.[43]

Pursuant to the CALEA, most third-party providers are required to assist law enforcement agents conducting authorized interception of communications transmitted through their services. By law, a wiretap order automatically directs third-party providers not to disclose the existence of the wiretap or the contents of intercepted communications to unauthorized parties.

The Pen/Trap statute's and Wiretap Act's rules for obtaining evidence of live electronic communications are summarized in Table 7.2.

7.5   OBTAINING EVIDENCE LOCATED IN ANOTHER STATE

For most crimes, investigations and prosecutions usually occur in one jurisdiction. If someone steals a wallet in Philadelphia, it will be the Philadelphia Police Department, the Philadelphia District Attorney's Office and the Philadelphia court system that handle the case from start to finish.

Cybercrime cases, on the other hand, commonly involve evidence and individuals in more than one state. This tendency raises questions for investigators about how to gather evidence in another jurisdiction. If a law enforcement officer in New York learns that a device located in Florida was used in the crime, what can she do to have the device seized and returned to New York to be used as evidence? What if the company that maintains records of the suspect's emails is headquartered in California?

Getting evidence from other states involves a combination of longstanding procedures and customs that have evolved since the country's founding, and newer application of provisions of the ECPA statute and state laws.

---

[43] There are consent and third-party provider exceptions to the normal wiretap application and court order process. If one party to the communications consents to a wiretap, no court order is needed (except in those states requiring all-party consent). Third-party providers can monitor their networks, including users' communications, to protect their own property or other rights, or to maintain cybersecurity. The cybersecurity exception was added in the Cybersecurity Act of 2015, Pub. L. No. 114–113, 129 Stat. 2242.

7.5.1   FEDERAL INVESTIGATIONS

When federal agencies conduct investigations, their jurisdiction is national and is not affected by state boundaries. A federal subpoena duces tecum under the Federal Rules of Criminal Procedure can be served on any individual or entity within the United States.[44] The same holds true for search warrants and 2703(d) Orders under the SCA. A federal judge with jurisdiction over the offense being investigated can issue a 2703(d) order or SCA warrant for accounts, data, property, or locations within the United States.[45] The Pen/Trap statute also allows federal courts to authorize pen/traps nationwide.[46] The Wiretap Act gives federal courts the ability to authorize wiretaps on landlines within their territorial jurisdictions, and on mobile devices that might travel anywhere in the country as long as the communications are intercepted in the judge's territorial jurisdiction. This is generally accomplished by having the listening post in that jurisdiction.[47]

In the case of electronically stored information or storage media, the judge can issue a warrant to use remote access to conduct the search in certain limited circumstances. Remote access situations arise if the location of the media or information has been concealed through technological means, or if the case involves protected computers (under the CFAA) that have been damaged in five or more districts.[48]

7.5.2   STATE AND LOCAL INVESTIGATIONS

Individual states do not have nationwide jurisdiction. While the SCA authorizes state subpoenas, 2703(d) Orders, and search warrants to obtain electronic communications evidence, these tools may be limited by the boundaries of state jurisdiction under varying state laws. However, there are five general ways that state and local investigators can obtain evidence from another state:

1. *Consent.* If the individual or business with the records/items is in another state, the first option is simply to ask for them. Quite often, companies and organizations are willing to assist a criminal investigation consensually, especially if the records/items involve information with few privacy considerations, or the records/items involve a customer who has violated the terms of service. Consent may be impractical when it is questionable who has legal authority to consent, or when asking for consent might alert suspects to the investigation.
2. *Consent to service of subpoena and to jurisdiction of the subpoena.* Sometimes it is a complicated issue of fact and law as to what type of service is proper, and whether a subpoena can compel action by certain out-of-state businesses. Some businesses may make this issue moot by agreeing to accept service by email, and by agreeing to provide the records rather than contest the matter. In many ways, this practice is a form of consent and cooperation.
3. *Subpoena, order, or warrant based on actual presence within the state.* When it is not possible to obtain consent, the next question is whether the company or individual with the records/items has a presence in the investigating state (an office or store, for example). If the business has an "actual presence" within the state, it falls within the state's jurisdiction, and the normal process for seeking those records can be used. Subpoenas, 2703(d) Orders, or search warrants – depending on the nature of the records or items – can be issued directly to the business or individual. It is

---

[44] FRCrP Rule 17.
[45] 18 U.S.C. § 2703.
[46] 18 U.S.C. § 3123(a)(1).
[47] 18 U.S.C § 2518(3).
[48] FRCrP Rule 41(b)(6).

always worth taking the time to determine whether the relevant business/individual has a presence in the state.

4. *State laws that honor out-of-state subpoenas, orders, and warrants for electronic and wire communications evidence.* Some states have passed laws authorizing Internet service and communications providers that are incorporated or registered within the state to honor out-of-state subpoenas, court orders, and search warrants. States with such laws often are homes to large Internet communications businesses that are bombarded with records requests from around the nation. By accepting other states' subpoenas and court orders, these companies do not have to worry about sorting out multi-state jurisdictional law, and law enforcement officials do not have to "domesticate" their search warrants with a prosecutor's office in the state with the records (see below). States with such laws include California, Florida, Minnesota, and Massachusetts.[49]

5. *Subpoena, order or warrant domesticated in another state.* The next option for obtaining evidence located in another state is to "domesticate" a subpoena or court order in the state where the evidence is held. Domestication means having a court with jurisdiction over the evidence issue the subpoena, order, or search warrant on the out-of-state investigation's behalf. In order to domesticate, the investigator must seek assistance from a prosecutor's office within the state where the evidence is located or where the business or individual controlling the evidence has a presence.

7.5.3 SEARCH WARRANT CONSIDERATIONS FOR OUT-OF-STATE DEVICES AND PHYSICAL PREMISES

As we have learned, subpoenas and searches of out-of-state records evidence do not have to be performed by a law enforcement investigator. Instead, a representative of the company will identify the specified records and provide copies of them to the investigator. But if an investigator successfully domesticates a search warrant for a physical location or device in another state, there are some legal and investigative factors to consider in getting the physical search done:

- *Authorization for case investigator presence.* A search or seizure generally must be conducted by law enforcement officials with jurisdiction over the location/item, meaning the investigators in the state where the device or premises are located. The search warrant application, however, can seek authorization from the court to have officials from the investigating state present during the search or seizure. Court approval forestalls any future defense allegation of impropriety.[50]
- *Transporting the evidence to the investigating state.* Case investigators usually want to transport any items found in the out-of-state search back to the investigating state so they can be used as evidence. However, seized items normally are "returned" to the court that issues the search warrant and stored by law enforcement in that jurisdiction. When transportation of seized evidence to the investigating state is needed, there must be explicit authorization to do so within the search

---

[49] California Code, Penal Code §1524.2(c); Florida Statutes, §92.605(3) (2018); Massachusetts General Laws, Ch. 276, §1B(d); Minnesota Statutes, §626.18 (2018).

[50] When a search warrant is obtained for an out-of-state location, it can be very helpful for the case investigator(s) to travel to the other state and be present at the search. They know what evidence is important to the case, and then can testify at any future proceedings about what occurred.

warrant. In some states, a separate application and court order may be needed to obtain this authorization after execution of the initial search warrant.

- *Authorization for forensic search of devices.* The search warrant should authorize forensic analysis of computer devices in the manner preferred by investigators. Typically, the case investigators would prefer to bring the seized computer devices (and other evidence) back to the home state and conduct the forensic analysis using the facilities and resources there. If so, the search warrant should authorize the case investigators to transport the evidence and conduct this search. Note that another search warrant for the device may be required in the home state. Occasionally, case investigators would prefer to have the forensics conducted by the out-of-state officials. Whatever scenario is preferred, authorization for that plan should be obtained in the search warrant.

7.6   OBTAINING EVIDENCE STORED OVERSEAS BY U.S. ENTITIES: THE CLOUD ACT

The Internet is an international network with few technical obstacles to communication or information-sharing among computers, servers, and mobile devices anywhere in the world. When crime occurs in this digital environment, investigators following a trail of online activity often find out that needed evidence is located in a foreign country. In many instances, records of various kinds are stored by U.S. businesses using servers and other equipment located in foreign locations.

Until recently, investigators facing this situation either were provided with the records by the U.S. business, or were forced to go through the complex and laborious process of obtaining evidence through the international diplomatic process described in the next section. Even though the records belonged to a U.S. company, their storage overseas could mean that access to the records was governed by the laws of the country where they were stored. Because of this issue, some companies would decline to comply with U.S. legal process.[51]

Today, the Clarifying Lawful Overseas Use of Data (CLOUD) Act of 2018 makes obtaining that evidence much easier for law enforcement.[52] The CLOUD Act amended the SCA to specifically cover all data and communications records stored by U.S. companies, no matter if they are stored in the U.S. or abroad.[53] In other words, the same procedures outlined in the SCA for obtaining subscriber, sensitive non-content, and content information now apply when the data controlled by a U.S. company is stored in a foreign country.

The CLOUD Act's other significant change is the creation of a new type of treaty – called a "CLOUD Act Agreement" – that can be formed between the U.S. and foreign countries to facilitate the sharing of third-party data in criminal cases. These agreements would supplement any existing legal assistance treaties and require approval by the U.S. Attorney General and Secretary of State (rather than traditional Congressional approval for treaties). Under a CLOUD Act agreement, there would be mutual sharing of third-party provider data through direct requests rather than a lengthy diplomatic process.

---

[51] In one notable case, the U.S. government sought records from Microsoft that were stored in Ireland, and Microsoft declined to provide them on the grounds that Irish law did not permit their disclosure. The FBI needed these records for a criminal investigation. The CLOUD Act, resolved this litigation. *See United States v. Microsoft Corp.*, 584 U.S. ___ (2018).

[52] 18 U.S.C. §2523.

[53] For a review of the CLOUD Act, see Stephen T. Mulligan, *Cross-Border Data Sharing Under the CLOUD Act*, Congressional Research Service (2018). https://fas.org/sgp/crs/misc/R45173.pdf.

Providers can object to certain requests based on privacy concerns. The CLOUD Act contemplates agreements only with those countries that follow privacy laws and regulations as strong or stronger than those in the United States.

The U.S. and the United Kingdom signed the first CLOUD Act agreement in October 2019.[54] As more agreements are established, they will provide far more direct and speedy compliance with law enforcement requests for third-party provider records and data held by foreign entities.

7.7 OBTAINING EVIDENCE LOCATED IN ANOTHER COUNTRY

During some cybercrime investigations, records, devices and other items implicated in the case may be outside the United States, whether belonging to victims, suspects, or unsuspecting individuals whose equipment has been surreptitiously coopted by cyber criminals to use as storage or communication hubs. And, of course, suspects themselves may be operating from homes or other locations in one or more countries to orchestrate their crimes.

In this section, we will look at the primary methods for gathering evidence located in other countries:

- Presence of Evidence or its Custodian Corporation in the United States
- Mutual Legal Assistance Treaties (MLATs)
- Letters Rogatory
- Informal Assistance
- Egmont Request.

Given the sensitive diplomatic nature of international criminal investigations, the process of obtaining evidence from foreign countries largely is overseen by the Office of International Affairs (OIA) in the Department of Justice. Federal and state law enforcement officials and prosecutors can contact OIA with requests for information, records, and other evidence in foreign countries. OIA advises investigators about the type of assistance that is available from a particular country, the procedures for obtaining the evidence, and the likely timetable. International evidence acquisition can take a long time.[55] In some instances, OIA will advise that the evidence is unobtainable from a particular foreign government.

Guidance for international matters, obtaining assistance from OIA, and all these matters is outlined in the Department of Justice Manual, and can be obtained on specific cases through direct contact with the OIA.[56]

There are some situations in which OIA assistance is not required to obtain evidence or information from foreign jurisdictions, such as when the CLOUD Act applies, when the evidence or its custodian has a presence in the U.S., or when the Egmont request or an informal method can be used. Otherwise, to obtain evidence admissible in court, OIA assistance is required.

[54] *U.S. and U.K. Sign Landmark Cross-Border Data Access Agreement to Combat Criminals and Terrorists Online,* U.S. Department of Justice (October 3, 2019), www.justice.gov/opa/pr/us-and-uk-sign-landmark-cross-border-data-access-agreement-combat-criminals-and-terrorists.

[55] Information about OIA, the international processes for gathering evidence, and the assistance OIA provides to state and federal law enforcement can be found at: www.justice.gov/criminal-oia.

[56] *See* www.justice.gov/jm/criminal-resource-manual-278-informal-means.

7.7.1 PRESENCE OF EVIDENCE OR ITS CUSTODIAN CORPORATION IN THE UNITED STATES

When evidence of criminal activity is held by a foreign individual, company or entity, the first question is whether the records or items are being stored in the United States, perhaps in a server or storage facility on U.S. territory or through an affiliated U.S. corporation. The "presence" question arises most frequently with records of foreign commercial or communications services. If a foreign company is keeping the needed evidence in a place subject to U.S. laws, it must comply with appropriate federal or state legal demands, including subpoenas, court orders, and search warrants. No international process would be required to obtain the evidence.

The next question is, even if the data is stored outside of the U.S., is it within the control of a foreign entity with a presence in the U.S.? Since the CLOUD Act does not make distinctions between U.S. companies and foreign companies with a physical presence in the U.S., it is possible the CLOUD Act might permit service of the legal process upon a custodian corporation for data it controls stored outside of this country. Of course, the company might raise other jurisdictional or procedural issues in response to the legal process.

7.7.2 MUTUAL LEGAL ASSISTANCE TREATIES (MLATs)

When evidence is located in a foreign country, none of the above techniques are feasible, and admissible evidence is needed, then investigators must seek the help of OIA. The primary method available for obtaining records, or to seize or search items or locations, is through international Mutual Legal Assistance Treaties (MLATs) that establish the steps each country will take to assist the other. The United States has entered into MLATs with countries around the world. Depending on the country, treaty, and relationships, there may be extensive cooperation or merely minimal aid. Usually, to invoke an MLAT's assistance provisions, the crimes must be serious and prohibited in both countries. There are many countries that do not have MLATs with the U.S., in which case an investigator must look to using Letters Rogatory.

MLAT procedures can require significant time and effort for investigators. The investigator must provide legal and factual justifications for the requested actions, and months, even years, can elapse before a request is accepted and completed.

It is possible to preserve the evidence pending completion of the MLAT process. The Computer Crime and Intellectual Property Section (CCIPS) at the U.S. Department of Justice operates a 24-hour help desk, through which preservation requests can be communicated to the relevant foreign provider or business.[57]

Searches of locations and seizure of evidence require even more cooperation from authorities in the other country, as well as coordination with U.S. federal law enforcement. While international searches and seizures can be done, they usually take more time and effort to accomplish than records requests.

7.7.3 LETTERS ROGATORY

If the country where the evidence is located does not have an MLAT with the United States, then OIA will need to try other approaches, such as the submission of a formal

---

[57] *See*, the Department of Justice Manual at www.justice.gov/criminal-oia. Also, the CCIPS at the U.S. Department of Justice is the point of contact for the "24/7 Network", a group of approximately 70 member countries that provides investigative collaboration. See, Mysti Degani and Louisa Marion, Making the Most of Your Statutory Electronic Evidence Toolbox, *United States Attorneys' Bulletin*, Vol. 64, No. 3 (May 2016).

diplomatic request through a mechanism called a Letter Rogatory. This process is usually lengthier than an MLAT request and can be denied outright by the country receiving the request.

7.7.4   INFORMAL ASSISTANCE

On a practical level, informal communication with law enforcement agencies and other authorities in the foreign jurisdiction can lead to the sharing of useful, timely intelligence and investigative support. For example, a police agency within the country may be willing to obtain needed records and share them with law enforcement investigators in the United States. Some countries may not have an MLAT with the United States but may still be willing to assist criminal investigations. Whether to engage in this type of contact outside of an official process is always a strategic decision, weighing the potential benefits to the investigation against the possibility of local authorities intentionally or unintentionally alerting a suspect.

Law enforcement officials may also contact Interpol, an international policing organization with 192 member countries. Interpol works to facilitate police cooperation across international borders. While it does not have the diplomatic or judicial authority of the MLAT process, Interpol can connect investigators with police agencies on the ground in the country where evidence is located. In some instances, support from local law enforcement in the foreign country can help move diplomatic proceedings forward.

No matter what type of evidence is sought from another country, it is possible the other nation will take its own interest in the criminal matter once it has been informed. For example, if a country learns through the MLAT process or an Interpol contact that one of its citizens is suspected of conducting cybercrimes from its soil, that country might initiate its own investigation into the matter or even alert the suspect. To the extent possible, once a request for evidence is made, it is essential to communicate with local authorities (with guidance from OIA), to ensure the U.S. investigation is not compromised, and to gain access to evidence or leads uncovered by local law enforcement. In some instances, local authorities' instinct to protect their citizens, or a culture of corruption, may lead OIA to advise against local contact.

7.7.5   EGMONT REQUEST

Finally, investigators should be aware of the Egmont request, a mechanism available through the Financial Crimes Enforcement Network (FinCEN).[58] Named for The Egmont Group, an international network of government financial intelligence units, an Egmont request seeks assistance from FinCEN's counterparts in participating countries to obtain financial information from those countries promptly. The information is supplied in an uncertified format and cannot be used in court, but it can be used to further other investigative steps. If admissible records are desired, investigators can follow up with an MLAT request through OIA.

7.7.6   SUSPECTS LOCATED IN OTHER STATES AND FOREIGN COUNTRIES (PREVIEW)

In Chapter 17 we will learn about the methods for arresting a defendant located in another state or country, as well as how to extradite the defendant to the jurisdiction

---

[58] *See*, FinCEN, The Egmont Group of Financial Intelligence Units, www.fincen.gov/resources/international/egmont-group-financial-intelligence-units.

conducting the investigation and prosecution. The handling of international suspects, in particular, involves some of the same rules and methods as those used to obtain evidence.

7.8 CONCLUSION

We now have assembled the legal toolkit for conducting a cybercrime investigation, and gain a sense of the many complexities in this area of the law. The first step was to consider the key underlying legal concepts around the reasonable expectation of privacy and consent. From there, we saw how the available investigative steps are deployable based on the privacy levels associated with needed evidence. From open online investigation of public information, gaining consent of the owner, to using one of the several legal processes – there are many methods of gathering cybercrime evidence. Statutes like ECPA provide guidance on which method to use for different types of evidence related to electronic communications.

Because cyber cases involve so many connections to other states and to foreign countries, we have also reviewed the procedures for obtaining evidence found outside an investigation's jurisdiction. Methods for interstate evidence-gathering are well established and relatively routine, although they often involve assistance from agencies within the other state. Getting evidence from a foreign country can be more complex, usually involving the United States Department of Justice's international assistance program.

8 Cyber Investigations Linked to Nation-States or Terrorists

This chapter is for those curious about:

- What happens if the cybercrime you are investigating leads to a foreign government or terrorist
- The spectrum of laws and actions that might apply to nation-state and terrorist actors.

8.1 INTRODUCTION

It might surprise some investigators to know that crimes reported to them may lead back to the actions of foreign governments and terrorists. Nation-states[1] and terrorists conduct a range of cyber activities, from familiar forms of cybercrime to espionage and covert actions, any of which might be detected by private or public cybercrime investigators. A discussion of cybercrime investigations is not complete, therefore, without a general understanding of the international level of cyber conflict and the laws and norms that exist to address this conduct.

To give investigators some general insight into this sphere of cyber activity, this chapter presents an overview of government-sponsored cyber actions and how they fit into existing bodies of domestic and international laws. The legal options for addressing nation-state actions may include criminal prosecution, civil suits, international treaties, and even war. We also examine actions along this continuum that may not fit neatly within the law, including sanctions, diplomatic pressure, espionage, and other secretive covert or clandestine operations.

Next, we will look at some of the motives behind nation-state cybercrimes, including generating funds, commercial espionage, infrastructure attacks, and advancing strategic interests; we then tie those concepts into various cyber actions. We examine a range of cybercrime activities engaged in by other nations to target this country that have been exposed through investigations, prosecutions, and media reports.

The chapter also discusses the motives behind cyber activities conducted by terrorist groups and the online actions taken to further them, and concludes with information about what an investigator should do when he or she encounters potential nation-state or terrorist involvement in a case.

---

[1] There is an international law custom that refers to nation-states as "States", but in this book we refer to them as "nation-states" so as not to confuse the reader with the states within the United States.

2007 Cyber Attack on Estonia

One of the first cyber incidents instigated against another nation occurred in 2007 when Estonia was hit with a series of devastating cyberattacks. The impetus for the attacks was Estonia's decision to move a Soviet-Era war memorial from central Tallinn to a less prominent location. After protests from some ethnic-Russian Estonians and at the Estonian embassy in Moscow, the cyberattacks began. Over the next few days, massive denial of service attacks were launched against websites and email systems for government, banking, and news sites throughout Estonia. Though Estonia blamed Russia for the attacks (or for organizing or facilitating them), direct evidence was hard to come by and Russia denied its involvement.

These cyberattacks brought worldwide attention to the realm of cyber conflict. In 2008, following the creation of a unified policy on cyber defense, NATO established the Cooperative Cyber Defence Centre of Excellence in Tallinn (the CCDCoE), and that city has become a world leader in the study of cyber conflict.[2] The CCDCoE has produced the *Tallinn Manual 2.0*, a resource for policy and legal experts on how international law applies to cyber incidents.[3]

8.2 LAWS AND MEASURES RELATING TO NATION-STATE AND TERRORIST ACTIVITY

To put nation-state or terrorist conduct into context, let us first review existing laws and practices regarding conduct between nations, and how they might be applied to cyber actions and conflict.

There is no single body of law on this topic. Instead, several legal systems and international conventions are drawn upon to address such cyber actions, and as we will discuss, their application can be ambiguous. Applicable areas include:

- Criminal laws (federal and state)
- Civil laws and the Foreign Sovereign Immunities Act
- Military tribunals
- International treaties, agreements, and judicial processes
- International laws about starting and waging wars
- Principles surrounding espionage, clandestine, and covert operations.

These laws and measures span the spectrum from domestic legal action to international alternatives of increasing intensity. While these avenues may allow governments to take some legal, diplomatic, or operational action against state and terrorist-sponsored cybercrime, there is increasing international attention to the considerable gray areas with respect to what constitutes a lawful response.[4] Legal analysis is further complicated by the fact that nations are never transparent when their online activity is covert.

---

[2] For a full account of the events in Estonia, the CCDoE's overview can be found in: Rain Ottis, *Analysis of the 2007 Cyberattacks against Estonia from the Information Warfare Perspective*, https://ccdcoe.org/uploads/2018/10/Ottis2008_AnalysisOf2007FromTheInformationWarfarePerspective.pdf.

[3] The *Tallinn Manual 2.0* can be found at: https://ccdcoe.org/research/tallinn-manual/.

[4] Michael Schmitt, Grey Zones in the International Law of Cyberspace, *Yale Journal of International Law* (October 18, 2017), https://papers.ssrn.com/sol3/papers.cfm?abstract_id=3180687.

8.2.1 CRIMINAL LAWS

Many cyber actions by a foreign nation-state or terrorist will violate the criminal laws we covered in Chapter 6. In addition, federal and state codes have specific statutes relating to terrorism and espionage. Given the nature of the cases and resources involved, criminal investigations and prosecutions of nation-state and terrorist actors are more likely to be handled by federal authorities.[5] In this chapter, we will review some examples of recent federal charges against nation-state actors for cybercrime activity, including from North Korea, China, Russia, and Iran. We also will discuss cybercrime in the context of economic and strategic espionage.

At times, the U.S. Government has brought criminal actions against nation-state cybercrime actors knowing that an arrest was extremely unlikely, and knowing those chances would be lessened even further once the charges were made public. The publication of these indictments reflects a decision to use the "name-and-shame" technique. Through criminal charges, the U.S. exposes the attacking nation-state, letting the world know of its alleged wrongdoing. Occasionally, cases are revealed because a private party decides to publicize its investigative conclusions.

While the charged individuals may never be apprehended, naming and shaming allows the government to hold the foreign nation accountable in the court of public opinion, and may open up the possibility of alternate remedies, whether political, diplomatic, or economic. The name-and-shame approach also may lay the foundation to justify more secretive counteractions by the U.S. Government. We will discuss some of the considerations behind naming and shaming when we discuss charging decisions in Chapter 17.

8.2.2 CIVIL LAWS AND THE FOREIGN SOVEREIGN IMMUNITIES ACT (FSIA)

Legal action for damages against other nations is restricted by the Foreign Sovereign Immunities Act (FSIA).[6] This federal law limits the ability of individuals and corporations to sue foreign countries in U.S. courts.[7] Under FSIA, foreign sovereign countries have immunity from civil suit, but as with most rules, there are exceptions. One significant exception allows suits alleging a tort (civil wrong) committed on U.S. soil. In other words, if another nation-state's act causes injury, damage, or loss within the U.S., the injured parties can sue for damages or other relief in a civil action.

Whether a cyberattack committed by a foreign nation-state against victims in the U.S. is a tort committed on U.S. soil is an ongoing legal question. Recent cases have indicated that FSIA immunity applies to government attacks conducted from abroad, although there are strong arguments that FSIA should be interpreted differently for cyber activity.[8] Some legal analysts suggest FSIA would have to be amended to allow civil suits for cyber misconduct emanating from overseas.

We will talk about civil liability for cybercrime in greater detail in Chapter 9.

---

[5] The laws of at least 33 states contain charges for terrorism and some prosecutions may occur in state court. See Lisa Daniels, Prosecuting Terrorism in State Court, *Lawfare* (October 26, 2016), www.lawfareblog.com/prosecuting-terrorism-state-court.

[6] Foreign Sovereign Immunities Act, 28 U.S.C. §§ 1602–1611.

[7] The law does not limit the ability to sue individuals who work on behalf of a foreign nation-state, nor does it limit the ability to sue terrorist organizations since they are not sovereign foreign states.

[8] Scott Gilmore, Suing the Surveillance States: The (Cyber) Tort Exception to the Foreign Sovereign Immunities Act, *Columbia Human Rights Law Review*, Vol. 46, No. 3 (2015). Available at SSRN: https://ssrn.com/abstract=2622184.

Testing the Protections of the FSIA against International Cybercrime

The Democratic National Committee (DNC) filed a civil lawsuit in April 2018 against Russia, members of Russia's military, Wikileaks (a nonprofit organization that publishes leaked and stolen news and data), and members of the Trump campaign team. The complaint accused these parties of conspiring to hack into the DNC's email accounts, steal information, and publicize it in order to influence the outcome of the 2016 presidential election. The suit alleged these acts violated several federal cybercrime laws, including the Wiretap Act and Stored Communications Act (discussed in Chapter 6), as well as other federal and state crimes. The DNC sought damages for many forms of injury caused by the hack, an injunction against the defendants, as well as punitive damages.[9]

On July 30, 2019, the court dismissed the DNC's case. As to the counts against Russia, the court found that the FSIA barred the lawsuit because the tort exception does not apply unless the whole tort occurs in the U.S. In this case, Russia's alleged hacking activity was conducted from Russia. The causes of action against the other defendants were dismissed on various grounds, including First Amendment protections for the publication of stolen documents.[10]

8.2.3 INTERNATIONAL TREATIES, AGREEMENTS, AND JUDICIAL PROCESSES

International treaties, agreements, and judicial processes also play a part in the legal approach to nation- and terrorist-sponsored cybercrime.

Treaties. Some international defense or policing treaty-based organizations, such as NATO (the North Atlantic Treaty Organization) and Europol (the European Union's policing agency), may initiate an international response to a cyberattack upon a member nation. NATO, a political and military alliance between the U.S., Canada, and 27 European countries, has increased its focus on cyber threats. It now includes cyber defense as part of its core mission and is building a cyber command center that will be capable of mounting its own cyberattacks.[11] NATO is still clarifying its role with regard to different levels of potential cyberattacks. International alliances such as these may become integral to pre-empting cyberattacks among nations.

Diplomacy and sanctions. Diplomatic agreements also are used to counter nation-state cybercrime. For example, in the 2015 Obama–Xi agreement, the U.S. and China agreed to stop supporting cyber theft of intellectual property and trade secrets from one another.[12] Beyond official agreements, countries might use a range of diplomatic options to stop cybercrime, including negotiations, international pressure, and economic sanctions.

---

[9] For an overview of the DNC suit and its description of Russian cybercrime activities, see Brian Barrett, DNC Lawsuit Reveals Key Details about Devastating 2016 Hack, *Wired* (April 28, 2018), www.wired.com/story/dnc-lawsuit-reveals-key-details-2016-hack/.

[10] The DNC's complaint and the court's order of dismissal of July 30, 2019 can be found through: www.courtlistener.com/docket/6368549/democratic-national-committee-v-the-russian-federation/.

[11] Robin Emmott, *NATO Cyber Command to be Fully Operational in 2023*, Reuters (October 26, 2018), www.reuters.com/article/us-nato-cyber/nato-cyber-command-to-be-fully-operational-in-2023-idUSKCN1MQ1Z9.

[12] James A. Lewis, *Economic Impact of Cybercrime – No Slowing Down*, Center for Strategic and International Studies (CSIS) (February 2018), www.csis.org/analysis/economic-impact-cybercrime. Some instances of Chinese violations of this agreement have been reported in the U.S. media.

International courts. International courts have some power to adjudicate accusations of state-sponsored acts that injure or attack another nation. The International Court of Justice (the judicial branch of the United Nations)[13] and the International Criminal Court (created by the Rome Statute in 1998)[14] are bodies established to resolve violations of international laws among member states. No cyber case has yet been reviewed by these bodies, but increasing international pressure to resolve state-initiated cyberattacks may result in increased involvement of these international bodies.

8.2.4   LAWS AND PRINCIPLES OF SOVEREIGNTY AND WAGING WAR

Established laws relating to war and conflict between nations can apply to cyber activities. These are laws nations are supposed to consider before using military force (e.g. incursion, invasion, missile strike, etc.), and are now relevant to cyberattacks and responses to cyber-attacks. It might seem odd that wars – which include the intentional killing of people – are waged under the umbrella of laws, but this body of law exists to create diplomatic and humanitarian constraints when war is contemplated and pursued. And it is because of those laws that the many violent war-time acts, if done according to the rules of war, do not constitute crimes. The wars of today and tomorrow will unquestionably include cyberat-tacks, as illustrated by Figure 8.1.

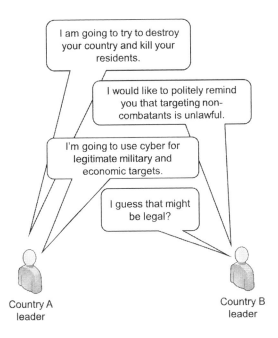

FIGURE 8.1   Cyber Operations and the Law of War.

---

[13] 193 of the 195 recognized countries in the world are members of the United Nations. Information on the U.N.'s International Court of Justice can be found at www.icj-cij.org/en.

[14] 120 nations are members of the International Criminal Court (ICC). The United States is not a member. For more information on the ICC, see www.icc-cpi.int.

Modern international laws are grounded in the basic principle of sovereignty. This principle holds that countries should not intrude upon the domestic affairs of others, invade their boundaries, attack their people and agents abroad, or encourage third parties to attack. Various legal compacts, treaties, and conventions have developed in an attempt to prevent wars between sovereign nations, and govern conduct during conflicts.

The first prong of the Law of War is *jus ad bellum*, the law governing conflict management and when nations can go to war or use force, as reflected in the United Nations Charter.[15]

The second law of war prong is *jus in bello*, which applies during a conflict and requires nation-states to adhere to targeting laws and customs (within the fight). This means targeting only necessary military objectives, distinguishing between military and civilian targets, and complying with principles of humanity and proportionality, while taking precautions in the attack.

Importantly for the purposes of this book, these laws of war frame acceptable responses to cyberattacks.

- When cyberattacks are conducted by foreign governments, do they violate the sovereignty of another nation?
- When would they constitute armed attacks to which nation-states can respond in self-defense; specifically, are the effects of the cyberattack tantamount to a kinetic attack which causes injury, death, or significant damage?
- What response by the victim state is authorized under the law?

In addition to contemplating questions of armed conflicts, it is important to recognize that economic attacks or data thefts may fall below these thresholds of armed conflict. Governments may call upon a range of other options, including responses in kind, other covert and clandestine operations, criminal prosecution, "name and shame", diplomatic, and economic responses.

8.2.5   Terrorism-Related Measures

Terrorists fall outside of traditional laws related to international conflict because they are not acting on behalf of a sovereign nation. Whatever their goals, they reject all laws of war by targeting, torturing, and killing civilians, noncombatants, prisoners, and children.

Terrorists can be criminally prosecuted using standard criminal statutes and procedures, as well as dedicated criminal statutes prohibiting terrorism. They also can be prosecuted under special procedures for terrorism cases within military tribunals, which are courts run by military personnel with fewer protections of defendants' rights than civilian courts.

Beyond prosecution in tribunals, there is an increasing continuum of measures that have been taken by the U.S. Government against terrorists, including extended detention and targeted killing. When these actions are pre-planned, classified documentation prior to the action typically sets forth the facts and legal authority to take the action.

---

[15] See U.N. Charter Article 2(4) and Article 51 for a further discussion of the concepts of sovereignty and self-defense.

8.2.6   Espionage, Clandestine and Covert Operations, and Propaganda

Espionage, including cyber espionage, is conducted by many nations but there is no international law that allows it. Much nation-state cyberactivity can be placed within this category, or within the related categories of clandestine, covert, or propaganda operations.

Espionage always has involved stealing information. Learning about another nation's sensitive military, technology, infrastructure, or communications information gives the spying nation the opportunity to adapt or enhance its own plans and equipment. Because governments store so much highly sensitive information digitally, nation-states use cyber actions, such as intrusions and data breaches, for espionage. Some nations also use their successful cyber infiltration and collection of intelligence to earn bragging rights over the victim nation and its security technologies. Other actors with interests in such material, such as terrorists and political insurgents, may use cybercrime to gain an intelligence advantage. Digital espionage also can aid with cultivating and blackmailing people who will become sources or agents for the spying country.

Two other areas of secretive nation-state activity that now extend to the cyber realm are clandestine and covert operations. A *clandestine* cyberattack (concealed from the target country and not detected) might mean infiltrating a nation's power grid and maintaining a secret, undetected ability to shut it down should the need arise. A *covert* cyberattack (where the effects are noticed but the attack cannot be attributed to an actor) might involve using malware to destroy a nuclear centrifuge, or using a cyberattack to engage the self-destruct mechanism during a missile launch.

Finally, propaganda operations might target a broader populace to influence their thoughts or votes, or sow discord.

If any of these cyber operations are detected and proven, they might be addressed through a continuum of options including criminal prosecution, counter-action in kind, and diplomatic or economic action.

East Germany, the Former Soviet Union, and the Cuckoo's Egg

In 1986, when computers were primarily found in universities, government agencies, and the largest corporations, one of the first cybercrime investigations took place. Clifford Stoll, a scientist at a national laboratory in California, started looking into a billing anomaly of 75 cents for use of the lab's computers. In trying to figure out the source of this small charge, he eventually uncovered a nation-state cyber attacker who was repeatedly committing electronic intrusions and espionage against university and military computers. At the time, the government was not equipped for this type of investigation, and so Stoll undertook most of the investigation himself. The attacker turned out to be an East German spy within the ambit of the former Soviet Union. Stoll tells the whole story in a fascinating book.[16] The methods of cybercrimes he describes have become a commonplace form of espionage today.

---

[16] Clifford Stoll, *The Cuckoo's Egg: Tracking a Spy through the Maze of Computer Espionage* (New York, Doubleday, 1989).

8.3 THE MOTIVES AND ACTIONS OF NATION-STATES

Now that we have examined the legal and diplomatic framework through which nations might take action, let us focus on the motives and actions of nation-states attacking organizations and individuals within our country. Nation-states represent significant cyber threats because they are motivated and resourced to invest in training, personnel, and equipment, and are willing to expend the time and effort to target an individual or organization or to achieve a result.

In Chapter 2, we introduced different forms of cybercrime and discussed the various motives of cybercrime actors. As we narrow our focus to nation-states, their motives bear both similarities and stark differences to those of the typical cybercriminal. These motives include:

- Generating funds
- Commercial espionage and theft of intellectual property
- Threatening or damaging infrastructure
- Advancing strategic interests.

Let's examine each of these motives, the types of cybercrime actions undertaken to further them, and some recent examples of how these government objectives have played out on the world stage.[17]

One important note first: No matter the actor or motives, the cybercrime economy is a consistent factor in this activity. Just like individual cybercriminals, governments (and terrorists) may obtain cybercrime services from criminals who are motivated by profit. A nation-state with any motive or objective can find tools and services within this economy, such as stolen data, the personal information of a target, malware, "hacker for hire" services, or virtual currency exchange services. As a result, state-sponsored cyber actions may intersect with the cybercrime economy and profit-minded cybercriminals.

8.3.1 GENERATING FUNDS

The characteristics of cybercrime that entice individuals to commit cyber offenses – profitability, anonymity and remote execution – make it an attractive method of illicit fundraising for some nations.

Corrupt nation-states. Governments that are not recognized by the international community or who are subject to economic sanctions may need additional revenue streams to fund military and domestic programs. Cybercrime conducted through state-sponsored operations can generate needed funds, often with the added satisfaction of stealing from an adversary. The anonymity of cybercrime allows such nation-states to maintain a veneer of respectability, and the ability to plausibly deny criminal activities.

Governments giving tacit approval. Ostensibly, legitimate governments may maintain their official distance from cybercrime-for-profit, yet turn a blind eye to it to obtain the benefits these crimes provide to their countries. For example, a country may allow thousands of cybercriminals within its borders to operate freely, so long as they confine their theft to victims *outside* the host country. These cybercriminals might collectively "earn" hundreds of millions of dollars, enhancing the country's economy by spending their ill-gotten gains on merchandise, eating at nice restaurants, and hiring contractors to improve houses. As indicated in Figure 8.2, an aggregate cyber theft from another country is an "import" of money, injected into the financial system and eventually spent in the local economy – a cybercrime version of trickle-down economics.

---

[17] For a listing of major cybercrime incidents, many of them involving nation-state activity, see the timeline maintained by CSIS at *Significant Cyber Incidents*, www.csis.org/programs/technology-policy-program/significant-cyber-incidents.

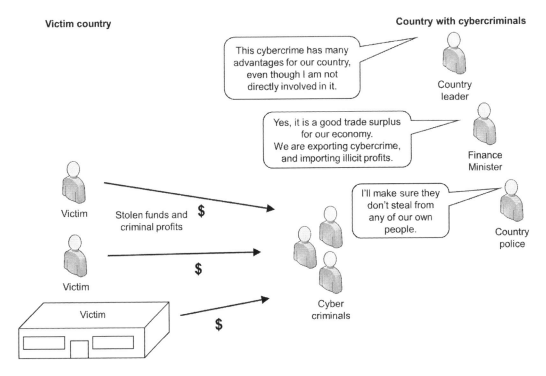

FIGURE 8.2   Cybercrime Profits Aid an Economy.

North Korea Uses Cybercrime for Profit

North Korea has become a formidable nation-state cyber actor, even as most of its population lives in poverty and without computers or access to the Internet. Some of North Korea's cybercrime activity was exposed in June 2018, when the U.S. filed a criminal complaint against Park Jin Hyok, a member of a North Korean "hacking team".[18] The complaint describes a wide variety of criminal acts, some for profit, some targeting the U.S. entertainment and defense industry. The investigation outlined in the complaint determined the defendant was acting under the direction of the North Korean government.[19]

The profit-motivated attacks included the theft of $81 million dollars from the central bank of Bangladesh. In February of 2016, Hyok and his team compromised the bank's computer terminals that interfaced with SWIFT, an interbank communication system. Using this access, the North Korean team fraudulently authorized over $850 million in funds transfers from the Bangladesh Bank to financial accounts they controlled in other Asian countries. A total of $81 million in transfers went through, and those funds ultimately were

[18] Press Release, U.S. Department of Justice, *North Korean Regime-Backed Programmer Charged in Conspiracy to Conduct Multiple Cyberattacks and Intrusions* (September 6, 2018), www.justice.gov/usao-cdca/pr/north-korean-regime-backed-programmer-charged-conspiracy-conduct-multiple-cyberattacks.
[19] For a description of North Korea's state-sponsored cyberattacks used to generate funds in violation of UN sanctions, see Edith M. Lederer, *UN Probing 35 North Korean Cyberattacks in 17 Countries*, Associated Press (August 12, 2019), https://apnews.com/ece1c6b122224bd9ac5e4cbd0c1e1d80.

unrecoverable. Further thefts were thwarted when the bank handling what would have been the next transfer out of Bangladesh detected a typo in the authorization instructions.[20]

The criminal complaint also alleges that Park and his co-conspirators helped develop "WannaCry", a form of ransomware that spread rampantly in 2017, encrypting user data, rendering it unusable, and extorting victims for a payout. The malware disrupted North Korea's adversaries around the world.

Aside from the profit-motivated bank fraud and ransomware activity, the complaint also alleges that Hyok and his government-sponsored hacking team attempted to compromise U.S. defense contractors by sending them malicious phishing emails in an attempt to access their computer systems.

8.3.2   NATION-STATE COMMERCIAL ESPIONAGE

As we discussed earlier, nation-states may use the reach of the Internet to gather intelligence and commit acts of security-related espionage. Some nation-states also use the Internet to engage in economic espionage and theft. Governments with central economies may have special motivations to use national resources to steal corporate intellectual property, using their cyber resources to steal various types of commercially valuable information from U.S businesses to benefit their state-owned enterprises.

A recent estimate of intellectual property theft through cybercrime puts the United States' annual losses at $10–12 billion, with many of these crimes emanating from China.[21] Some nations steal corporate intellectual property (such as scientific formulations, production methods and product designs) to give a competitive advantage to businesses in their own countries, which are likely to be state-controlled or otherwise provide benefits to nation-state leaders. Victim businesses and nations suffer when the products or services they have created and produced show up in the market at a cheaper price from companies in the thieving nation.

Corporate Espionage by the Chinese Military

In 2014, the U.S. Government took the unprecedented step of indicting Chinese military personnel for espionage and theft of intellectual property. The case, which was investigated by the FBI and prosecuted in federal court in the Western District of Pennsylvania, alleges that five officers in the Chinese army breached the computer systems of U.S. companies and stole data between 2006 and 2014.[22] The targeted companies were in the nuclear power, solar power, and steel industries, and the stolen data included trade secrets, communications, and other intelligence that benefited Chinese competitors,

---

[20] Serajul Quadir, *How a Hacker's Typo Helped Stop a Billion Dollar Bank Heist*, Reuters (March 10, 2016), www.reuters.com/article/us-usa-fed-bangladesh-typo-insight/how-a-hackers-typo-helped-stop-a-billion-dollar-bank-heist-idUSKCN0WC0TC.

[21] James A. Lewis, *Economic Impact of Cybercrime – No Slowing Down*, CSIS (February 2018), www.csis.org/analysis/economic-impact-cybercrime.

[22] Press Release, U.S. Department of Justice, *U.S. Charges Five Chinese Military Hackers for Cyber Espionage … for Commercial Advantage: First Time Criminal Charges Are Filed against Known State Actors for Hacking* (May 19, 2014), www.justice.gov/opa/pr/us-charges-five-chinese-military-hackers-cyber-espionage-against-us-corporations-and-labor.

including state-owned businesses. No defendants have been apprehended, and it is probable such apprehension was never a serious consideration. Still, the indictment represents a public statement by the U.S. that they investigated these thefts and found proof identifying Chinese Army personnel as the culprits.

8.3.3   ATTACKS ON INFRASTRUCTURE

At times, state-sponsored interest in cybercrime goes beyond preserving or advancing national interests, and it is used to weaken or damage rival countries. Attacks on critical infrastructure – utilities, communications networks, travel services, and financial systems – are a focal point of such cyber warfare. Consider the consequences if attackers could breach a network and gain access to control systems for a power grid, nuclear power reactor, or dam. A compromise of this nature has the potential to cause catastrophic damage and loss of life. Many other critical systems are controlled by computers and are theoretically susceptible to cyberattack, including air traffic control systems, traffic signals, subway controls, 911 emergency call and dispatch systems, processing networks for financial transactions and market trades, as well as computerized functions within individual planes, trains, and automobiles.

With any direct cyber-strike upon infrastructure, attackers also might attack methods of communication and conduct influence operations to increase the fear and confusion caused by such attacks.

There already have been several instances of nation-state attacks on critical infrastructure, including the below examples.

Stuxnet Attack Attributed to the U.S. and Israel

Stuxnet was a malware program discovered in 2010, which many believe was created by the U.S. and Israel to target Iran's development of nuclear capabilities. Stuxnet was designed to replicate and spread, but only take action if it encountered certain targets, including nuclear centrifuges made by Siemens, a major international engineering company. When Stuxnet found these centrifuges, it altered their speed, causing vibration and destruction. The attack is considered one of the first known forms of cyber sabotage by a nation-state, and Stuxnet is often described as a "cyber weapon".[23]

The methods of the Stuxnet attack may reveal something about the motives and actors behind it. The U.S. and Israel were immediate suspects because of their joint interest in stopping Iran from developing nuclear weapons. The nations who deployed Stuxnet also were motivated to hinder Iran without a physical strike and resulting casualties, and in an untraceable manner that avoided public and diplomatic backlash. Investigators and researchers consider factors such as these, as well as technical and physical clues to determine who is responsible.

[23] Kim Zetter, *Countdown to Zero Day: Stuxnet and the Launch of the World's First Digital Weapon* (New York, Crown Publishers, 2014).

Iranian Attack on New York Dam

In 2016, seven Iranians were indicted in federal court in New York for a variety of state-sponsored cyberattacks.[24] The charged activity included denial-of-service attacks against 46 U.S. companies, primarily in the financial sector. In addition, one defendant was charged with breaching the information and control systems for a dam located in the suburbs of New York City. The defendant repeatedly accessed information about the dam's operation and gained the ability to manipulate dam controls. Fortunately, the defendant was unable to open the dam's gates because, unbeknownst to him, manual repairs were being made at the time.

Russian Attacks on U.S. Infrastructure

As a final example, in 2018, the Russian Government conducted cyberattacks against the energy, nuclear, commercial facilities, water, aviation, and critical manufacturing sectors within the United States.[25] Using spearfishing emails, invitations to malicious websites, and other techniques, Russian actors spread malware to gain unauthorized access to critical infrastructure systems.

8.3.4   ATTACKS TO ADVANCE STRATEGIC INTERESTS

Along with generating funds and conducting espionage, nations engage in cybercrime for the purpose of furthering their strategic interests. On the global level, every nation wants to protect and advance its positions along the spectrum of allegiance and conflict that exists between countries. At one end of the spectrum is peace, harmony, and alliance, while at the other end is full-scale war. Cyber operations play a role everywhere on the spectrum, whether for intelligence-gathering, partnership-building, propaganda, espionage, attacks, or defense, as depicted in Figure 8.3.

Cyber actions taken to further a country's perceived interests may be spurred by nationalistic perceptions of pride, superiority, or resentment. Unlike profit-motivated cybercrimes, which generally follow predictable, short-term objectives, these motives might spur a country to devote considerable resources to accomplish specific ends, making their actions potentially more dangerous. An infiltration, attack, or capability may remain secret for years, waiting for special circumstances to arise.

With the Internet as a ready vehicle, nation-states (and terrorists) are increasingly working to improve their strategic positions by turning to online propaganda campaigns that can influence public perception and political outcomes, undermine stability, sow discord, instill fear, and recruit followers. Some cyber propaganda is conducted in illicit or illegal fashion through websites, social media, and email.

State-sponsored propaganda and psychological operations run the gamut from clumsy to sophisticated. Some efforts are poorly produced and disseminated, while others use the slick methods of commercial advertisers, marketers, and influencers to manipulate user perception and to optimize content for Internet search results and

---

[24] Press Release, U.S Attorney's Office, S.D.N.Y, *Manhattan U.S. Attorney Announces Charges against Seven Iranians for Conducting Coordinated Campaign of Cyber Attacks against U.S. Financial Sector* … (March 24, 2016), www.justice. gov/usao-sdny/pr/manhattan-us-attorney-announces-charges-against-seven-iranians-conducting-coordinated.

[25] Department of Homeland Security, Alert (TA18-074A), *Russian Government Cyber Activity Targeting Energy and Other Critical Infrastructure Sectors* (March 15, 2018), www.us-cert.gov/ncas/alerts/TA18-074A.

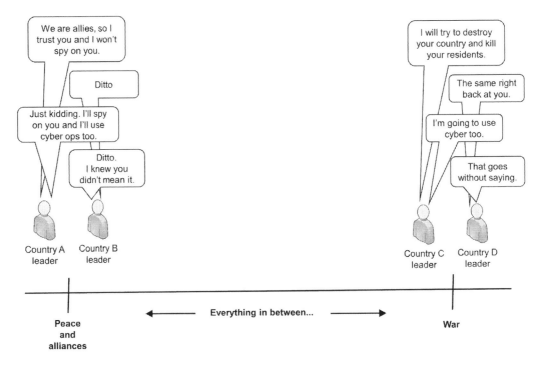

FIGURE 8.3   The Spectrum of Conflict.

high visibility on social media platforms. These techniques and results often are amplified using illegal means, such as false or stolen identities and hidden distribution methods (like botnets).

Below are some examples of cybercrimes undertaken by nations seeking to advance their strategic interests against other nations.

North Korea Cyberattacks for Revenge

We return to the 2018 criminal charges against North Korean Park Jin Hyok and his accomplices to see yet another motive in their prolific cybercrime conduct: revenge in response to a perceived personal and national insult.[26]

In addition to the other alleged crimes, Hyok and his team are charged with conducting a spate of cybercrimes against Sony Pictures, a major Hollywood movie studio. In late 2014 Sony Pictures was scheduled to release "The Interview", a comedy that lampooned North Korean leader Kim Jung-un and depicted his assassination. North Korea was not happy with this film, and soon Sony became the victim of a devastating cyberattack. Sony computers were damaged with malware and rendered inoperable, confidential and embarrassing emails were leaked to the public, unreleased movies were made available online, and acts of terrorism were threatened.

---

[26] Press Release, U.S. DOJ, *North Korean Regime-Backed Programmer Charged in Conspiracy to Conduct Multiple Cyberattacks and Intrusions* (September 6, 2018) www.justice.gov/usao-cdca/pr/north-korean-regime-backed-programmer-charged-conspiracy-conduct-multiple-cyberattacks.

Russian Interference in the U.S. 2016 Presidential Election

Intensive investigation by U.S national security agencies has made clear that the Russian Government took actions to influence public opinion and voter decisions during the 2016 presidential campaign and election, using technology for unprecedented reach.

The activity was first described in a public document from the U.S. intelligence community, which laid out how Russian President Vladimir Putin ordered an influence campaign in 2016 aimed at the U.S. presidential election, with a preference for then-candidate Donald Trump.[27]

Shortly thereafter, Robert Mueller was appointed by the U.S. Department of Justice as a special counsel to investigate Russia's actions and related issues. Over the next two years, his office investigated Russian and U.S. nationals for crimes related to the Russian cyber propaganda activity, and ultimately issued a report on the case in March 2019. The final report issued by Special Counsel Mueller clearly asserts that the Russian Government was behind some or all of the activities described in this indictment.[28]

The Mueller investigation resulted in two indictments directly exposing Russia's attempt to influence the U.S. election.

- In February of 2018, Special Counsel Mueller's office brought an indictment against three Russian businesses and 13 Russian nationals, accusing them of interfering with the U.S. presidential election and political process. The defendants were charged with wire fraud, bank fraud, and identity theft for posing as U.S. persons and creating false personas on social media in order to disseminate propaganda designed to manipulate the outcome of the election.[29] None of the individual defendants have been apprehended, though one of the organizations appeared in court through an attorney to contest the charges (and possibly to obtain information about the investigation).

- In July of 2018, Mueller's office brought an indictment against 12 members of Russian intelligence agency GRU for their alleged roles in computer hacking conspiracies aimed at interfering in the 2016 U.S. elections.[30] The indictment charges the defendants with computer crimes, identity theft, and money laundering. It alleges these intelligence officers, while acting in their official capacities, breached the computer networks of the Democratic Congressional Campaign Committee, the Democratic National Committee, and the presidential campaign of Hillary Clinton, stole information, and released it to the Internet. The defendants gained network access by conducting spear-phishing attacks, compromising email accounts and documents, and implanting malware, with the intent to steal data and interfere with the presidential election.

---

[27] In January 2017, the Office of the Director of National Intelligence issued a public, declassified document about Russia's actions. See Office of the Director of National Intelligence, *Background to "Assessing Russian Activities and Intentions in Recent US Elections": The Analytic Process and Cyber Incident Attribution* (January 6, 2017) www.dni.gov/files/documents/ICA_2017_01.pdf.

[28] Robert C. Mueller, *Report on the Special Investigation into Russian Interference in the 2016 Presidential Election* (Washington DC, March 2019), www.justice.gov/storage/report.pdf.

[29] The case is *U.S. v. Internet Research Agency LLC et al.*, (1:18-cr-32, District of Columbia) February 16, 2018.

[30] Press Release, Department of Justice, *Grand Jury Indicts 12 Russian Intelligence Officers for Hacking Offenses Related to the 2016 Election* (July 13, 2018), www.justice.gov/opa/pr/grand-jury-indicts-12-russian-intelligence-officers-hacking-offenses-related-2016-election

8.4 TERRORIST FUNDING, RECRUITING, VANDALISM, AND ATTACKS

Terrorists work to instill fear, cause disruption and damage, and inflict injury and death for the sake of an extremist agenda. They increasingly use cybercrime to accomplish these goals. Terrorists will attempt to use all of the tools and methods of both common cybercriminals and nation-states to earn money, recruit members, develop attack plans, and execute attacks on victims.

8.4.1 TERRORIST FUNDING

Terrorist groups need to fund their activities, so they look for secretive ways to earn, launder, and move money. The U.S. and the international community recognized the significance of terrorist funding activity after 9/11, where analysis of the money terrorists used to train, live, and travel was traced around the world. From this investigation, the discipline of counter-terrorist financing (CTF) was born.

Because cybercrime and identity theft are lucrative, and can be accomplished from any location, it is no surprise that terrorists use these crimes to generate funds. Frauds against hated countries also serve their ultimate goal of causing harm. Many cybercrime skills are applicable to terrorist operations and vice versa, including Internet anonymity and money laundering techniques. Along with earning money through cybercrime, terrorists use these skills to communicate with co-conspirators, disguise operational payments and funds transfers, spread propaganda or fear, and recruit new members.

Credit Card Fraud Funds al-Qa'ida in Iraq

In the early 2000s, a Moroccan-born teenager living in London helped Islamic extremists establish a major recruiting, operational, and communications presence online. Younis Tsouli began posting videos, weapons, and bomb information, and propaganda about terrorist activity that he found online. He also frequently talked about hacking and technology. Over time, he built websites and online forums for al-Qa'ida in Iraq. As the moderator, he enabled thousands of extremists and sympathizers around the world to communicate with one another, creating one of the earliest examples of broad integration of the Internet into terrorist operations.

To fund this jihadist web presence, Tsouli and two accomplices purchased stolen credit card account information from black market forums online. When arrested in 2005, the three men had a stockpile of over 37,000 stolen accounts through which more than $3.5 million in fraudulent charges were made. The group earned money by using the compromised accounts to gamble online on popular poker websites. They transferred their winnings to and between bank accounts to launder the funds. Some of the stolen money was used to pay for over 180 websites and hosting services. Other funds were used to purchase equipment for terrorists.[31]

[31] Michael Jacobson, Terrorist Financing on the Internet, *Combatting Terrorism Center (CTC) Sentinel*, Vol. 2, No. 6, West Point (June 2009), https://ctc.usma.edu/terrorist-financing-on-the-internet/.

8.4.2   Recruitment

The anonymity and reach of the Internet allow terrorist recruiters both to broadcast their agendas widely and direct their recruitment efforts individually. Using anonymous and encrypted online platforms, terrorist recruiters issue propaganda about their cause to attract the attention of potential sympathizers. When a newcomer engages, recruiters can switch to personalized messaging to develop relationships and start to indoctrinate. These tactics can be especially effective with vulnerable individuals, including teenagers and those who feel marginalized.[32]

8.4.3   Cyber Vandalism and Hacktivism

To promote their extreme positions and objections to particular organizations, governments or individuals, terrorist groups have used illegal access to deface websites, social media, and email accounts. At times, stolen data has been posted to embarrass or expose their targets. Extremist hacktivists also have conducted denial-of-service attacks.

8.4.4   Inciting Local Attacks

A disturbing recent trend is the use of the Internet to incite terrorist followers to conduct attacks in their local communities. This approach leads to unpredictable threats that could be carried out anywhere in the world. Instead of engaging in operational planning that requires time, money, and preparation, terrorist groups can simply encourage their online recruits, who devise and fund their own attack scenarios.

Cyber Terrorist was a Hacker, ISIS Recruiter, and Attack Promoter

The activities of Junaid Hussain, a British resident of Pakistani descent, demonstrates the role of cybercrime in the world of terrorism. A reclusive gamer growing up, Hussain got into hacking as a way to retaliate against other players stealing from his game accounts. As a teenager in 2010, he took interest in reports of violent attacks against Islamic countries and began to use his technical skills against those he held responsible. He eventually formed a hacktivist team with other teenagers and targeted the websites and computer systems of government agencies and right-wing groups. Many of his hacking exploits were undertaken in collaboration with other hacktivist groups, like Anonymous. Eventually, he worked up to stealing and publicly posting U.K. Prime Minister Tony Blair's digital address book, as well as launching a successful denial-of-service attack against the U.K.'s Counter Terrorism Command. Hussain was arrested in 2012 and briefly went to jail for these crimes.

Not long after his release Hussain traveled to Syria where he joined up with the Islamic State (ISIS). He became a prolific online recruiter and the head of the "Islamic State Hacking Division". Hussain coached several recruits in the U.S, U.K., and Australia to conduct physical attacks in their local areas. These included attempted shootings and stabbings of police officers in Boston, Massachusetts and

---

[32] The online recruitment efforts of the Islamic State (ISIS) are described in Tailored Online Interventions: The Islamic State's Recruitment Strategy, by J.M. Berger, *CTC Sentinel*, Vol. 8, No. 10, Combating Terrorism Center at West Point (Oct. 2015), https://ctc.usma.edu/tailored-online-interventions-the-islamic-states-recruitment-strategy/.

Garland, Texas (the recruits were killed in the return fire), and planned mass shootings, bombings, and attacks on military personnel in several different countries. Hussain also posted a list of over a thousand U.S. military personnel, culled from stolen
customer data, and threatened to kill them.

In 2015, at the age of 21, Hussain was killed by a U.S. missile while leaving an Internet café in Syria.[33]

8.5   WHAT TO DO IF THE INVESTIGATION LEADS TO A NATION-STATE OR TERRORIST

As this chapter has addressed, a cybercrime under investigation might ultimately lead to
evidence of nation-state or terrorist involvement. As we have seen, government and terrorist
actors engage in cyber frauds to earn money, and may use the general cybercrime economy
to obtain data, tools, or launder funds. They also commit cybercrimes for a host of other
reasons, including to penetrate corporate networks and accounts to view or steal data. Such
activity might be reported to or detected by investigators at any level. If the ensuing investigation suggests nation-state or terrorist cyber activity, investigators should recognize this
case is a national security matter and know what to do and whom to contact.

If investigation reveals facts tending to implicate a nation-state or terrorist group, the
FBI must be notified, and it may also be appropriate to notify the Department of Homeland Security. The FBI is a lead law enforcement agency for such crimes and is also our
domestic intelligence agency. It has the resources and experience to evaluate investigators'
suspicions of nation-state or terrorist involvement and, if needed, can enlist the assistance
of other intelligence agencies such as the Central Intelligence Agency and National Security
Agency. Consulting and coordinating with the FBI ensures investigative actions and disclosures are in accord with national security interests, and that these attacks receive the special
investigative attention they deserve.

8.6   CONCLUSION

Nation-state and terrorist cybercrime activity is prolific, though much of it never sees the light
of day. Still, cybercrime investigators might happen upon it while investigating. Such activity
might be simple fraud or a sophisticated intrusion. It might be low or high-impact, motivated
by the desire to influence, embarrass, scare, disrupt, or even cause injury and death.

There are many areas of law that might come to bear on state and terrorist-sponsored cyberattacks. Diplomatic or economic pressure, criminal charges, civil complaints, military tribunals,
and international law may be used to determine appropriate responses to cyberattacks.

Nation-state attackers are formidable but also fallible, and many criminal investigations and
prosecutions have brought their motives and actions to light. State actors and terrorists use cybercrime as a powerful tool for many objectives, including generating funds, stealing intellectual property, vandalizing websites, issuing propaganda, and attacking infrastructure. Because these crimes
may victimize everyday people or companies, investigators may run across pieces of these schemes.
Any suspicion of nation-state or terrorist involvement should be reported to the FBI.

---

[33] John P. Carlin and Garrett M. Graff, *Dawn of the Code War: America's Battle Against Russia, China and the Rising Global Threat* (New York, Public Affairs, 2018).

9 Civil and Regulatory Implications of Cybercrime
Cyberlaw in the Civil and Regulatory Sectors

This chapter is primarily for:

- Investigators seeking to understand cybercrime's impact in the context of civil law and liability
- Investigators interested in regulations related to cybercrime and their enforcement
- Law enforcement considering a civil asset forfeiture action and those wishing to learn about asset forfeiture procedures.

9.1 INTRODUCTION

Cybercrime is unlike most other crimes in that it frequently implicates aspects of civil law and regulatory law, so an understanding of these legal disciplines is valuable for any cybercrime investigation. In this chapter we will survey civil and regulatory concepts and requirements relating to cybercrime.

Because cybercrime so often involves theft of data and money, affected parties often turn to civil remedies to recover their losses. Those harmed by cybercrime may look to compensation from three places: the cybercriminal who committed the intentional crime (tort), another victim whose negligent cybersecurity may have allowed the crime to occur, or an insurer who contractually promised to cover the loss. Other contractual relationships also may lead to civil litigation if they include conditions related to cybersecurity. We will review civil actions for intentional harm, negligence, and breach of contract in this chapter, as well as cybercrime-specific statutory causes of action.

Federal and state governments have instituted numerous regulations requiring businesses, organizations, and public agencies to maintain certain levels of cybersecurity and to report the compromise of consumer data. Additional regulations govern specific industries, such as the financial and healthcare sectors, requiring safeguards for the sensitive information they maintain. This chapter will provide an overview of those regulations.

9.2 ATTORNEY–CLIENT PRIVILEGE

The principle of attorney–client privilege protects the confidentiality of communications between attorneys and clients. The privilege allows clients to provide candid, accurate information to their attorneys without worry that detrimental information will be exposed to the public or an opposing party. Attorneys, in turn, can objectively investigate on behalf of their clients and provide an accurate assessment of the facts, which is essential to guiding the case. This is a principle with legal authority. Courts will protect attorney–client confidentiality unless there is a compelling need otherwise (such as to protect someone's safety or if the communications are about ongoing criminal activity).

Attorney–client privilege can be very important for civil and regulatory cybercrime investigations. If a private sector investigation is conducted under privilege – such as an attorney-directed investigation in anticipation of litigation – negative facts might be shielded from discovery. Attorney–client privilege is not absolute and cannot be used by a client to selectively and misleadingly provide only helpful information during litigation.

If privilege applies, it belongs to the client. If the client is a company or other entity, the privilege belongs to the entity, not to individuals working on behalf of it. In other words, employees facing civil or criminal liability might need their own attorneys to engage in privileged communication and receive legal advice.

Whether or not attorney–client privilege is asserted, investigative reports and statements might still become part of the litigation. For example, a court might rule the privilege does not apply, or the client might waive the privilege to publicize favorable facts. A corporate client also might be encouraged or pressured to waive the privilege when the target of government investigation.

9.3 CIVIL LAWSUITS AGAINST CYBERCRIMINALS: ACTIONS FOR INTENTIONAL TORTS

Someone who commits a cybercrime not only has violated a criminal law, but likely also has committed a civilly wrongful act (intentional tort) against an organization or individual, as we covered in Chapter 5.[1]

Where private parties are wronged by intentional cyber torts, there may be instances when they may consider bringing a civil action against the individual(s) believed to be responsible. Some such suits arise from instances of:

- Harassment
- Stalking
- Defamation
- Revenge porn
- Computer system intrusion or data theft, including that committed by a former employee, partner, or significant other.

Victims of crimes might prefer that law enforcement conduct the investigation and bring a prosecution, but that outcome is not always possible. Although private investigation and civil litigation can be expensive, victims might undertake these measures when there is no law enforcement investigation, the investigation is limited, or the identity of the perpetrator is clear.

There are often many hurdles to bringing a successful civil action against criminals, especially in cybercrime cases. For example, the cybercriminal might not be identifiable, or might be beyond the practical power of a civil court. Even when the identity of the

---

[1] In Chapter 8, we mentioned a civil lawsuit for intentional torts related to nation-state cybercrime activity in which the Democratic National Committee (DNC) filed a civil lawsuit against Russia, Russian nationals, and others for hacking them (and conspiring to do this) during the 2016 presidential election campaign. Suing a nation-state involves additional legal issues, including the concept of sovereignty and protections under the Foreign Sovereign Immunities Act.

cybercriminal cannot be determined, however, parties still might bring a civil action for an intentional tort committed by the unknown actor. Such lawsuits might be filed in order to:

- Seize or disable information systems being used to commit crimes
- Disable spam servers, botnets, and servers that control malware
- Issue subpoenas to third parties, particularly to learn the criminal's identity.

A suit against an unidentified defendant for these purposes is known as a "John Doe" lawsuit. We will discuss how these suits work in more detail in Chapter 12. Whether this type of civil litigation is warranted or reasonable depends upon the circumstances and goals of the litigant.

Microsoft's John Doe Lawsuits to Issue Subpoenas and Dismantle Botnets

Microsoft, the giant of computer operating systems and software, has been leading the way in civil actions against unidentified cybercriminals, using the power of the civil courts to fight cybercrime.

Microsoft started these efforts in 2008, suing anonymous botmasters and obtaining court orders to seize their domains.[2] With these orders, Microsoft has been able to redirect botnet traffic from victim computers to servers controlled by Microsoft, thereby alleviating the harm of the malware and botnet, and gathering valuable intelligence. The company is filing these suits using civil causes of action under the Computer Fraud and Abuse Act (CFAA) and Electronic Communications Privacy Act (ECPA) (statutes we discussed in Chapters 6 and 7), as well as intellectual property laws relating to trademark and copyright.

In August 2016, Microsoft sued a number of John Doe cybercrime defendants known collectively as "Fancy Bear" or "Strontium" and believed to be affiliated with Russia's foreign intelligence agency (GRU).[3] This group engaged in phishing activity to create phony political websites designed to influence elections in the United States. The indictments and the report of Special Counsel Robert Mueller (discussed in Chapter 8) seem to confirm that this group was, in fact, made up of GRU officers.

Microsoft has continued similar civil legal actions, including against groups associated with Iranian hackers.[4]

9.4 "HACKING BACK": INTENTIONAL ACTS BY CYBERCRIME VICTIMS THAT COULD INCUR LIABILITY

In Chapter 5, we introduced the concepts of self-defense, justification, and necessity, including that the law generally allows self-defense from physical attacks when reasonable and necessary.[5]

---

[2] Microsoft Digital Crimes Unit, https://3er1viui9wo30pkxh1v2nh4w-wpengine.netdna-ssl.com/wp-content/uploads/prod/sites/358/2019/01/DCU-Overview-2019_.pdf.

[3] For an example of one of Microsoft's John Doe civil complaints, see its filing regarding Strontium at *Microsoft v. John Does 1–2 Controlling a Computer Network and Thereby Injuring Plaintiffs and its Customers*, Civil Action No: 1:16-CV-993 (U.S. District Court, EDVA), www.noticeofpleadings.com/strontium/#.

[4] Tom Burt, New Steps to Protect Customers from Hacking, *Microsoft on the Issues* (March 27, 2019), https://blogs.microsoft.com/on-the-issues/2019/03/27/new-steps-to-protect-customers-from-hacking/.

[5] For contrast, consider that in Chapter 8 we introduced the discussion about what nation-states might have the power to do when faced with cyberattacks, including responding in-kind. Individuals and private entities do not have this legal power.

The defense of justification is not just about using physical force, but can arise regarding property rights, such as if a person claims an otherwise unlawful property crime was justified and lawful due to necessity. Suppose a family breaks into an abandoned apartment for shelter to avoid a rising flood. If this act was done to save their lives, and they had no other choice, it might be a valid defense to criminal charges of trespass or burglary. From a civil perspective, they might still be required to compensate the owners.

Along these lines, there are some who advocate for a private right or ability to "hack back" or attack cyber attackers in order to defend oneself from and combat cybercrime. Under this theory, the victim, due to necessity, might take otherwise unlawful action to reveal clues about the attacker's identity, destroy or disable the attacker's system, or erase stolen data so that the attacker cannot use it. The necessity justification might be based on the urgency of the situation and government's lack of response.

While a victim's temptation to hack back is understandable, it is likely to expose the victim to civil and criminal liability.

First, any legal justification to defend oneself against physical threats is usually defined by statute. Whether current statutes on justification apply to cyberattacks is an open legal question. If they do not apply, any action by the victim to hack back likely will constitute a criminal offense under federal and state law.

Even if justification law does apply in the cyber realm, consider that even the well-established principle of justification in a physical encounter is typically hotly contested.[6] The issues surrounding justification will be all the more complicated when the actions in question are conducted through cyberspace. For these reasons and more, the U.S. Department of Justice advises not to attack back, advising that doing so would likely be illegal under U.S. and foreign laws.[7]

The victim also would assume all civil legal risks, including for potential torts against the original cyber attacker or for intruding upon the rights of innocent third parties.

9.5   CYBERCRIME STATUTORY CAUSES OF ACTION

Victims of cybercrime also can take action against cybercriminals using civil causes of action that are set forth within federal and state statutes. These statutory claims, often included within criminal laws defining cybercrime offenses, typically allow victims (or other affected individuals and entities) to seek monetary compensation for losses suffered, as well as court-ordered injunctions to stop ongoing harmful activity.

Under federal law, cybercrime-related civil claims are available for violations of several statutes, including:

- The Computer Fraud and Abuse Act, 18 U.S.C. § 1030(g)
- The Stored Communications Act, 18 U.S.C. § 2707
- The Wiretap Act, 18 U.S.C. § 2520
- Sexual Exploitation of Children and related laws, 18 U.S.C. § 2255
- Racketeer Influenced and Corrupt Organizations Act (RICO), 18 U.S.C § 1964.

Many state laws also authorize civil causes of action for cybercrime conduct. In some states, civil claims may be filed for specific forms of cyberattack, such as dissemination of

---

[6] Although reasonable physical force is generally legally allowed to defend oneself from a physical attack, in practice such instances can be highly controversial. A person may claim she used force lawfully but still face civil or even criminal charges.

[7] U.S. Department of Justice, *Best Practices for Victim Response and Reporting of Cyber Incidents*, Version 2.0 (September 2018), www.justice.gov/criminal-ccips/file/1096971/download.

malware or spyware, phishing emails, transmission of spam communication, and computer intrusions of various kinds. Other state laws offer victims the opportunity to make civil claims for traditional offenses that can be committed online, such as identity theft, harassment, stalking, and menacing.[8]

9.6 NEGLIGENT CYBER TORTS: THE REASONABLE PERSON AND THE STANDARD OF CARE

Much civil litigation relating to cybercrime concerns the issue of cybersecurity negligence and whether security measures were reasonable. A cybercrime victim might allege negligence for allowing a data breach or fraud to occur. For example, a consumer whose personal information was stolen from an organization in a data breach may sue the breached party for damages. Or, an entity that had money stolen because of a cybercrime may sue a business partner whose lax security unwittingly allowed the crime to happen.

We introduced the concept of negligence in Chapter 5, as well as the three elements of a civil action for negligence: existence of a *duty*, *breach* of the duty, and *harm* caused by the breach. Whether there was a breach of duty owed to another depends upon the "standard of care" that a "reasonable person" would have used under the circumstances. In other words, if someone had a legal obligation to exercise care towards another, what would a sensible, reasonable person (or company) have done in that situation? When it comes to negligence leading to cybercrime, technology and information security principles inform the appropriate standard of care and what is reasonable.

So, to allege negligence as a cause for cybercrime, the factual and legal questions that need to be examined include:

- *Did the defendant have a legal duty to the plaintiff relating to the cybercrime and cybersecurity?*
- *Was that duty breached?*
  - *Was the level of security reasonable?*
    - *What was the level of security of the defendant?*
    - *What should the level of security of the defendant have been?*
- *Did the breach of that duty (the existence of a lower-than-reasonable security level) cause the harm?*

The mere fact that a harm occurred, or that someone is victimized, does not by itself mean negligence liability exists for that harm. After all, a review of the facts and applicable standards might indicate that a person or company behaved reasonably. Getting to these facts requires investigation, as indicted in Figure 9.1.

9.6.1 NEGLIGENCE THAT DIRECTLY CAUSES THE HARM

Before we examine negligence claims stemming from cybercrime activity, let us look at some examples of traditional negligence and how they might compare to the cyber world. In doing so, it is important to consider technology basics (covered in Chapter 3) and information security principles (covered in Chapter 4). Analyzing the potential civil consequences of a cybercrime depends upon an understanding of technology and the best practices to secure it.

---

[8] For a listing of states with civil laws against harassment and stalking, see: The National Center for Victims of Crime, https://victimsofcrime.org/our-programs/stalking-resource-center/stalking-laws/civil-stalking-laws-by-state.

FIGURE 9.1   Arguing Civil Liability and Negligence.

Most cases of negligence involve a single actor. One person or business does something without using reasonable care, and that action causes harm to another. In brick-and-mortar liability situations, we consistently use our everyday knowledge to analyze these types of situations and apply the principles of negligence law to them.

For example, drivers who cause an accident by violating traffic laws, or by making poor or inexperienced driving decisions, may be civilly liable for any resulting injuries or property damage. They were negligent, they caused the injury, they bear liability.

Landlords or property owners who do not maintain their premises safely may be civilly liable to tenants, workers, or guests if the unsafe conditions cause injury or damage (or if they allow criminals to enter and cause harm, as we will discuss shortly).

Similarly, to analyze single-actor civil liability following a cybercrime, we would want to understand the relevant technology and standards for information security and cybercrime prevention methods. We also would want to know whether human error was a factor (like with the driver), as well as whether security risks were adequately calculated and addressed (like with the landlord). We then could assess the facts surrounding the cybercrime and evaluate whether the defendant's technology and security met the applicable standards and, if not, whether that deficiency (or something else) is what caused the harm to the plaintiff.

9.6.2   NEGLIGENCE THAT ALLOWS THE COMMISSION OF A CRIME BY A THIRD PARTY

Now let's look at negligence with respect to the actions of third parties.

Consider three sets of fact patterns. These are situations where the negligent party's action does not directly cause harm but enables a third party to cause harm to others. In these examples, we are focusing only on the negligence liability, and do not examine the liability of the criminal (third party) committing the harmful act.[9]

9.6.2.1 Theft of Automobile

First, consider traditional negligence regarding the criminal theft of an automobile by a third party and resulting harms under two scenarios:

- Andy Victim is driving his car reasonably and safely, but is carjacked at gunpoint and thrown out of the car. The carjacker is chased by police, flees, crashes, and injures bystanders, who eventually sue everyone involved, including Andy Victim, the carjacker, and the police. There probably would be no civil liability for Andy Victim.
- Bradley Victim leaves his car running and unlocked in a busy street in a high-crime neighborhood, in violation of a state law that prohibits leaving keys in an unattended car. He did this to run into a store and make a quick purchase. The car is stolen, and the thief causes a collision that results in injuries to innocent bystanders, who sue everyone. There would probably be some civil liability for Bradley Victim, for negligently failing to secure his car.

9.6.2.2 Premises Liability

Next, let us look at intentional criminal acts by a third party with respect to premises liability, and the landlord's duty to maintain a certain degree of security.

- Building Manager Aardvark Real Estate has invested in security protections, including security cameras, secure and functioning locks on the outer doors to the building and individual apartment doors, and safety training for residents and staff. A criminal gains entry by "piggybacking" behind a resident who enters through the building's front doors. Then the criminal tricks a resident into opening his apartment door, enters, assaults, and robs the resident. It will be difficult to show Aardvark Realty is civilly liable for these harms.
- Building Manager Broken Properties has not repaired the security cameras or front door lock that were vandalized long ago. A criminal walks in through the unlocked front door, goes to the victim's apartment, easily kicks in the door (the lock and door frame are weak), and then assaults and robs the resident. Here, it could be argued that building security was inadequate and negligent, which could mean civil liability for the building manager.

9.6.2.3 Cybercrime Liability

Finally, we turn to civil liability with respect to cybercrime. Consider two lawyers who each have a duty to protect their clients and safeguard client funds, confidences, and communications. One is more likely to bear some civil liability for their acts or omissions.

---

[9] Previously, we covered civil liability for intentional cybercrimes, such as for the intentional tort of theft if a criminal stole from a victim. Here, we focus on negligence liability. Each example involves a criminal committing an intentional crime and tort that was enabled by another party's negligence. The role of the negligent party is significant if a victim seeks to recover money damages, as the criminal would likely be "judgment proof", meaning unwilling or unable to pay anything if found civilly liable.

- Lawyer Coy Rohn does not understand technology, is unaware of common frauds that target lawyers, does not warn his clients about these frauds, has malware on his computer, and has poorly secured his email account. His email account is compromised ("hacked"). The cyber attacker impersonates Rohn and directs Rohn's client to wire funds to criminal associates, which the client does and the funds are stolen. When the fraud is detected, Rohn does nothing to investigate or recover the funds.
- Lawyer Darrence Clarrow has taken reasonable steps to secure her systems, warns her clients about common frauds, and takes reasonable measures to prevent intrusion of her computer system and email accounts. A cybercriminal impersonates Darrence in order to misdirect and steal funds. When Darrence learns of this, she takes steps to prevent the fraud and investigate and recover the funds.

From these scenarios, we get a sense of how negligence might be evaluated when a cybercrime occurs. In determining whether a person or business met the reasonable standard of care, or whether the party might be civilly liable for negligence, investigators might consider:

- *What cybersecurity was in place?* Were appropriate hardware and software being used, were security policies and protocols created and enforced, and was human error a factor?
- *What security would a sensible, reasonable party have used?* Here, the answer requires analysis of standards imposed by information security principles, regulation, best practices, and commonsense risk evaluation. Sometimes even the best security can be compromised by cyber attackers, and if the security was appropriate and reasonable, there would be no liability.
- *Did the party's actions cause the harm in question or enable someone else to cause the harm?* In cybercrime-related cases, this analysis can be complex. First, there must be evidence tying the insufficient security to the cybercrime, and then evidence tying the cybercrime to the damages. Answering this question may require technical expertise and other forms of expert analysis.

This process of investigating negligence liability is demonstrated in Figure 9.2 using the business email compromise fraud we just discussed.

9.7 ACTIONS UNDER CONTRACT LAW

Contracts and agreements for services between organizations and individuals may specify conditions that would be relevant in the event of a cybercrime.[10] If a party to a business or services contract becomes the victim of a cybercrime, the contract may be analyzed for promises relating to security and remediation.

Some contracts are entered into with deliberation and negotiation and are affirmed with signatures. Other contracts are accepted almost by default, such as when we open an email account, social media account, or download software, and we click on an "accept" button to indicate we agree the company's terms of service. These default conditions are "take it or leave it" boilerplate requirements the user must accept if he or she wants to use the service or product.

Both types of contract may have relevant provisions if a cybercrime occurs and would have great weight in evaluating liability. If either party's conduct was in breach of the

---

[10] As we learned in Chapter 5, the law generally allows parties to enter into agreements with one another and set the terms of those agreements, so long as the terms are legal and meet basic standards of fairness.

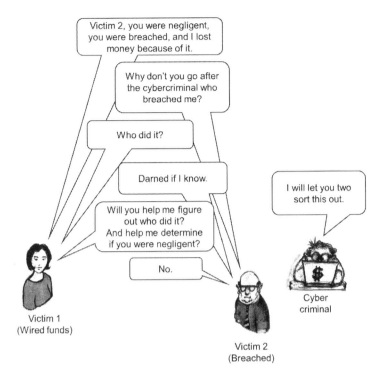

FIGURE 9.2 Why Civil Liability.

promises and conditions made in the contract, it might be liable for the resulting damage. But if the contract limits or disclaims liability, it may be impossible to recover anything.

Contracts that might implicate cybercrime include "terms of service" that users accept without reading, boilerplate agreements small businesses must accept if they want to do business with a vendor, and complex contracts between large businesses where all terms are bargained for. Subjects of these contracts may include:

- Internet and phone services
- Email services
- Website hosting services
- Cloud computing services, including data centers
- IT maintenance services
- Any other type of IT service or cybersecurity service.

Contracts might have clauses specifically anticipating cybercrime and its potential consequences, such as:

- Security requirements and standards
- Promised availability for a service (e.g. permissible downtime following a cyberattack, financial responsibility for outages that cause losses)
- Duties of each party in the event of a data breach or other cybercrime, including notification and investigation requirements
- Agreements about who bears what costs, including the costs of investigation, remediation, and indemnification (liability to third parties)
- Limitations of liability for cybercrime incidents.

When a cybercrime occurs, the victim can examine any contracts with parties who have a connection to the cybercrime to determine whether they breached the terms of the contract and might be liable for the resulting damages.

9.7.1   CYBER INSURANCE POLICIES

Insurance policies are a form of contract that are of considerable importance with regard to cybercrime. An insurance policy is a contract between the insured and the insurance company. The insured makes certain representations that help the insurance company gauge potential risk, and the insurance company promises to cover the cost of certain adverse events. Older policies may not have anticipated cybercrime, leading to ambiguity about what cyber injury they cover if an incident occurs. Nowadays, insurance companies sell policies specifically designed to cover costs relating to cybercrime.

After a cybercrime, the insured may submit a claim for reimbursement. The terms of the insurance policy (contract) and the surrounding facts will be important to the insurance company's determination of whether to honor or deny the claim, including:

- Whether the policy specifically includes or excludes cybercrime events or is ambiguous
- Whether the insured provide accurate information about its cybersecurity posture when it applied for or renewed the policy?
- How the cybercrime occurred.

For cyber-insurance policies, the insurance company will probably inquire (both before issuing a policy and after a claim) about the insured company's cybersecurity practices. Questions likely will include whether the insured has written policies regarding information security, what steps the company takes to securely transfer funds, and whether it uses two-factor authentication for its online accounts. If the insured company says these measures were in place, but investigation reveals the crime occurred because these protections were *not* in place, the insured may have difficulty collecting on the claim.

9.8   CIVIL ACTIONS FOR ASSET FORFEITURE BY THE GOVERNMENT

Prior chapters discussed the criminal prosecution of cybercriminals, a powerful legal tool that can be used to detain individuals and seize evidence for use at trial. But despite its power, criminal law often struggles to address the illegal profits and assets successful criminals amass, including cars, boats, houses, businesses, and funds.

Civil actions by the government can recoup these illegally obtained assets, allowing prosecutors to ensure criminals do not profit from the crimes, as illustrated in Figure 9.3. These actions can temporarily freeze assets to prevent them from being secreted away, as well as permanently seize property, bank accounts, and even Internet domains.

9.8.1   FEDERAL AND STATE LAWS

Federal law provides prosecutors with convenient and powerful tools for civil asset forfeiture. Federal forfeiture can be pursued within a criminal proceeding (criminal forfeiture), through a separate civil suit (civil judicial forfeiture) or as an administrative action for certain contraband, funds, and vehicles (administrative forfeiture).[11] Many state laws are less

---

[11] For a description of the types of asset forfeiture proceedings used by the U.S. Department of Justice's Asset Forfeiture Program, see www.justice.gov/afp/types-federal-forfeiture.

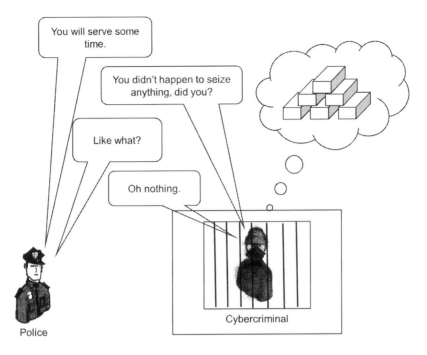

FIGURE 9.3   Asset Forfeiture.

accommodating to the government, and there are major differences among them. Some states require the defendant to be criminally convicted before civil forfeiture of his property can be pursued. Moreover, even with strong forfeiture laws, state prosecutors may lack the resources to conduct civil litigation.[12]

9.8.2   TEMPORARY RESTRAINING ORDERS (TROs)

Civil law has mechanisms to deal with defendants who might hide and dissipate their assets to keep them from being seized. One method is to seek an *ex parte* temporary restraining order (TRO), which is a type of injunction. To obtain a TRO, the government goes to the judge *ex parte* (without the knowledge of the defendant) and makes a showing that the government is likely to win an asset forfeiture lawsuit, and that the defendant is likely to intentionally dissipate or hide assets. If the court is convinced, it issues an order to restrain (freeze) designated assets. The order is then served upon financial institutions and the defendant, along with the civil forfeiture complaint. The defendant can litigate the TRO by arguing that it lacks merit, or that he or she will eventually prevail in the lawsuit.

9.8.3   BURDEN OF PROOF

Asset forfeiture proceedings may use different burdens of proof, depending on the type of litigation and jurisdiction. Many states use a preponderance-of-the-evidence standard,

---

[12] For a listing of state asset forfeiture laws, see https://criminal.findlaw.com/criminal-rights/asset-forfeiture-laws-by-state.html.

which is just enough evidence to tip the scales in favor of the plaintiff. Some states use other standards, like "clear and convincing evidence". In contrast, a prosecutor needs to prove a criminal case beyond a reasonable doubt, the highest legal standard.

Sometimes, resolution of a parallel criminal proceeding will resolve many issues within an asset forfeiture action. If the prosecutor obtains a criminal conviction by guilty plea or jury verdict, the legal doctrine of *res judicata* ("the thing has been decided") greatly narrows the issues in the civil case. Under that doctrine, factual matters resolved in one court are typically deemed resolved in other courts. Therefore, in this scenario, the defendant's commission of the criminal acts would no longer need to be litigated in the civil case.

Western Express and Civil Asset Forfeiture

We obtained the first Grand Jury indictment in the Western Express case in 2006. It charged the virtual currency exchanger Western Express and its owners for illegal money transmitting and related offenses. We also brought a parallel civil asset forfeiture proceeding which sought forfeiture of the defendants' funds in bank accounts and cash we recovered during the execution of a search warrant.

This civil asset forfeiture proceeding was conducted in a civil court, a different court from where the criminal case was being heard, because that is how the New York City (and many other) courts are organized. The Manhattan DA's Office (DANY) is an office of sufficient size that it has a dedicated unit to conduct asset forfeiture litigation. Prior to the arrests and search warrant executions, the DANY asset forfeiture unit obtained a TRO in the civil court. Once we started making arrests and executing search warrants, the unit began serving the TRO on various banks to prevent the defendants from transferring money out. We served the TRO and civil complaint on the defendants also, ordering them not to transfer or dissipate any assets without the permission of the court. Many criminal defendants will not be inclined to obey a civil court order, so it is important to serve the orders upon the banks and other third parties who may hold the assets, as they will be more likely to comply and freeze or turnover assets.

In Western Express, the civil action did not freeze all of the defendants' assets, but did ultimately result in the forfeiture of a million dollars in ill-gotten gains. Without the TRO, these funds would have been available for the defendants to enjoy while the criminal case was pending and after the case's conclusion.

9.9 GENERAL CIVIL LAWS AND REGULATIONS REGARDING CYBERSECURITY AND PRIVACY

Civil laws and regulations are increasingly significant in creating cybersecurity and privacy standards for individuals, businesses, and industries. Organizations may face a civil action and fines from the government if they fail to comply with relevant rules and laws. Further, non-compliance with a law or regulation might constitute evidence that an entity was negligent in allowing a cybercrime to occur.

In this section, we will discuss laws relating to cybersecurity and privacy that are generally applicable to businesses or individuals.

Federal and state laws. There is no overarching federal standard for information security, data breach notification, or privacy (though there are federal requirements for specific sectors). In this vacuum, individual states have enacted laws on these topics.[13]

This patchwork of federal and state laws and regulations covers varying topics, with different levels of authority over the business sectors, geographic regions, and consumers they seek to protect. Some organizations might need to comply with the laws of multiple states, depending upon where they are headquartered, where they do business, and where their customers are located.

Federal and state laws empower many different agencies to create and enforce laws and regulations related to information security and cybersecurity. On the federal side, one primary agency with authority in this area is the Federal Trade Commission (FTC), which enforces many privacy-related rules. At the state level, the Attorney General of each state typically performs similar functions.

General concepts. Many data security and privacy laws incorporate two key concepts:

- "Reasonable" security (recognizing this term may be subject to interpretation)
- Protecting "personal identifying information" (PII), non-public information (NPI), "private information", or other terms for data that can identify an individual or be used to assume another's identity, including financial account numbers, birth dates, and social security numbers.

We cannot summarize every state's laws, nor keep up with the rapid changes in this area, but the following sections provide an overview of the types of laws and regulations of which investigators should be aware.

9.9.1 DATA DISPOSAL LAWS AND RULES

We start with data disposal laws because they are the early precursor to today's information security and data breach laws. Data disposal laws were enacted in response to irresponsible companies that disposed of sensitive data by leaving it on the curb for trash pickup (and for anyone to rifle through), or by selling used computers with sensitive data still stored within them. A slight majority of states have data disposal laws, which generally require sensitive data to be securely destroyed and erased.[14]

The FTC also enforces its Disposal Rule, which became effective in 2005 and requires a host of covered entities to securely destroy sensitive information and documents, such as credit records.[15]

9.9.2 INFORMATION SECURITY LAWS

About 15 states now have general information security laws that essentially require businesses and organizations to take reasonable measures to protect defined categories of

---

[13] Over the years, there have been a number of federal bills introduced regarding information security, data breach notification, and privacy, but none have been enacted into law. Burgeoning state laws may create more incentive for the federal government to pass such legislation. If federal laws are enacted, it remains to be seen if they will operate in parallel with state law or preempt aspects of state law.

[14] *See* National Conference of State Legislatures (NCSL), *Overview of Data Disposal Laws* (December 1, 2016), www.ncsl.org/research/telecommunications-and-information-technology/data-disposal-laws.aspx.

[15] FTC, *Disposing of Consumer Report Information? Rule Tells How* (June 2005), www.ftc.gov/tips-advice/business-center/guidance/disposing-consumer-report-information-rule-tells-how.

personal information.[16] The scope of the laws and definitions vary greatly among the states. "Personal information" or "personally identifiable information" usually means information containing general or specific facts about an identifiable individual (such as name, address, date of birth, and Social Security number). Next we discuss data breach notification laws, and organizations should consider that notifying the government of a breach could trigger an investigation into the sufficiency of their cybersecurity.

9.9.3   DATA BREACH NOTIFICATION LAWS

Every state, plus the District of Columbia, Guam, Puerto Rico, and the U.S. Virgin Islands has a data breach notification law.[17] As mentioned, there is no general federal rule on this topic.

California passed the first such law in 2003, which created the first legally mandated procedure to inform the public about massive data breaches. Until data breach notification laws were enacted, the only reason a breached corporation would tell anyone would be for transparency, good corporate citizenship, and to aid law enforcement. Companies that focused on potential negative publicity or lawsuits remained silent, sometimes not even telling law enforcement about the serious crimes that had occurred. Today, most data breaches involving personal information require notification of law enforcement and the consumers whose data was stolen. Depending upon how the particular data breach statute is worded, it might apply to companies based in the state, with a presence in the state, or with customers in the state.

Data breach reporting requirements create a legal duty to report, which implies a requirement to properly investigate the cybercrime in order to provide an accurate report. Upon receiving a report of cybercrime, the government and affected consumers will want to know the cause of the breach and whether the level of cybersecurity was adequate. Organizations likely will find themselves in the position of justifying the reasonableness of their security posture. Ensuing cybercrime investigations, both internal and government-led, may focus on root causes and whether proper security was in place.

9.9.4   PRIVACY LAWS AND WHO ENFORCES THEM

Data privacy laws and rules concern what businesses and government actors do with information about us – what information they collect, how they use it, when they can intentionally share it with a third party, how long they store it, and how they protect it from theft. Consumer privacy cannot be protected if the organization has poor security and allows customer data to be stolen. A data breach lawsuit will likely allege violation of privacy rights as well as inadequate information security. Later in this section, we will look at some recent laws in the European Union and the U.S. that create stricter privacy protection requirements for businesses.

[16] *See* NCSL, *Overview of Data Security Laws – Private Sector* (December 5, 2017), www.ncsl.org/research/telecommunications-and-information-technology/data-security-laws.aspx. These states include Arkansas, California, Connecticut, Florida, Indiana, Kansas, Maryland, Massachusetts, Minnesota, Nevada, New Mexico, Oregon, Rhode Island, Texas, and Utah. In July 2019, New York became the sixteenth state when it enacted the SHIELD Act, amending NY General Business Law 899-aa to strengthen data breach reporting requirements, and adding 899-bb, a data security requirement, www.nysenate.gov/legislation/bills/2019/s5575.
[17] *See* NCSL, *Security Breach Notification Laws* (March 29, 2018), www.ncsl.org/research/telecommunications-and-information-technology/security-breach-notification-laws.aspx.

9.9.4.1 FTC and State Attorneys General

In the absence of specific federal privacy legislation, Section 5(a) of the FTC Act is the federal government's main privacy rule and is enforced by the FTC.[18] Under this rule, the FTC can bring civil actions against defendants engaged in unfair or deceptive trade practices. For example, a company that falsely advertises ironclad cybersecurity for its customers, or that falsely describes how they collect, store, or share personal information, may be engaging in a deceptive practice. States, through state Attorneys General, may bring civil enforcement actions under similar state statutes.

The FTC also enforces the Children's Online Privacy Protection Rule (COPPA).[19] Companies with a website or "app" need to have a policy and protocols in place to avoid collecting personal information from children under the age of 13 or to obtain parental consent before doing so.

The FTC enforces the Red Flags Rule as to those who create and use credit reports. This rule requires financial institutions (who are separately regulated) and those using the credit information to have a program to detect identity theft red flags.[20] The FTC also enforces the Safeguards Rule (a part of the Gramm-Leach Bliley Act, covered shortly) as to certain companies.

9.9.4.2 GDPR

The European Union (E.U.) General Data Protection Regulation (GDPR) became effective in May of 2018 and made important changes regarding data privacy regulation.[21] It affects businesses in the E.U. and any business with customers in the E.U., which caused many U.-S. businesses to pay sharp attention to privacy issues. Violations can result in significant fines. Some key terms to understand from the GDPR are data controller, data processor, and data subject.

The *data controller* is the entity that obtains information about data subjects and determines why, how, and where personal data will be processed.

The *data processor* is an entity that processes personal data on behalf of a controller. The data processor might be an external third party, such as a payroll company making payments as directed by the data controller. The data processor might be within the same company as the data controller.

The *data subject* is the individual whose personal information is being collected and used. The GDPR gives data subjects a number of rights, including:

- Personal information can be used only with their consent, which requires clear notice in plain language
- Convenient methods to withdraw consent
- Notification of a data breach within 72 hours of detection
- Access to personal data being stored about them, in a convenient format
- The ability to correct inaccurate personal data
- Ability to transmit their data to another controller (portability)
- The "right to be forgotten" – to have data about them erased.

---

[18] *See* FTC Act § 5(a), 15 U.S.C. § 45(a)(1). *See also*, FTC, *A Brief Overview of the Federal Trade Commission's Investigative and Law Enforcement Authority* (Revised, Oct. 2019), www.ftc.gov/about-ftc/what-we-do/enforcement-authority.

[19] *See* FTC, *The Children's Online Privacy Protection Rule: A Six-Step Compliance Plan for Your Business* (June 2017), www.ftc.gov/tips-advice/business-center/guidance/childrens-online-privacy-protection-rule-six-step-compliance.

[20] See 16 CFR Part 681, available through www.ecfr.gov.

[21] E.U. 2016/679. The text of the regulation can be found at https://gdpr-info.eu.

The GDPR also requires that the data processor and data controller maintain the data with proper security.

Following the implementation of GDPR, the California and Colorado state legislatures created laws similar to the GDPR, and other states also are considering doing so.[22]

9.9.4.3   California Consumer Privacy Act

The California Consumer Privacy Act (CCPA) was passed in June 2018 and took effect on January 1, 2020.[23] It was amended shortly after its passage, and more change is anticipated. The CCPA is described as a landmark privacy bill similar to the GDPR, that gives consumers many privacy rights, including:

- Ability to request information about the data being held about them
- Right to erasure (right to be forgotten)
- Ability to object to sale of their data
- Non-discrimination against consumers who exercise their privacy rights
- Enforcement by the state Attorney General
- Private civil right of action for consumers whose data is breached under certain circumstances.

Businesses covered by the CCPA are required to "implement and maintain adequate security procedures and practices".[24] This law applies to for-profit companies with over $25 million in revenue, or holding personal data of 50,000 people, or whose business primarily involves the sale of personal data.

9.9.4.4   Colorado Protections for Consumer Data Privacy Act (PCDPA)

In May 2018, Colorado enacted a data protection law which took effect in September 2018 and has similarities to the GDPR. It requires companies to have a written policy for disposing of documents and data containing personal information. Companies also must maintain "reasonable security procedures" to protect personal information that are appropriate for the size and nature of the business, and must ensure these security measures are implemented by third party companies that work with their data. Companies must notify affected consumers within 30 days of identification of a data breach. If the breach affected more than 500 residents, they must also notify the Colorado Attorney General.[25]

9.10   CIVIL LAWS AND REGULATIONS FOR SPECIFIC SECTORS

Some business sectors and industries are directly regulated, which means the government entity that licenses and regulates them may set forth specific rules that relate to information security in that particular business environment. We will cover the financial and health sectors here. Other sectors with information security and cybersecurity regulation include power and communications utilities, critical infrastructure services, and defense contractors.

---

[22] For example, New York has introduced a sweeping data privacy bill that has not yet been passed. NY Privacy Act (S-5642), www.nysenate.gov/legislation/bills/2019/s5642. Issie Lapowsky, New York's Privacy Bill Is Even Bolder Than California's, *Wired* (June 4, 2019) www.wired.com/story/new-york-privacy-act-bolder.

[23] California Civil Code § 1798.100–199.

[24] California Civil Code, § 1798.150.

[25] The Colorado Attorney General's Office provides information on the state's data and privacy laws and regulations at https://coag.gov/resources/data-protection-laws/.

9.10.1   FINANCIAL SECTOR

The financial sector is heavily regulated in order to ensure the safety and soundness of individual financial institutions and the financial system as a whole, as well as to prevent money laundering and protect consumers.

9.10.1.1   GLBA: Gramm-Leach-Bliley Act

The Gramm-Leach-Bliley Act (GLBA), also known as the Financial Services Modernization Act of 1999, created privacy and security requirements for financial institutions. Requirements include an information security and incident response program to protect customer information, and disclosure to customers about how their personal information is used, shared, and protected.[26]

GLBA's implementation rules include the Safeguards Rule (to protect consumer information) and the Privacy Rule (regarding disclosure of consumers' nonpublic personal information).[27] GLBA compliance for financial institutions is generally overseen by their regulators.

9.10.1.2   FFIEC and SEC Requirements

The Federal Financial Institutions Examination Council (FFIEC) establishes common standards for use by many financial sector regulators, including requirements for cybersecurity to protect consumers and ensure the cyber-safety of financial institutions.[28] These financial regulators include the Federal Deposit Insurance Corporation (FDIC), the Office of the Comptroller of the Currency (OCC), the Federal Reserve System (the Fed), the National Credit Union Administration (NCUA), and the Consumer Financial Protection Bureau (CFPB). Significant parts of these FFIEC standards are mapped to the NIST Cybersecurity Framework, which we discussed in Chapter 4.

FFIEC regulations include GLBA compliance and measures to ensure institutions' "safety and soundness", which includes a review of their information security posture.

Financial organizations also must comply with the "Red Flags Rule", a federal regulation that requires certain businesses (such as financial institutions and those who issue or use credit reports) to implement a written program to detect and combat identity theft.[29] The program must include reasonable policies and procedures to detect the red flags of identity theft, such as the use of forged identification or stolen personal identifying information. Financial institutions must have procedures in place to investigate and respond when they detect identity theft. Policies and procedures must be kept current, taking into account new fraud trends. Regulation of the Red Flags Rule for financial institutions is handled by the relevant financial regulator.

---

[26] FTC, Gramm-Leach-Bliley Act (updated September 4, 2015), www.ftc.gov/tips-advice/business-center/privacy-and-security/gramm-leach-bliley-act. FTC.

[27] FTC, *Financial Institutions and Customer Information: Complying with the Safeguards Rule* (April 2006), www.ftc.gov/tips-advice/business-center/guidance/financial-institutions-customer-information-complying; FTC, *Financial Privacy Rule*, www.ftc.gov/enforcement/rules/rulemaking-regulatory-reform-proceedings/financial-privacy-rule (with link to 16 CFR Part 313).

FTC, Safeguards Rule, www.ftc.gov/enforcement/rules/rulemaking-regulatory-reform-proceedings/safeguards-rule (with link to 16 CFR Part 314).

[28] For more information about the FFIEC, see www.ffiec.gov/. The FFIEC provides institutions with a Cybersecurity Assessment Tool to identify cyber risks and preparedness. www.ffiec.gov/cyberassessmenttool.htm.

[29] See FTC, *Fighting Identity Theft with the Red Flags Rule: A How-To Guide for Business* (May 2013), www.ftc.gov/tips-advice/business-center/guidance/fighting-identity-theft-red-flags-rule-how-guide-business.

The Securities and Exchange Commission (SEC) has regulatory and enforcement over-sight regarding securities, investment companies, hedge funds, and public corporations. Oversight areas include information security, protection of customer records, identity theft red flags compliance, and the security and integrity of their technology infrastructure.[30]

Other regulators, such as the Commodity Futures Trading Commission and the Finan-cial Industry Regulatory Authority, impose comparable requirements.

9.10.1.3   New York Information Security Requirements for the Financial Sector

The New York State Department of Financial Services issued cybersecurity regulations for all financial services institutions regulated by the state, which became effective in March 2017.[31] These regulations are titled "Cybersecurity Requirements for Financial Services Companies", and require banks and other financial institutions to have information security policies; protect the confidentiality, integrity, and availability of their information systems; certify compliance with the regulation annually; have an incident response plan; and notify the government promptly upon a cyberattack. Given that many financial services companies are located in New York, this law affects the finances and data of consumers all over the world.

9.10.2   Health Sector Regulations: HIPAA and HITECH

Federal law requires special handling of patient medical and personal data, as set forth in the Health Insurance Portability and Accountability Act of 1996 (HIPAA), which was amended with the Health Information Technology for Economic and Clinical Health Act of 2009 (HITECH).[32] HITECH was designed to increase the use of technology to store med-ical records, with added privacy and data breach notification requirements and penalties. These rules apply to doctors and medical offices, hospitals, and anyone else working with medical and patient data. HIPAA was one of the earliest laws protecting personal informa-tion and privacy.

9.11   CONCLUSION

This chapter has provided an overview of civil laws related to cybercrime that could be used to seek redress. Civil litigation plays a large role in the legal response to cybercrime through lawsuits relating to intentional tortious acts, negligent cybersecurity, or breach of contract,

We also surveyed some of the growing number of regulations and laws pertaining to information security, privacy, and cybercrime response. Organizations must comply with these rules or face potential action by the government. Failure to meet government stand-ards could provide grounds for private civil actions as well.

Before private parties take legal action, they will look for evidence to support their case. Investigators play a key role in determining whether a defendant failed to comply with an applicable law, regulation, or norm.

---

[30] *See* Regulation S-P, 17 C.F.R. § 248.30, and Regulation SCI, 17 C.F.R. § 242.1000–1007. The SEC has additional information on their website, SEC.gov.

[31] *See* 23 NYCRR 500, *Cybersecurity Requirements for Financial Services Companies*, www.dfs.ny.gov/docs/legal/regu lations/adoptions/dfsrf500txt.pdf.

[32] HIPAA, Pub. L. 104–191, Stat. 1936. Web. August 11, 2014.

HITECH, Pub. L. 111–5, div. A, title XIII, div. B, title IV, February 17, 2009, 123 Stat. 226, 467 (42 U.S.C. 300jj et seq.; 17901 et seq.).

Part III

The Cybercrime Investigation

10 Embarking on a Cybercrime Investigation

The Three Perspectives and Key Areas of Focus

This chapter is for:

- Investigators of all types and titles in the public and private sector.

10.1 INTRODUCTION

In the first two parts of this book, we learned about cybercrime conduct and related technical/security factors, as well as the laws underpinning a cybercrime investigation (criminal, civil, regulatory, and international).

This chapter begins Part III – The Investigation, where we will take all the information from earlier chapters and use it to understand the nuts and bolts of how to investigate a cybercrime. Throughout this book, we have centered our discussion around the three groups primarily responsible for cybercrime investigation – the private sector, law enforcement, and government regulators. This chapter introduces the big picture of the investigation from all of these perspectives, giving a sense of broad goals and how each sector works to further individual and common objectives. Each group has a different focus and capabilities, and it is helpful for each to know something about the others. We discuss investigative techniques applicable to all types of investigators in the next chapter (Chapter 11). Then we get deeper into the discussion of aspects specific to each perspective – the private sector (Chapter 12), law enforcement (Chapter 13), and regulators (Chapter 14).

In this chapter, we also give an overview of the investigative methods and goals that require special focus in the cyber context. These topics get detailed treatment in later chapters within Part III.

10.2 CYBERCRIME INVESTIGATION FROM THREE PERSPECTIVES: PRIVATE SECTOR, LAW ENFORCEMENT, AND REGULATORY

Like few other types of cases, cybercrime investigations require cooperation between the private and public sectors. When businesses and organizations become victims of cybercrime, they rely on law enforcement to perform the criminal investigation, but may expend private resources for significant investigative work (which then might be shared with law enforcement). From the law enforcement side, no criminal cybercrime investigation can be done without records and evidence from the private sector. And many private sector entities are regulated by government agencies that both provide guidance to prevent cybercrime, investigate when it occurs, and require reporting to law enforcement.

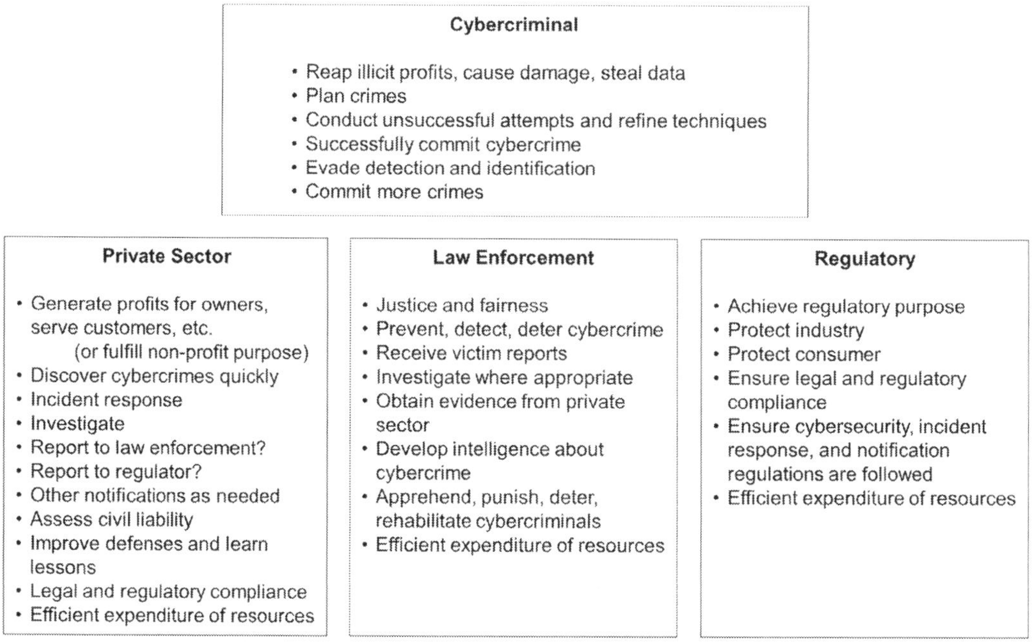

FIGURE 10.1   General Goals Surrounding Cybercrime and Investigations.

In a perfect world, each group's investigation would support and complement the others' work. The private sector would forward all leads to law enforcement, and law enforcement would investigate every complaint. Law enforcement would have easy access to private sector evidence and records. Information would be shared among regulators and all law enforcement agencies to create effective prevention and response to cybercrime.

Unfortunately, this perfect synergy is not always achievable. Motives and goals for different players often diverge. Each of these broad groups is made up of many different organizations with their own priorities, and resources and experience may vary. A cybercrime investigation might cross into all three groups' authority, and it might be difficult for one entity to judge the significance or global relevance of facts at the time they are discovered. No matter the individual purpose or interest, therefore, all parties are best served when the integrity of the investigation is paramount.

The general goals of each group, both intersecting and differing, are illustrated by Figure 10.1. Next, we summarize the three perspectives on cybercrime investigation. We start with the private entities since they are most likely to discover the crime first.

10.2.1   PRIVATE SECTOR

Private entities are on the front line of cybercrime and the investigation of it. They typically encounter cybercrime because they belong to one or more of the below groups:

- *Victims*, whether of an outside attack or the misconduct of an employee, associate, or other insider
- *Regulated businesses* that are monitoring for cybercrime and are subject to government information security and data breach notification requirements
- *Services cybercriminals use to facilitate crime against other victims* and that may have records or other evidence of the cybercrime.

Private entities in any of these situations are often the ones to initiate a cybercrime investigation. They might investigate to restore their systems and business, identify the culprits or compromised users, recover stolen funds, determine liability, protect their reputations, and comply with laws and regulations such as data breach notification rules. These investigative goals may be undertaken while assisting law enforcement and regulators with their investigations. A private entity's investigation also may explore another private organization's compliance with security regulations and reasonable practices, with a focus similar to a regulatory investigation (discussed later).

Certain private entities, such as service and communications providers, often are used by criminals to commit cybercrimes and might hold evidence relevant to crimes, while not being directly affected themselves. These entities may conduct their own internal investigation to determine how their services are being compromised or misused.

We will cover details specific to private sector investigations in Chapter 12.

10.2.2   LAW ENFORCEMENT

Law enforcement agencies investigate cybercrime to prevent, deter, detect, investigate, and prosecute criminal conduct. Unless there is law enforcement action, no cybercriminal will be apprehended, prosecuted, or punished for his harmful acts.

Law enforcement usually undertakes an investigation into cybercrime because of:

- *Victim reports* (by individuals or businesses) to local police departments, federal law enforcement, and government agencies that monitor cybercrime activity
- *Private sector reports of data breaches and other cybercrime activity* made in compliance with laws and regulations mandating notification
- *Referrals* from other law enforcement and government agencies that learn of cybercrimes they cannot investigate or with which they need assistance
- *Press accounts* that bring cybercrime activity to public light
- *Proactive investigations* to identify and prosecute individuals or groups committing cybercrime.

Law enforcement investigation into cybercrime is particularly meaningful because public perception may be that these offenses are unstoppable. When law enforcement officials bring cybercriminals to justice, then victims, Internet users, the public at large, and other criminals learn that there can be consequences.

In Chapter 13, we will cover the investigation from law enforcement's perspective.

10.2.3   REGULATORY

As we discussed in Chapter 9, federal and state laws authorize certain government agencies to regulate businesses and organizations, and these regulations often involve information security standards and cybercrime notification requirements.

Regulatory investigations may be triggered by:

- *Mandated reporting* by regulated entities of a network intrusion or data compromise
- *Voluntary reporting* by regulated entities of suspicious activity that may affect other businesses or organizations
- *Regular monitoring* of some industries, such as financial markets, utilities, and critical infrastructure
- *Referrals* from law enforcement and other public agencies
- *Press reports* of cybercrime that bring potential regulatory violations to public light.

Regulatory agencies may investigate under these circumstances to determine root causes and whether regulatory or legal requirements were met.

We cover regulatory-type investigations in Chapter 14.

10.3 KEY INVESTIGATIVE TOPICS

Cybercrime investigations performed by the private sector, law enforcement, and regulators may have different perspectives and goals, but some investigative strategies and challenges are important to all three. As discussed in Part III, they include:

- Organizational tools and techniques, open-source and records-based investigation, and email analysis for cybercrime cases (Chapter 11)
- Financial investigation – following the money trail (Chapter 15)
- Identification of a suspect and attributing cybercrimes to the correct individual (Chapter 16)
- Apprehending identified suspects and related jurisdictional issues (Chapter 17).

We concentrate on these topics because they are critical to solving cybercrimes and they require an investigative approach that often differs from the techniques and needs of a traditional case.

Investigations are a process with a beginning and an end, evolving through many intervening stages. Every investigation is unique and unpredictable, and few progress neatly through various phases. Instead, many are fluid, frenetic, and occasionally chaotic. Knowing what to expect about the information a cyber investigator will encounter allows for a more productive assessment of an unfolding investigation during the continual cycle of searching for, obtaining, and analyzing evidence.

10.4 ENDING THE INVESTIGATION: SUCCESS OR EXHAUSTION OF LEADS OR RESOURCES

What constitutes a "successful" cybercrime investigation? When should an investigation be terminated? How an investigation "ends" varies with the categories we have established.

10.4.1 THE END OF LAW ENFORCEMENT'S INVESTIGATION

In one sense, a law enforcement investigation succeeds when it is fair, ethical, and complies with laws and rules. In fact, any effort to investigate cybercrime may be considered a success because the more law enforcement develops experience and gathers intelligence, the more overall pressure is created to prevent and stop these crimes. Ideally, a law enforcement investigation brings some cybercriminals to justice with appropriate criminal charges backed by sufficient proof, resulting in convictions and appropriate punishment for the offenders. In many cases the ideal result may not be reached, and the case ultimately is closed for lack of resources or leads.

It is important to recognize that in the world of cybercrime, even a closed investigation can produce positive results. For example, even if a suspect could not be identified or charged, the investigation may have gathered intelligence useful for future investigations, and identified attack methods or trends that help the public protect themselves.[1] The evidence gathered in any

---

[1] Still, law enforcement is not in the information security business and should not neglect their enforcement role. There are many organizations that focus on information security and help with public awareness, but only law enforcement has the ability to bring criminal charges.

cybercrime investigation may end up assisting a case in another jurisdiction. And, the investigative process itself may deter criminal conduct by other potential cybercriminals, who now are aware that these offenses will garner law enforcement attention. In other words, while identifying, finding, and arresting criminal offenders will always be the primary law enforcement goal, cybercrime requires a broader, longer-range view of investigative success.

Some factors in deciding to conclude a law enforcement investigation are:

- Will further investigation reveal helpful information about the crime, the identity of the perpetrator, other crimes committed, and other suspects?
- What is the effort and cost of further investigation compared to the likely benefits?
  - Benefits include investigation progress, victim assistance, enhanced experience and knowledge for the investigator, and the potential to assist other investigators with similar cases.

10.4.2   THE END OF THE PRIVATE SECTOR INVESTIGATION

The private sector investigation may end when the goals of the entity or individual affected by the cybercrime are reached – whether the focus is on prevention of future attacks, remediation of damage, or identification of the criminal(s) involved. Business decisions about the expenditure of resources also play a significant role in determining whether to continue an investigation. Some factors to determine whether the investigation should be concluded include:

- Have the attack methods and system or user vulnerabilities been sufficiently identified to stop the current attack and better prevent one in the future?
- If the cybercrime was initiated by an employee or associate, has the investigation identified the offender and recovered the relevant internal evidence?
- Has the investigation thoroughly pursued the recovery of stolen funds or data?
- Has the investigation been sufficient to comply with relevant laws and regulations, including government agencies' follow-up requests for information or evidence?
- Have the affected customers been identified and notified of the data breach?
- Have available leads and evidence been identified and presented to law enforcement?
- Did the investigation uncover facts relevant to bringing or defending against a civil suit, or defending a regulatory action?
- Will the costs of continued investigation outweigh the likely positive results?

10.4.3   THE END OF THE REGULATORY INVESTIGATION

A regulatory investigation may be cursory if the information reported by a regulated organization is accurate and involves a relatively minor event, or it may be lengthy and detailed, examining the security measures of the organization to see if it was in regulatory compliance. Where discrepancies are detected between a report and the organization's practices, the investigation also may focus on the accuracy of the reporting to the regulator about the initial incident.

Factors in concluding a regulatory investigation include:

- Has sufficient information and evidence about the cybercrime been obtained from the regulated entity and external sources?
- Have the required notifications about the crime been made to law enforcement and consumers?

- If the organization was found to be non-compliant with regulations, has it been brought into compliance?
- Has intelligence been shared to better accomplish the objectives of the regulation?
- Have all regulatory proceedings concluded and fair advice or punishment for non-compliance been imposed?

10.5 CONCLUSION

This brief overview outlines the different perspectives that may be involved in a cybercrime investigation, and some overarching characteristics.

The following chapters will provide detail for each perspective and information on investigative methods and stages of special importance to cybercrime investigators.

11 General Investigation Methods

Organization, Open Source, Records, and Email

This chapter is primarily for:

- Everyone
- Any investigator wanting to use the information available to all of us on the Internet
- Any investigator getting and analyzing records or email evidence
- Any investigator gathering evidence that might be used in litigation.

11.1 INTRODUCTION

In this chapter, we cover some of the key investigative methods involved in conducting a cybercrime investigation that are applicable for investigators in all sectors.

The first part of the chapter looks at tools and techniques investigators can use to manage the flow of cybercrime evidence effectively. Part of the process includes anticipating that evidence might be used in a court proceeding, and taking steps to ensure its admissibility. It is hard to look for clues if the evidence is not collected and organized in a sensible way. And discovering clues is no good unless investigators can find them later in the pile of evidence. As investigators document and report on the unfolding investigation, being able to write clearly and logically about suspects, victims, accounts, and criminal activity greatly increases the efficiency of the investigation.

We then discuss three aspects of investigation that are important to most cybercrime cases: open source investigation, records evidence, and email evidence. These sections focus on finding and preserving information that is openly available online, organizing and analyzing records of Internet and financial activity, and locating valuable evidence within both individual email headers and large volumes of email evidence.

Finally, we turn to methods investigators can use throughout an investigation to take advantage of existing cybercrime intelligence, while also building and sharing intelligence from their own cases. Working cybercrime cases one at a time without the benefit of intelligence resources is a tough proposition.

11.2 CYBERCRIME INVESTIGATION: THE CYCLICAL PROCESS OF BUILDING EVIDENCE

As with traditional criminal cases, a cybercrime investigation is a continuous process of searching for evidence and leads. But unlike traditional street crime investigations, even a simple cybercrime case typically involves piecing together clues from a variety of sources, including records evidence from Internet service companies and financial institutions. More complex cases require investigators to build a web of circumstantial evidence with many strands, each comprised of multiple evidentiary links. The strength of this web depends upon each and every link.

These qualities mean a cybercrime investigation is a detail-oriented process that requires organization and continuity. While great technical skills are wonderful resources and may be needed at some stages of a cyber case, the primary qualifications of a good cybercrime investigator are a desire to get to the bottom of the crime and a willingness to follow the trail wherever it leads. Investigators of any background who are good analytical thinkers, clear writers, and determined sleuths are tremendous assets to these cases.

The Cyclical Process. Finding evidence in a cybercrime investigation is best thought of as a cyclical, iterative process. Many investigations of traditional crime are essentially linear. One piece of evidence leads directly to another in a relatively straight line to an identified suspect and the legal basis for an arrest. Cybercrime investigations, on the other hand, often start with little concrete information about the criminal or even the crime. One small clue – such as a piece of information found online or in a set of records – leads to another clue, which prompts another online search or a subpoena for another set of records, and so on. As each clue is reviewed and analyzed, additional leads are generated and followed until enough rounds of evidence-gathering have occurred to develop an identifiable suspect and proof of his crimes. Figure 11.1 illustrates this process.

To conduct a data and records-based investigation efficiently, investigators need a method for organizing and following leads. Such a system can evaluate the case at the present time, what leads are available to be pursued, how to prioritize those leads, and what steps should be taken for follow-up.

Of course, an investigation exists within the context of finite resources. Rarely does any investigation receive all of the resources needed to follow every single lead. Public resources are limited, and private sector investigations cost money, whether through internal personnel time and resources or outside contractors who may charge by the hour or project.

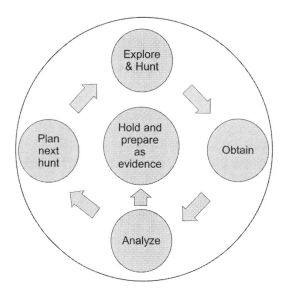

FIGURE 11.1   The Cyclical Investigative Process.

As new information is learned – through results of a witness interview, subpoenaed records from a communications provider or other private entity, or analysis of evidence – it needs to be incorporated into the investigation, to see what assistance it provides, and what additional leads are revealed.

Time Sensitivity. This cyclical, iterative process takes time, a significant issue for investigators because certain evidence becomes harder to obtain as time goes by.

Some of the time-sensitive evidence commonly important to a cybercrime investigation includes:

- Witness recollection
- Data within a computer's volatile memory (see Chapter 3)
- Data stored in a computer's fixed (persistent) memory (see Chapter 3)
- Records of Internet service providers and communications companies (before they are purged)
- Security video recordings from relevant retailers or government-operated cameras
- Fingerprints or DNA when devices or other physical evidence are obtained.

With few exceptions, evidence and leads are best obtained shortly after the event. That said, life rarely follows best practices. Investigators will find themselves trying to obtain evidence, wishing it had been done long before. Lawyers will prepare for a hearing or trial, wishing certain evidence had been obtained during the investigation.

11.3 MANAGING CYBERCRIME EVIDENCE: READILY AVAILABLE VS. PROPRIETARY INVESTIGATION TOOLS

During a cybercrime investigation, investigators inevitably will encounter many types of information from many different sources. In fast-moving investigations with limited resources, having a system to store and organize this data is essential so that it can be logically analyzed and used as evidence if needed. A good system tracks all the gathered information, knowing some pieces ultimately will not be helpful, some will be of general use, and some will contain crucial facts that must be referenced within legal documents and ultimately admitted into evidence at trial.

Many tools can be used to manage the evidence in a cybercrime investigation – from specialized software available for purchase to the applications readily available within most of our computers. The important thing is to have a system in place that organizes and preserves the evidence and allows it to be reviewed by colleagues and supervisors. An investigation and its conclusions will be used to take serious actions, making it crucial to avoid sloppy methods that might damage the weight or admissibility of evidence down the line.

11.3.1 PROPRIETARY TOOLS

Several brands of case management databases and software tools are available for purchase from a number of companies. These products are designed to help investigators store and analyze data, as well as present evidence and exhibits in court proceedings. The companies that create these tools are excellent at explaining the merits of their proprietary systems, so we will leave the details of each software package to them.

The cost of certain investigative software may be out of reach for some. Further, each tool involves an investment not just of funds, but of time to configure it, import data, and master its functions. Some fall into the trap of thinking that an expensive tool will do the investigation for you – that you dump in data, push a button, and the indictment or civil complaint rolls out, complete with proof. But while proprietary tools can be very helpful, no investigator should believe that a program (no matter how expensive) will magically make a case or substitute for training, experience, diligence, and effort.

When contemplating the use of any software tool, consider these factors that affect its cost and usefulness:

- Initial and recurring price and license fees
- Number of licenses that need to be purchased and who can use the licenses
- Training for users of the tool – time and cost
- Whether trained and competent people will be available consistently to use the tool
- Consequences when trained users leave their positions
- Amount of effort and work to get data imported *into* the tool
- Effort and work to get data *out of* the tool if needed, or to transition to another tool
- Level of difficulty to verify and articulate results and output.

11.3.2   READILY AVAILABLE TOOLS

Before considering the purchase of proprietary software to store and analyze data and records, remember that we all have powerful tools for handling case information within our computer operating systems and business suite of applications. Here are some ways these readily available tools can be used to successfully store, organize, and analyze the evidence collected during a cybercrime investigation.

Word processing documents. Word processing documents are good for making profiles of individuals, as well as summaries of investigative steps and information. Text narrative can accompany graphics inserted in a document, including screenshots and photos of suspects or locations (see Chapter 16 for discussion of creating cybercrime pedigree documents). Of course, word processing documents are essential for legal submissions, including subpoenas, search warrants, complaints, indictments, motions, and exhibits. When investigations become lengthy and complex, some documents may benefit from a cover page that describes the contents and where it fits into the case.

Spreadsheets. Spreadsheets are essential for organizing and analyzing large sets of data, as well as keeping track of suspect accounts, investigation events, charges, suspects, witnesses, subpoenas, and evidence. Rows and columns set up to record specific details allow investigators to sort and filter the collected data more powerfully, and can yield important investigative leads.

File naming. A consistent file naming system that accurately describes the contents of a document, spreadsheet, or folder can ensure that files are easy to identify and can be sorted as needed. This is especially important in a team setting.

Folder structure. A good folder structure helps organize files and folders in a logical fashion, maximizing efficiency for storing and retrieving documents and spreadsheets. The goal is the efficient middle ground between creating too many folders and having so many files within a particular folder that it is hard to find what is needed. As a case progresses towards Grand Jury, civil complaint, or trial, the folder structure may become more detailed. Evidence may have to be stored in both electronic and paper versions, and they should have cohesive and parallel organization. Consider creating initial folders for:

- Each source of data, information, or evidence as the place to store the data in its original form
- A "work copy" of the original data that can be used for analysis, cross referencing, or summaries

- Each suspect or target, to hold supporting evidence, including about pedigree information
- Each physical location from which evidence is recovered or seized to hold related documents, photos, and data
- Each device that is forensically searched to store the resulting data and analysis
- Each website from which evidence is preserved
- Evidence summaries
- Subpoenas sent, search warrants obtained, and other legal processes
- Court proceedings, like motion practice or calendar appearances
- Correspondence with other investigators, attorneys, witnesses, and other relevant individuals or entities.

Wiki tools. A wiki is a digital tool that allows users to edit and add information collaboratively in a manner that is organized, categorized, and linked. We are all familiar with Wikipedia, the online encyclopedia, which allows multiple people to contribute knowledge and information, edit entries, and conduct quality control. The wiki method can be used by any organization to privately store and organize information, analyze data, and collaborate as a team. Investigators can create a very simple intranet wiki site (using the open source Wikimedia platform, which Wikipedia runs on, or one of dozens of other Wiki platforms) that enables multiple investigators to add and track information as the investigation unfolds. Remember, these writings may be discoverable during litigation.

Western Express and Software Tools

The Western Express investigation lasted years and uncovered many cybercriminal suspects and targets. Ultimately, 17 individuals and the Western Express corporation were charged by indictment, while over a hundred other suspects were identified, but not charged. For those who were charged, a long litigation ensued. As the case inched towards trial, it was John's task to cull through the massive data and records and select what was relevant for trial, as well as identify the witnesses or certifications that would render the evidence admissible.

This trial preparation was possible because we had a system to store and track evidence throughout the span of the investigation. The system included dual paper and electronic versions of records, which were organized and accessible during both the investigative and trial phases.

Notably, the Western Express investigation was done mostly without specialized tools or software. The analysis was conducted and trial evidence was presented using readily available applications such as Microsoft Word, Excel, Visio, Mozilla Thunderbird, and a Windows folder structure. (If your office doesn't use Microsoft products, it probably uses an equivalent office software package.) The point is, complicated cases can be made with basic tools, just like craftsmen hundreds of years ago used hand tools to build strong houses that are still standing today.

If an agency or organization has the resources to invest in software tools, they can be very useful in organizing and analyzing data and evidence. But, like any tool, it is only as good as the human using it. A person guides the software and analyzes the output, and a person must be able to explain and articulate the results to investigators, prosecutors, judges, and juries. Developing these skills requires training, both in technology and investigative methods. Too often, money is invested in tools but not the time to master their complex functions.

Experience has shown us that just because an expensive tool is used, it does not necessarily mean the investigative process is more efficient or the analysis is more accurate.

11.4   EVIDENCE ADMISSIBILITY IN LITIGATION

As we delve into information about how to find, store and analyze different forms of evidence as a crime is investigated, it is important to keep in mind what happens at the end of the case. Ultimately, any evidence that is found may be needed in a court proceeding to prove criminal offenses or support a civil or regulatory action.

The federal and state "rules of evidence" dictate when evidence can be used, or "admitted" into a court proceeding, and it is the judge's role to make this decision. Investigators can maximize the likelihood evidence will be admissible by considering three important concepts as they look for and preserve clues:

*   *Relevance.* Evidence must be relevant to be admitted in court, meaning it must tend to prove or disprove a fact that is at issue. That said, it can be hard to predict what facts will be relevant at some future proceeding, and so it may be prudent to treat every piece of evidence as potentially relevant.
*   *Authentication.* Evidence must be authenticated to be admissible, meaning the party seeking to admit the item must show that it is authentic and reliable, and not a forgery or fraud. Often, evidence is authenticated by having a witness (like an investigator) testify about the source and preservation of the evidence.
*   *Weight.* The judge decides if an item can be admitted into evidence, so that it can be used by the court or jury as it decides the case. Then, it is up to the jury (or judge, if it is a pre-trial hearing or a non-jury trial) to determine how much weight should be given to that evidence. In other words, the admissibility of evidence is essential. But once it is admitted, the evidence must be valuable and strong enough that juries and judges rely on it to make their decisions.

When investigators think about the relevance, authentication, and weight of the evidence they are collecting, storing, and analyzing during the investigation, they not only create a strong and reliable chain of evidence to solve the cybercrime, they develop evidence that can support future litigation.

11.5   WRITING FOR CYBERCRIME INVESTIGATIONS

Writing is a surprisingly important factor in conducting a successful cybercrime investigation. From documenting evidence and investigative steps, to drafting affidavits for search warrants and other legal submissions, writing is a constant component of an investigator's work. Thoughtful writing helps avoid confusion and miscommunication, especially when discussing cybercrime evidence that may entail lengthy and complicated chains of information.

Effective written information in any investigation stands on its own, without requiring the reader to refer to other documents, prior emails, or earlier conversations to discern its true meaning. A summary written today should be understandable a year later, and require minimal additional explanation or context.

Investigators can strengthen the written materials created during a cybercrime investigation by:

- *Writing clearly.* Describe names, dates, and events fully. Avoid pronouns (him/it/etc.) that make it difficult to follow the information being documented. Paragraphs and sentences should thoroughly cover one topic at a time, and avoid inferences about other materials or sources that are mentioned. A good rule of thumb is whether the writing might be confusing or misleading to someone unfamiliar with the case, including a future juror.
- *Using diagrams.* Diagrams can be very useful tools for demonstrating how an investigator got from Point A to Point Z in the trail of evidence, or how different pieces of evidence are connected to one another.
- *Using screenshots.* As the saying goes, a picture is worth a thousand words. It may be easier to view a screenshot of a source of evidence, rather than to read through a description of that evidence in a report or other document. But while a screenshot supplements good writing, it never replaces it.
- *Documenting sources.* When evidence is gathered from records or witnesses, these sources should be clearly noted and referenced so that, if necessary, they can be found and the evidence verified by a third party.
- *Using accurate account names.* Be clear in describing any email, social media, financial, or other accounts when writing about them. The full account name should always be referenced, rather than vague descriptions like "the email account". For example:
  - Hotmail/Outlook email account john[@]hotmail[.]com, or
  - PayPal account with user name john[@]hotmail[.]com.

A complete description will avoid confusion when, over time, numerous accounts are uncovered and documented. A description such as "his email account", on the other hand, will make it difficult to follow which account is being discussed and the related chain of evidence.

- *Distinguishing facts from opinions and conclusions.* Investigators should express clearly whether statements in a report, legal submission, or other writing describe a fact or the investigator's hypothesis or conclusion. Opinions and conclusions can be important to moving the investigation forward, but should not be presented as fact.
- *Explaining conclusions for the reader.* A report or other writing about a cybercrime may include the investigator's summary of several connected pieces of evidence. When presenting such conclusions, it is important to articulate them in a manner that clarifies the factual basis, as well as the steps of the investigator's analysis. For example:
  - *Less effective*: The identity of Cybercriminal X is Frank Smith based on the information on Webpage Y.
  - *More effective*: A review of the ShadowCrew website at Webpage Y indicates that on 1/1/2020, User X posted that his name was Frank Smith and provided a mailing address of POB 123, New York, NY, 10013. Follow-on searches will be performed relating to this information to further establish whether User X is in fact Frank Smith.

11.5.1 THE DANGERS OF AUTOMATIC HYPERLINKING

One pitfall that investigators will encounter when writing about a cybercrime case is the automatic hyperlink feature within many types of software. A hyperlink is a link to a website, file, folder, or email address that, when clicked, takes the user to the linked location, or creates a new, pre-addressed email. Our word processor and email applications may automatically create hyperlinks for webpage addresses and email addresses, and having these hyperlinks in documents can be dangerous for cybercrime investigations.

Imagine that your target is Suspect@gmail.com, with website SuspectWebsite.com, and you are building a case. You write these addresses in summaries, reports, affidavits, and warrants, and exchange emails discussing the case with investigators and lawyers. Your word processing software and email programs automatically convert any references to the email and webpage addresses into hyperlinks.

Now the danger arises that you or the users receiving your emails and documents could accidentally click on the links and visit the target's webpage, or even start to draft an email to the target. The inadvertent triggering of the hyperlinks could alert the suspect about the investigation and those working it.

A two-step approach will prevent accidental hyperlink compromises:

1. Turn off default hyperlinking to webpages and email addresses on your own systems, to prevent you from clicking a link, and
2. Write account and website addresses differently, so that hyperlinks will not be generated automatically when others view the documents. For example:

Suspect@gmail.com	becomes	Suspect[at]gmail[.]com
SuspectWebsite.com	becomes	SuspectWebsite[.]com

These small extra steps, which quickly become routine, can save an investigation from devastating accidents.

Clear and Effective Writing

Here are some examples of the types of information that cybercrime investigators might write about, and the clearer, safer methods of doing so, as laid out in Table 11.1.

TABLE 11.1
Cybercrime Writing

Less Effective	More Effective
Account descriptions like: @JohnTBandler Account 123456789 Info@ abcdefg.com	Account descriptions like: Twitter account @JohnTBandler Chase Bank Account 123456789 Email account: Info[at]abcdefg[.]com Medium blog account: Info[at] abcdefg [.]com
Antonia, I preserved his LinkedIn account, here it is! This proves he's the one we are looking for!	Antonia, Today I preserved the LinkedIn profile page and activity of LinkedIn account found at https[:]//www[.]linkedin.com/in/FredSmith45/, and the files are attached as LinkedIn FredSmith45 profile 2019-8-29.pdf LinkedIn FredSmith45 activity 2019-8-29.pdf. The profile states he is currently employed as a freelance IT specialist and that he went to school in New York. We'll have to confirm this information, but it is consistent with what we know about our suspect, Fred Smith.
His bank account received $100,000 last month.	Chase Bank account 123456789, Account holder Fred Smith, received $100,000 in Nov 2019.

TABLE 11.1 (Cont.)

Less Effective	More Effective
Antonia, We just got those subpoena returns you had asked about! I filed them away!	We just got the subpoena returns for FredSmith1234[at]gmail[.]com! The records show the account was opened on 4/1/2019 from IP address 123.123.123.123, and the alternate email address is StolenCards5678[at] yahoo[.]com and had regular logins for the last 30 days from IP address 123.123.123.123 and 111.111.111.111. I filed them here: G:/case data/compliance returns/gmail I checked on those IP addresses and: IP address 123.123.123.123 belongs to Verizon IP address 111.111.111.111 belongs to Comcast Should I prepare subpoenas to Yahoo, Verizon and Comcast?
The person who posted the Yelp review's name is David Jones and he lives in New York City.	I reviewed the Yelp profile at https[:]//www[.]yelp.com/user_details? userid=123456789 for user "David Jones" and the profile indicates he is in New York, NY.

11.6   OPEN SOURCE INVESTIGATION

Investigators always have used sources of information that are free and openly accessible to the public, like newspaper articles and public records maintained in paper files by local governments and court systems. The Internet has created millions of publicly available digital sources of information. Searching online through these open sources has become a staple for anyone looking into criminal activity, and cybercrime investigators must become especially adept in this area. Like any potential evidence, information found online needs to be reviewed critically to assess its reliability and relevance to the case being investigated.

Because of the enormous amount of searchable data, open source investigation can result in rapid redirection of searches, where the investigator starts on one path that yields clues or items of curiosity, and then zigzags through layers and layers of follow-on searches. In this section, we will look at practical methods for effective online searching, as well as for preserving information found online to ensure its admissibility in future court proceedings.

11.6.1   OPEN SOURCE INVESTIGATION RESOURCES

There are seemingly infinite open sources online for investigators to explore, and many methods of approaching online searching. We will not attempt to list actual sources here because entire books have been written on this topic and Internet sources change rapidly.[1] Instead, we will summarize places and categories that are useful both to start an investigation and to conduct follow-on searches.

- *Popular search engines*, such as Google, Bing, Yahoo, and DuckDuckGo
  - ○ Search engines "crawl" the Internet, indexing webpages and material to be retrieved during a search engine query.

---

[1] See for example, Michael Bazzell, *Open Source Intelligence Techniques: Resources for Searching and Analyzing Online Information* (CreateSpace Independent Publishing Platform, 2018), https://inteltechniques.com/.

○ There are many ways to customize search terms or "key words" to look for information. Search too broadly and you will get millions of results and find nothing; search too narrowly and you will get no relevant results, and perhaps miss clues. Crafting search terms that allow for possible mis-spellings of names, places, or other details often can lead to better results.

○ Remember that the "Deep Web" and "Dark Web" refer to Internet sites and data that are *not* indexed by traditional search engines. If data is there, an investigator will not find it through Google, but rather must go directly to the source's Internet address.

○ Safety alert: Depending upon the search engine, web browser, privacy settings, and whether a user is "logged in", the search terms used for investigation may be stored in the device being used to search and also may be tracked by search engines. Further, any location someone visits on the Internet can learn information about him or her, including the devices and Internet path used to get there.

- *Social media* (like Twitter, Facebook, LinkedIn, and YouTube)
- *News* and other media outlets
- *Online forums and communities* (whether for criminality or legitimate subjects and hobbies)
- *Court records* for criminal and civil cases of all types
- *Property ownership records* including deeds, liens, and mortgage information
- *Marriage, birth, death, voting, and other public records* maintained by local governments
- *Online maps* (traditional and photographic)
- *People search engines* that provide information like phone numbers and addresses
- *Professional licensing databases* (for doctors, attorneys, security guards, hairdressers, and other professions requiring licenses under federal, state, or local law)
- *Corporation look-up databases*, with details on incorporation status, location, and corporate officers (including from government sites)
- *Documents, images, blogs, and media* posted on searchable online platforms
- *Website databases* containing information about domain name registration, IP addresses, and website security certificates
- *The "Wayback Machine"* (archive.org) for historical website information.

The "Wayback Machine" can be especially useful to investigators. This open-source tool is provided by The Internet Archive, a non-profit organization that maintains a digital library by archiving websites and other digital media. Archive.org takes digital snapshots of thousands of websites at different periods of time. Investigators looking for website evidence that no longer appears to be available online may well find an archived version in The Wayback Machine's historical website records.

11.6.2 VIEWING AND PRESERVING OPEN SOURCE CLUES

Investigation through open sources found online is a search through different types of websites for information and activity that can offer leads and intelligence.

Some common ways in which evidence appears on open source webpages include:

- Displayed text, images, or videos
- Postings or comments from named individuals, Internet accounts, or nicknames
- Links to other websites of significance to the case.

The content of webpages, however, is temporary. Data might be altered or removed at any time by the website administrators or through automatic cycling of content. It can be crucial to an investigation, therefore, to preserve a website for the evidence it contains at a particular date and time.

Viewing safety. When looking at websites for evidence, investigators should take steps to ensure they are viewing them securely and safely. Some websites may be malicious and could infect the investigator's computer. Also, websites can track the users who visit them, learning information about the visitor's IP address and computing device (even developing a virtual "fingerprint" of it). For all these reasons, investigators should view websites using techniques that hide any information traceable to their agencies, employers, or the investigator personally. For example, websites can be viewed through a computer that is not registered to the investigator or her employer. Similarly, viewing can be conducted using an Internet service provider that is not linked to the investigator or employer (such as through a hot spot subscription, or a publicly available Wi-Fi network).

Preservation. When a website contains useful information to the investigation, it should be preserved as evidence. There are specialized software tools available for purchase that are designed to preserve webpages, and even entire websites, but these tools can require expense, configuration, and training, and this type of investment is not always practical or possible. Our everyday computers, however, come with their own tools that often are adequate for documenting websites as evidence.

Here are some simple methods for preserving evidence on a website using readily available tools:

- *Take a screenshot.* Most computer and mobile device operating systems include a screenshot function. For Windows, there is the snipping tool, Macs have screen capture, and mobile devices offer the same function in various forms. A screenshot will preserve a view of the website as a user would see it at the date and time it is taken.

  ○ Save the screenshot as an image, with a clear, descriptive filename.
  ○ Paste the screenshot into a document, with a helpful caption that includes the date, time, and webpage address. A supplemental method for certain cases is to simply take a photograph of the screen.

- *Copy and paste text found on a website into a document.* This process will make the text searchable, and facilitates future quoting of the material.
- *Print the webpage.* Another way to quickly capture a webpage is to print the page to a PDF file. This process can create a document that contains the basic content of the webpage in a stable format. When using this approach, investigators should ensure the webpage address, date, and time also are printed.
- *Save the webpage.* Instead of printing, investigators can use the "save" or "save as" command to save the webpage as an individual HTML or PDF file.
- *Document with narrative text.* Investigators can document what they see online with a clear, concise summary of relevant information, including date, time, URL (webpage address), what was observed, a listing of critical information or accounts, and notation of any witnesses who also observed the webpage at the same time. See Table 11.2.
- *Hash the preserved webpage data.* As we learned in Chapter 3, data can be run through a hashing algorithm to ensure that it was not altered or tampered with after the time of preservation. Depending on the nature of the webpage, hashing may be useful if there is any concern that the authenticity of the preserved data will be challenged. However, hashing can become a cumbersome process that ends up

TABLE 11.2
Summarizing What is Observed Online

Less Effective	More Effective
I preserved the webpage of his Facebook account today.	I preserved the webpage of Facebook account https[:]//www[.]facebook[.]com/johnbandlerbooks/ (Facebook UserID 123456789123456) today on 5/30/2019, saved it as Facebook JohnBandlerBooks 2019-5-30.pdf, and confirmed it was preserved accurately. Cyrus Miley witnessed it. This is believed to be the account belonging to John Bandler. The post (dated today) describes a book he plans to write on investigating cybercrime.

     inhibiting investigative curiosity and documentation of leads, and often is not necessary for webpage evidence.

- *Spreadsheets.* When investigators begin preserving multiple webpages, spreadsheets can be used to track the preserved information. Spreadsheets help investigators quickly see what has or has not been preserved, as well as identify investigative leads and patterns to follow up.

When using preservation methods, it can help to have multiple investigators or witnesses see the evidence contained on the webpage at the time it is preserved. The more people that view it live, and verify the preservation (if possible), the better the chance of defeating any challenge to the accuracy of the evidence should the case ever be litigated.

Website content and visitor data also can be obtained through a legal demand served upon the business administering or hosting the website. Using this method is a strategic decision. Time may pass in obtaining a subpoena or search warrant during which data may be altered or deleted. More importantly, although using a legal demand may allow investigators to collect more detailed webpage evidence, it also potentially will alert those associated with the website of the investigative interest.

11.6.3   PRACTICAL TIPS TO MAXIMIZE THE ADMISSIBILITY OF OPEN SOURCE DATA

Sometimes online investigation leads to a "eureka" moment, and when that happens, investigators will need to document where this great information was found and how they got there. More often, it is hard to know where information discovered during the investigation might lead, but it is worthwhile to accurately store it in case it turns out to be important later. Either way, if this information is ever to be used as evidence, it must be legally admissible.

Here are some things to think about during the investigative stage to maximize the future admissibility of open source data:

- *Authentication*

When obtaining or preserving evidence for potential use in court, consider how the evidence will be authenticated. For evidence found through open source investigation, authentication means demonstrating that the preserved image or other documentation of the webpage is a legitimate, unaltered depiction (not a misrepresentation or forgery).

Preserved open source evidence typically is authenticated by a live witness, most often the investigator who preserved the webpage. The authentication requirement will be met if the investigator (or another witness to the preservation) can testify that the preserved web-page is a "fair and accurate depiction" of the original as it appeared on the date the witness saw it. If website evidence was obtained through a subpoena or other legal demand, it can be authenticated by a representative from the company that provided the records who can attest to the reliability of the company's record-keeping practices.

If additional steps were taken to document or preserve open source information, including a process to prevent tampering (such as hashing), those facts also could be elicited.

- *Hearsay*

Throughout the investigation, and in summarizing evidence, investigators should be aware that federal and state rules of evidence generally prohibit the use of hearsay (sometimes called the "hearsay rule"). Under this general rule, the law prefers live witness testimony – meaning statements made in court, under oath, and subject to cross examination. Generally, out-of-court statements should not be introduced into evidence for their truth unless an exception to the hearsay rule is found (and many such exceptions exist).

Websites often contain past statements of various people. These statements were not made in court or under oath, so they may be hearsay. Further, the authors of these statements (declarants) often will not be available to testify in a court proceeding, heightening the hearsay concerns. Noting and documenting certain details about statements contained in preserved webpages (or anywhere else) can help prepare for hearsay issues. Details to be documented include:

- The fact that a statement was made
- Indications of who might have made the statement
- Whether the statement is truthful (or if that still needs to be determined)
- Whether the truthfulness of the statement matters.

If a hearsay statement is ever offered into evidence for its truth, then an exception to the hearsay rule must apply – such as the exception for "excited utterances" (things said in a state of excitement), "present sense impressions" (things said to describe an ongoing event), statements that are against the interests of the speaker or writer (such as admitting to a crime), or statements in furtherance of a conspiracy.

More often, however, the statements found in open source material will be admissible because their truthfulness does not matter, and so they are not hearsay. Perhaps the fact the statement was made is what is important, or the statement helps explain why an investigator or witness took certain action.

11.7   RECORDS EVIDENCE

The crux of a cybercrime investigation often comes down to records – the information compiled and stored by Internet service and communication providers, financial institutions, merchants, and other businesses and organizations documenting the trail of crime online. One set of records generates leads that require more sets of records, starting a continuing cycle of seeking and analyzing records until the crime is solved and the criminal identified.

Because records are often the most important type of evidence in a cyber case, this chapter focuses on the two key aspects of handling records evidence. First, we will look at methods for gathering and organizing records evidence to efficiently keep track of the information coming in to the investigation. And second, we will discuss techniques for analyzing records to get the most information and evidence possible.

11.7.1 THE WORKFLOW FOR RECORDS EVIDENCE

The workflow for seeking and reviewing records looks something like this:

- Start a Grand Jury investigation, civil suit, or administrative case
- Send a Letter of Preservation (if warranted)
- Determine what legal tool should be used to get the needed information
- Obtain that legal process (subpoena, search warrant, etc.)
- Serve the legal documents
- Await response
- Analyze records
- Repeat.

1. *Start a Grand Jury investigation, civil suit, or administrative case.* Investigators seeking records from a business or organization usually get them using some form of legal demand in connection with an official case or investigation. In most criminal cases, the process starts with opening a Grand Jury investigation through the prosecutor's office that has jurisdiction. For private sector investigations, issuance of legal process (subpoenas) may require filing a civil lawsuit. Government agencies with administrative subpoena authority will create a case or investigation within their internal system.

2. *Send a letter of preservation if warranted.* When an account or event connected to the case is identified, investigators should consider sending a letter of preservation to the company holding the relevant records. As we learned in Chapter 7, this letter alerts the company that the designated records should be found and maintained pending the receipt of future legal process compelling their disclosure (such as a subpoena or search warrant). When there is a delay in starting a case or obtaining legal process, the letter of preservation may ensure records are not deleted.

3. *Determine what legal tool should be used to get the records.* In earlier chapters, we learned about the legal tools available to private, regulatory, and law enforcement investigators to compel individuals and businesses to produce records. Which tool to use depends upon the type of investigation, the nature of records, the type of entity that possesses them, and the pertinent laws and statutes regulating law enforcement or other parties' access. Remember that consent is often an option to consider. Occasionally, records can be obtained just by asking for them.

4. *Obtain the necessary legal process.* Once investigators have determined what tool should be used, they must take the necessary steps to obtain the subpoenas or court orders.

5. *Serve the legal documents.* Legal process needs to be served properly according to federal or state rules, though many organizations and individuals will waive some of these requirements. Most Internet and phone service providers, financial institutions, and retail chains have dedicated units for receiving subpoenas, search warrants, and other court orders.

6. *Await the response.* When the subpoena or court order is properly obtained and served, the person or entity to which it is directed has a specified timeframe within which to comply. The timeframe may depend upon relevant state or federal law, and would be indicated on the document.

7. *Analyze the records.* We will cover more details on how to conduct the analysis later, but here we state the obvious – there is no point going through the trouble of obtaining records if they are not carefully reviewed for evidence and new leads.

8. *Repeat*. The process of obtaining records through legal process is cyclical, and likely will involve many iterative rounds.

Starting Out on the Records Trail

A rookie cybercriminal used a stolen credit card to make a purchase online from Cybrseller.com. To do this, he accessed the Internet, opened his web browser, then typed "Cybrseller.com" into the address bar. The domain name system routed him to the server where the Cybrseller website was hosted. He then conducted the fraudulent transaction with the stolen credit card data.

A law enforcement investigator receives a report about this crime from the credit card's owner. The investigator asks the local District Attorney's office to open an investigation in the Grand Jury, and then obtains a Grand Jury subpoena directed to Cybrseller, demanding all information about the purchase, all information provided by the purchaser, and any IP addresses used.

Cybrseller responds with the information requested. The company's records indicate that the fraudulent purchase was made on December 1, 2019, at 4:45 pm EST by a user with IP address 71.123.165.147 (a public IP address, of course).

Now a new round of records work begins. The investigator needs to find out who was using that IP address at that specific date and time. First, the investigator has to figure out which Internet service provider (ISP) has been assigned this IP address. There are several open source (free) and reliable IP address look-up services online, such as the ARIN Whois IP Address Database search tool and the website search.org. The investigator types in the IP address supplied by Cybrseller and the search tool provides the name of the Internet service provider to which the IP address has been assigned.

The investigator sees that IP address 71.123.165.147 is administered by Great Cable LLC, and prepares a Grand Jury subpoena for Great Cable, asking for all subscriber information about the customer who was using that particular IP address at that date, time, and time zone.

When this IP address information is gathered, it will inevitably create new questions and data points that require another round of investigation and records – and the hunt will continue as the circle closes.

11.7.2 TRACKING RECORDS REQUESTS

With the first inkling that records are going to be needed in an investigation, it is incredibly helpful to create a simple system that organizes the requests made and responses received. Without a system, investigators can quickly lose track of these requests or inadvertently request the same material twice. A tracking system is especially important when more than one investigator or staff member is working on obtaining records evidence. It can be amazing how quickly one subpoena for some subscriber information or credit card transactions quickly turns into a dozen follow-up requests, and on and on.

Tracking can be as easy as creating a spreadsheet, a log, or even a poster on the wall. Some key details to include in the tracking system are:

- Description of the information sought in each records request
  - Account names, type of information sought, date range, etc.
- Entity/person providing the requested records/items

- ○ The email provider, phone service provider, bank, etc.
- • Letters of Preservation sent and date
- • Type of legal tool used
  - ○ Subpoena, 2703(d) Order or search warrant
- • Date legal process was issued
- • Date material due from provider/business
- • Date material received from provider/business
- • Presence of non-disclosure order
- • Expiration date of non-disclosure order
- • Continued non-disclosure orders and expiration dates.

Routinely noting these details in an organized system will ensure the investigation receives the correct information, that entities are complying with the requests in a timely manner, and that non-disclosure orders are being obtained and kept up-to-date. The response time from providers can be a major factor slowing down a cyber investigation, so alerting providers when material is past due can help keep the investigation moving.

11.7.3   Organizing the Records

As investigators engage in the cycle of records requests and analysis, the pile of records (digital and paper) quickly becomes deep. Keeping the growing stack of records organized is another important step in making sure they are efficiently analyzed and retained for future use.

A simple, consistent system that is easily adopted by everyone handling the records is ideal. For example, records might be organized and stored by the business providing the record, then by the account name or number for which records were obtained.

This approach is effective because one business may be subpoenaed many times, supplying records about multiple accounts. The paper or digital file for each account should hold the records in original form, with a copy of the subpoena, other legal process, and any correspondence. Copies of the records (not the originals) should be used for analysis.

An organizational system of this nature helps investigators find and review records as the investigation proceeds, and helps organize the records as evidence, should the case proceed to litigation.

11.7.4   Analyzing the Information in Records

Analyzing the evidence in records can be likened to putting together a jigsaw puzzle. Each piece of information gives a new, but incomplete, glimpse of the picture, and spurs the investigator to find the next piece that will fit. But receiving responses to records requests can feel like staring at the pile of jigsaw pieces, wondering where to start. Records often contain a blast of names, numbers, and dates, and it can be difficult to know what to look for in all that data. Of course, no investigation ever recovers every piece of the puzzle.

To jumpstart the analysis, it can be helpful to look at records in three stages.

1. *Quick review.* Skim through the records looking for information that jumps out. The victim's name. An email address that appeared in another part of the case. A location of interest. A new email address or clue worthy of follow-up. Grab those quick leads and take the next steps (more subpoenas or other investigative work).
2. *Deeper dive.* Set aside more time and really comb through the data. Pay attention to details that seem important or unusual. Conduct careful open-source searching

that may shed light on names or locations in the records. Make notes about anything that should be investigated further.

3. *Data analysis.* Use keyword searches, spreadsheet functions, analytical software or whatever tools are available to extract useful information from the data. This process is especially useful with large pools of records (whether from one subpoena or search warrant, or combining the results of several records requests).

Throughout the records analysis, there are three general ideas that can help pinpoint evidence of a crime or new leads to follow:

- Connections
- Nuggets
- Opportunities for physical legwork.

Connections. When analyzing records, investigators should constantly look for connections between accounts, events, and individuals. Did the users of two accounts contact each other, or a third? Those accounts are probably significant. Was the same stolen information or fake name used in two crimes? Does the same purveyor of stolen identity information or malicious code come up repeatedly? Sometimes, just one connection is enough to start unraveling the mystery. As connections come together, they eventually fit the puzzle pieces together into a coherent picture of the case. They also will provide highly persuasive evidence should the case ever be presented to a judge, Grand Jury, or trial jury.

Nuggets. Cybercrime investigations often turn on nuggets of evidence in a sea of records and data. So often, the tiniest inconsistency or outlier, gleaned from a detailed review of records, opens the door to identifying a suspect or putting the case together cohesively. A name misspelled the same way twice, one unusual IP address among a thousand – nuggets like these can suddenly change an investigators' understanding of a case, and how it should be pursued.

Opportunities for physical legwork. So much of a cyber case is focused on the data side of an investigation – looking for those nuggets and connections in the records and following new leads by obtaining more records. But investigators should always be on the lookout for intersections between the records data and the physical world. Was a local store used to transmit fraudulently earned funds? Do a suspect's email records lead to an IP address nearby? Is there a new victim who can be interviewed? Taking advantage of any real-world aspect of the case is critical to solving these mysteries. Real-world clues found through records analysis can lead investigators to an identified victim, location, or suspect. They can turn the virtual mystery into a tangible arrest.

11.7.5 ADMISSIBILITY OF RECORDS EVIDENCE IN LITIGATION

Records evidence usually is admissible in a court proceeding under federal and state rules of evidence so long as certain legal steps are followed. Assuming the records are relevant to the litigation, the only hurdle to admissibility is their authentication.

Authentication can be accomplished through testimony of a live representative from the organization that provided the records, who also can give any explanation of the records that might be helpful to the court or jury.

Some jurisdictions allow records to be authenticated without a live witness, instead relying upon a written certification from a representative of the organization. The certification typically states that the records were kept in the ordinary course of business and that they are reliable consistent with a business duty to accurately make and store such records.

To ensure the records can be authenticated using either of these methods, investigators should:

- Save all correspondence to and from the entity providing the records
- Save the records provided by the entity in their original form
- Provide the business the opportunity to review all records and correspondence in advance of the court proceeding.

11.8   EMAIL EVIDENCE

Emails can be a significant source of evidence in cybercrime cases. Email might be the method through which a crime is committed, such as a phishing scam or business email compromise. Cybercriminals also might use compromised email accounts or create accounts that impersonate victims to send emails. Beyond email-centered crimes, cyber-criminals use email to communicate with their colleagues, vendors, friends, and families, just like everyone else.

11.8.1   READING EMAIL HEADERS

Along with the content of the messages, emails contain information about where they came from and how they were routed to their destinations, which can be useful leads and evidence (analogous to the postmark on a letter but more informative).

Our email applications typically display information in a friendly format. We normally see the sender and recipient, the names of other people copied on the email, the date, and the subject line. These elements, however, are actually only a small portion of what is called the full email "header". The full header contains the basic information we see when we open the email, but also many other raw details, such as the IP address from which the email was sent, and the route it took through the Internet to its destination. This header information can provide clues about where the email was created, who sent it, and whether it is genuine.

Criminals can manipulate the way an email displays header information to trick recipients into believing the email came from a legitimate person or organization. By looking at the full header information many of these tricks can be exposed.

Viewing Email Headers

You can practice viewing headers for incoming emails using the common email applications we use to send our own email:

- Gmail (via web browser): click on the options dots and select "show original message".
- Hotmail (via web browser): click on the options dots and select "view message source".
- Yahoo (via web browser): open the message and select "view raw message" in the email options.
- Microsoft Outlook: open the message, navigate to the "file" tab, view properties, navigate to the "Internet headers" box.

When you view the full headers, read from the bottom up to view the message's path from when it was sent to when it was received. The first (bottom) IP address listed may be that of the sender, which could be crucial evidence for a case. Note that many email providers protect the privacy of their customers by substituting the email provider's IP address for the sender's IP address.

For example, imagine Victor Victim receives an email that looks like this:

To: Victor Victim
From: Alert@BankName.com
Subject: Important Account Notice
Date: February 19, 2020, 5:42 p.m.

At first glance, this email appears to be from Victor's bank, but the name in the "From" field is merely the "friendly" name the sender manipulated for display. When the full email header is viewed, it may give the true sender information, making it possible to detect the email's true source and providing additional clues.

11.8.2 ANALYZING LARGE SETS OF EMAILS

Public and private sector investigators may come across enormous troves of email records as a case proceeds. Criminal investigators may find them after serving a search warrant upon an email provider for a suspect's account, or after doing a forensic search of a suspect's computer device. Private sector investigators may obtain internal corporate emails that need to be reviewed.

Large sets of email data present challenges and opportunities for investigators. The challenge is finding relevant evidence in a haystack of irrelevant data. The opportunity is that large amounts of data offer the potential to get to the heart of the conduct being investigated. Somewhere in that big data set might be the evidence showing wrongful conduct, or evidence demonstrating a suspect's identity or ownership of certain devices.

Thousands of emails would take a year to read so investigators need a system to review these emails in an efficient and effective way. That system ideally would:

* Review emails to and from individuals relevant to the investigation
* Review emails a suspect or target sends to himself
* Conduct keyword searches for important terms.

The simplest way to find this information in large quantities of email is to view them with an email application, and then analyze them using the same methods we use for our own email accounts.

Mozilla Thunderbird is a free email application that can be used for this purpose. It can be configured such that it does not access the Internet (meaning, without the capability to send or receive emails, and without the ability to load images from remote servers). This configuration is an important precaution so that investigators do not accidentally send an email to an account within the suspect's email data. Once loaded into the application, the suspect's emails can be viewed and read, filters applied, and searches conducted to narrow the results according to:

* Sender
* Recipient

- Date
- Keywords in subject line
- Keywords in body of the email
- Attachments.

While this simple, readily available method is very effective for reviewing emails, there also are proprietary software tools designed for email and forensic evidence review.

Western Express: Email Review and Admissibility

The Western Express investigation led to the review of tens of thousands of emails among cybercriminals, identity thieves, and money launderers. This email evidence allowed us to track the various and shifting Internet accounts of the targets – including instant message, virtual currency, and new email accounts that were created. Email evidence provided clear examples of the group's criminal conduct, the exchange of stolen data, and the use of it for fraud.

We used the Mozilla application described above to conduct most of the email analysis in the case. Although the crimes we investigated proved to be complex, this simple, free method was very effective in distilling the thousands of email records into leads we needed to follow and evidence that would prove the case.

At the indictment stage and through the eventual conviction of the defendants who went to trial, the email records were admitted into evidence after being authenticated by representatives of the email service providers. Relevant emails were extracted from the pool of records in both electronic and paper format and assembled into dozens of binders so that jurors could see the extent of the criminal conduct. Summaries also were prepared to make the highlights of the evidence easy to understand.

11.9 THE IMPORTANCE OF CYBERCRIME INTELLIGENCE

The importance of cybercrime intelligence cannot be overstated, especially for those tasked with identifying and prosecuting cybercriminals. It is often impossible to solve significant cybercrime cases working them one case at a time – receiving a report of crime, then working from scratch to develop suspects and prove a case. Given all the evidence that can be gathered among many investigations (from open sources, records, and email), developing and sharing information about crimes, actors, and criminal methods is the most effective way to battle these crimes.

Anyone investigating cybercrime can both create intelligence resources and benefit from developed and shared intelligence. Creating intelligence involves simply recording information about the people and activity uncovered through an investigation in a shareable format. Some useful ways of organizing case information into shareable intelligence include:

- *Profiles* of significant cybercriminal actors that come up during the investigation (personal identifiers, communication accounts, financial accounts, criminal and personal history)
- *Associations* between criminal actors, as well as with other relevant people or businesses (the connections may be personal, geographical, and/or financial)

- Explanation or diagram of how a group of criminals is *organized*
- *Photos* of key individuals and locations.

When investigators create intelligence documentation and analysis in this manner, the effort results in an aggregated knowledge base within their agencies that helps develop leads and evidence in the case. Agencies and organizations also can utilize this accumulated knowledge in future investigations, with each case adding to and benefitting from this base of intelligence.

Some of the crucial benefits for investigators of sharing and using cyber intelligence to investigate cybercrime are:

- *Saved time and resources* when investigators can use information already obtained in other cases
- *Better investigation results* by receiving data on subjects that may otherwise have been unavailable, and because of the assistance and referrals available through intelligence sharing
- *Connecting dots* by offering data that might indicate a cybercrime is linked to events and people being investigated by other groups.

There are many agencies, organizations, and services that build information-sharing communities, including:

- Private sector intelligence businesses (paid services)
- Government and public–private partnerships such as:
  - *IC3*. The Internet Crime Complaint Center (FBI site) analyzes and shares cybercrime reports for intelligence and investigative purposes
  - *FBI Cyber Watch*. CyWatch is a 24-hour command center run by the FBI to receive threat and incident reporting and facilitate communication with the appropriate responders
  - U.S. Secret Service Electronic Crimes Task Forces (ECTFs), regional interdisciplinary groups
  - Anti-Phishing Working Group: an international coalition
  - CERT. The Computer Emergency Response Team is part of the Software Engineering Institute affiliated with Carnegie Mellon University
  - Information Sharing and Analysis Centers (ISAC), including Multi-state Information Sharing and Analysis Center (MS-ISAC), etc.
  - InfraGard. InfraGard is a partnership between the FBI and members from the private sector.

Remember that laws and rules may govern what information can be shared, what it can be used for, and information may need to be independently confirmed.

11.10 CONCLUSION

All cybercrime investigators benefit from creating systems to organize, track, and analyze the information and data they gather. In this chapter we explored proprietary and readily available tools that can assist in this process, as well as the steps that ensure evidence eventually will be admissible in court. As we have seen, recording and documenting the information clearly is essential to a cybercrime investigation.

Several types of evidence are integral to all cybercrime investigations, including open source information, records from private companies, and email evidence. Mastering the methods of finding, preserving, organizing, and analyzing these types of evidence both strengthens a cybercrime case and creates intelligence that can be shared with other investigators.

12 Private Entity's Cybercrime Investigation

This chapter is primarily for:

- Private organizations, corporations, and individuals, plus the investigators, consultants, and lawyers hired to assist them
- Law enforcement and regulatory officials who want to know more about how a private sector investigation might proceed.

12.1 INTRODUCTION

In this chapter we explore what a private entity (or individual) can do to investigate cybercrime. While private entities lack many of the tools and resources of law enforcement (such as search warrants and ready access to subpoenas), they do have the benefit of internal data, tools, and focused resources on a particular case.

The chapter begins with a discussion of incident response, which includes prior response planning and even prevention. Then we look at the steps of a private sector investigation from the view of the entity or person victimized by the crime. The investigative steps covered include discovery of the incident; establishing investigative goals; activating necessary personnel (internal and external); notifications to law enforcement, regulators, and affected parties; identifying potential witnesses and evidence; and collection of internal and external evidence.

Any type of private entity can be affected by cybercrime, including businesses, non-profit organizations, financial institutions, Internet service providers, and communications services. Some entities may be direct victims, while others might be used as tools by cybercriminals to victimize others. Depending on the size and nature of the entity, some investigative steps may be handled internally or by contracting with third-parties. Chapters 5 and 9 give investigators a background on some of the legal considerations involved in a private sector investigation.

12.2 INCIDENT RESPONSE (AND PREVENTION)

By preparing in advance, private sector entities can help prevent cybercrime incidents, improve investigations, and mitigate any harm. We cover incident response planning in Chapter 4, and return to it now since, ideally, it serves as the foundation of a private sector investigation. All organizations should have an incident response plan that is appropriate to the size of the organization and the threats faced. The plan should be part of a broader and comprehensive information security program that addresses diverse areas like training, identification of threats and vulnerabilities, and threat monitoring.

Sound response preparation includes a written plan that is routinely practiced, reviewed, and improved.

To recap the stages of planning and response:

- Creation of an incident response plan that is part of a comprehensive information security program, and customized to the organization
- Preparation for an incident
  - Evaluate information security program and devices
  - Make regular data backups
  - Monitor and detect attacks
  - Identify and train an incident response team, including those charged with investigation, forensics, legal, compliance, communications, and notifications to outside parties
- Identification and detection of a cyber incident
- Containment of the threat
- Eradication of the threat
- Recovery and resumption of normal operations
- Reporting to government and affected parties
- Communications to the public and interactions with the media
- Aftermath and lessons learned.

Each of these steps impacts a private entity's investigation of a cybercrime incident. The better the preparation, the more likely an attack will be detected and stopped quickly, with a rapid investigative response that finds and preserves evidence.

12.3 DISCOVERY OF CYBERCRIME INCIDENTS BY PRIVATE PARTIES

Businesses, organizations, and individuals discover a cybercrime event when they detect it themselves or are informed by an outside party about suspicious events. When discovered, it typically comes as a rude shock. Although ideally the entity has been monitoring its systems and data for abnormal activity, the actual targeting or infiltration by cybercriminals may occur in unexpected ways. Detection by private sector organizations commonly occurs when employees notice:

- Emails received impersonating other employees or entities (*phishing* or *spearphishing*)
- Strange computer activity, including after clicking on links within emails from unknown or impersonated senders (*malware transmission*)
- Unauthorized emails sent from an account, possibly reported by colleagues/friends who receive them (*email account compromise*)
- User is locked out of an email account (*email account compromise*)
- Confidential information or other data has been changed or copied (*network intrusion, malware*)
- Theft of funds from financial accounts, or transferred funds do not reach the intended recipient (*account compromise, identity theft*)
- Computers and devices spontaneously shutting down or other irregular device activity (*malware detection*)
- Data, files, or drives cannot be accessed and/or communications received demanding ransom (*ransomware*)
- Customers or employees cannot access the entity's websites or online services (*denial of service attacks*)

- Unknown users operating within a network (*network intrusion*)
- Online threats on social media or harassing communications received through the entity's website or communications accounts (*cyber harassment or stalking*).

Larger organizations tend to devote greater resources to information technology and information security. Major financial institutions, for example, have entire divisions devoted to the task of monitoring all information systems for indicators of cyberattacks. Regardless of organization size, an individual employee who has no specific duties relating to cybersecurity or cybercrime might be the person who discovers an attack, and so training for employees at all levels is essential.

The bigger the organization, the more complex their information technology (IT) systems become. Companies large enough to have dedicated IT personnel, whether in house or out of house, may use different methods for detecting cybercrime incidents than smaller companies, including:

- Help desk inquiries from employees indicating the possible presence of malware, ransomware, or other suspicious activity
- Monitoring tools that report
  o Malware on computers or devices
  o Suspicious network traffic
  o Suspicious email traffic, including phishing emails
- Data loss prevention (DLP) tools reporting unauthorized removal of data
- Systems that detect and prevent the connection of unknown devices
- Other security and event monitoring tools.

Private entities also might be informed by outside parties regarding a potential cybercrime. Sometimes these notifications merely provide clues, while other warnings provide clear indicators of a crime. Examples include:

- Inquiries from suppliers, business associates, or customers regarding suspicious emails or transactions, or payments that have not been received
- Alerts from partner businesses (like suppliers, communications services, and credit card processors) about cybercrimes affecting their own organizations
- Contact from law enforcement, regulators, cybercrime victims, or security researchers
- Intelligence notifications from government, academic, or industry organizations tracking the spread of malware and other forms of cybercrime.

12.3.1   Is This a Crime the Private Entity Can and Should Investigate?

Private sector entities face a continual flood of attacks at the hands of cybercriminals. Some organizations (such as financial institutions) may be subject to thousands of network intrusion attempts and malicious email attacks. In a legal sense, each attack, even if unsuccessful, is itself a serious cybercrime since criminal attempts are crimes as well. But with so many attacks, how does a private entity decide whether it can or should investigate each crime?

Although the answer will be different depending on the size and nature of the organization (or for individuals), each entity must set a reasonable and realistic threshold for investigation. Most businesses and individuals will work to identify and investigate serious incidents that cause financial or reputational harm, or as required by law or regulation.

Beyond the most serious cases, organizations must evaluate the types of incidents that merit investigation resources.

As entities determine their thresholds for investigation, these decisions form the foundation of their incident response plans. Both the thresholds and response plans may change over time, another reason that practicing response actions is so important.

Cost is a major factor in deciding what to investigate and how thoroughly. Every private investigation costs money, time, and resources, and the potential benefits need to be weighed against these costs. For smaller organizations, the cost of investigating the root causes of a cybercrime may be prohibitive. Instead, these entities might better spend available funds on improving their cybersecurity, restoring their systems, and regaining customer trust. Larger companies, on the other hand, especially those under government regulation or responsible to shareholders, may be under a legal obligation to investigate.

Monitoring for cyberattacks also plays a significant role in determining investigative thresholds because more attacks are detected. Many organizations profess they have never been cybercrime victims and have nothing to investigate. It is worth considering whether these statements are accurate, or whether the organizations are not detecting such attacks sufficiently or defining them appropriately (as depicted in Figure 12.1).

An organization that ignores every cybercrime merely to save resources or avoid damage to its public reputation is simply ignoring the inevitable. Even if they have not yet been victimized, they almost certainly have been the subject of unsuccessful cybercrime attempts. Monitoring unsuccessful attacks could prevent them from morphing into successful ones, and could yield clues about what data the criminals are targeting and the methods employed.

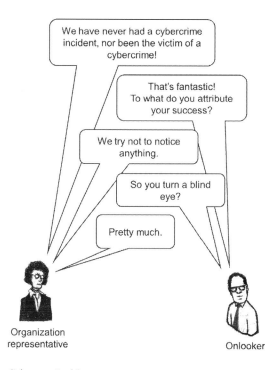

FIGURE 12.1   What is a Crime or Incident.

12.4   DETERMINING INVESTIGATION GOALS AND SCOPE

When a private sector entity decides a cyber incident should be investigated, the next step is to determine the goals and scope of the investigation (a decision that will need to be continually re-evaluated). Depending on the type of cybercrime incident and size of the organization, there may be trade-offs between collecting evidence and getting the organization running again so that it can continue its work, serve clients and earn revenue.

Some of the goals of a private sector investigation might include:

- Determine what was compromised and the extent of the compromise
- Determine or rule out insider involvement
- Secure networks and devices to avoid continued or repeated attack
- Collect internal and external evidence of the attack
- Determine identities of cybercriminals
- Assist law enforcement in identification, apprehension, prosecution of perpetrators
- Rapid resumption of normal activities
- Recovery of stolen funds
- Restore business reputation and customer/client trust
- Identify root causes to correct them
- Fulfill regulatory and legal requirements
- Satisfy owners/shareholders
- Minimize investigative costs.

The investigative need to preserve and collect evidence of a crime often conflicts with the business goals of limiting damage and keeping things running. For example, investigators might want to image all computer devices to preserve evidence, taking days before the process of restoring backup data can begin. Others in the organization may want to get computers running faster, preferring to quickly wipe them clean and restore backups.

To analogize this dilemma, a business facing a fire will want to focus on putting the fire out, and will not immediately be concerned with figuring out how it started and preserving that evidence.

Private entities often weigh these competing investigative goals in working out the scope of an investigation. While all the goals might be worthy, they must be evaluated within the context of the general factors that affect the organization as a whole. Factors that determine which goals will be pursued and to what extent include:

- *Scope of the incident itself.* The extent of the damage to systems, the amount of revenue or funds lost, the number of customers affected, whether data was encrypted or damaged, intellectual property stolen, etc.
- *Breadth and timeline of the likely investigation.* Does the incident appear to be relatively confined (such as the work of one disgruntled employee) or a complex scheme executed by sophisticated cybercrime actors? Are investigative steps necessary to resume normal activities? Is the scope of the investigation likely to change as more information is learned about an attack?
- *Extent of forensics to be performed.* To what extent will digital forensics play a role in this investigation? Was an entire network compromised, or does the compromise seem limited to certain devices? What is the likely timeline of the forensic work? How much disruption to entity functions will it involve?
- *Projected cost of the investigation.*

FIGURE 12.2 Determining Scope.

- ○ Internal resources (including time) needed for the investigation
- ○ Cost projections for third party investigators or experts.
- • *External demands.* Is investigation necessary to satisfy law enforcement, regulatory compliance, reports to shareholders, media inquiries, customer complaints, or lawsuits?

As the response to an incident unfolds, the urgency of certain goals and the projected costs are often the most significant factors in deciding the ultimate scope of the investigation, as depicted in Figure 12.2. Entities with limited funds, or with business needs that override investigative goals, may decide to conduct an investigation of lesser scope.

Investigation and Business Goals: The Inherent Tension

Dogged investigators like to pursue every lead and turn over every stone, knowing they might turn over 20 stones and find nothing, or one could conceal a valuable lead that makes the case. Anyone can speculate about what *might* have been under a stone, but doing thorough investigative work is what finds the answers.

Private sector entities generally do not like long-term costs with an unpredictable ending. Neither do they like having their employees toiling on tasks that might not yield solid results. Sometimes it can be hard for an investigator to convince a client or manager that spending time and money on a cybercrime case is worthwhile.

Herein lies the basic tension that defines many private sector investigations: thoroughly investigating a cyberattack versus cost, work, and disruption. Because of this frequent source of conflict, it often is not advisable for someone with little or no investigative experience to dictate what investigative leads should be pursued. At the same time, reasonable decisions have to be made about the resources spent, and the goals and scope of an investigation.

While the solution is not simple, one answer might be to budget a certain number of hours for basic investigative tasks, allowing those with investigative experience to have discretion on what leads to follow. Decisions about major investigative expenses – like computer forensics work – can be made through ongoing evaluation of the needs of the investigation and the entity's recovery.

12.5   ACTIVATING NECESSARY PERSONNEL: IN-HOUSE AND EXTERNAL

As goals are determined and the investigative scope takes shape, the people who will conduct or assist in the investigation must begin their work. Ideally, these investigators are the personnel designated within the entity's cybercrime incident response plan and have prepared to take on their pre-assigned response roles. Of course, some cybercrime incidents may result in unexpected investigative needs, requiring an organization to obtain assistance from other sources.

Whether planning for future incidents or responding to one at hand, the first consideration in assigning and activating personnel is whether the right people already work for the entity ("in-house" employees) or must be hired from outside the organization ("external" services or consultants). Much of this determination depends on the size of the private entity. Smaller organizations victimized by cybercrimes may not have employees with the necessary investigative expertise on staff. Large organizations may have the choice of using in-house personnel or external investigators.

Some reasons organizations use *inside* personnel for the investigation include:

* Resources exist in-house and can operate as a separate investigative function
* In-house personnel are part of the incident response team and are trained for this type of investigation
* Lower cost, meaning additional expenses are not incurred, just expenditure of employee labor (also known as retrospective or "sunk" costs)
* Fewer people involved, less confusion and moving parts
* No reason to believe insiders (employees) are involved in the criminal activity.

Some reasons organizations use *outside* personnel for the investigation include:

* Resources or expertise do not exist in-house
* Resources exist in-house, but the organization:
  ○ Wants to avoid bias, interest in the outcome, ethical conflicts (or the appearance thereof)
  ○ Wants to solidify a claim of attorney/client privilege for the investigation by separating the investigation from traditional employee duties (see Chapter 9)
  ○ Wants to avoid making their own employees witnesses who might have to testify
  ○ Cannot pull employees from their ordinary duties to perform investigative tasks
  ○ Cannot rule out insider involvement, either intentional or due to negligence.

Entities looking to hire outsourced investigative personnel have a number of options ranging in quality, expertise, and size, from solo forensics specialists and attorneys to publicly traded investigations firms. Any outside lawyer, consultant, or investigator serves at the direction of the client, while complying with the ethical and legal norms and requirements.

Therefore, many investigative decisions rest with the client, including notifications, reporting, and information sharing.

Hiring an external attorney to supervise an investigation may add expense, but also may bring much of the investigation under the umbrella of the attorney–client privilege. Attorney-supervised investigations in anticipation of litigation provide some confidentiality for facts discovered, allowing investigators to seek information whether it helps or hurts the client's cause. We discuss legal privilege in this context in Chapter 9.

12.5.1 External Services to Consider

Whatever an organization's individual and organizational resources, it is always worthwhile to consider whether external assistance would be beneficial. Some cyberattacks raise unexpected or unusual forms of damage, or raise internal concerns the entity cannot address on its own. Some specialized services pertinent to cybercrime investigations include:

- *Background investigations.* Many investigation firms conduct background inquiries on individuals or corporations, both by searching proprietary databases or through interviews and surveillance.
- *Asset location.* Some firms specialize in locating and investigating assets held by suspects.
- *International investigations.* Attorneys and investigators in other countries can use investigative tools and the legal process within that country to obtain information about suspects and financial transactions.
- *Digital forensics.* Forensics experts who can image and analyze computers, networks, and devices are increasingly affordable and can be found in most areas.
- *Financial intelligence.* A variety of products and services can assist entities in the tracing of virtual currency payments, as well as other monetary transactions.
- *Cybercrime intelligence.* A variety of organizations monitor the "dark web" and cybercrime underground, and potentially can provide intelligence about an attack on a private entity.
- *Forensic accounting.* Accountant services that can unravel discrepancies within an entity's financial accounting or explain the money movement within the financial records of suspects.

These types of services range greatly in cost, often depending on the nature and volume of work that a particular investigation will entail. At times, the cost of hiring an external service turns out to save money, as their work may quickly and conclusively resolve important aspects of the case.

In House or External?

Consider these scenarios where an organization might turn to external investigative resources.

Company A is the victim of a cyberattack with devastating consequences. Part of the investigation will address whether the company's information security defenses were adequate and whether the systems were working properly. If the investigation is conducted by members of the in-house information security or information technology team, they might be tempted to emphasize facts or conclusions that absolve them of responsibility, such as by attributing the incident to user error or the work of a sophisticated nation-state.

Company B is the victim of insider crime, where an employee has stolen or damaged information assets. Company employees normally assigned to certain investigative actions might have a personal relationship with the suspect. If this personal relationship is friendly, it might influence their eagerness to explore all leads. If the relationship is unfriendly and the case proceeds towards criminal or civil litigation, the insider could claim the investigation was biased, or that the company tried to frame the employee out of retaliation or animosity.

In situations such as these, the organization ideally might be better off using external investigators. But there still are all the general factors to consider, especially cost. If external resources cannot be used to investigate, an organization may consider establishing clear, finite investigative goals with supervision that better ensures accurate results.

12.6 REPORTING AND NOTIFICATIONS TO LAW ENFORCEMENT, REGULATORY AGENCIES, AND OTHER PARTIES

Private sector entities that encounter cybercrime have another important investigative consideration – reporting the incident to other sectors and parties. Reporting outside of the entity can take two forms:

Voluntary reporting. Whether or not the organization embarks on its own investigation, the option of voluntary reporting to law enforcement, relevant regulatory agencies, and to other affected parties (like customers or business partners) is always available. Voluntary reporting may be undertaken to obtain investigative help, contribute intelligence to industry security groups, or to inform agencies, parties, or the public about the nature of the cyberattack, thereby allowing them to take investigative or security actions of their own.

Mandatory notification. As we covered in Chapter 9, some laws and regulations require private entities to notify law enforcement, regulators, and affected individuals or businesses following certain cybercrime events. Mandatory notification rules usually are intended to ensure that customers, regulators, and the public are made aware when data is compromised that could lead to identity theft or other damage to consumers, and to give law enforcement the chance to investigate.

Organizations need to evaluate at an early stage whether or not the incident should be or must be reported to government agencies and outside parties. If required, they should make the notification within the specified time period of the applicable state or federal rule, and retain documentation of the report to show compliance with the rule's requirements. With discretionary reporting, organizations can decide whether to report based on the facts of the case and their investigative and business goals. Documenting voluntary reports of cybercrime is also useful for any potential litigation surrounding the incident.

When an entity decides *not* to report a cybercrime, that decision should be continually re-evaluated in light of new facts that are learned during the entity's investigation. When cyberattacks are not reported, the organization may find itself in the position of defending that decision should future events bring the attack to light.

12.6.1 REPORTING TO LAW ENFORCEMENT

There are many reasons a private sector organization might report a cyberattack (or other cybercrime exposure) to law enforcement, with both investigative and business goals in mind. These reasons include:

- Enlisting investigative help
- Apprehending perpetrators
- Compliance with laws and regulations
- Demonstrating commitment to properly investigating the incident

- Documenting the cyberattack and incident response for later use, including
  - Future litigation as plaintiff, defendant, or witness
  - Insurance claims
  - Reports of losses for tax returns
  - Justification for personnel decisions, including if an employee violated policy or is suspected of intentional wrongful acts.

Reporting to law enforcement agencies can be done in many ways. For voluntary reporting, the most direct method is to contact the local police department, FBI office, or prosecutor's office (especially if it is an office with a process for directly reporting crimes). Online reports can be filed with the FBI through the Internet Crime Complaint Center (IC3) though it may be some time before the victim receives a response. If identity theft occurred, online reports can be filed through the Federal Trade Commission's Identity Theft Clearing House.[1]

For mandatory notification to law enforcement about a data breach or other cyberattack, organizations should review the notification requirements of their home state and the states where they do business. An entity may be obligated to notify law enforcement in states where their customers reside. Notification laws and regulations usually instruct entities to notify specific law enforcement agencies, and also indicate what type of reporting is mandated. For example, in addition to notifying regulating agencies, federal regulations require financial institutions to file a SAR (Suspicious Activity Report) in the event of cyber-enabled crime.[2]

When reporting a cybercrime to law enforcement, private entities can enhance both their own and law enforcement's investigation by anticipating certain aspects of working together:

The reporting entity's assistance will be needed. Reporting a crime to law enforcement does not mean handing the investigation over and wishing the officers and agents luck. Instead, notification carries an implied responsibility to assist in the criminal investigation. The complexity of many cybercrimes may require greater investigatory assistance and sharing since the reporting entity has direct knowledge of its systems and employees, and law enforcement resources are limited. Entities that are reporting primarily to satisfy regulatory requirements or business goals (like public relations strategies) should understand that the report is not just a formality, but that a law enforcement investigation will be initiated that requires their participation.

Crimes must be reported accurately. A report to law enforcement is required to be accurate to the best of the organization's (or individual's) knowledge, with the understanding that all the facts may not be known in the early stages. Knowingly making a false report or providing false information wastes law enforcement resources and may subject the reporter to criminal or civil penalties.

Reporting is not a one-step, seamless process. Law enforcement agencies are busy handling a continuous stream of crime reports. Agencies often are divided into various units with a hierarchy of supervision, and so the reporting process may require repeating information to different officials (along with follow-up from the organization to ensure an investigation is underway). Documenting details about each step in the reporting process is useful as

---

[1] IC3's reporting page can be found at www.ic3.gov/. The FTC's identity theft reporting page can be found at www.ftccomplaintassistant.gov. When reporting through online portals, users may not be provided with an email confirmation or other convenient method of confirming the report. Printing the screen to electronic PDF format (or paper) as you progress is sometimes the best method of documentation.

[2] *See e.g.* FinCEN Advisory FIN-2016-A005, *Advisory to Financial Institutions on Cyber-Events and Cyber-Enabled Crime* (October 25, 2016), www.fincen.gov/sites/default/files/advisory/2016-10-25/Cyber%20Threats%20Advisory%20-%20FINAL%20508_2.pdf.

these may be needed later. Obtaining a case number helps ensure that the complaint has been officially recorded by law enforcement.

Good communication is essential. When making the report and during the course of any law enforcement investigation, good communication with the reporting organization greatly improves the results. Providing law enforcement officials with designated contacts within the organization can ensure calls and emails are directed efficiently. Clear channels of communication are especially important when the interests of the organization and law enforcement potentially conflict, such as over access to the organization's sensitive systems or data. All that said, law enforcement agencies may not respond as quickly or thoroughly as a private entity might prefer, and the entity may have to be persistent in its follow-up.

Information sharing is usually one-way. While the reporting entity may be asked to share information about the cyberattack, information systems, and incident response with law enforcement, it is likely that law enforcement will not share information reciprocally. For example, much of the evidence law enforcement gathers is through Grand Jury subpoenas, and this information generally cannot be shared due to rules of Grand Jury secrecy. Private entities should be aware that they will not always be kept apprised of every stage of law enforcement's work.

Getting to Know Law Enforcement

Cybersecurity experts, law enforcement representatives, and government resources frequently recommend that private sector businesses and organizations get to know their local federal agents before an incident occurs, so that they know who to call when cybercrime strikes. This is indisputably good advice, and most law enforcement agents are dedicated and wonderful professionals who it is a pleasure to know.

This advice, however, also points to the inherent problems with our current approach to investigating cybercrime. First of all, the advice is unrealistic. It is not possible for law enforcement agents to get to know every potential cybercrime victim – that is to say, every business and resident of the country.

But even more significantly, advising us to get to know law enforcement before the cybercrime occurs is an acknowledgement that it can be hard to report these crimes and get an adequate response. It concedes that law enforcement is not readily accessible for individuals and organizations *unless they already have a personal connection.* If someone suggested we apply this logic to brick-and-mortar crimes, we would reject it. We expect that we can readily report street crimes and get a law enforcement response, even without having any personal connection.

The moral of this story is twofold. It is good to get to know law enforcement and they deserve our cooperation, respect, and appreciation for their service. However, our country needs to get to a place where every cybercrime can be readily reported and investigated, even without personal connections.

12.6.2   REPORTING TO REGULATORS AND AGENCIES ENFORCING SIMILAR LAWS

Private sector organizations affected by cybercrime also might report the events to government agencies tasked with enforcing civil laws and regulations applicable to private sector entities. Much of this regulatory reporting is mandated when certain types of cybercrime occur, although entities also might voluntarily report cybercrime events as part of an effort to share information and intelligence.

Regulated industries. Organizations within regulated industries must follow the procedures spelled out by the regulator in the event of a cybercrime. Depending on the nature of the incident, notification to the regulator may be required, as well as to law enforcement and affected parties. If so, the regulator will probably want to investigate the circumstances of the crime, the results of the regulated entity's investigation, and the entity's security posture.

Laws affecting all industries and organizations. All private sector entities may be required to report data breaches and other cybercrime compromises of consumer information in accordance with state law. As we covered in Chapter 9, all 50 states have mandatory data breach notification laws. Organizations with customers in multiple states may be required to comply with those states' laws as well. In many states, this form of mandated notification must be made to the state Attorney General's office within a certain number of days of the crime or crime discovery. Each state's data breach law provides the specific guidelines for the mandatory notification process.

These mandatory notification requirements have implications beyond mere reporting. They imply a duty to conduct an investigation to figure out what happened. As with notifications to law enforcement, the reporting process does not end with the making of the report. Regulators and other investigators are likely to follow up with requests for information and assistance to examine the root causes of the cybercrime, as well as the information security measures that were – or were not – in place. If the organization is subject to regular review of its information security practices, the next regulatory review may include heightened scrutiny based upon the prior cybercrime incident.

12.7   IDENTIFYING POTENTIAL WITNESSES AND EVIDENCE: INTERNAL AND EXTERNAL

All investigations into cybercrime are an ongoing effort to locate witnesses and evidence that might shed light on the crime and its perpetrators. Private sector investigations, however, must view all potential evidence through one central distinction: is the evidence internal or external to the organization?

Internal witnesses and evidence are tremendous resources for investigators working on behalf of private entities. Employees generally are available to be interviewed. Data and records from internal accounts and devices can be accessed and viewed without having to obtain subpoenas or other legal demands compelling their disclosure. As discussed in Chapter 5, many private entities retain all ownership and privacy rights over devices and communications accounts assigned to employees. Internal evidence also may include company-owned data that is stored with a third party.

External evidence and witness interviews also may be crucial to a private organization's investigation, but often are harder to obtain. In the following sections, we will look at methods and considerations for private sector investigators collecting internal and external evidence.

Taking the time to develop an overview of what evidence is available through internal access and what is external to the entity can give investigators a game plan for how to proceed. This evidence review will continue to develop as the case develops and new leads and information accumulate.

12.8   COLLECTING EVIDENCE AVAILABLE INTERNALLY

The easiest evidence for private sector investigators to collect is the internal information over which the organization has control. By definition, no consent or legal process is required to collect and examine this evidence. The entity has full authority to make it available to its investigators, whether these are existing personnel or investigators hired from outside the organization.

In general, this internal evidence includes the recollections of employees, records, and data owned or retained by the organization, and devices the organization owns or controls. The following sections discuss collecting each of these forms of internal evidence.

12.8.1 INTERVIEWING INTERNAL PERSONNEL

Cybercrime investigations are similar to traditional investigations in that they start with people and finding out what they saw, heard, or experienced in connection with the crime. Asking questions is one of the most effective ways to uncover the truth about an event and additional leads and witnesses, although it is sometimes overlooked in the rush to find technological evidence of cybercrimes.

In a private sector cybercrime investigation, internal personnel very often are a key source of evidence about what happened to the organization and how to locate other evidence of the crime. When investigators interview internal employees regarding a cybercrime event, some topics of inquiry might include:

- *Firsthand accounts of what happened.* The employee's experience of when and how an attack occurred, and the chain of events observed before, during, and after the incident.
- *Contributing events.* What actions (by them or others) or other events may have contributed to the crime (for example, password sharing or clicking on malware links)?
- *Systems and data.* Knowledge of internal computing systems and data, and any technological repercussions from the crime.
- *Changes or problems.* Do any data, communications, or financial records appear different or amiss? Is there anything unusual in the records the employee has noticed that could be connected to the crime?
- *Understanding of employee functions.* Employees can provide a ground-level perspective on data access, job assignments, and unusual employee activity (particularly if another employee is suspected of playing a role in the crime).
- *Admissibility of other evidence.* Is the employee in a position to verify the integrity and accuracy of data and records?

Accurate documentation of the interview is important. Remember that interview notes might have to be disclosed if future litigation occurs. Inaccurate notes about the interview could be used by opposing parties to discredit the witness.

Along with questions targeting specific areas of an internal witness' knowledge about the entity or the crime, it is always helpful to give employees a chance to share their insights into the incident and ideas for potential leads. To this end, some useful open-ended questions include:

- Who else should I speak to who might have information to share?
- What do you think the investigation should look at?
- Aside from what you witnessed/know, what do you think might have happened?
- Is there anything else I should ask or you want to tell me?

12.8.2 INTERNAL RECORDS AND DATA

Access to a private entity's internal records and data provides a major source of evidence for investigators. For example, records for internal email accounts, social media accounts, financial accounts, customer transactions, and help desk reports may be key areas of focus in a cybercrime case. There are some important considerations for private sector investigators who are obtaining and analyzing this type of records data, including:

Locating data and records. While a private sector investigator may have access to the entity's data and records, locating them is often another story. An organization's information governance is never perfect, so locating data on both internal and cloud networks can be an extreme challenge.

Obtaining timely access. In the early stages of an investigation, having prompt access to evidence can be critical. Sometimes organizations may delay investigative access due to business needs (like an unwillingness to shut down systems or divert employees to pull records). If the incident response plan did not foresee these needs, investigators may have to persuade an organization's management about the timely need for certain records and data.

Ensuring records collected are complete. When records and data are received, investigators should ensure they obtained a complete set of the relevant information. Otherwise, time and effort can be wasted searching incomplete data sets. Some criteria to check include date ranges and account names.

12.8.3   Forensics on Internal Devices and Networks

As we covered in Chapter 3, computer forensic investigations are undertaken by qualified professionals with extensive training and experience. Here we discuss managing that process for a private entity's investigative purposes.

When an organization's computing devices potentially contain evidence of a cybercrime, or may have been used to commit one, there are several general facts to establish and decisions for the organization's management and investigators to make.

- Devices involved and legal authority to seize and search them
- Whether certain devices should be disconnected from the network
- Whether any devices should be forensically imaged (preserved)
- After a device is imaged, whether the contents should be analyzed
- Use of in-house forensic experts or external consultants
- How long to allow for the forensic imaging process and any subsequent analysis
- Projected cost of the needed computer forensics
- Business reasons that conflict with investigative needs (e.g. taking devices offline and/or forensically imaging them might interfere with business processes)
- Employees that must be notified regarding the taking or search of devices
- Whether passwords should be changed or other measures taken to avoid intruder or employee access
- On-site or off-site forensic imaging, considering cost, time, and space.

Preserving digital evidence takes time and resources. Imaging one laptop or smartphone may be a small job, but imaging 10, 20, or hundreds of devices increases the scope, time, and costs. These factors, and the likelihood that relevant evidence will be found, influence the decisions about what to image and analyze.

As the investigative process continues, more decisions may have to be made about whether additional digital evidence should be preserved. Prompt forensic analysis of some devices can help determine whether the scope of the forensic investigation should be expanded.

When multiple devices are imaged and analyzed, it is helpful to keep track of when each device was imaged, who imaged it, and any helpful evidence found (or likely to be found). It is also useful to note devices that were not imaged (and why), As more devices become potentially relevant, and more forensic examiners become involved, tracking all of this information ensures the details needed for future use of the imaged data in the investigation or litigation is maintained.

12.9 COLLECTING EVIDENCE FROM EXTERNAL SOURCES

Although private entity investigations may begin with and center on internally available evidence, information also is likely to be needed from external parties and sources. In this section, we will look at common forms of external evidence, as well as some of the investigative and legal issues that arise for private sector investigators seeking to obtain it.

12.9.1 OPEN-SOURCE RESEARCH REVISITED

Chapter 11 provided an introduction to open-source investigation, a technique that can be especially helpful to private entity investigations. Needless to say, open-source information is freely available with no legal process required. Open-source investigation can provide leads on:

- Scam typologies
- Phone numbers
- Email addresses
- IP Addresses
- People
- Companies
- Online discussion about the entity or by entity employees.

If open-source research produces leads about important evidence, decisions can be made about performing more in-depth or costly investigation, or obtaining civil subpoenas (discussed later in this chapter).

12.9.2 REQUESTING DATA AND INFORMATION FROM THIRD PARTIES

Private entity cybercrime investigations routinely lead to data and information that is owned or held by external parties. External evidence of this nature includes subscriber and account records for email, cellphone, or social media accounts; subscriber records for IP addresses assigned by Internet service providers; and account and transaction records from banks or credit card companies.

Because private sector investigators generally cannot rely on subpoenas to legally demand records and data from third parties, they must use requests and persuasion to obtain needed third-party information. Essentially, this process requires gaining an external party's consent, as depicted in Figure 12.3. Some individuals and organizations may assist if there is no concern over privacy interests in the material. Others will flatly decline, raising issues that include the legality of sharing the data or records. And others may be unsure or seek to delay the response. Persuasion is an important skill, and investigators can use it to appeal to a third-party's sense of professional or moral duty, while minimizing any expense or inconvenience to them.

Requests to external parties for records or other evidence should be done in a timely fashion, and the request and response should be documented. Even if the result is "no" or a claim that no such evidence exists, it is possible they may change their mind at a later date.

If the answer to a request for information or data is "no", the next step could be a formal letter of preservation, requesting the party to conduct an internal investigation and preserve the data and information for potential litigation. Along with hopefully ensuring the data is preserved, such a letter may serve to persuade the entity to comply with the request, rather than embroil itself in other parties' litigation.

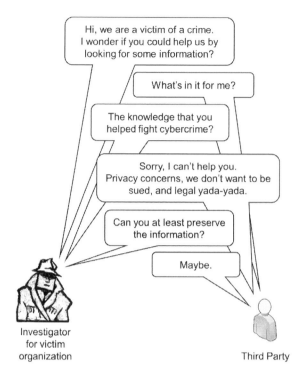

FIGURE 12.3 Getting Information from Third Parties.

If the sought-after information is critical for an investigation, then private entities may consider a John Doe civil lawsuit in order to obtain subpoenas to compel the third party to divulge the information, as outlined in the next section.

Conversely, the organization may face a request from an outside party for information, records, or evidence relating to a cybercrime. For example, if the organization's information systems were breached, or used to commit a crime, third parties may request information about the incident. Depending on the outside party and the information requested, the organization may be *required* to provide it, be *prohibited* from providing it, or be somewhere in between. For example, we covered mandatory notification and reporting earlier, and privacy, health, or bank secrecy laws may prohibit sharing of certain information.

12.9.3 CIVIL LEGAL PROCESS TO COMPEL EXTERNAL PARTIES TO PRODUCE EVIDENCE: JOHN DOE LAWSUITS AND SUBPOENAS

In contrast to law enforcement investigators, a private cybercrime investigator, or attorney working with her, cannot easily issue subpoenas to third parties to compel disclosure of evidence.[3] Instead, private sector investigators must take many steps to obtain external evidence and each is time-consuming and costly, especially if the entity is paying out-of-pocket for outside counsel to do this work.

---

[3] In earlier chapters, we discuss the powerful and convenient legal tool that criminal investigators have, the Grand Jury subpoena duces tecum. Needless to say, the private sector lacks this tool.

Private third-party civil subpoenas can be issued only in connection with ongoing litigation. This means a lawsuit has to be filed, and then one party to the suit can ask the court to issue a subpoena to individuals or businesses (that are not part of the lawsuit) for items or data that could be evidence in the case.[4]

When a private organization is investigating a cybercrime, and subpoenas are needed to obtain evidence about the crime and who did it, the organization can bring a lawsuit naming an anonymous "John Doe" as defendant. This mechanism allows the investigating entity to begin a civil case and get the court's permission to issue subpoenas to third parties who might have evidence relevant towards identifying the responsible cybercriminals.

These civil actions generally require an attorney to file the lawsuit, properly advise on the legal options at all times, and comply with the rules and procedures of the jurisdiction (which vary by state and federal district).

When filing a John Doe suit, private organizations can benefit from considering these aspects of the process:

- *Information in the complaint is public.* Lawsuits usually are public information, potentially available online to the public, and monitored by news organizations. Consider how much information should be placed in any filings.
- *Long timeline for issuing subpoenas and receiving a response.* The process of filing a John Doe suit, receiving court permission to issue subpoenas, and submitting them to third parties can take a significant amount of time, and third parties receiving civil subpoenas may not react promptly. Third parties also may charge money for records production, and might notify the ultimate target of the records request to give them an opportunity to object.
- *Informal connections can save time and effort.* Establishing informal connections with representatives in the third-party organization can be beneficial for investigators, and might yield clues about what records are stored and whether a subpoena would result in fruitful evidence or be a waste of time.

Cyber Threats Case

We learned of a case that highlights the real-life importance of investigative decisions around subpoenas, and the working relationship between the private sector and law enforcement. A private investigator was investigating the crime on behalf of a teenage girl who was receiving threats via social media, essentially threatening to kill her and her family in a gruesome way. Other girls in her school also were receiving similar threats.

An obvious and important cybercrime investigation step was to subpoena the social media provider (e.g. Facebook or Instagram) for subscriber information about the person posting the threats, as well as for the Internet Protocol (IP) addresses logging-in to the accounts sending the death threats.

However, the police agency's detective was reluctant to obtain a criminal subpoena. First the detective speculated that it would be pointless, perhaps leading to an overseas criminal that could not be apprehended. Then the detective claimed that state laws did

---

[4] We discuss civil litigation in Chapters 5 and 19. If the perpetrator of a cybercrime is sued, then subpoenas could be requested in that lawsuit to be served upon third parties. Evidence also can be obtained from the defendant through the discovery process without a subpoena.

not allow a subpoena to be used for these records, that a search warrant was required, and that the search warrant was almost impossible to obtain.

In the face of this reluctance, one option the private investigator considered was a John Doe civil lawsuit in order to issue a subpoena and get the evidence through the civil process. However, that method would have been expensive, lengthy, and could have publicized the investigation, perhaps alerting the perpetrator. This option was determined to be a last resort which, in the end, did not have to be exercised.

Instead, the investigator researched the laws of that state and discussed it with prosecutors there. Together, they convinced the police agency that the responsible next step was to obtain and serve a criminal subpoena on the social media company. The social media records made identification of the suspect simple. It was not a mysterious overseas criminal threatening these girls, but a student in the same school. A confession was promptly obtained by the detective, the suspect was deemed not to be a physical threat, and the case ultimately was resolved in an appropriate fashion.

12.9.4   RESPECTING THE RIGHTS OF THIRD PARTIES

For some private sector investigators in the midst of unraveling a cybercrime, the denial of requests for evidence by third parties can be both frustrating and potentially damaging to the case. As a result, there may be temptations to find ways to obtain the needed data without adequately considering criminal or civil laws. Those temptations should be resisted. History has shown that some private investigators overstep the bounds of the law in the course of an investigation, resulting in violations of third-party rights and potential criminal charges or lawsuits for fraud, extortion, wiretapping, invasion of privacy, and other offenses.

In the cybercrime context, one investigative temptation might be to digitally trespass on a third party to gain access to information. As we learned in Chapters 5 and 9, this type of conduct is illegal and has no recognized legal defense. If a private entity does not have permission or control over a system, it cannot invade it. Put simply, a victim is not justified in breaking the law to investigate the crime against him. Further, any perceived short-term gain from investigative misconduct is negated by the long-term negative effects. The investigation and investigators will be tainted and their credibility diminished. The investigators, whether in house or third-party contractors, will find themselves in a conflict of interest, torn between a duty to their client/employer and a need to protect themselves from criminal or civil liability.

Any investigating entity must obtain and access information and evidence lawfully. Investigators working on an organization's behalf should have a clear understanding of relevant laws and regulations, civil and criminal law principles (like privacy and consent), and workplace policies.

The Improper Search

Organization A is the victim of a crime, and it learns the cybercriminal created a "throw-away" email account to help commit the crime. Employee B is eager to investigate and tries to log in to this email account, correctly guessing the password. Employee B gains access and reviews the contents of the emails, which reveal additional leads about new email accounts used by the attacker and new schemes that are in progress.

Employee B shares this investigative victory with Employee C, but then they start discussing potential consequences. Has Employee B committed a state and federal crime by logging into the email account? Has Employee B put his digital fingerprints on that email account, and might law enforcement suspect him for committing the original crimes? Has the employee, and by extension the organization, committed a civil tort by accessing and obtaining information unlawfully?

Now Employee B is worried he could get in trouble with law enforcement and fired by his organization. He starts to think about whether he should come clean to his manager and truthfully report the mistake he made. Or, should he keep quiet, or even lie about what he did, and also delete some of the digital traces of his prior actions. If he lies or deletes evidence, he may be committing additional crimes.

Here, the investigation into the cybercriminal has already been compromised and tainted. In the event the cybercriminal is identified and arrested, defense attorneys will have fertile grounds to attack the integrity of the evidence and the entire case. The credibility of the organization and the investigation is damaged.

12.10 CONCLUSION

Private entity investigations may serve many purposes, and may be interconnected with law enforcement or regulatory investigations. They start with an organization's incident response as the crime is detected and initial decisions are made about whether to investigate. Private entities may have to make investigative decisions that weigh the needs of the case against business requirements and costs to the entity. In many ways, a private sector investigation can be divided into internally available investigative resources and information, and those that need to be obtained from external sources. At all times, investigative steps can anticipate the evidentiary and procedural requirements of potential litigation.

13 Law Enforcement's Cybercrime Investigation

This chapter is mostly for:

- Law enforcement
- Other readers who want to learn more about law enforcement cyber investigations.

13.1 INTRODUCTION

Thousands of times a year, law enforcement agencies across the country are alerted to cybercrimes that impact individuals, businesses, organizations, and government agencies. In this chapter, we will look at how law enforcement receives and responds to these reports – from assessing the first-known facts and initiating an investigation, to using the range of investigative steps available to find out what happened and who is responsible.

Much of this discussion, and, indeed, much of law enforcement's work, is an application of the legal and investigative concepts discussed in earlier chapters to the particular facts and circumstances presented by each unique case. This process results in a combination of routine procedures and individualized assessment through which law enforcement makes decisions on the best investigative approach. As this chapter will explain, these decisions hinge upon an array of practical and legal factors.

13.2 HOW CYBERCRIME COMES TO LAW ENFORCEMENT'S ATTENTION

Cybercrimes come to the attention of law enforcement agencies in several ways. Some of the common paths are:

- *Individual victims reporting to local police.* Direct reporting by individuals is the most common method through which law enforcement learns of cybercrime activity. Many of these reports are related to financial fraud and identity theft, with victims reporting the discovery of fraudulent accounts, charges, withdrawals, or other misuse of their personal and financial information. Cybercrimes involving stalking, harassment, or dissemination of private or pornographic images also typically are reported by individual victims.
- *Reports to complaint clearing houses.* Several government agencies – including the Internet Crime Complaint Center (IC3), the Federal Trade Commission (FTC), and state agencies – document reports of cybercrime from individual and business victims, as well as third parties. This information is then analyzed for patterns and trends, and can lead to public alerts or law enforcement referral.

- *Financial institution reports.* Financial institutions also report cybercrime to the Treasury Department's Financial Crimes Enforcement Network (FinCEN) and to law enforcement, either following a cybercrime event or when their internal investigations reveal a pattern of fraud with a geographical nexus or common perpetrator. Banks, credit card companies, credit unions, and financial services companies frequently are the ultimate victims of financial cybercrimes, since they often bear the cost of any fraud inflicted on their customers. Fraud costs financial institutions and merchants billions of dollars each year.
- *Private sector reports of network attacks and data breaches.* Businesses, including financial institutions, may report attacks on their networks or communication systems. These types of cybercrimes – including intrusions, denial-of-service attacks, cyber vandalism, and malware attacks – might be reported to law enforcement agencies with the specialized capabilities needed to investigate such events. For intrusions involving the compromise and theft of customer data, law enforcement must be notified under the mandatory reporting requirements of various state and federal laws and regulations.
- *Press accounts.* In some situations, the media may publicize a cyber incident before the individual or corporate victim has informed law enforcement. These press accounts can trigger a law enforcement investigation if the described incident appears to be a crime.
- *Law enforcement referrals.* State or local agencies may refer cases that are reported to them, but turn out to be within the jurisdiction of another state or county, or are connected to another agency's investigation. At times, when more than one agency has jurisdiction over a case, the decision may be made to consolidate the investigation with one agency. Law enforcement agencies in other countries also report cyber incidents to federal law enforcement agencies that cross international borders, or may be emanating from the United States.
- *Proactive investigations.* Law enforcement agencies sometimes initiate investigations into cybercrime. Proactive investigations of this nature can occur when a suspect or criminal conduct is discovered through an unrelated investigation or through cyber intelligence.

13.3   WAS THERE A CRIME?

Whenever an incident is reported to law enforcement, the first question investigators face is whether the events that occurred constitute a crime. Answering this question requires a thorough understanding of the criminal code – federal or state – under which a potential offender might be charged. As we learned in Chapter 6, each state and the federal government has its own set of laws covering a variety of crimes applicable in the cyber context. And each crime within a particular code contains definitions and elements, each of which must be provable with evidence. Often, even the most complicated cybercrime scenarios can be reduced to traditional criminal acts like theft or identity theft.

An investigator should be careful to distinguish the question of whether there was a crime from the issue of how to prove the crime and find the identity of the perpetrator. All too often, it is clear a crime has been reported, but the challenges of cyber evidence-gathering make law enforcement reluctant to open a case. Proof and resource concerns are important, but the first question to assess is whether a crime has occurred. That determination creates a fair and accurate foundation for the next decisions about whether and how to investigate the report.

The initial evaluation of whether a crime occurred within the jurisdiction (and what statute might have been violated) can be difficult for law enforcement. Many reports are made by victims who know only that their identities or financial information were used, but have no further details about how, when, or where any fraud or compromise took place. The problem is compounded further when the victim, officer, or both parties lack the technical expertise to properly assess the events as a particular form of cybercrime, or to know what statutes they might violate. Law enforcement officials in this position can readily learn the necessary skills with training, practice, and experience, and should always consider seeking assistance from other investigators and prosecutors who may specialize in cybercrime.

When there are insufficient facts to show a crime occurred, or the reported events suggest a civil dispute, law enforcement agencies may decide a case is not a criminal matter and law enforcement investigation is not warranted (for example, if the victim is reporting a customer who is late paying a bill, or a business is complaining about an inaccurate online review).

13.4   IS THIS A CRIME THAT LAW ENFORCEMENT CAN AND SHOULD INVESTIGATE?

When law enforcement officials determine a reported cyber incident was likely a crime, the next questions are whether the event is something that law enforcement can and should investigate.

There are several key factors to weigh in deciding whether and how to take on a cybercrime investigation, including:

- Nature and extent of the harm
- Nature of the available evidence (and the evidence that investigation may reveal in the future)
- Jurisdictional analysis
- Resources and personnel needed
- Likelihood of apprehending suspects
- Civil versus criminal approach
- Impact on society and deterrence.

13.4.1   NATURE AND EXTENT OF THE HARM

Reports of cybercrime, especially those involving financial fraud, can encompass varying degrees of damage and identity compromise. In some cases, the nature of the harm is clearly serious and the need for an investigation is obvious. In many cyber cases, however, the initial reported harm may be so minimal that investigators will question whether an additional investment of time and resources is merited. That logic often makes sense from the perspective of the individual report, but it does not take into account the characteristics of cybercrime, More often than not, a single reported event is the proverbial "tip of the iceberg", and some basic investigative steps are likely to reveal additional theft, frauds, and victims. Gaining some sense of the extent of the criminal activity is crucial in deciding whether and what kind of resources should be expended on an investigation. It also is worth the time and effort to contact federal and statewide law enforcement groups to determine whether this case fits into a larger, existing investigation. One small reported incident may be a piece of another investigator's puzzle.

13.4.2   NATURE OF INITIALLY AVAILABLE EVIDENCE

In many cybercrime cases, there is an investigative starting point derived from clues about how a reported crime was executed. Emails, fraudulent transactions, harassing social media posts, and other types of Internet activity leave a trail that can be followed. With some cybercrime reports, however, the available evidence about the event provides little for law enforcement officials to analyze. The victim may not have saved the emails, text messages, or posts by which crime-related communications were conducted. Enough time may have passed between the event and the report such that retail records, security video, and other forms of evidence are no longer obtainable. In these situations, there may be so little viable evidence that further investigation is not feasible. A report of a crime with no initial leads and low probability of developing future evidence may not be a good use of resources.

13.4.3   JURISDICTIONAL ANALYSIS

A major factor in deciding whether a law enforcement agency can or should begin an investigation is whether there is a sufficient jurisdictional nexus. In many instances of cybercrime, multiple jurisdictions may have a legal basis for jurisdiction.

Ideally, the agency with the strongest geographical connection is the best one to handle the case. For example, imagine a criminal who is cyberstalking victims he meets online, with each victim living in a different state. Legally, the counties where each victim resides have jurisdiction to begin a separate investigation and prosecution. But once the extent of his conduct is known, the strongest place for this investigation might be within the defendant's home jurisdiction, where all his criminal activity could be addressed in one case. There are times, however, when the place with the strongest basis for jurisdiction does not pursue an investigation, most often because of limited resources.

Unfortunately, the fact that cybercrime jurisdiction often can be found in multiple locations leads to the "hot potato" phenomenon, which occurs when a victim goes to a law enforcement agency and is told this is not the right place to report the crime. The victim is then referred to another agency, where he is told the same thing, and so on. This regrettable practice is a disservice to victims, and results in many solvable crimes being ignored.

13.4.4   RESOURCES AND PERSONNEL NEEDED

Most cybercrime investigations require a greater investment of resources than an equivalent street crime. These cases typically depend upon extensive review of service provider records, as well as data obtained through search warrants and forensic analysis of seized devices.

Cyber investigations also benefit from dedicated personnel with accumulated familiarity with the evidence. Such long-term investigative assignments are typical for detectives or agents handling serious violent crimes, but are unusual for all but the most serious cybercrimes, if even those.

Investigators might consider other resource and personnel options for cyber cases. These options include utilizing personnel already working on technology-focused assignments (such as digital body-camera evidence), partnering with other law enforcement agencies that have more cyber-related resources, and building regional task forces or working groups to pool resources and staff on cyber investigations.

13.4.5   LIKELIHOOD OF APPREHENDING SUSPECTS

The geographical reach of cybercrime, and the ability of cybercriminals to hide their identities online, mean that locating and apprehending subjects in cyber cases can be challenging. For agencies with scarce resources, the likelihood of ever apprehending some suspects is too low to justify the case. This reality is frustrating, as there are far too few regional or national agencies to handle the volume of cybercrime.

However, the initial perception about the difficulty of identifying and locating a suspect should not be the only factor in deciding to investigate. In a percentage of cases, some preliminary steps might reveal the defendant is an identified, local individual. If there are good investigative leads pointing to an out-of-state or foreign offender, the suspect can be apprehended with creative approaches and partnerships, as well as the assistance of the Office of International Affairs in the U.S. Department of Justice (see Chapter 17). Or, after an initial investigation is conducted, promising cases can be referred to other agencies. If no one tries to find them, cybercriminals will continue to victimize individuals and businesses with impunity within each investigator's jurisdiction.

13.4.6   RELATED CIVIL IMPLICATIONS

Cyber incidents often have both criminal and civil components, with complicated questions of civil liability (as covered in Chapters 9 and 12). For example, an employee of Company A goes to work for Company B, and brings with her some proprietary internal data about Company A's customers or products. There may be grounds to consider a criminal investigation into whether the employee stole Company A's data. Separately, the complainant may consider civil remedies, such as an action for intentional torts or breach of contract. The decision to proceed with a criminal investigation should be made on the merits of a potential criminal case and the law enforcement duty to justice. A complainant's desire to pursue civil remedies should neither prompt nor preclude a criminal investigation, though law enforcement can always consider the motives of the parties. Obtaining appropriate restitution from a criminal defendant for the financial loss suffered by his victim is a legitimate goal of law enforcement, and might save the victim from the cost of pursuing a private civil action.

13.4.7   IMPACT ON SOCIETY AND DETERRENCE

Other important considerations for law enforcement are whether taking on a cyber investigation will act as a deterrent to future criminals, and whether the crime's impact on the community calls for law enforcement action. Conducting cybercrime investigations can change the common public perception that reported crimes are being taken seriously by the government.

The deterrent effect of law enforcement is quite powerful. Most criminals (cybercriminals included) guide their conduct based upon self-interest. They will commit crimes if it will benefit them and if they perceive the risk of being caught and punished as slim. As we emphasize throughout this book, we must investigate cases if we hope to solve them. Investigation is what can help both catch and deter cybercriminals.

13.4.8   ADVISING THE VICTIM

Law enforcement investigators will make a decision on whether to pursue a case or not, and for how long. No matter what is decided, investigators should let victims know, and offer them guidance about how to protect themselves and obtain other assistance by providing the following:

- Instructions on other places the crime can be reported, including the IC3 and FTC identity theft clearing house
- Information about how to prevent such crimes in the future
- Resources and steps to mitigate or prevent identity theft risks, such as free annual credit checks and free credit freezes

- Suggestions about agencies or companies the victim should notify about the compromise of his personal information, including the Department of Motor Vehicles, Social Security Administration, or financial institutions where he has accounts
- Contact information for the newly assigned investigators if the case was referred to another agency.

Western Express: An "Impossible" Case that Was Possible

The Western Express case started with a report of a single incident of credit card fraud that many law enforcement agencies would not have bothered to investigate – either because the amount stolen was small, because the credit card company covered the cost of the fraud loss, or because the agency did not have the personnel or resources to work on any kind of financial fraud case. But we decided to take preliminary investigative steps using simple subpoenas and research, which revealed dozens of similar incidents of credit card fraud. At that point, the organized and extensive nature of these frauds could not be ignored. It was clear that further investigation was needed.

As we got deeper into the Western Express investigation, and realized some of their most culpable customers were located in Eastern Europe, it was daunting to think about identifying, indicting, and apprehending them. Back then, it rarely had been done by any prosecutor, and (to our knowledge) never by a local prosecutor's office.

If there could be a slogan for cybercrime investigators it might be, "Where there's a will, there's a way." There are so many potential obstacles, like those we ran into in this case. But the desire to solve the mystery of these crimes, and to end them, spurred us to keep looking for help and inventive solutions. This outlook led to our partnership with the U.S. Secret Service and gaining assistance from the DOJ's Office of International Affairs, and these collaborations often made the difference. At other times, the difference boiled down to ingenuity and persistence. The lesson learned? These cases can be solved with the right mindset and the willingness to look for help when needed.

13.5 OPENING A CASE

Once the decision is made to pursue a cybercrime investigation, there are three typical actions involved in opening an official investigation: generating a new case file, assigning personnel, and opening a Grand Jury investigation (though these steps will vary greatly by agency depending on size and resources).

- *Creating a new case number/file for the investigation.* For most agencies, "opening a case" starts with creating a unique case number for the investigation within the agency's case management system.
- *Assigning someone to investigate.* The agency also must assign officers, agents, or detectives to handle the investigation. Cyber cases often are assigned to staff in an investigative division of the agency, if it exists. Ideally, there is someone in the department who receives training about cybercrimes and develops experience investigating them.
- *Initiating the legal process for issuing subpoenas.* The third key step in setting up new cyber investigations is initiating the process to issue subpoenas. For most law enforcement cases, that means opening a Grand Jury investigation, usually through the appropriate prosecutor's office. As we covered in Chapter 5, the Grand Jury is empowered to conduct investigations, and can issue subpoenas for witnesses to appear

and/or produce documents and physical evidence. Through this legal process, third-party service providers, other businesses, and individuals can be directed to preserve and provide digital evidence. Certain federal and state agencies and commissions also have statutory authority to issue administrative subpoenas in criminal investigations.

13.6   ASSESSMENT OF INITIAL EVIDENCE: WHAT DO WE HAVE, WHAT DO WE NEED?

When a case has been opened, the next step is to conduct an assessment of the initial evidence to identify leads about what happened and who is responsible.

The initial evidence of a reported incident will vary, depending on the crime that occurred. Some of the common types of evidence available at the beginning of a cybercrime investigation are:

- Emails, text messages, or social media postings in furtherance of a fraud or threat
- Communications or notifications from retailers, financial institutions, Internet service providers, or other companies describing new or unauthorized account activity
- Fraudulently purchased items and/or retailer receipts for such items
- Computer or mobile device malfunction
- Unauthorized changes to network function or security settings
- Missing, altered, or encrypted data.

In a typical cyber case, the initial evidence comes from the victim – whether an individual, private company, financial institution, or service provider. It is crucial to speak directly with victims, and not simply rely on information from financial institutions or other third parties. Through conversations, investigators learn the victim's explanation of the events, what evidence the victim has kept or preserved, and whether there are additional actions the victim should take to immediately retain evidence vulnerable to deletion or tampering. If a victim's personal/corporate Internet or financial accounts are involved, the victim can take steps to preserve and obtain data and records that will be needed as evidence. When a victim's device is affected, law enforcement might take immediate steps (with appropriate consent) to protect evidence within the device from alteration, deletion, or tampering.

After evaluating the evidence available at the outset of a case, investigators can identify missing pieces and the next investigative steps. If an Internet account was used in connection with criminal activity, law enforcement may send a letter of preservation to ensure evidence is retained. These letters were explained in Chapter 7, and also will be discussed further in this chapter.

13.7   GETTING READY TO INVESTIGATE: A RECAP OF THE TOOLS

In Chapter 7, we learned about the law surrounding privacy, how ECPA interprets privacy for electronic and wire communications (like email, voicemail, and text messages), and the nine legal tools in law enforcement's investigative toolbox. As a reminder, the nine tools are:

1. Open-source investigation
2. Consent
3. Letters of preservation (if additional process is contemplated)
4. Non-disclosure or delayed-disclosure orders
5. Subpoenas
6. 2703(d) Orders

7. Search warrants
8. Pen registers and trap/trace devices
9. Wiretaps.

Now we will briefly review the tools and how to use them in an investigation. For each tool, we first provide a brief summary of the related law (explained in Chapter 7). Then, we provide a brief summary of how the tool can be used in an investigation.

Two important points about using tools in cybercrime investigations:

- *Be careful.* Many investigative acts might alert the suspect or create other risks, so each step should be taken with consideration.
- *Undercover investigations.* Undercover methods are another available investigative tool, but they are not covered in this book due to their legal and technical complexities. However, law enforcement should be aware they are an option in cybercrime cases, while recognizing the preservation, legal, and technical challenges that will ensue. When contemplating using undercover methods, consider asking agencies with experience in undercover cyber work for guidance and assistance.

13.7.1   OPEN-SOURCE INVESTIGATION

What it is. Looking for and finding publicly available information.

Legal summary. Open-source investigation can be done without any legal analysis because the information is publicly available with no expectation of privacy.

Investigative takeaway. Throughout a cybercrime case, open-source research is a fundamental investigative tool. As investigators learn information from various sources, they can research online for more details or related leads. The more investigators use open-source investigation techniques, the faster and more skilled they become. Useful types of information available through open-source investigation, as well as investigation techniques, are covered in Chapter 11.

13.7.2   CONSENT

What it is. A victim, witness, or suspect agreeing to give law enforcement access to otherwise private spaces, items, communications, or accounts.

Legal summary. Consent must be voluntary and informed and must be given by an owner, or someone else with legal authority to give consent.

Investigative takeaway. Whether to obtain evidence through consent is a strategic decision. In some situations, asking for consent may be the easiest and fastest way to acquire evidence that comes with an expectation of privacy. Victims and witnesses often voluntarily provide access to data, accounts, communications, and spaces to aid the investigation. If the evidence is controlled by a potential suspect or someone whose role is unknown, investigators might not try to gain consensual access because doing so would tip off the cybercriminals to law enforcement's interest. Instead, investigators could use a search warrant. If the owner is a potential suspect who might be charged (or anyone who might allege later that the consent was obtained unlawfully), a search warrant is the safer method. Search warrants are authorized by judges and presumed lawful, whereas the consent of a future defendant could be challenged in court. Any consent is best documented in writing or on video.

13.7.3   LETTER OF PRESERVATION (IF ADDITIONAL PROCESS IS CONTEMPLATED)

What it is. A formal request that an organization preserve information. These letters are used to ensure email, cloud storage, or other third-party companies maintain account records until law enforcement provides legal process to obtain them.

Legal summary. Electronic communications and storage providers are legally required to comply with Letters of Preservation issued by law enforcement. When served with a preservation demand, these companies must preserve the specified account evidence for a period of up to 90 days (plus an extended period of 90 days if needed).

Investigative takeaway. Letters of Preservation are essential tools for obtaining electronic evidence that a user has stored with an online service provider. Once a target account is identified, it might take days or weeks for investigators to obtain legal process to get the account records (Grand Jury subpoena, 2703(d) Order, or search warrant). A Letter of Preservation helps ensure that electronic evidence will be available, and not purged by the service provider or deleted by the account user while investigators obtain the necessary legal demand. These letters are typically form letters that investigators can quickly complete with details about a particular case, service provider, and target account. Most Internet service providers produce Law Enforcement Guides to inform investigators about where and how to send a Letter of Preservation and other legal process.

13.7.4   NON-DISCLOSURE ORDER AND REQUEST

What it is. A court order that tells the relevant company not to inform the customer (or anyone else) that it has received a subpoena or other legal process about an account.

Legal summary. A judge can issue a Non-disclosure Order when law enforcement demonstrates that disclosure presents a compelling risk to someone's safety or to the ongoing investigation. With pen/trap and wiretap orders, non-disclosure is automatically provided for by law. Investigators also can make Non-Disclosure Requests to companies asking them not to disclose the legal process (but without the force of law).

Investigative takeaway. Whenever alerting the customer might compromise an investigation or present a safety risk, law enforcement investigators must consider obtaining a Non-disclosure Order from the court to accompany subpoenas and other legal demands. This step is important because, pursuant to the company's legal policies or user agreements, some providers will notify customers about the receipt of a subpoena or court order about their accounts. Certain tools automatically provide for such non-disclosure orders; others require investigators to apply. Either way, the investigator must ensure the non-disclosure language is present in the legal demand if it is needed. This "do not disclose order" need not be a separate document, but may be contained within the relevant legal process. When grounds do not exist to seek a court order, investigators can request that companies withhold from disclosing information (a request that does not legally require the company to do anything).

13.7.5   SUBPOENA

What it is. A form of legal process used to compel companies and individuals to supply specified records, books, documents, or other physical items relevant to a case or investigation.

Legal summary. There are three types of subpoenas: (i) Grand Jury subpoenas, drafted and signed by a prosecutor's office for an open Grand Jury investigation; (ii) trial court subpoenas, issued by the court once a defendant has been criminally charged in an indictment or information; and (iii) administrative subpoenas, issued by government agencies authorized by federal, state, or local laws to investigate certain crimes (pursuant to internal approval procedures).

What evidence can it get? Subpoenas can be used to obtain:

- Subscriber and session information from cellphone, electronic communication, and social media providers
- Subscriber and session information from cloud and other Internet storage providers
- Customer and transaction records from financial institutions and retailers
- Security video from retailers and public agencies
- Other records and items from businesses and individuals.[1]

Investigative takeaway. In cyber cases, subpoenas arguably are the most important tool. They are used for obtaining records from companies that frequently figure in cybercrime cases, such as Internet service providers, financial institutions, and retailers. These records provide evidence about customers, transactions, communications, and many other vitally important areas to unraveling a cybercrime. Issuing subpoenas is a constant feature of the investigation, from start to finish.

13.7.6 2703(d) ORDER

What it is. An order that compels electronic communications companies to provide non-content information about customer accounts beyond the records available via subpoena.

Legal summary. A 2703(d) Order (a specialized court order authorized by the Stored Communications Act) can be obtained when law enforcement shows specific and articulable facts providing "reasonable grounds" to believe the non-content information will be relevant and material to an ongoing criminal investigation. This standard is lower than the probable cause standard for a search warrant. Though the language of the SCA may indicate these orders can be used to obtain the content of communications, a search warrant should be used for content because the SCA language does not reflect court decisions and evolving norms.

What evidence does it get? A 2703(d) Order can be used to obtain sensitive non-content data from Internet service providers, such as:

- Account names, numbers, or addresses with which the target account has corresponded
- Full header information for email and other electronic messaging (not including the subject line)
- Contacts and buddy lists
- Subscriber, session, and payment information available by subpoena.

Investigative takeaway. Practically speaking, 2703(d) Orders are of limited use. If investigators already have enough proof to meet the standard for a search warrant (probable cause), it is not worthwhile to get a 2703(d) Order. A search warrant can obtain anything the 2703(d) Order can obtain (sensitive non-content information) *plus* the content of the messages. However, if investigators do not have enough evidence of criminality to support a search warrant application, then these orders are a good interim step and might build enough evidence to show there is probable cause to search the accounts.

---

[1] Though the language of the Stored Communications Act (SCA) may indicate subpoenas can be used to obtain communications content over 180 days old, investigators should use a search warrant instead (see Chapter 7 for more information).

13.7.7   Search Warrant

What it is. An order from a court with jurisdiction over the investigation permitting law enforcement officials to search a location (physical or virtual) and seize specified items found therein.

Legal summary. Law enforcement investigators can obtain a search warrant if they demonstrate there is "probable cause" to believe criminal evidence will be present in the target location, or that criminal activity is occurring there. Probable cause essentially means there are reasonable grounds to believe (it is more likely than not) the evidence will be found there.

What evidence does it get? A search warrant can be used to look for any kind of evidence within a location protected by an expectation of privacy. Some common physical locations search warrants are used to access include:

• Homes
• Vehicles
• Places of business
• Containers (like suitcases, safes, storage areas).

In the cyber context, the SCA and court decisions direct law enforcement to use a search warrant to obtain:

• The content of *stored* online communications
• The content of online storage repositories (accounts, networks, servers)
• Information stored on electronic devices (smartphones, tablets, computers)
• Location data kept by service providers (cell-site tower transmission data, GPS, and other geolocation data).

A search warrant also can be used for evidence that is obtainable by subpoena or 2703(d) Order. In other words, if an investigator applies for a search warrant, he or she can include subscriber or other non-content information as well, instead of using multiple forms of legal process.

Investigative takeaway. When law enforcement investigators have gathered enough information to show an account, device, or location probably holds information about criminal activity, they should always consider obtaining a search warrant. Search warrants are powerful investigative tools that allow investigators to lawfully look for evidence in private spaces. Of course, criminals are more likely to keep incriminating information in locations they believe are private or hidden, and so search warrants frequently are the tool that uncovers significant proof of criminal conduct and identification. Developing sufficient proof to support search warrant applications is an ongoing process throughout a cybercrime investigation.

Investigators should think of search warrants for three general purposes, (i) obtaining electronic data stored by third parties, (ii) searching physical locations for physical items of evidentiary value, and (iii) searching electronic devices (computers, cellphones) for digital evidence.

13.7.8   Pen Register and Trap/Trace Device (Including with Location Data)

What it is. Tools authorized by a court that are used to gain real-time subscriber and dialing information about the communications coming in and out of a phone or Internet account.

Legal summary. Law enforcement investigators can obtain a pen register and trap-and-trace device (pen/trap) if they establish proof the pen/trap will provide information relevant to an ongoing criminal investigation. This legal standard is lower than probable cause. If location data is desired through the pen/trap (cell-site, GPS, etc.), an investigator's application must establish probable cause to believe the location data will provide evidence of criminal activity (a higher standard).[2] A pen/trap order typically allows up to 60 days of monitoring, with the opportunity to extend the order as needed.

What evidence does it get? A pen/trap monitors and collects *live*, non-content information about communications into and out of a phone, cellphone, or Internet account. These details include:

- Email addresses, phone numbers, account names with which the account corresponds
- Internet protocol (IP) addresses used by the target account
- IP addresses of accounts with which the account corresponds
- Email header information (except for the subject line)
- Other forms of dialing, addressing, routing, and signaling data pertinent to different communication services
- Location data (only with a showing of probable cause).

Investigative takeaway. Once a suspect's communications accounts are identified, a pen/trap order is relatively easy to obtain and can be highly useful in building a case. By providing real-time monitoring of communications to and from a known target account, a pen/trap can potentially reveal ongoing crimes, pinpoint a suspect's location or movement, and identify potential associates and victims. Pen/traps are also utilized as one of the precursor investigative steps supporting a wiretap application. Evidence from pen/traps also is useful to support search warrant applications, or to identify targets (or confirm their identities) in a faster moving investigation.

13.7.9 WIRETAP

What it is. A court order allowing live law enforcement monitoring of communications related to criminal activity

Legal summary. To get a wiretap order, law enforcement investigators must detail the course of the investigation and show probable cause that the interception will yield evidence of specific serious felony offenses. The application also must explain that all other investigative options have been exhausted, except for those that appear too dangerous or too unlikely to succeed. The identity of the target must be specified if known, as well as details about what communications will be intercepted and from where, and the time period the wiretap is to last. A wiretap order typically allows up to 30 days of monitoring, with the opportunity to extend the order as needed.

What evidence does it get? A wiretap captures the content of *live* communications to and from a phone, cellphone, or Internet account (oral or written, including photos, videos, and any other types of insertions or attachments). Companion pen/trap and location data orders can be obtained to supply non-content and location information in tandem with a wiretap.

---

[2] Some law enforcement agencies use the term "prospective location data warrant" for authorization to obtain location data in conjunction with a pen/trap.

Investigative takeaway. A wiretap is always the tool of last resort because investigators must show that every other method of investigation has been exhausted or cannot be implemented. Drafting the application and implementing the order are complicated, labor-intensive undertakings from both a legal and investigative perspective. The expenditure of resources is enormous for any wiretap implementation, meaning they are pursued in only a tiny percentage of cases. Soon after the conclusion of a wiretap, individuals whose communications were overheard must be notified. This notification requirement means arrests and physical searches usually must occur during or immediately after the wiretap is conducted. For many good practical and privacy reasons, the wiretap tool is used sparingly. Consider that if a search warrant is like panning for gold, a wiretap is like blasting open a mountain to reach a gold mine.

13.8   SIMPLE: THE SIX-STEP INITIAL MINI-PLAN FOR LAW ENFORCEMENT

Here are six basic steps we recommend for every law enforcement investigator whenever a cybercrime incident is reported. These steps are simple and quick, so even agencies with scarce personnel and resources can do them. By going through these minimum steps, investigators can provide much-needed help to victims, solve some cases, and gain experience with cyber investigations.

The Six-Step Initial Mini Plan for Law Enforcement ("SIMPLE") consists of:

Step 1. Interview the victim and/or main witnesses. Find out what really happened, don't rely on the first report.

- ○ Some incidents turn out to be easy to resolve (for example, the victim is mistaken about what happened, or there is a non-criminal explanation for the events).
- ○ Some victims and witnesses will offer good clues and leads for what to do next. These clues and leads may not have been included in the initial verbal report or written form.

Step 2. Assess the evidence. What kind of cyber situation is this?

- ○ Although the case may be "cyber", the evidence may suggest a simple, local explanation (like an online bank fraud by the victim's relative or caregiver; or a credit card used online after the victim's wallet was stolen at the gym).
- ○ Many cyber incidents will not have readily apparent origins.

Step 3. Identify any Internet accounts involved.

- ○ Accounts belonging to victims or witnesses (like email or social media accounts).
- ○ Accounts from which perpetrators communicated or acted.
- ○ Relevant online financial accounts.

Step 4. Send a Letter of Preservation (if needed).

- ○ Notify the companies providing those accounts to save and protect the evidence within them (for example, letting Google know to maintain the contents of a Gmail account that was used to scam the victim).
- ○ This is a form letter! Investigators can adapt the same letter for every account and case.

Step 5. Subpoena records.

- o Contact the local prosecutor's office with a description of the case, the list of accounts, and a request for the records needed (and/or whatever other procedure the prosecutor uses).
- o Subpoenas should ask for subscriber records, log-in information, and whatever other material a subpoena can legally obtain. This is a form request that you can use over and over again.

Step 6. See what you get! When the subpoenaed records arrive, review them. What do you see?

- o Is the criminal the victim's family-member, friend, neighbor, or co-worker?
- o Do the records suggest there are other victims?
- o Are there indications about the criminal's location? E.g. local, other state, out of country.
- o Are there references to other Internet accounts, suggesting a potentially complex crime?

Now an investigator can make an informed decision by evaluating if the case fits within one of these three categories:

A. We have a lead. In a percentage of cases, these six steps will be enough to either identify the perpetrator or to determine that the crime is local in nature and can be solved with a few more investigative actions. Investigators can make the easy decision to pursue those leads.

B. It's a crime, and it's part of a bigger scheme. In many cases, the records will show that the victim's case is one of many frauds or attacks. The victim clearly is one of many, or the reach of the criminal(s) involved is revealed to be wide and complex. Now the investigator and agency can decide – Is this a case we can and should take on (maybe because the other victims are local, too)? Is there a task force, prosecutor's office, or partner-agency that could collaborate to investigate further? Is there a state or federal agency that is already looking into this crime ring and wants this piece of the puzzle?

C. The records didn't answer our questions. In some cases, the records will provide little or no information that sheds light on what happened to the victim. Often the records simply identify additional Internet or financial accounts that are part of the scheme. If the criminal was smart enough to use accounts with fake or minimal information, the records might offer no new information at all. Now the investigator can decide. Continue pursuing what leads there are? Check with other agencies if the case fits a pattern being investigated? Make a report to IC3 or other cybercrime data clearinghouses? Close the case as unsolvable?

Whatever the investigator decides to do, the decision will be based on real information. The total time spent on these six steps can be a couple of hours. But the result can be a solved case, a referred case, or at least factual answers for both the victim and the case file.

13.9   THE RECORDS PHASE: DIGGING FOR CLUES AND CONNECTIONS

After these first steps of getting and analyzing the initial records, a law enforcement agency may find there are clues that should be followed. Subscriber and session information for an email account may show an IP address through which the account was accessed, or bank records may show a new fraudulent transaction at an ATM machine. The next phase of the investigation focuses on following leads by getting more information from other records. This cyclical process of uncovering leads and getting the records to explain them will continue throughout the investigation.

Using subpoenas. In the records hunt, law enforcement's key investigative tool is the subpoena. Subpoenas can be used to obtain records from most companies, as well as from private individuals. During a cybercrime investigation, subpoenas are used most commonly to obtain subscriber and session information (from communications providers) and customer and transaction information (from banks, credit card companies, and retailers). Investigators also can use subpoenas to get security video and other items when initial reports involve (or follow-on records reveal) conduct that occurred at stores, banks, or other physical locations.

Investigation Strategies. Investigators working their way through records evidence should keep four strategies in mind:

1. *Look at the records for what they reveal and where they might lead.* In this phase, law enforcement investigators are using records to develop more information about the criminal incident and its perpetrators (as discussed in Chapter 11). While following the records trail, investigators should note both evidence that directly tells something about the event and evidence that is a breadcrumb in the trail to more information. Some important details include:
   - Accounts used to commit the crime (communication and financial)
   - Other accounts linked to those initial accounts, and accounts linked to those accounts (and so on)
   - Names, addresses, phone numbers, and other identifiers associated with those accounts
   - How fees are being paid to maintain accounts used to conduct criminal activity
   - IP addresses from which accounts are accessed
   - Stores, banks, and other locations where fraudulent transactions were conducted in person.

2. *Use open-source investigation to support information being uncovered in records.* Routinely incorporating open-source investigation into the records analysis process allows investigators to greatly expand upon the information the records supply. Open-source research is a quick, free, and highly effective way to figure out more about names, accounts, and locations discovered in subpoenaed records. Before assuming any detail is a dead-end or can only be explained by more records, investigators should check online for what public sources might know about it.

3. *Create an organizational system and use it consistently.* As covered in Chapter 11, keeping track of each records demand, with all the associated dates, recipients, letters of preservation, subpoenas, and non-disclosure orders, requires an organizational system. This system should be created as soon as the first letters of preservation or subpoenas are sent, and updated when a response is received and new requests are made. The system later can incorporate search warrants and other investigative steps.

4. *Develop information that might support a search warrant.* The evidence in records, in combination with open-source information, may end up being the factual proof needed to obtain a search warrant. One goal of records analysis is to identify connections from the crime to a particular email or phone account that provides probable cause to search it.

13.10 THE DATA SEARCH PHASE: ZEROING IN ON INTERNET ACCOUNTS AND THE CRIMINALS USING THEM

As investigators go through the repeated process of getting and analyzing records, certain Internet accounts may begin to stand out. Multiple crimes might trace back to particular email or cellphone accounts that were used either to commit the crimes or for crime-related communications. There may be links from criminal activity to financial or communications accounts, which, in turn, are linked to identifiable data storage accounts (such as cloud accounts). In some cases, sources (such as witnesses or victims) may help bring attention to accounts earlier in the investigation, without the need for extensive records review.

When the significance of specific online accounts becomes clear, the next phase of the investigation is to zero in and see what evidence they contain. The information contained in communications and stored data accounts can expose the breadth of the criminal activity under investigation, the locations from which criminals are operating, as well as the identities of the culprits.

Using search warrants for data. Finding out the content of messages stored in an online communications or data account requires a search warrant. A search warrant also must be used to get the location data showing where past calls and messages were transmitted. A search warrant for data is obtained just like any other. Law enforcement investigators provide an affidavit or sworn testimony to a court with jurisdiction showing they have uncovered facts that support probable cause to search a specific account. There are some special issues regarding data search warrants that investigators should keep in mind:

- *Non-disclosure.* Investigators can ask the court to include a non-disclosure order in the search warrant, provided they demonstrate that disclosure presents a risk to the ongoing investigation or a person's safety. This step is recommended with search warrants to prevent Internet companies from informing targets that their accounts are being searched.
- *Specificity in the application: evidence sought and listed crimes.* Applications for search warrants must include a specific description of the type of information for which law enforcement is searching, as well as the specific criminal statutes the conduct under investigation may violate. Law enforcement should specify all relevant information for any crimes they can establish.
- *Ownership and control evidence.* The search warrant should seek evidence demonstrating a suspect's ownership and control of the electronic account. It will not be enough for investigators to find evidence of criminality if the defendant then claims the account was controlled by someone else.
- *Searching with specificity.* Investigators must apply these specific criteria when searching content information obtained through a search warrant. In other words, if the warrant authorizes searching only for evidence of fraud crimes, investigators should not be reading emails from the subject about how much he loves cats (though that might be relevant to demonstrate ownership and control of the account). In practice, finding ways to comb through content without overbroad searching is a difficult juggling act – especially with cybercriminals, who may use coded language or hidden text to communicate.[3]

---

[3] If a search warrant specifies searching for records related to one crime, but investigators discover evidence of other crimes, an application can be submitted to the court to amend the search warrant to expand the range of the search.

- *Drafting the warrant for third-party compliance.* Search warrants for data are served upon third-party companies to obtain the account contents, but law enforcement officials will conduct the actual analysis of the electronic data for the evidence specified by the warrant. Consider spelling out this two-part procedure in the search warrant.
- *Timing.* Law enforcement must comply with the rules of their jurisdiction concerning the timetable for serving the warrant on the provider, and can request that the provider copy and turn over the stored data promptly.

A note on 2703(d) Orders. In some cases, when probable cause cannot be established, a 2703(d) Order is helpful to obtain evidence that might support an application for a search warrant. However, a 2703(d) Order should not be used to obtain the contents of communications (a search warrant demonstrating probable cause should be used).

Investigative strategies for communications accounts. Investigators using search warrants for communication accounts can consider these strategies:

1. *Analyze the contents by reading and searching.* The message being expressed in emails, voicemails, text messages (and their attachments) is the portion of a communication most likely to provide direct evidence in a criminal investigation. Reading (or hearing) the messages is incredibly valuable. Not only might the content itself offer useful nuggets and connections, but how the messages are written or spoken can give a sense of the accountholder's speech, age, and first language. Many accounts will have large numbers of messages within them, and content information sometimes must be reviewed quickly. As described in Chapter 11, investigators can load the content of the target account into a free email program that allows for specific keyword searching. When reading or searching through the content of messages, useful areas of focus are:

   - Names, addresses, and identifiers of any kind
   - Nicknames, and any associations with real names
   - Family and friends
   - Criminal associates
   - Any discussion of criminal activity (past and future)
   - Victims' identities
   - Stolen data (PII, etc.)
   - Criminal vendors and their wares
   - Financial information
   - Travel references or plans
   - Photos and videos (look for data showing where/how these were taken)
   - Documents and other attachments
   - References to other accounts used by targets
   - References that show who owns or controls the target account (even by nickname)
   - Other accounts corresponding with the target
   - IP addresses used by the target account.

2. *Look for connections to the physical world.* The content of communications may reveal devices and physical spaces connected to the criminal activity. With enough detail, this information might provide probable cause to obtain a search warrant for these areas.

Investigative strategies for stored data. There are numerous types of online data created and stored by individuals, organizations, businesses, and government agencies. In this category, we generally are considering documents, spreadsheets, databases, code, photos, videos, and other forms of digital information. Some common online storage locations include:

- Cloud and other online storage accounts
- Personal servers and networks
- Business/organization servers and networks
- Websites.

Many of the strategies for searching the contents of communications work well for other types of online data. In addition, investigators searching the contents of data storage accounts might focus on:

- *File names and storage organization.* How the user has organized and named the information being stored may shed light on its use, importance to the user, and connection to other evidence.
- *Dates items were stored.* Investigators can use these dates as a timeline through the stored information.
- *Log-in and session information.* These details may have been obtained through earlier subpoenas about the target account, but now may be more meaningful as investigators can correspond log-in dates, times, and IP addresses with items being stored and accessed.

Investigative strategies for location data. Location data obtained with a search warrant details the physical areas from where past calls or messages were sent. Much location data centers on phones and mobile devices (cell-site transmissions, GPS tracking, E911 information). When investigators receive this information through a search warrant, some investigative strategies include:

- *Mapping a target's movements.* By looking at the user's calls, the times they were made, and the cell-towers through which they were transmitted, investigators may be able to develop a map of a target's movements.
- *Comparing location data to message contents.* Investigators may be able to learn information from seeing where a suspect was when he sent a particular text message, voicemail, or email.

13.11   THE PHYSICAL WORLD PHASE: SEARCHING SPACES AND DEVICES

After the review of a suspect's communications, online storage accounts and location data, investigators may reach a point where they have identified a physical location or a device tied to the criminal activity. In some cases, locations and devices quickly come into play, such as when they belong to victims. Devices and places also may enter the investigation with the arrest of a low-level member of an organization or through the final arrests and searches near the end of the case. In any of these scenarios, the next phase of the investigation involves finding out what evidence is within those spaces and devices.

Using search warrants for locations and devices. To search a private location or device, law enforcement must use a search warrant. Search warrants for premises must describe the target location with specificity, and require significant planning to confirm the correct place has been identified and to determine how to enter and secure the site.

Search warrants for electronic devices must include a description of the device to be searched, the evidence (information) sought, and anticipate law enforcement's needs during the forensic search process. Doing so may forestall future legal challenges about whether the searching process conformed with the parameters authorized by the court.

Using a pen/trap. While pen/traps are typically thought of as a tool for the end-game of an investigation, they also can be useful tools for developing probable cause for search warrants. Pen/trap orders are relatively easy for investigators to obtain and use. Investigators may have sufficient evidence to meet the pen/trap's lower legal standard before they have probable cause to search an account, device or location. Once a pen/trap order is obtained from the court, it is implemented by the phone or Internet communications provider. The dialing, subscriber, and other information (for communications going in and out of the target account) is made available to investigators in real-time through a software platform. When a pen/trap is up and running, it becomes a powerful gateway to more traditional forms of investigation. Investigators can use the ongoing flow of communications and location data to conduct surveillance, prepare retailers or financial institutions for potential criminal activity, and determine how suspects are traveling.

Investigative strategies. When investigators are working on search warrants for physical spaces and devices, these are some strategies to consider:

1. *Double-checking the physical location in cyber cases.* Most cybercriminals practice anonymity and will take steps to thwart the methods law enforcement might use to track their locations and identify them. The attribution process of law enforcement must be strong, as we cover in Chapter 16, especially if it is the basis for obtaining a search warrant for a physical location.

   For example, criminals might use the wireless networks and communications accounts of unsuspecting victims and conduct their criminal business through these channels. Their online criminal activity then might trace back to this unsuspecting victim. For these reasons, additional investigative steps to learn more about the accountholders are essential. IP addresses are merely one strand of proof leading to a suspect, and can sometimes be deceiving.

2. *Traditional physical evidence.* With the search of a device or premises, law enforcement can take advantage of some traditional forms of evidence associated with tangible locations and items. Fingerprints, DNA, witness interviews, and other forms of hands-on investigation may lead to valuable identification evidence. If physical items are recovered, they might be traced back to fraudulent purchases (such as with stolen merchandise, forgery equipment), or to data compromises (stolen or forged credit/debit cards or checks, or other forms of stolen personal identifying information).

3. *Search warrants in the physical world expose the investigation.* When a search warrant is executed in a physical location, the suspect and others will know. Not only will people see the officers on site, the law requires them to leave a copy of the search warrant and list of seized items with the owner or occupant. Simply put, there is no "non-disclosure" option in the physical world. Therefore, searches of physical places often are undertaken at the same time that suspects are being arrested. In other cases, they are conducted when the exposure from a particular search is unlikely to upend the investigation (such as the search of the home of a low-level criminal that will not necessarily reveal the entire criminal organization is under investigation).

4. *Planning ahead for seizing devices.* If investigators have reason to believe computing devices will be recovered in a premises search, they should draft the warrant accordingly and plan ahead about how to seize them. Certain investigators might be tasked

with securing those devices properly (including knowing whether to keep them powered on or connected to a network, how to avoid encryption or data destruction, how to conduct an evidence preview in the field, or even the forensic imaging itself).

5. *Working with the forensic analyst.* Devices usually are searched by an expert in digital forensics, as described in Chapter 3, and this search is done best when a case investigator collaborates with the forensic analyst. The investigator can provide a brief overview of the case, the main suspects, and key search terms, and assist throughout the process. An informed and invested examiner will do a better analysis of the device.

Searching Devices with Consent

Obtaining consent to search devices is a common law enforcement practice, especially when the device belongs to a victim who wants to give law enforcement access in order to investigate how it was compromised.

For a suspect's device, seeking consent is a more complex issue. Here, consent is an important option when the device in question is encrypted,[4] and a password, fingerprint, or other authentication mechanism is required to access the data. Without consent (including unlocking the encryption), it might be impossible for law enforcement to obtain access to it.

Consent from a suspect is likely to be litigated. If the suspect is later prosecuted, he may claim the consent was obtained improperly and move to suppress the evidence found in his device. A "belt and suspenders" option is to obtain the consent to gain access and image the device, and then also obtain a search warrant. The pros and cons of using a suspect's consent are described in Table 13.1.

TABLE 13.1
Searching Devices of Suspects or Potential Suspects – Consent vs. Search Warrant

	Pros	Cons
Consent	+ Fast + Access encrypted devices + Establishes cooperation with law enforcement	− Validity and scope of consent can be challenged in court − Consent may be withdrawn
Search Warrant	+ Preferred method. + Presumptively lawful. + Very difficult to challenge the admissibility of recovered evidence.	− Slower − Takes resources and people to draw up a warrant (investigator, prosecutor, judge, etc.) − Encrypted devices may not be searchable

[4] As we covered in Chapter 3, encryption protects the confidentiality of data by encoding it, and is deployed on many computing devices.

Documenting Consent (Verbal, Written, Recorded)

Consent is best obtained in written or video-recorded form, using a formal consent agreement between the investigator and the person giving consent. Many law enforcement agencies create a form for consent agreements to ensure all the necessary legal points are properly included and documented – including the consenter's acknowledgment that she has authority to consent and is acting knowingly and voluntarily.

An owner's verbal approval of a law enforcement action is a less-desirable method of obtaining consent because if the legality of consent is later disputed, a judge may have to decide who is telling the truth, law enforcement or the suspect.

13.12   THE WIRETAP PHASE: SPECIAL CASES USING LIVE MONITORING OF TARGETS' COMMUNICATIONS

A few investigations will proceed to the point where a wiretap order is contemplated, the legal tool to monitor a suspect's live communications. Live information is helpful when investigators have reached the stage in which they believe a crime is about to be committed, seek to locate a known suspect, or need to defeat security measures. At this point, the investigation likely has identified key phone and Internet accounts used by criminal actors on an ongoing basis in connection with criminal activity.

Using a pen/trap. Investigators considering a wiretap typically obtain pen/trap orders first. A pen/trap (especially with location data) provides valuable real-time information about a target's activity, movement, and associates, helping the investigation prepare for a wiretap. If gathering evidence from a pen/trap does not lead to the arrest of the target, it helps satisfy a wiretap's exhaustion requirement as an investigative method that was tried and failed.

Using a wiretap. Wiretap evidence is some of the most productive and compelling evidence of criminal activity. Investigators can see or hear, in real time, exactly what a target is planning, admitting to, and conspiring with associates. Wiretaps are also extremely difficult to use. Even after the extensive application process, implementing a wiretap requires numerous other steps, including setting up the wiretap with the service provider, establishing a physical facility with the technical equipment to monitor the wire, sufficient staffing to conduct 24/7 monitoring, training procedures for the monitoring investigators, and regular reporting about the wiretap's activity to the court. At the conclusion, investigators must notify all individuals whose communications were intercepted and provide recordings of all monitored communications to the court.

Investigative Strategies – when investigators are working on wiretaps, some strategies might include:

1. *Wiretapping voice conversations: minimization and amendment.* When conducting the wiretap monitoring of communications, law enforcement agents must establish procedures that "minimize" the interception to only the information approved by the court order. In other words, if the wiretap order is to monitor a cellphone for activity related to identity theft, then the agents listening to the calls must have a procedure to check for that information without needlessly listening to calls about other topics. If an agent is listening to a call and happens upon information about different crimes, the wiretap application must be amended and re-authorized by the court to allow for interceptions related to this new crime. The same procedures must be implemented for email and other text-based wiretaps.

2. *Wiretapping written communications versus voice communications.* In some cyber cases, using a wiretap solely for written (text) communications (such as emails or text messages) has fewer technical and practical demands than a wiretap for voice communications. When the monitoring involves only reading messages as they come through, fewer investigators are required, even with multiple intercepted accounts. In addition, the goals for a text wiretap may be different than for voice interceptions. A text wiretap can gain evidence and perhaps identify a cybercriminal, but may not be needed to coordinate surveillance or other real-time investigative activities. Thus, 24/7 monitoring may not be required, and leads can be pursued at a pace more amenable to the regular schedules of investigators.

13.13   TRADITIONAL SHOE LEATHER TECHNIQUES

The tried and true investigative techniques used for all types of crimes are also needed in cybercrime investigations, and are especially useful at the beginning of a cyber case. When first reported, a cybercrime often involves a live person and/or a physical device that has information about a crime. After assessing the initial evidence, cyber investigators often will conduct interviews, crime scene evaluation and searches – in other words, the traditional methods that are universally applicable.

Beyond the initial stages, there can be many points along the course of a cyber investigation that require investigators to get out from behind the computer screen and use traditional "shoe leather" investigative methods. Some of the traditional techniques that are used frequently in cyber investigations are:

- Victim or witness interviews
- Recovery of computing devices as evidence
- Recovery and review of security videotape or other surveillance video
- Recovery of stolen/forged credit cards and fraudulently purchased property
- Surveillance of locations and suspects.

Investigation Skills in a Cybercrime Investigation

The lead DA's investigator on the Western Express case always made clear that technology was not his forte, but nevertheless he was an experienced and dogged investigator in all respects and he wore down a lot of shoe leather during the investigation. New-York-City-based cybercriminals and identity thieves were using mail drops and Internet cafés around the area. One of the investigator's roles was to visit those locations and gather evidence about the suspects' activities. He interviewed the managers and attendants and, through the personal connections he made, was able to obtain leads that helped identify suspects and further the investigation. He also did all the important things that investigators do to build a case, including surveillance and coordinating search warrants and arrest.

Simply put, investigative skills and people skills are as essential to a cybercrime investigation as any technological expertise.

13.14   WRITING FOR LAW ENFORCEMENT INVESTIGATIONS

In the course of obtaining evidence of cybercrimes, prosecutors and investigators will have to draft affidavits and documents to justify the issuance of various types of legal process, including for non-disclosure orders, search warrants, pen registers, and wiretaps.

No matter who is at the keyboard writing the initial draft or editing it (law enforcement officer or prosecutor), creating these documents can be a complex task because the facts uncovered in a cyber investigation often need to be woven and linked together. In Chapter 11, we introduced the concept that cybercrime investigations require clear writing throughout the entire process. Needless to say, good legal writing can demonstrate the strength of the evidence and convince the court to issue the appropriate legal process.

If all goes well, the court will authorize an order leading to valuable evidence – evidence that may eventually result in the arrest of a cybercriminal. But if affidavits are poorly drafted, they later can be attacked by the defendant's attorneys as misleading or insufficient. Defense attorneys will file motions to suppress the evidence, and the affiant will be cross-examined based upon the information to which he swore.

To that end, investigators and prosecutors should ensure that all legal documents are written clearly and logically. Consider these criteria:

- Wording that is understandable and verifiable by the investigator or other affiant. The affiant must read it, understand it, and swear under penalty of perjury to the accuracy of the statements.
- Writing that is understandable to the judge who will review it and, hopefully, issue the requested order. Remember, the judge is probably learning about the case for the first time in the affidavit.
- Years later, the investigator may be on the witness stand, being cross-examined about the contents of the affidavit. The investigator's memory may have faded, and he or she will be under courtroom stress. The language and statements in the document need to survive this test of time, and be clear and self-explanatory to the investigator, prosecutor, judge, and jury.
- Photos may assist in describing a complicated textual or technological issue to the court. When it comes to making connections among layers of digital records, a screenshot can be worth a thousand words.[5]
- For any factual issues relating to identification of a suspect or a physical place, consider the concepts reviewed in Chapter 16.

13.15 WORKING WITH THE PRIVATE SECTOR

Investigating cybercrime rarely is a solo effort by law enforcement. The very nature of crimes that take place through the Internet means a continual intersection with the private sector. Private sector individuals and entities are often the first to discover, to gather evidence of, and to investigate a cyber-related incident. Ongoing threat information frequently comes from private sector observations that are then communicated to law enforcement.

The ultimate success of law enforcement's efforts to track new and growing criminal trends, and investigate individual crimes, requires a collaborative approach with the private sector. Without a good working relationship, law enforcement may never find the proof needed to arrest and prosecute cybercriminals. Creating a mutually positive relationship starts with understanding the common roles of private sector actors in an investigation, including:

---

[5] During the Western Express case, screenshots were used to demonstrate what we were describing within the text of search warrant affidavits, extradition paperwork, and appellate motions. Rarely before were such images used in legal documents, but the approach was helpful to explain what were then very new crime typologies and concepts.

- Victims, both individuals and organizations
- Companies that maintain records relating to cybercrime
- Witnesses
- Resources and experts (those who possess information or technical capabilities that can assist law enforcement).

As discussed in Chapters 10 and 12, private sector companies or individuals sometimes have different interests or motives than those of law enforcement. Understanding these private sector responsibilities is vital to working out solutions that address the needs of both law enforcement and the affected companies and individuals. There are times when law enforcement may decide to take certain actions – such as executing a search warrant – even if the involved private parties disagree. But, in practice, an investigation is more likely to achieve better results through communication and collaboration with the private sector.

13.16   CYBERCRIME INTELLIGENCE AND LAW ENFORCEMENT INVESTIGATIONS

We covered cybercrime intelligence in Chapter 11, but the issue deserves special emphasis for the law enforcement perspective. It is nearly impossible to solve significant cybercrime cases working them one case at a time. Instead, law enforcement agencies (both independently and collectively) need to build deep background knowledge about cybercrime trends and the individuals and groups committing these crimes. After all, many cybercriminals are attempting their schemes on a repeated basis, every day, over the course of years. Limiting an investigation to a single reported crime (as is often done with many "street crimes" and some cybercrimes) ignores the vast number of clues and evidence that might be obtained from shared intelligence.

For law enforcement, there are several concrete ways to incorporate cybercrime intelligence throughout an investigation.

- *Create your own intelligence database.* Document important details, trends, and suspect pedigree.
- *Check outside intelligence sources.* Using public and private intelligence resources; investigators can check whether the facts in their cases mirror existing investigations or trends.
- *Share intelligence with others.* One agency's old or unsolved case could well provide clues for a new case that pops up in a different jurisdiction.
- *Develop personnel and processes.* Training investigators to handle cybercrime cases and building internal procedures for handling them allows agencies to gather intelligence in a cohesive manner.

13.17   CONCLUSION

Law enforcement agencies learn of cybercrimes in many ways, and must determine whether and how deeply to investigate. Because cyber investigations are more complex and resource intensive than most other cases, the decision about what to do with a cybercrime report often rests on the practical realities of the technical and human resources available.

When an investigation is initiated, it requires law enforcement investigators to combine traditional and analytical investigative methods, relying heavily upon records and data. The processes of obtaining these records and maximizing their investigative effectiveness are the foundation of any cyber case. The work often requires painstaking, dogged dedication, but is essential if we hope to catch any of these cybercriminals and stop their crime spree.

Remember that these chapters also have essential information for law enforcement investigators:

- Chapter 11 on general investigative techniques, including open-source investigation, tracking records requests, and email evidence
- Chapter 15 on developing the money trail
- Chapter 16 on developing suspects and attributing criminal conduct to an individual.

14 The Regulator's Investigation

This chapter is for:

- Regulators (federal or state) responsible for ensuring that regulated entities comply with data breach notification and cybersecurity requirements
- Regulated entities, who want to understand regulator's responsibilities
- Companies of all kinds covered by data breach and other regulatory-type laws
- Law enforcement, to better understand cybercrime reports spurred by regulatory rules and laws.

14.1 INTRODUCTION

This chapter addresses cybercrime investigation from the perspective of federal and state regulators who ensure compliance with laws and regulations related to data breach reporting, cybercrime reporting, and cybersecurity. These evolving guidelines apply to regulated entities and now – more and more – to all organizations who face regulatory-type laws generally enforced by state Attorneys General.

A regulator's work comes into play both before and after a cyberattack occurs. Before an attack, regulators may inspect a regulated organization to assess the sufficiency of its information technology and information security programs. Regulatory agencies and state Attorneys General also play a role in educating businesses on how to comply with reporting requirements and improve their cybersecurity to prevent compromise. Deficiencies in required security protocols can result in regulatory consequences, like fines, additional inspections, and license revocation.

After a cybercrime attack, a regulatory investigator's focus is not to identify the individuals responsible for a cyber incident, but rather to determine whether a regulated business had reasonable cybersecurity measures in place, and whether the business complied with reporting requirements. The investigation into a business' actions may require examination of how the cybercrime occurred.

A regulatory investigation will, in many ways, delve into the same issues that a victim might examine in making the decision to bring a civil lawsuit. Violations of legal or regulatory requirements regarding cybersecurity or reporting may support a victim's claims of negligence or breach of contract against the business under investigation.

14.2 REGULATORY RECAP: REGULATED INDUSTRIES AND REGULATORY-TYPE LAWS

As we covered in Chapter 9, some industries are directly regulated by federal and state agencies regarding a variety of business practices (including cybersecurity). These industries and their primary regulators include:

- Banks, securities brokers, money transmitters, and other financial services
  - Federal Deposit Insurance Corporation (FDIC)
  - Office of the Comptroller of the Currency (OCC)
  - Financial Crimes Enforcement Network (FinCEN)
  - Federal Financial Institutions Enforcement Council (FFIEC)
  - Federal Reserve System (The Fed)
  - Securities Exchange Commission (SEC)
  - Commodity Futures Trading Commission (CFTC)
  - Federal Trade Commission (FTC)
  - Other federal regulators
  - State agencies regulating state-chartered or licensed services, often in conjunction with federal regulators
- Hospitals, doctors, and other businesses providing healthcare services
  - Department of Health and Human Services (HHS) (federal)
  - State and local healthcare regulatory agencies
- Utilities and other entities that provide critical infrastructure
  - Federal Energy Regulatory Commissions (FERC) and other federal regulators
  - Local or regional public utility commissions
- Telecommunications services
  - Federal Communications Commission (FCC) and other federal regulators
  - State or regional public utility commissions.

For these important industries, regulatory requirements now include cybersecurity, cybercrime prevention, and reporting of cybercrime events to regulators and consumers.

Then, there are industries that are not regulated, but fall under regulatory-type laws enforced by federal and state agencies. The Federal Trade Commission (FTC) regulates many types of businesses in the areas of unfair or deceptive trade practices, consumer protection, and data security practices. Every state has laws requiring that consumer data breaches be reported to the state government, whether or not the organization is part of a regulated industry. Many states also have cybersecurity requirements for all businesses, regulated or not. Often, it falls to the state Attorneys General to receive these reports, investigate their sufficiency, and take action when an organization fails to report. In other words, a non-regulated organization may face a regulatory-type inquiry concerning compliance with these overarching laws.

Lifelock and the FTC

LifeLock is a U.S. identity theft protection company. Beginning in 2010, the corporation came under various Federal Trade Commission (FTC) rulings and court orders requiring it to better secure personal information and to advertise its services truthfully. However, according to the FTC, LifeLock failed to establish a comprehensive information security program while falsely advertising the extent of its protections against identity theft crimes. LifeLock exposed personal data and was sued by consumers and the FTC. In 2015, the company ended up settling with the FTC and paying $100 million towards reimbursing consumers and other consumer protection.

The FTC decision noted that the reasonableness of information security will depend on the facts and circumstances of each case. While LifeLock claimed that its information security systems had PCI DSS certification (this cybersecurity framework is discussed in Chapter 4), that assertion was insufficient alone to satisfy the company's obligations in light of the other evidence.[1]

14.3 A CYBERCRIME OCCURS: REVIEWING THE REPORT OF THE AFFECTED BUSINESS

A regulator's investigation into cybercrime typically begins when a business reports a cyber incident – like a data breach or security compromise – pursuant to regulations or state laws. Affected business typically must submit a notification of specific types of cybercrime to the agency in charge of enforcing the laws or regulations. Sometimes, however, regulators might learn of a cybercrime from other sources, such as impacted customers or media reports.

Assessment of a cybercrime notification starts with the applicable laws and regulations for reporting and cybersecurity, and also may be informed by information security best practices and frameworks. Regulated industries often have detailed compliance requirements, including rules, advisories, and guidance. With laws applicable to all businesses, whether regulated or not, the compliance requirements may be more generalized. Most regulations and laws related to cybersecurity include provisions describing:

- *Types of businesses* that must comply
- *Proactive security measures* a regulated business must undertake to be in compliance
- *Specified cybercrime-related actions or events that must be reported* to regulators, law enforcement, affected customers, or to the public
- *Procedures and timeline for notifying* regulators, law enforcement, customers, and the public should a specified cyber event or internal action occur.

Based on these provisions, regulators review the submission to see whether it was filed correctly, meaning within the stated time frame and using the mandated procedures. This review also examines whether the notification contains the details the law or regulation requires. In the early stages of an investigation, businesses may have incomplete facts at their disposal, but their cybercrime notifications should include whatever required information can be provided and an explanation for why some details could not be determined. If the notification is missing information or was submitted improperly, regulators may demand further reporting or explanation from the business. If a business makes no notification about a specified cyber event, or makes it long after the required time frame, the business may be subject to regulatory sanctions for failing to comply with these requirements.

14.4 INVESTIGATING THE CYBERCRIME: SUFFICIENCY OF CYBERSECURITY MEASURES AND ACCURACY OF THE REPORT

Once regulatory investigators have reviewed the cybercrime report, they might determine that further investigation is warranted. Key areas of concern are whether the business was

[1] *LifeLock to Pay $100 Million to Consumers to Settle FTC Charges it Violated 2010 Order*, FTC (December 17, 2015), www.ftc.gov/news-events/press-releases/2015/12/lifelock-pay-100-million-consumers-settle-ftc-charges-it-violated.

in compliance with industry regulations or state-level regulatory-type laws and whether the business accurately reported the nature and extent of the cyberattack.

For example, a company's report that data was exposed through a cyberattack on its servers may trigger questions about the company's pre-existing cybersecurity, current cybersecurity, and reporting duties (express and implied). For example:

- Did the regulated entity *detect* the breach promptly?
- Did the regulated entity *report* the breach promptly and accurately as required to the regulator, law enforcement, and affected parties?
- Is the regulated entity investigating the breach diligently to determine the cause and after-effects?
- To the extent information is not known at the time of initial reporting, what follow-up information will be provided after further investigation?
- Did the regulated entity have adequate information security measures at the time of the breach? Was it in compliance with applicable laws and regulations? Or, did deficiencies in information security practices, in violation of regulation, allow the data breach to occur?
- Did the organization make false representations to the public about its level of cybersecurity? If so, that conduct might constitute an unfair or deceptive business practice.
- Is the entity incorporating lessons learned from the breach into its information security program?

Depending upon the nature of the reported event, and the duties created by the relevant law or rules, regulators must decide the extent of any regulatory investigation into the business' conduct and whether additional steps must be taken by the business to mitigate the effects of the attack.

When a regulator determines that additional investigation is needed, steps will be taken to gather the needed evidence related to the business' security and reporting, as well as the incident itself. While each government agency has its own process, the primary evidence-gathering methods used in a regulatory investigation include interviewing witnesses and reviewing records and data. These witnesses and records may come from within the business, or from sources outside the business that have knowledge or information pertinent to the investigation.

Some laws and regulations require businesses to make their internal employees and records available to the investigating regulatory agency. In addition, some agencies have the power to issue administrative subpoenas, or obtain criminal or civil subpoenas, to compel witnesses or entities to testify and produce records.[2] The existence of such powers makes voluntary cooperation all the more likely.

Depending on the investigation findings, action might be taken by the business or regulator. Some examples of these actions include:

- *Voluntary steps* by the business to change its practices or assist affected customers
- *Corrective actions* mandated by the agency
- *Administrative sanctions* against the business following a regulatory hearing or other agency proceeding

---

[2] Examples of the investigative process can be found on the websites of regulatory agencies, such as the Securities and Exchange Commission (SEC) at www.sec.gov/enforce/how-investigations-work.html, or the Department of Health and Human Services (HHS) at www.hhs.gov/hipaa/for-professionals/compliance-enforcement/examples/how-ocr-enforces-the-hipaa-privacy-and-security-rules/index.html.

- *Civil lawsuits brought by the agency* to obtain court-ordered sanctions or remedies against the business
- *Civil lawsuits brought by the business* to dispute an agency's findings or sanctions.

If voluntary or corrective actions by the business are not completed, regulatory agencies are likely to pursue administrative or civil enforcement measures.

Data Breach Report Example

Bank A is regulated by both federal and state regulators. It experiences a data breach where customer and employee information is compromised. As required, the bank reports the breach to the regulators and to law enforcement. It also files a suspicious activity report (SAR) with FinCEN. The regulators determine they need more information about when and how the breach initially occurred, when it was identified, and how the bank responded by securing its systems, so they request more information.

Further investigation reveals the attackers took advantage of a vulnerability in one of Bank A's software systems that had been identified over a year prior, and for which a patch (update) was available. Previously, regulators had warned the Bank about the need to improve its process for software patching, and the Bank had provided assurances about both the patching process and the status of pending software updates.

The regulators now want to know why the patch was not implemented, and whether this patching failure allowed the attack. They also investigate to determine if this one deficiency is a symptom of broader weaknesses in the Bank's information security program. The Bank works to demonstrate that its information security program (and patch process) is strong. The Bank might argue either (i) there was a valid business and IT reason why this patch was not be implemented, or (ii) this was an isolated oversight in an otherwise strong information security program.

Depending upon the results of the investigation, the regulator might issue a finding of inadequate cybersecurity and fine the bank, or might be satisfied that the Bank's information security program is adequate and that the breach occurred despite their best diligent efforts.

14.5 BALANCING THE ROLES OF COMPLIANCE AND ENFORCEMENT

When a business or organization experiences an event that triggers regulatory scrutiny, regulators often have to balance their roles of encouraging compliance and taking enforcement action.

One purpose of data breach reporting rules (required by many regulations) is to ensure that the public, regulators, and law enforcement are informed of potentially harmful criminal events. Knowing that breaches will have to be disclosed is a powerful incentive for organizations to improve their security to prevent them.

Another purpose of regulations is to prevent cybercrime, protect the privacy of consumers and employees, and protect the regulated industries as a whole by improving cybersecurity.

From these perspectives, the regulator's goal is to encourage businesses to take the steps that will bring them into compliance, thereby achieving the purpose of the regulations.

When an organization notifies regulators about a data breach or security compromise, it is fulfilling the regulatory requirement to report these events. Doing so, however, exposes the organization to a potential regulatory investigation and subsequent penalties. Because compliance with one regulation (reporting) opens an organization to other regulatory enforcement action (investigation and punishment), regulators have to consider the potentially conflicting implications of these rules.

Breached entities, having been victimized by a major crime, face serious business impairment, high costs, reputational damage, and potential lawsuits, and reporting rules are an additional burden. If regulatory requirements are excessive or enforced too rigidly, they might unfairly punish organizations who accurately report information, while rewarding companies who withhold information or shade the facts to put themselves in a better light.

In the arena of cybercrime, the dual powers of requiring reporting and enforcement of security standards can leave regulators facing complicated issues following a data breach or similar attack including:

- Who are the victims?
  - The breached organization.
  - The organization's customers, clients, and others (who may not be adequately represented by the breached entity).
  - Business partners/suppliers of the breached organization (which may face increased security risks due to the compromise).
- What does the exposure of the incident say about the company?
  - When initial evidence of a breach or security compromise comes from outside of the affected business (such as through impacted customers), questions are raised about why the business itself did not report. Some organizations fail to report data breaches in ignorance of the event or the reporting requirements; others deliberately hide the fact that it occurred.
  - When affected businesses report data breaches and cyber incidents, they are not only complying with the rules, they are doing a public service. Regulators should encourage businesses to make reports of cyberattacks, and to investigate the crimes diligently and accurately. Finger-pointing and blame may discourage reporting.
- Was compliance adequate or deficient?
  - Were there prior incidents or red flags involving this organization?
  - Did the organization have adequate cybersecurity and incident response planning and did it follow its plans and policies?
  - Though a cybercrime might indicate poor cybersecurity, organizations with excellent cybersecurity can still be victimized.
- Are regulatory measures sufficient?
  - Do current regulations sufficiently achieve security and reporting?
  - Is the regulator adequately advising organizations about their duties and the risks of cybercrime?
  - Is the regulator properly incentivizing good faith information security measures and honest reporting?
  - Is the regulator properly addressing organizations whose security and reporting is deficient?

14.6 CONFIDENTIALITY AND INFORMATION SHARING

Regulators investigating an entity's compliance with data security or notification rules may come into possession of sensitive information about the organization, including its security measures and personal data about customers and employees. Regulatory agencies and organizations need to evaluate how this information will be protected from further sharing.

For example:

- *FOIA/FOIL records requests.* If an individual, organization, or journalist seeks information from a regulatory government agency under the Freedom of Information Act (FOIA) or similar state laws, consider what information from or about the breached entity might have to be provided under the law, and what can be withheld.
  - What information might expose security details of the breached entity?
  - What information might compromise an ongoing criminal investigation?
- *Civil lawsuits.* If civil suits from private parties ensue as a result of the reported cyber incident, what information might be provided or withheld in response to a civil subpoena?
- *Other regulatory actions.* If another regulator requests information, what can be provided?
- *Law enforcement demands.* If law enforcement requests or subpoenas information, what can be provided?

Third-party victims, law enforcement, or the media may be highly motivated to obtain regulators' reports or investigative data. A civil litigant might argue that regulatory requirements establish a standard of care, and that an organization's failure to comply with these requirements demonstrates failure to meet this standard and, thus, potential liability to the third-party victim.

14.7 CONCLUSION

Regulatory investigations into cybercrime focus on incidents that impact businesses within regulated industries or within the scope of overarching laws regarding data breaches and cybersecurity. Regulations and laws (federal and state) typically require such businesses to notify regulators, law enforcement, and/or the public regarding the occurrence of specific cyber incidents. Regulatory investigators must review these notifications, determine whether the business has reported the events as mandated, and conduct the ensuing investigation into whether the business was in compliance with required cybersecurity measures. Their decisions often create new guidance for all regulated companies about the regulatory and legal requirements around cybersecurity and cybercrime reporting. Regulators who supervise an industry also are in a special position to aggregate information and inform regulated entities about threats, vulnerabilities, and methods to mitigate risks.

15 Financial Investigation
Following the Cybercrime Money

This chapter is for:

- Everyone.

15.1 INTRODUCTION

We have dedicated this chapter to investigating money movement and illegal income connected to cybercrime because of the importance of the topic to anyone conducting a cybercrime investigation. As we discussed in the early chapters, most cybercrime is done for profit, and all types of cybercrime may require payments to conduct fraudulent transactions, purchase criminal tools and supplies, and pay criminal associates. Cybercriminals seek to hide the nature of these payments and the proceeds of their criminal activity using a wide variety of money laundering techniques.

For all the elusive qualities of cybercrime, the prominent role of value transfer presents an opportunity for investigators to find and analyze clues. Cybercrime yields billions of dollars in revenue annually for cybercriminals and money launderers, meaning there is a huge potential to find money-movement evidence. Following the money can lead investigators to the perpetrators at various levels of a criminal operation, including those participants working as money launderers. By exploring the financial aspects of cybercrime, investigators also can develop proof that specific criminal offenses were committed (including the crime of money laundering), as well as the grounds to seize illegally obtained assets.

In this chapter, we will look at methods of picking up and following the money trail. We start with an introduction to money laundering to learn why criminals move and hide money, and how these actions may be a separate crime. Next, we discuss traditional currency and virtual currency, as both are important tools of cybercriminals for committing crimes and laundering profits. Then we apply these concepts to cybercrime investigations, looking at different types of financial evidence that can be used to identify cyber-suspects and prove crimes (including money laundering).

15.2 MONEY LAUNDERING 101

Money laundering is the process successful criminals use to conceal their illicit profits and payments.[1] We start this chapter by explaining money laundering because it is a major

---

[1] For an overview of money laundering, see John Bandler, Money Laundering Investigations, article in the *Encyclopedia of Security and Emergency Management* (Springer) (August 2018) (DOI 10.1007/978-3-319-69891-5_26-1), https://link.springer.com/referenceworkentry/10.1007%2F978-3-319-69891-5_26-1.

component of cybercrime. Most cybercrime is committed for profit, and the cybercrime economy requires payments between the participants.[2] A good cybercrime investigation recognizes that financial transactions are key investigative clues, and that criminals may disguise the purpose of transactions from law enforcement and regulators.

There are four general reasons why criminals need to hide the money they make from crime.

- *The money itself can be proof that crimes were committed.* Evidence that certain funds were paid, earned, or otherwise used to facilitate a crime can help establish the commission of that crime.
- *Financial transactions can help identify criminals.* Sending, spending, and receiving funds for criminal or personal purposes can unveil the identity of a cybercriminal who is trying to operate anonymously.
- *The money trail can be a roadmap to the criminal operation.* How money was paid, stored, or transferred can reveal the different roles and associations within a criminal organization, and the breadth of the group's criminal activity.
- *Income (legal or not) is taxable.* Hiding earnings from the government is illegal, and likely constitutes the commission of separate crimes.

Although money laundering has been occurring for as long as income has been taxed and crime has been profitable, government investigation of this activity has evolved over time. Money laundering investigations started in the 1930s with the novel prosecution theory that criminals must pay taxes on illicit income or face the consequences. Al Capone was convicted not for the murders, bribery, and bootlegging, but for failing to declare his illegal income on his taxes. After Capone, it became incumbent upon successful criminals to file taxes and declare some of their ill-gotten gains, disguised as legitimate income.

In 1986, the crime of Money Laundering became a distinct offense and government investigators were given a more powerful mechanism for punishing the concealment of illegal profits and money movement. As we learned in Chapter 6, both federal and state criminal codes now directly criminalize money laundering efforts. Essentially, the crime of money laundering is committed if someone knows that funds are the proceeds of criminal activity and they conduct transactions with the intent to conceal the source, destination, or ownership of those funds.

Financial institutions play a significant role in uncovering money laundering by monitoring transactions and reporting suspicious activity to the government. This function started in 1970 when the United States enacted the Bank Secrecy Act (BSA), which has been amended and strengthened many times. The BSA requires banks to monitor, investigate, and report on criminal activity and funds touching their systems. Other laws require financial institutions and money service businesses, such as money transmitters, to be licensed by the state and/or federal government, and often to register with federal regulatory agencies.

These licensing and regulatory requirements include a duty to have an appropriate anti-money laundering (AML) program that will identify and report suspicious transactions potentially related to criminal activity or money laundering. Financial institutions and money service businesses may be required to submit suspicious activity reports (SARs) regarding questionable transactions and currency transaction reports (CTRs) summarizing cash transactions above a certain amount. Effectively, these laws deputize financial institutions and their AML experts to assist the government by detecting this criminal activity.

---

[2] John Bandler, Stemming the Flow of Cybercrime Payments and Money Laundering, *ACAMS Today* (Law Enforcement Edition), Vol. 16, No. 3 (June–August 2017), www.acamstoday.org/stemming-the-flow-of-cybercrime-payments.

Money laundering statutes and regulations governing financial institutions recognize that criminals can move funds, generate profits and conceal their source using a number of mechanisms for storing or transferring value. Conduct that conceals illicit profits is criminalized whether the funds are in the form of currency (cash, bank wire, etc.), property, or other value – including virtual currency (discussed in the next section). The U.S. Financial Crimes Enforcement Network (FinCEN), a bureau within the U.S. Treasury Department dedicated to combatting money laundering, also recognizes the threat of money laundering in any form of value, whether it is currency or a substitute for currency.[3]

Following the Money on Television and in Real Life

Television and movies have some great examples concerning money laundering.[4] Consider HBO's *The Wire*, where the Baltimore Police Department is investigating drug trafficking, but having difficulty making a case against the leaders of the drug crew. Detective Lester Freamon directs the team to follow the paper trail, concluding with:

> In this country, somebody's name has got to be on a piece of paper ... and here's the rub. You follow drugs, you get drug addicts and drug dealers. But you start to follow the money, and you don't know where the [heck] it's going to take you.[5]

Although *The Wire* is a fictitious story, we have seen firsthand the truth of Detective Freamon's wisdom. In Western Express, the money trail began with one fraudulent online purchase using the credit card account of a New York resident. By getting information about that transaction from the credit card company and the retailer, we eventually identified the person who received shipment of this merchandise. With more research, we learned this person received many other such items, all fraudulently obtained using credit card information of other victims. After more investigation, we learned this person used virtual currency to pay another cybercriminal for the stolen merchandise, which he then resold at a profit. We also learned this was a massive and growing scam. We could have pursued many merchandise receivers and ended the case right there. But like in the drug business, following the stolen merchandise leads cyber investigators to only the lowest levels of the criminal pyramid.

So, instead, we followed the money. We learned about virtual currency, which back then was not well known. We used subpoenas for banks and money transmitters to learn more about the payments made in connection with this fraud, including their source and destination. We kept tracing the path of the money through many layers, and it led us around the country and world. Following the money from one minor, local fraud led to the unravelling of a major international cybercrime and money laundering conspiracy.[6]

When we began looking into that run-of-the-mill credit card fraud, we had no idea where it would take us. But we would never look at any case involving cybercrime and money as "run-of-the-mill" again.

---

[3] See *New FinCEN Guidance Affirms Its Longstanding Regulatory Framework for Virtual Currencies* (May 9, 2019), www.fincen.gov/news/news-releases/new-fincen-guidance-affirms-its-longstanding-regulatory-framework-virtual.

[4] See John Bandler, Lawyers, Drugs and Money: AML in Popular Media, *ACAMS Today*, Vol 17, No. 2 (March 20, 2018), www.acamstoday.org/lawyers-drugs-and-money-aml-in-popular-media.

[5] *The Wire*, "Game Day," Blown Deadline Productions/HBO (2002).

[6] John Bandler, Dirty Digital Dollars, *Fraud Magazine*, a publication of the Association of Certified Fraud Examiners (July/August 2016) www.fraud-magazine.com/article.aspx?id=4294993652.

15.3   TRADITIONAL CURRENCY AND VALUE

Now that we know why criminals need to launder money, let us explore some fundamental concepts about value and currency. When criminals make payments, move money, and hide profits, they are transferring and storing value. In this section, we will look at the idea of value and the official definition of currency.

First, it is worth reflecting upon humankind's history of storing and exchanging value. For millennia, long before any currency was issued, people established value through bartering goods or services, or by using precious items like gold and salt. Over time, the idea of abstract value developed. For example, over a thousand years ago (and continuing in some regions today), people began paying one another across long distances through the process of Hawala and its Hawaladars, a network of independent agents facilitating the transmission of value (similar to modern-day money transfer systems such as Western Union or bank wires).

Eventually, governments started issuing currencies, which originally were backed by precious physical items like reserves of gold. As the power of these currencies took hold, many countries left the gold standard and their currencies were based simply on the full faith and credit of the government. These government currencies are called "fiat currencies", examples of which are the U.S. dollar, E.U. euro, and Japanese yen. According to the U.S. government's own definition, currency means the coin and paper money of the United States or of another country that issues its own official coins and bills. Anything not issued by a government cannot meet this official definition of a "currency".

The establishment of official currency greatly improved commerce, creating a simple national payment system for goods and services. Official currencies also have facilitated international commerce and travel, since the fiat currencies of different countries can be exchanged to pay for goods and services around the world.

Over time, systems developed to make it easier to spend and save official currency. Banks emerged to allow people to save their currency in a safe place and from there, new methods evolved to help people pay for things using the funds saved in their bank accounts. These methods include:

- Checks
- Wire transfers
- Money orders
- Credit cards
- Debit cards
- Online payment systems linked to credit/debit cards or bank accounts (such as PayPal, Venmo, and ApplePay).

All of these traditional currency payment methods (as well as cash itself) are used routinely to commit cybercrimes and launder the profits.

15.4   VIRTUAL CURRENCY AND CRYPTOCURRENCY

Virtual currencies are a relatively new way to transfer value, and are frequently used in connection with cybercrime. Cryptocurrencies are a type of virtual currency, with Bitcoin being the most popular.[7] Virtual currencies are not issued by governments but rather by individuals and organizations that decide to create their own payment systems. So long as people believe a virtual currency has value and are willing to accept it or exchange it, then it has value.

---

[7] A cryptocurrency is a type of virtual currency that uses encryption (cryptography) to secure transactions. Some cryptocurrencies use a distributed ledger to record transactions and "blockchain technology".

The first step in using virtual currency is to create an account within that particular virtual currency platform. Once a user has an account, there are two ways to get units of the currency into it. A user can be paid virtual currency by someone else, or a user can go to a virtual currency exchanger and exchange regular (fiat) money for units of the virtual currency. Virtual currency exchanges are often independent dealers or businesses that charge a fee for exchanging virtual currencies and fiat currencies. Western Express was an early virtual currency exchanger.

Virtual currency has a number of general characteristics that make it appealing for cybercrime and identity theft.

- *Internet based.* Since cybercrimes are committed or facilitated through the Internet, being able to make payments through the Internet is also essential.
- *Anonymous.* Cybercrime participants need to send and receive payments anonymously, and will take advantage of any opportunities to do so with virtual currency.
- *Instant.* With virtual currencies, online payments can be made and verified instantly, or at least faster than most conventional transactions. This feature provides assurance to cybercriminals doing online deals with anonymous criminal associates.
- *Irreversible.* Virtual currency payments are final once sent, another important quality for payments among anonymous criminals. A criminal cannot trick his counterpart by making a payment, and then trying to take the payment back.

Virtual currency is used by cybercriminals in a number of ways, such as:

- *Payment among participants in the cybercrime and identity theft economy.* Virtual currency allows participants to offer criminal services and goods in a capitalistic environment. Since virtual currency transactions can be conducted anonymously, cybercriminals can transact with one another without identifying themselves.
- *Ransomware and other extortion.* Criminals looking to extort victims using ransomware, denial of service attacks, and other cybercrimes can demand payment through virtual currency.
- *Money laundering.*

Suppose an identity thief wants to obtain virtual currency in order to buy some stolen credit card data. He might send traditional money to a virtual currency exchanger, tell the exchanger what account to fund, and then have the virtual currency units added to his account, as depicted in Figure 15.1. He then can purchase the stolen data without identifying himself to the data seller (or vice versa), and in a manner difficult for law enforcement to trace back to him.

15.4.1 History of Virtual Currency and Its Evolving Terminology

The term "virtual currency" essentially acknowledges that it is a virtual representation of currency, not a real "currency" issued by a government. While this is a generally accepted term used by regulators and lawmakers, terminology continues to evolve. The Financial Action Task Force (FATF) – an international consortium working to fight money laundering – now uses the term "virtual asset", perhaps recognizing that the word "asset" is broader than "currency".[8] FinCEN's recent guidance puts emphasis upon the transfer of "value that substituted for

---

[8] FATF, *The FATF Recommendations*, Adopted 2012, updated June 2019; www.fatf-gafi.org/media/fatf/documents/recommendations/pdfs/FATF%20Recommendations%202012.pdf; FATF, *Guidance for a Risk-Based Approach to Virtual Assets and Virtual Asset Service Providers* (June 2019), www.fatf-gafi.org/media/fatf/documents/recommendations/RBA-VA-VASPs.pdf.

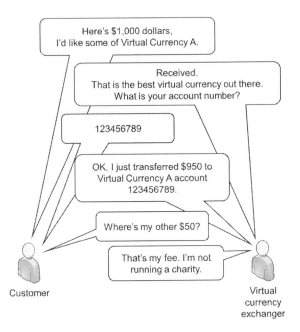

FIGURE 15.1 Virtual Currency Exchange.

currency" which has a broad meaning, and deemphasizes the specific language and terminology that participants may use, and which may be subject to debate.[9]

In other words, even experts debate the correct terminology, and laypeople often use virtual-currency-related terms and descriptions loosely. Moreover, organizations seeking to avoid certain regulations or seeking to garner public interest or investment may name and describe their products to suit their own interests, rather than follow evolving norms. For example, a group hoping to avoid a particular law or regulation might describe their offering as something other than a virtual currency or a virtual asset. Alternatively, a company might describe its product as a "cryptocurrency" to stir up investment interest when it really is not. Our view of the important categories and relevant terminology is depicted in Figure 15.2. Note the bright line distinction between government-issued "currency", and "value that substitutes for currency", and how virtual assets, virtual currency, and cryptocurrency are subcategories.

While virtual currencies are a relatively recent phenomenon to the public eye, they have been around for decades and have a fascinating history.[10] In 1996, Egold was founded and is credited as the first widely adopted virtual currency. Egold's marketing claimed that it was backed by a reserve of real gold. In 1998, Webmoney was founded in Russia and is still in existence. After Egold and its founders were indicted and convicted by the federal government, Liberty Reserve emerged around 2009 (based in Costa Rica). Each of these platforms became very popular with cybercriminals and identity thieves.

---

[9] FinCEN, FIN-2019-A003, *Advisory on Illicit Activity Involving Convertible Virtual Currency* (May 9, 2019) www.fincen.gov/sites/default/files/advisory/2019-05-10/FinCEN%20Advisory%20CVC%20FINAL%20508.pdf;

FinCEN, FIN-2019-G001, *Guidance on Application of FinCEN's Regulations to Certain Business Models Involving Convertible Virtual Currencies* (May 9, 2019) www.fincen.gov/sites/default/files/2019-05/FinCEN%20Guidance%20CVC%20FINAL%20508.pdf.

[10] John Bandler, Cybercrime and Digital Currency, *ABA Information Law Journal*, Vol. 7, No. 4 (Autumn 2016), www.americanbar.org/content/dam/aba/administrative/science_technology/2016/ilj_volume7_issue4.authcheckdam.pdf.

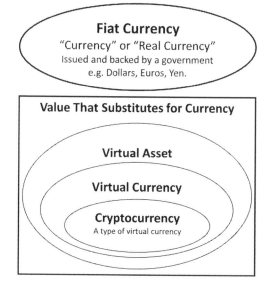

FIGURE 15.2 Terminology and Categories.

These early virtual currencies were "centralized", meaning the transactions were administered by a central entity. From a law enforcement and regulatory perspective, a centralized entity (and its executives and employees) can be subpoenaed, arrested, and held to account for criminal activities. Using these methods, the U.S. government eventually shut down both Egold and Liberty Reserve for enabling money laundering.

Bitcoin, the first cryptocurrency, went live in 2009 and has become the most popular virtual currency to date. Bitcoin is also the first "decentralized" virtual currency, functioning through blockchain technology and the concept of the decentralized ledger. Unlike prior virtual currencies, no one is "in charge" of running Bitcoin. Rather, the currency is managed through open-source software that handles the payment transactions and stores the records. A subset of Bitcoin users operates this software, confirming Bitcoin transactions and storing transaction records on the "distributed ledger". This ledger consists of "blocks" of transaction records, which are "chained" together, hence the term blockchain. For law enforcement and regulators, this decentralization means there is no one at the virtual currency itself to hold accountable if it is used criminally. Instead, investigators need to look to the individuals and exchangers who use Bitcoin or other decentralized cryptocurrencies.

Aside from Bitcoin, there are currently thousands of different virtual currencies, some created in the image of Bitcoin, some that are centralized currencies, some that may not fit a particular mold, and some that may not be accurate in how they describe themselves. No matter the terminology or type, however, investigators looking at virtual currency transactions should focus on how value gets transferred, who is transferring it, and the underlying purpose of the transactions. These fundamental questions about any currency payments apply equally to virtual currency transactions in any form.

The pros and cons of virtual currency are frequent topics in the media, so it is worth taking a moment to put virtual currency in perspective. Some argue that virtual currency is a bad invention, largely unregulated, that allows anonymous accounts and payments mostly useful only for criminals. Others argue these virtual currencies are the answer to an overly regulated, monopolistic and stodgy financial system. Perhaps the truth is somewhere in between.[11] Clearly, financial regulation has many benefits, including consumer protection and the prevention and detection of money laundering – and the absence of such regulation has risks.

Government regulation of virtual currency has come to the United States but is still evolving. But even with regulation, criminals have shown throughout time that they will exploit any form of value storage or value transfer. Whether cash, bank wire, virtual currency, diamonds, gold, or even the currency within online videogames, criminals will use it if it suits their interests. It is too late to wish virtual currency away. Learning how to best glean clues and leads from virtual currency is a necessary step to making strong cases against cybercriminals.

Western Express: Virtual Currency Exchanger and Launderer

Western Express was a virtual currency exchanger and a money launderer. We seized the company's computers and paper records, but it was still extremely difficult to follow the flow of funds among their customers because they deliberately did not keep records of customer identity, and did not use any of the record-keeping practices of a legitimate financial institution or money transmitter.

Eskalibur, a cyber wholesaler of stolen credit/debit card account information, laundered hundreds of thousands of dollars of virtual currency through Western Express. The company's recordkeeping was sparse, so the bulk of the evidence was found in instant message chat logs and Egold and Webmoney virtual currency payment records. Another cybercriminal laundered over a million dollars through Western Express, using a combination of Egold, Webmoney, and bank wires to over a dozen different bank accounts around the world.

The information we gathered about this money movement was a financial puzzle. With additional evidence gathered over the course of the investigation, and the work of a fantastic financial investigator, all communications, bank wire records, and Egold and Webmoney records were pieced together to match each incoming payment with an outgoing payment through Western Express.

This analysis also showcased a technique of verifiable, transparent records analysis that went step-by-step (discussed further in Chapter 18). Beginning with the raw evidence, from whatever source, this method highlighted key portions of the transaction records while connecting them with other evidence in the case.

This technique also underscored a reality of financial investigations involving criminals and money launderers – you will rarely find every piece of the puzzle, and not every penny can be accounted for. But sometimes, discrepancies in the trail of transactions can be clues to a missing puzzle piece.

15.5 GETTING STARTED ON THE MONEY TRAIL: HOW FINANCIAL DETAILS CAN PROVE CRIMES AND THE CRIMINAL'S IDENTITY

When an investigation turns to financial activity connected to a crime, a helpful first step is to think about how financial transactions reflect events in the course of the crime or the life of the criminal. Through this lens, investigators can more effectively evaluate the

---

[11] Aside from value transfer, there are other potential uses for blockchain technology and the distributed ledger, such as tracking the ownership or origin of property.

information contained in the records kept by banks, credit card companies, money transmitters, and virtual currencies for proof of criminal activity and the suspect's identity.

From that viewpoint, it is worth reflecting on why criminals receive and spend money. Let us start with some reasons connected to their criminal activity, and how evidence of these transactions provides proof a crime was committed. These reasons include:

- Earning money through fraud and other crimes
- Paying for products and services that facilitate their crimes
  - Stolen personal identifying information (names, DOBs, SSNs, account info)
  - Equipment to make forged IDs
  - Forged IDs made by criminal specialists
  - Hacking services, spam, malware, botnets
- Paying criminal employees/associates for their roles in the criminal activity
- Moving money through accounts or purchases to launder its origins.

But criminals also send, spend, and receive money for all the reasons the rest of us do. The financial window into a suspect's personal life can be the thread that leads to identification. For example, criminals may use financial transactions to:

- Pay for items and events in their personal lives
  - Bills for phone, Internet, rent
  - Travel and vacations
  - Food and restaurants
  - Entertainment
  - Gifts
  - Cars, boats, jewelry, and other luxury purchases
- Give or receive loans
- Earn payments from legitimate work.

Payments indicating travel can contain significant clues. Some travel payments might directly show flight or hotel details leading to identifiable individuals (such as friends or relatives of the suspect). Other payments might reveal that a suspect was traveling in a certain country, information that matches the suspect to other evidence in the case (like emails from an anonymous account discussing travel to that country).

Financial transactions with a connection to a suspect's regular life, no matter how small, are always worth investigating. If the cybercriminal is a beginner, they might be a direct link to his identity. If the cybercriminal is a professional, these money trail clues can be the momentary mistake that breaks apart his cyber anonymity.

15.6   FINDING AND FOLLOWING THE MONEY

Now that we have an understanding of value, currency, and virtual currency, as well as the way financial transactions might contain key evidence about crimes and criminal actors, we can look at how investigators can search for this evidence.

The journey along the money trail begins with a single step. Often, all an investigator has at the beginning is a single transaction connected to fraud or cybercrime. Whatever information is available can be used as the starting point. From there, the goal is to follow the money to uncover as much information about the crimes and suspects as possible.

Every investigator can conduct important financial investigation steps. Looking at bank, credit card, or other similar records is just a commonsense hunt for two kinds of clues,

(i) information that says something about the crime or suspect under investigation, and (ii) information that provides further leads to additional crimes, accounts, evidence, or suspects.

15.6.1   WHERE TO FIND EVIDENCE OF FINANCIAL ACTIVITY

When looking for and following the money trail, it is helpful to think about these forms of financial evidence:

- *Bank account records.* Bank account opening and transaction records, including deposits, withdrawals, checks, debit card payments, and bank wires.
- *Credit card records.* Credit card account opening and transaction records, including purchases, cash withdrawals, and bill payments.
- *Pre-paid card account records.* Pre-paid card account opening and transaction records, including purchases, cash withdrawals, and bill payments.
- *Credit reports.* Credit reports provide a financial history of both victims and suspects, and are worth obtaining where possible. For victims, credit reports can reveal accounts fraudulently opened using their identity information. Information from credit reports may be aggregated into reports from subscription-based services used for background investigations or credit checks.
- *Money transfer records (Western Union/MoneyGram).* Western Union, Money-Gram, and other money transmitters are services for sending funds both within the United States and internationally. These companies often have monetary limits per transaction and sometimes require identification. Cybercriminals regularly use these services to purchase stolen data or virtual currency, using fake names or employing individuals (money mules) to send or receive funds. This practice can make the records analysis more complicated, but patterns of activity can be detected.
- *Money order records (U.S. Postal Service and others).* Some fraudulent schemes involve purchasing money orders using cash or stolen accounts and identifiers. Money orders also can be used as a layer in the money laundering process. Because many money orders require some form of identification, they can be a fruitful avenue of investigation when they appear on the money trail.
- *Payment services linked to a conventional financial account.* PayPal, Venmo, ApplePay, Google Pay, Amazon Pay, and many others are examples of payment services linked to conventional financial accounts (such as bank accounts and credit card accounts). Typically, a bank has taken some due diligence steps towards a "know your customer" (KYC) review before opening the bank or credit account, and the payment service relies partly upon the bank's review. The records of the payment service may have considerably more transaction information than the underlying financial account.
- *Payment methods not linked to a conventional financial account.* Some payment methods might not be linked to a conventional financial account, and thus no conventional KYC process occurred. Nevertheless, transfer of value occurred and can be investigated.
- *Virtual currency records (virtual assets/value other than currency).* Two sources of records relate to virtual currency – records from exchangers and transaction records.
  - *Exchangers.* In the United States, AML regulations require virtual currency exchangers to get information about their customers. A subpoena or request to the right exchanger might yield additional leads about a suspect's virtual currency activity. Criminals who wish to evade this scrutiny may provide forged identification or purchase their virtual currency from exchangers outside of the U.S.

○ *Transaction records.* Decentralized cryptocurrency transaction records (e.g. for Bitcoin) are stored publicly on the blockchain distributed ledger. With the right knowledge, effort, or tools, transactions and transaction patterns can be examined. Centralized virtual currency transactions also could be obtained with a subpoena to the administrator, if they will submit to the jurisdiction and comply with the subpoena (or request).

- *Retail purchase and transaction records.* At times, receipts, delivery records, bank/credit card records, or physical items point to retail purchases that are connected to criminal activity. Retailer transaction records (including security video) can be useful evidence and provide leads to additional criminal activity.
- *Cash.* Cash is always going to play a role in money laundering, even for some cybercrime activities. One cybercrime that routinely generates cash is the ATM cash-out scheme, where criminals steal credit and debit card information, create forged cards, and withdraw cash from ATM machines. Cybercriminals in one country often partner with criminals in the U.S. to conduct the cash out. They then share the proceeds, often paying one another through money transmitters, bank wires, or virtual currency. This crime is decreasing as ATM machines and credit cards slowly switch to microchip authentication ("chip and pin" or "chip and signature").

Like all areas of investigation, following the leads from financial records can be a continuing, cyclical process, as we covered in Chapter 11. Clues from bank records might lead to a credit card account, the credit card account might lead to a clue about a new bank account, a conventional transaction might reveal the existence of a virtual currency account, an email might reveal existence of more accounts, and so on.

When a suspect is developed, the investigation can turn to a full analysis of his or her financial activity. Investigators can look at the suspect's personal and business activity and look for links to the crimes under investigation.

When a virtual currency exchanger is being investigated for criminal conduct, such as money laundering, the financial analysis required might be quite extensive (as it was during Western Express). This type of suspect typically has numerous customers and, therefore, engages in a large number of financial transactions through multiple accounts.

Investigators looking at financial transactions should consider how to prioritize leads and whether a lead is worth following. For example, a bank wire or check might be to or from an account controlled by the suspect or a co-conspirator, and worthy of obtaining. On the other hand, if bank records for one account show the issuing of a hundred checks that were then deposited in a hundred different accounts, investigators may consider whether records are needed for all the new leads. As a first cut, perhaps records should be obtained for a portion of the hundred new accounts.

15.6.2   Investigating Virtual Currency Transactions: Specific Tools and Resources

Investigators following a cybercrime money trail involving virtual currency may not be able to obtain information about a transaction directly from the virtual currency, but should consider the evidence to be found from other sources surrounding the transaction.

Some basic steps for investigating a virtual currency transaction are as follows:

- Identify the virtual currency being used (for example, Bitcoin or Webmoney).
- Determine all available information about the transaction.

- ○ The records, data, or other source that led the investigation to the virtual currency transaction may provide the date, time, account name or number used, amount, payor or payee, type of transaction (exchange, payment).
- If the virtual currency is centralized, determine what entity controls its records.
  - ○ If the virtual currency records are in the United States, subpoenas or other court orders could be used to acquire transaction records. Virtual currency is regulated in the United States, so exchangers transacting with virtual currency customers typically must obtain information about the customer to satisfy their AML obligations.
  - ○ If law enforcement is seeking virtual currency records located in another country, consider whether they are obtainable through the international legal process, with help from the U.S. Department of Justice's Office of International Affairs (discussed in Chapter 7).
- If the virtual currency is decentralized, determine if records are available through publicly available sources (like Bitcoin's public ledger data discussed below).
- Consider the other side of the transaction. What was the virtual currency payment made for? Stolen data? Services? Records may be obtainable from the other side of the payment.
- If the transaction involves an exchange of fiat currency funds for virtual currency, look for information about the fiat side of the exchange.
  - ○ Exchangers in the United States are regulated and can be compelled to provide records through subpoenas and other appropriate legal tools.
  - ○ Records can be subpoenaed from traditional financial institutions for money orders or bank/credit/debit accounts that may have been used to purchase the virtual currency, which may provide other leads about the case.

Information about virtual currency transactions can be found. Some transactions have enough connection to the traditional financial system to offer an investigative foothold. Some entities can be subpoenaed. And some, as we will learn in the next section, make information about transactions available to the public.

15.6.3 CRYPTOCURRENCY TRANSACTION RECORDS

Decentralized cryptocurrency transaction records are created and maintained differently than those of centralized virtual currencies or other financial records. Most cryptocurrencies use blockchain distributed ledger technology, creating a system that stores the records of transactions on publicly available ledgers distributed across many computers. In other words, anyone can go online to see all of the transactions ever made using that currency.

The good news for investigators is that the records are publicly available. But there are challenges when looking at these public records. For example, the transactions of an account are available, but investigators still have to determine who controls each account. Further, properly analyzing large volumes of data to identify a particular relevant transaction can be difficult.

Bitcoin has voluminous cryptocurrency transaction records available for inspection. Though there are publicly available free tools to analyze Bitcoin's ledgers, some companies now sell tools and services to analyze Bitcoin transaction data and participants. For certain types of investigations, these tools might be essential, especially when money is moving between various Bitcoin accounts.

Investigation is more difficult when users exchange funds between virtual currencies (e.g. from Bitcoin to Webmoney). The path of value transfer can be hard to track without assistance or records from the currency exchanger. In addition, some cybercriminals use money

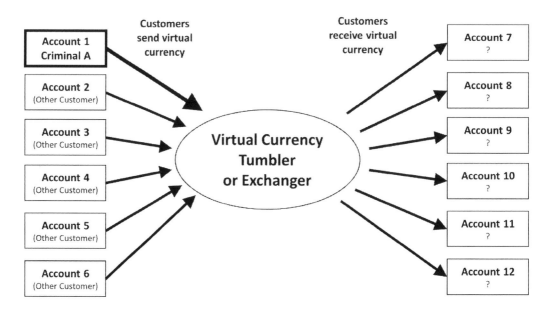

FIGURE 15.3   Virtual Currency Tumbler or Exchanger.

laundering services, such as "tumblers" whose purpose is to conceal and disguise the flow of value. Consider virtual currency payments from Criminal A, which go to a tumbler or exchanger. The payment from Criminal A is mixed with the payments from many other customers, and the tumbler service may take action to disguise the path of funds as they are recorded on the blockchain. Ultimately, the tumbler returns Criminal A's funds to a different account. This process is depicted in Figure 15.3.

15.7   CONCLUSION

Cybercrime investigators should pay careful attention to the financial aspects of all forms of cybercrime, including the theft committed, profits reaped, payments made, and flow of funds. All methods of transferring value should be evaluated, whether fiat currency, bank wires, virtual currency, money transfers, and other creative ways of sending value and funds.

The global cybercrime and identity theft economy is based on profits, and international cybercriminals look for ways to get illegal profits out of the victim country and back to their own. Knowledge of virtual currency and how it interacts with the conventional financial system will help investigators follow the trail of cybercrime.

We rarely obtain all pieces to a cybercrime puzzle, but the financial trail can provide some of the most important clues and buttress other avenues of investigation. Step by step, one transaction at a time, investigators can develop insight into crimes and criminals and integrate the financial evidence with other avenues of investigation.

16 Identification of the Suspect
Attributing Cyber Conduct to a Person

This chapter is primarily for:

- Law enforcement
- All investigators seeking insight into their attackers.

16.1 INTRODUCTION

One of the most interesting and challenging aspects of a cybercrime investigation is uncovering the true identities of individuals committing illegal acts online. Investigators might quickly learn that a criminal actor is committing all kinds of crimes. But identifying that actor can be a more difficult task since the Internet makes it so easy for criminals to conduct crimes with anonymity from anywhere in the world.

The process of identifying a cybercriminal is known as attribution. Cybercriminals do not want to be caught, so they conceal their activities and use nicknames, pseudonyms, or stolen identities. In this chapter, we will learn about investigative steps that help cut through those disguises and attribute cyber conduct to a particular person. These steps include identifying the criminal conduct that needs to be attributed, identifying cyber pedigree details associated with this conduct, and looking for connections that become links in a chain of identifiers and evidence that eventually lead to a real person.

Issues of proof are always central to a cyber identification. Because establishing a criminal's identity often relies upon a trail of interconnected pieces of evidence, this chapter also focuses on techniques for articulating the information in a clear and persuasive manner. We also will discuss the need to demonstrate that identity evidence meets the relevant burdens of proof that must be satisfied at various stages in law enforcement and civil cases.

16.2 DOING ILLICIT BUSINESS ONLINE: CYBER NICKNAMES AND PSEUDONYMS

Any criminal who wants to get away with his crime cannot risk being identified by victims, witnesses, or investigators. Criminal actors committing traditional crimes often take physical steps to hide their identities. They wear masks, operate at night, and cover security cameras. As identification technology improves, so do smart criminals' methods. They wear gloves so as not to leave fingerprints; they cover up or clean up so as not leave behind DNA.

For cybercriminals, hiding their identities is easier. They never have to physically visit the scene of the crime, but rather can operate from wherever they are behind the veil of the Internet. Using nicknames or fake or stolen identifiers is one method commonly used by cybercriminals to take advantage of the Internet's potential for anonymity.

Many established cybercriminals pick an online nickname ("nic") as their primary pseudonym. By conducting business under a consistent nickname, a criminal can develop a reputation in the marketplace as a reliable vendor, coder, forger, or other service provider. Sometimes criminals operate under different nicknames for different criminal purposes, or change their primary nicknames over time.

Of course, nicknames are not necessarily unique characteristics. Two individuals might separately come up with the same nickname, or an imposter might use the nickname of an established cybercriminal to try to steal his business. For investigators, discovering a suspect's nickname is highly relevant and should be investigated, but it should not be treated as a conclusive identifier. As discussed in the next section, the significance of a nickname and the weight to give it as an identifier depend greatly on the timing and specific platforms where a nickname was used, as well as on the other unique accounts that can be connected to it.

Some online activity requires criminals to supply personal identifying information, such as when opening certain online accounts or conducting certain types of transactions. When a name, physical address, phone number, birth date, or social security number is needed, cybercriminals likely will provide made-up or stolen information. This information may contain helpful clues. A cybercriminal or identity thief may use a particular pseudonym regularly for these purposes, or otherwise give information that indirectly ties back to them, such as a contact account for receiving email or text confirmations.

16.3 THE ATTRIBUTION PROCESS AND DEVELOPING A SUSPECT: MAPPING CRIMINAL CONDUCT TO CYBER PEDIGREE AND PHYSICAL PEDIGREE INFORMATION

To learn the identity of the real person committing a crime online, investigators sift through the evidence, finding and assembling nuggets of information until they point to a certain individual. This work requires attention to detail and a good system for keeping track of the information as it is discovered. Ultimately, the process means starting from the original criminal conduct, determining the identifying information directly involved in the commission of it, looking for follow-on pedigree information connected to those initial cyber identifiers, and tracing the conduct to a real person, as depicted in Figure 16.1.

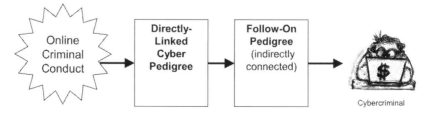

FIGURE 16.1 Attribution Process Overview.

16.3.1 TWO KINDS OF PEDIGREE INFORMATION: PHYSICAL AND CYBER

Law enforcement often uses the word "pedigree" to describe personal information about a suspect or defendant. Traditional *physical pedigree* information focuses on the characteristics of a suspect that identify him in the physical world, including the suspect's name, date of birth, address, phone number, physical description (height, weight, eye, skin and hair color), and other pertinent details that specifically describe the individual. Other types of physical pedigree information include photographs (including mug shots), fingerprints, and DNA.

Physical pedigree information is what law enforcement relies upon for identifying suspects in traditional crimes. In a cybercrime investigation, learning these physical identifiers – in other words, identifying a real person – is the desired end point of an attribution investigation.

Most cybercrimes require compiling the suspect's *cyber pedigree* information as a starting point for identification. Cyber pedigree information also describes a specific individual, but begins with a focus on his or her online characteristics and cyber identifiers. Cyber pedigree information includes any information used to commit the crimes, such as nicknames, email accounts, computing devices, IP addresses, instant message accounts, and phone numbers. Investigation into those names and accounts may lead to follow-on information about the suspect that is not linked directly to the criminal activity. As more information is found and analyzed, the goal is to ultimately uncover details leading to the physical human using these cyber identifiers.

Figure 16.2 lists some traditional physical pedigree, and also cyber pedigree information.

The process of examining cyber pedigree information to identify someone requires a certain amount of philosophical thought. We may take for granted what identifies us as who we are, because it is rarely challenged: name, date of birth, social security number, our parents and family, the experiences of our lives. Building an identification from cyber pedigree information depends on thinking broadly about what details might be a part of someone's identity online, including Internet accounts, devices used, IP addresses, languages used, and even spelling mistakes.

Now let us look at how investigators can take clues from a cybercrime to assemble a cyber pedigree summary that might trace back to a physical cybercriminal.

Traditional Physical Pedigree	**Cyber Pedigree**
Name	Email accounts
Date of Birth	Instant messenger accounts
Social Security Number	Social media user accounts
Parents & family	Virtual currency accounts
Home address	IP Addresses
Phone number	Device identifiers
Occupation	Nicknames
Work address	Pseudonyms
Physical descriptors	
Photograph (mug shot)	
Fingerprints	
DNA profile	

FIGURE 16.2 Traditional Physical Pedigree and Cyber Pedigree.

16.3.2   THE ID-PLUS ATTRIBUTION PROCESS: SIX STEPS TO LINK CRIMINAL
CONDUCT TO CYBER PEDIGREE AND PHYSICAL PEDIGREE

We have developed a six-step cyber attribution process, called the ID-PLUS process:

1. **Isolate** the online criminal conduct that is the investigative starting point.
2. **Determine** any pedigree identifiers *directly* linked to the crime.
3. **Pursue** follow-on pedigree identifiers, and keep looking.
4. **Link** a chain of articulable connections from the crime to an identifiable suspect (if you are able).
5. **Uncover** more links between the crime and suspect to confirm the suspect's identity.
6. **Summarize and articulate** proof clearly to meet increasing burdens of proof at each stage.

This process is summarized in Figure 16.3.

*Step 1. **Isolate** the online criminal conduct that is the investigative starting point.*

An attribution investigation starts with isolating the specific online criminal conduct for which a perpetrator needs to be identified, as indicated in Figure 16.4. This step may sound obvious, but being clear at the outset about what crime is being investigated is the anchor to organizing the attribution process and the chain of circumstantial identification evidence that will support it. Using this organizing principle allows the starting point of the evidence trail to remain in focus as an investigator gets deep into the minutiae of leads pointing in many directions. It also keeps the investigation focused on the criminal conduct that the identification ultimately will help prove in a criminal or civil proceeding.

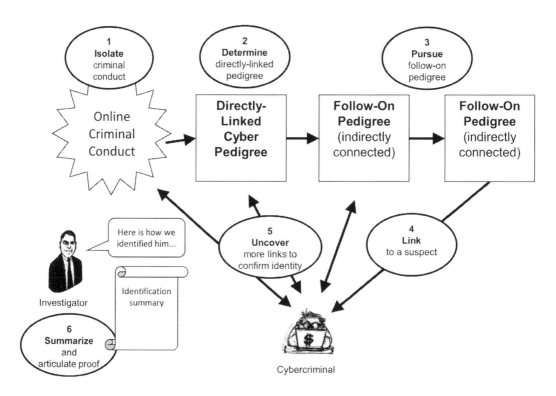

FIGURE 16.3   ID-PLUS Attribution Process: Six Steps to Identification.

FIGURE 16.4   Step 1: *Isolate* the Online Conduct Being Investigated.

The online conduct isolated as the attribution starting point might consist of a discrete event, a series of events, or a long-running criminal business. Examples include:

- Sale of credit cards delivered via email message
- Spam email
- Cyber intrusion into an organization's network
- Ransomware threats or actions
- Threatening online comments posted to a third-party website
- Threatening comments delivered directly to recipient by email or other messaging method.

*Step 2. **Determine** any pedigree identifiers directly linked to the crime.*

The second step is to determine the pedigree information directly connected to the online criminal conduct isolated for investigation in Step 1. These are the identifiers the suspect used to commit the crime, and so should be connected to the offending conduct with minimal inferences or conclusions. Once documented, these identifiers will form the start of the suspect's cyber pedigree information, and would include the email account address used to send stolen credit cards or threatening messages, the social media account used to post the public comment or personal message, the network connection used to commit the data breach, the virtual currency account used to conduct a criminal transaction, and other accounts, handles, or nicknames used to perform the specified crime. Figure 16.5 depicts this direct pedigree information.

Of course, investigators need to correctly identify the cyber pedigree information directly linked to the crime, and assess any uncertainty about this evidence. For example, with a phishing or harassment crime, a sending email address might be disguised to the casual user. Investigators would have to view the full email header for greater insight about the true origin of the criminal email.

Two quick points. First, the cyber identifiers documented during this step, and any inferences or conclusions drawn from them about leads or connections, need to be continually

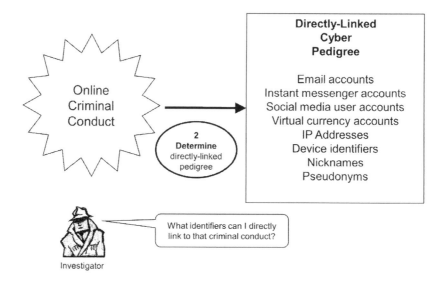

FIGURE 16.5   Step 2: *Determine* Directly-Linked Cyber Pedigree.

reviewed and reassessed as more information is gathered (as for all steps). Second, remember that in this step, we are looking only at the pedigree information *directly linked* to the crime and no further. The next step begins the process of looking at where this direct information might lead.

*Step 3. **Pursue** follow-on pedigree identifiers, and keep looking.*

The next step is to find follow-on pedigree information stemming from those direct links. Investigators can use the full range of investigative tools (such as open-source research or subpoenas) to look for new links from the direct identifiers. These new links are additional pedigree identifiers which become part of the suspect's cyber pedigree summary. Any newly discovered identifiers then become the basis for further follow-on searches with more connections to be made, as depicted in Figure 16.6. Each piece of new information spurs another round of investigation, in a continuous and cyclical search that might eventually lead to the physical pedigree of a suspect.

To put it another way, the cyber pedigree information learned in these follow-on searches is not directly connected to the criminal action, but rather requires an inference or conclusion to link it to the initial pedigree. Whatever the logical reason to believe the follow-on information is related to the initial pedigree, that connection usually must be investigated further to understand and verify it.

Each subsequent cyber identifier discovered is a successive link, which are all tied ultimately to the direct pedigree like multiple links in a chain. Each link requires another inference, or conclusion, about how it is connected that needs to be properly articulated and tested. Not every link is of equal weight, so some links in this chain will be stronger than others. Keeping track of the trail of follow-on investigative steps and pedigree information identified is essential to demonstrate how newly uncovered cyber pedigree links back to the original identifiers directly connected to the crime. This process may result in many paths of investigation; some will lead nowhere, but one may ultimately lead to a suspect.

For example, if an email address was used to commit the crime, that address would be cyber pedigree tied directly to the crime (identified in Step 2). A subpoena to that email provider for subscriber information and IP address information might lead to follow-on pedigree identifiers, including:

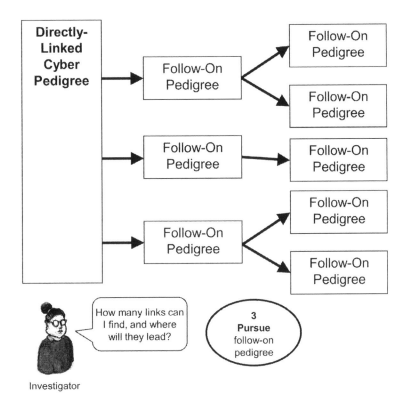

FIGURE 16.6 Step 3: *Pursue* Follow-On Pedigree Identifiers, and Keep Looking.

- An alternate (recovery) email account address, name, address, phone number, or other information that the user had provided to the email provider.
- IP addresses used to create and log in to the email account (identified by the email provider).

The investigator would then need to evaluate and investigate each of these items of follow-on (indirect) pedigree. The user-supplied information is a clue whether it is accurate or made-up. The IP address also is a clue, whether from a proxy computer, a VPN, TOR, or from a coffee shop or neighbor's Internet connection. Follow-on investigation will provide additional leads and pedigree information, one link further away from the direct pedigree with which we started.

*Step 4. **Link** a chain of articulable connections from the crime to an identifiable suspect (if you are able).*

Using many pieces of both directly-connected and follow-on pedigree information, an investigator *may* be able to create a circumstantial chain of evidence that leads from the crime to a suspect. The investigator needs to be able to articulate the entire length of this chain, the proof of each link, and any concerns about the proof and the inferences behind it. Perhaps there are multiple chains of proof, but often investigators start with just one. (*After* a suspect is identified, the work will continue in Step 5 to solidify the proof by developing more chains and interconnections). The identification at this stage will likely be tentative. As tempting as it might be to consider the case "solved", more work must be done.

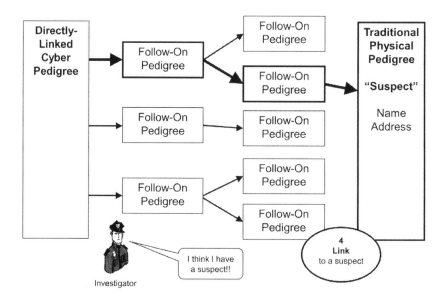

FIGURE 16.7 Step 4: *Link* a Chain of Articulable Connections from the Crime to an Identifiable Suspect (If You Are Able).

Figure 16.7 provides an example of how, with enough effort (and some luck), a path of logical connections might lead from the crime to a suspect. It would be great if every attribution investigation found a suspect this simply, but the important point is that, of many paths tried, one may eventually lead to a suspect.

Step 5. ***Uncover*** *more links between the crime and suspect to confirm the suspect's identity.*

Once a suspect is identified, the attribution investigation expands. Investigators now must confirm the suspect's identity working both ways – from the original crime to the suspect, and from the suspect's physical pedigree back to the crime (see Figure 16.8). This step requires utilizing all types of evidence to learn everything about the cybercriminal that might fortify and expand the links to identification. Where evidence is inconsistent, it must be tested and evaluated.

Ideally, this step produces multiple chains, as different pieces of information spawn their own links that either separately lead to the suspect or prove to be interconnected. Having multiple chains of evidence means building stronger, more-reliable proof. They also ensure an identification is not made because of tunnel vision about the outcome or because of unconfirmed conclusions.

For example, a single chain of circumstantial evidence may lead to a suspect in Step 4. That chain is made up of many links, each of which requires a logical inference or reason to connect it to adjacent links. This single chain might be insufficient to attribute the criminal conduct to the suspect because any mistake in assumptions or reasoning might mean arresting or suing the wrong person. Further, even if the chain of identification was correct, a single-strand identification is more vulnerable to attack. Likewise, identifications based on multiple strands may need additional investigation when some strands rely on evidence that is difficult to corroborate or admit into evidence at a trial. In all of these situations, investigators need to look for additional and independent chains of pedigree information linking the suspect to the crime.

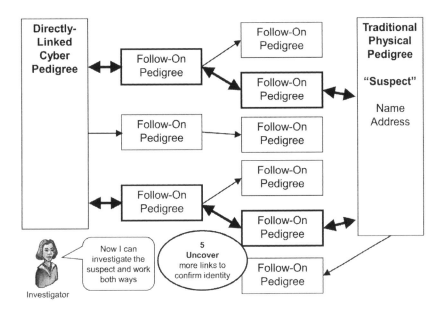

FIGURE 16.8 Step 5: *Uncover* More Links Between the Crime and Suspect to Test and Confirm Identity.

Working on Step 5 can be extremely fruitful for the investigation as a whole, especially if the suspect makes his living with cybercrime. This process both will solidify the identification and likely discover additional cybercrime and money laundering activity.

Step 6. **Summarize and articulate** proof clearly to meet increasing burdens of proof at each stage.

During a cyber attribution investigation (and in each of the earlier ID-PLUS steps), every piece of information discovered and added to the suspect's pedigree information should be recorded systematically and accurately (starting with cyber pedigree). It is important to document how each item of pedigree information is relevant, and how it is linked to other relevant pedigree information (e.g. whether it was directly linked to the crime or developed through follow-on investigation). The chain of reasoning leading from one follow-on detail to the next also should be clearly recorded, so that investigators both can retrace their steps and explain the progression to others. Once a suspect is identified (Step 4), additional, independent chains of proof confirming the suspect is the cybercriminal also should be developed (Step 5), and then documented clearly and accurately.

Step 6 focuses on summarizing and articulating the chains of logical inferences connecting the crime to the suspect, which must be done for varying audiences during the investigation as it progresses (as depicted in Figure 16.9). The identification evidence may need to meet increasing burdens of proof to continue the investigation, obtain a subpoena, apply for an email or physical search warrant, or to seek the arrest, extradition, or conviction of a suspect. As the case advances, the consequences for being wrong about the identification increase. The better the pedigree investigation is documented and corroborated, the stronger the proof will be.

In other words, Step 6 is an ongoing activity throughout the identification process. It recognizes that the entire six-step process is cyclical, leading to an ever-deepening analysis and understanding of each identifier uncovered. To summarize and articulate the evidence, investigators have to continually review Steps 1 through 5 to confirm and strengthen the proof.

FIGURE 16.9   Step 6: *Summarize and Articulate* Proof Clearly at Each Stage.

In the following sections, we will look at methods of creating and maintaining an attribution summary beginning with identifiers directly linked to the crime.

As Step 6 is repeated to meet higher and higher standards of proof, investigators may cycle through Step 5, looking for more links and chains to connect the crime to the suspect. Developing additional independent and interconnecting strands of such proof can be visualized as spinning a spider web connecting one post (the crime and directly-linked cyber pedigree) to another (the suspect and his traditional pedigree), as depicted in Figure 16.10. If the strength of one path of proof is tested, there are other paths that still lead to the suspect.

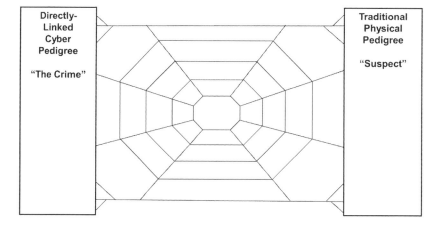

FIGURE 16.10   Spider Web of Identification Evidence Linking Suspect to Crime.

16.3.3 Example: Using **ID-PLUS** to Build an **Identification**

Now, let us walk through a simple cybercrime investigation to demonstrate how this ID-PLUS process might work.

Steps 1 and 2: **Isolate** online criminal conduct, and **Determine** directly-linked pedigree.

Imagine a victim reports that his credit card account was used to fraudulently purchase an expensive watch online. The victim gets some information from his credit card company, tries to get more from the online merchant, and eventually makes a report to law enforcement. Investigators obtain information from the merchant and learn that the watch was purchased online by a fraudster, who provided the email account Fred-Smith1234 [at] gmail.com, a ship-to address of 1234 Broadway, New York, NY, and used an IP address of 123.123.123.123. Given this information, we can perform Step 1 (isolate the online criminal conduct) and Step 2 (determine directly-linked pedigree), as depicted in Figure 16.11.

Steps 3 and 4: **Pursue** follow-on pedigree identifiers, and keep looking, and **Link** to a suspect.

The investigating officers take the simplest next investigative steps. They send a subpoena to Google for subscriber information and IP login data for the email address FredSmith1234 [at] gmail.com. They also send a letter of preservation (LOP) to ensure the content of any emails is preserved.

When the subscriber records eventually arrive, they show the account was accessed regularly from IP address 123.123.123.123 (a Verizon IP). The records also show the user provided Google with an alternate recovery email address of StolenCards5678 [at] yahoo.com, but no other subscriber information.

A subpoena and LOP are sent to Yahoo for the newly discovered Yahoo email account. When those records come back, they show access from many IP addresses, including the directly-linked IP address above, and also IP address 111.111.111.111 (Comcast).

A quick check online reveals that 1234 Broadway is a Mailboxes Etc. business, which offers mail receiving services and computers for customer use. A subpoena to Verizon for the 123.123.123.123 IP address reveals it is assigned to this Mailboxes Etc.

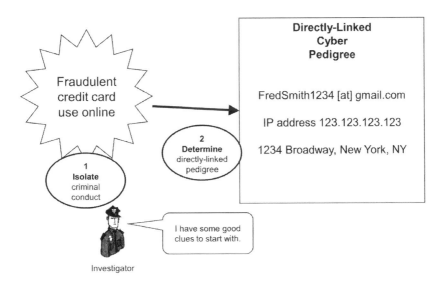

FIGURE 16.11 Example of Steps 1 and 2 to Isolate the Crime and Determine Directly-Linked Cyber Pedigree.

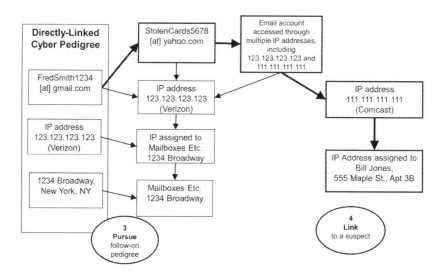

FIGURE 16.12 Example of Step 3 and Step 4: Pursue Follow-On Pedigree Identifiers and Link to a Suspect.

A subpoena to Comcast reveals that at the times the 111.111.111.111 IP address was used to access email account StolenCards5676 [at] yahoo.com, it was assigned to Bill Jones, 555 Maple St., Apt 3B.

In doing all of this work, investigators pursued follow-on pedigree (Step 3) and were even able to link all of that to a suspect (Step 4), as depicted in Figure 16.12.

Step 5: **Uncover** more links between the crime and suspect to confirm the suspect's identity.

Investigators now have a suspect, but the proof is untested and more work needs to be done. They have a lot of information and can pursue the following leads, among others:

- Open-source investigation on the two email accounts identified thus far, and on their suspect
- Check of government or proprietary databases regarding the suspect
- Subpoenas for records relating to accounts and IP addresses identified thus far
- Interviews with manager or employees at the Mailboxes Etc.
- Surveillance.

In this case, investigators would search online for information about Bill Jones at 555 Maple St. and find clues that seem to confirm he is a real person living at that address. An investigator could visit the mail receiving location at 1234 Broadway and speak to a manager about who is renting a mailbox there, and whether the rental application or store security video might provide further evidence.

As the investigators continue obtaining records, searching online, and taking traditional investigative steps, they are working to establish more corroborating chains between the fraudulent online purchase and Bill Jones.

Step 6: **Summarize** and articulate proof clearly to meet increasing burdens of proof at each stage.

Throughout the investigation into the fraudulent online purchase leading to Bill Jones, the evidence about the suspect's identity will have to be articulated and summarized at multiple stages.

For example, early on, a supervisor might ask the investigators to explain how this identification was made, and whether the evidence justifies further investigation into Bill Jones.

Investigators then might consider a search warrant for various email accounts associated with Jones, requiring investigators to describe the attribution evidence in more detail and to a higher standard of proof. Eventually, if investigators plan a search warrant of Mr. Jones' house, the attribution evidence must be articulated with even more precision. These searches might lead to a decision about whether to criminally charge Jones, prompting yet another, even more heightened review and summary of the identification evidence. And if the case against Jones ever goes to trial, the attribution proof needs to be prepared, summarized, and articulated for the jury to the highest standard possible.

16.3.4   EXAMPLE: A SAMPLE ATTRIBUTION SUMMARY (WORKING FROM THE CRIME TO A SUSPECT)

Let us briefly consider how investigators might articulate an attribution summary of the crime and their suspect at a particular point in time (such as before obtaining a search warrant). The attribution summary would have a list of pedigree information, briefly annotated to describe its relevance, and a narrative, explaining the connections from the crime to the suspect as set forth in Table 16.1. The attribution summary narrative would be modified continuously as more information about a particular identifier is uncovered during the investigation. We have created this example using the same crime discussed above, omitting certain details to streamline the presentation (such as specific dates).

More follow-on cyber identifiers could be listed as well.

TABLE 16.1
Sample Attribution Summary

Pedigree identifier	Comment/Annotation
— **Suspect** —	
Bill Jones, 555 Maple St., Apt 3B, New York, NY	*CAUTION – SUSPECT IDENTITY NOT CONFIRMED*
— **Directly-Linked Pedigree Identifiers (directly linked to cybercrime)** —	
FredSmith1234 [at] gmail.com	Email address provided to Online Merchant
Address: 1234 Broadway, New York, NY	Ship-to address provided to Online Merchant. A Mailboxes Etc. location
IP address 123.123.123.123, Verizon	IP address used to place order with Online Merchant (assigned to Mailboxes Etc. at 1234 Broadway)
— **Follow-On Pedigree** —	
Suspect: Bill Jones 555 Maple St. Apt 3B	*CAUTION – IDENTITY NOT CONFIRMED*
Names used: Fred Smith, Bill Jones, Victor Victim	
StolenCards5678 [at] yahoo.com	Recovery email address for FredSmith1234 [at] gmail.com
User "CardsForMerch" from SuspectWebsite[dot]com	Nickname of user on SuspectWebsite[dot]com who appears to use email address StolenCards5678 [at] yahoo.com
Nickname "CardsForMerch"	Online nickname possibly connected to StolenCards5678 [at] yahoo.com
IP address 111.111.111.111 (Comcast):	Used to access StolenCards5678 [at] yahoo.com and assigned to Bill Jones, 555 Maple St Apt 3B

Sample Attribution Summary Narrative

Summary of the crime. On Date 1, Victor Victim's Credit Card ending in 789 is used without permission for an online purchase of a watch (value $2,300) from Online Merchant. The purchase is made from IP address 123.123.123.123, with ship-to address 1234 Broadway, New York, NY, and contact email address of Fred-Smith1234 [at] gmail.com (direct pedigree).

On Date 2, Victor Victim reported the above crime. Online Merchant declined to provide Victor Victim with any details about this purchase.

On Date 3, law enforcement contacted Online Merchant about the above purchase, and their representative stated and provided records indicating that the purchase was made on Date 1 using Victor Victim's Credit Card ending in 789 from IP address 123.123.123.123, and that the watch was shipped to address 1234 Broadway, New York, NY, with a contact email address of FredSmith1234 [at] gmail.com.

On Date 4, open-source research on 1234 Broadway, New York, NY revealed it is the address of Mailboxes Etc., a business that receives and sends mail for customers, and has computers available for customer usage.

On Date 5, a subpoena and letter of preservation (LOP) were served on Google regarding email account FredSmith1234 [at] gmail.com. Subscriber records were provided on Date 6 and showed regular usage from IP address 123.123.123.123, as well as a user-provided recovery email address of StolenCards5678 [at] yahoo.com, but no other leads.

Open-source research on IP address 123.123.123.123 shows it is maintained by Verizon. On Date 7, a subpoena was sent to Verizon regarding subscriber information for this IP address on the relevant dates and times. On Date 8, those records were received and indicate it is a static IP assigned to Mailboxes Etc. at 1234 Broadway, New York, NY.

On Date 9, open-source research on FredSmith1234 [at] gmail.com reveals no leads.

Open-source research on StolenCards5678 [at] yahoo.com shows it appears on the website SuspectWebsite[dot]com, a website largely devoted to criminal activity. In a public post, a user with the nickname "CardsForMerch" offers to purchase stolen credit card information or receive merchandise for a fee. User "CardsForMerch" asks to be contacted directly at StolenCards5678 [at] yahoo.com.

Open-source research was conducted for other posts on SuspectWebsite[dot]com by user CardsForMerch, and across other websites to see if this nickname is used elsewhere [Investigator would summarize results here.]

On Date 10, a subpoena and letter of preservation (LOP) were served on Yahoo regarding email account StolenCards5678 [at] yahoo.com. On Date 11, records were obtained showing regular access from IP address 123.123.123.123 (Verizon) and IP address 111.111.111.111 (Comcast).

Also on Date 11, a subpoena was sent to Comcast regarding IP address 111.111.111.111. On Date 12, these records were received and show that on the relevant dates and times it was assigned to Bill Jones, at 555 Maple St., Apt 3B.

At this point, investigators have identified a suspect, and must work to develop more facts and chains of attribution. Steps might include:

- Visits to Mailboxes Etc. to speak to employees, get records
- Open-source research on the suspect, look for government records, confirm he is a real person
- Surveillance of 555 Maple St. to find and observe Bill Jones.

16.3.5 THE ATTRIBUTION PROCESS FROM ANOTHER LENS: TYPES OF EVIDENCE THAT CAN IDENTIFY CYBERCRIMINALS

With the ID-PLUS process, we outlined a step-by-step logical method to link discrete pedigree details together using reasoning and inferences to attribute conduct to a suspect. Here, we will look at identification from a different investigative perspective, focusing on certain categories of evidence and how they might help identify a suspect. While it is essential to pay attention to all of the information learned during an investigation (since any detail or interconnection might be significant), clues to the cybercriminal's identity are often found within:

- Content of communications
- Location information
- Data from devices.

Content of communications. If investigators can read the content of communications from an email, text message, instant message, or other account through which cybercrimes are known to be conducted, an enormous amount of information may be found. As information and early records are gathered about communications accounts directly-linked to the crime, one focus should be on developing probable cause to search the account's contents. For the purposes of developing identification evidence, some of the key details to look for include:

- *Personal information.* The suspect provides his name or other personal identifiers for some reason, perhaps thinking the innocuous communication has been deleted or will not be connected to his cyber nickname.
- *Personal information about criminal associates, family, or friends.* A suspect may be vigilant about hiding his own details, but less careful about screening what friends, family, and associates communicate to him. Learning about people with whom a suspect interacts can lead to the suspect himself.
- *Travel details.* A suspect may feel safe discussing subjects like his travel plans. Knowing where a suspect takes vacations or "business" trips can provide direct information proving identity, because most cybercriminals will not risk using forged identification documents to travel. Border and passport checks are logged. Airplane passenger manifests can be obtained. Hotel and car rental companies keep records.
- *Personal interests.* Cybercriminals have interests outside of crime and may discuss them in their online communications, thinking they are anonymous and these random topics will not attract attention. Learning that a suspect is a stamp collector, follows a particular sports team, or has another personal interest, can open doors to sources of identification the criminal may not have considered.

Information specifying location or place of origin. In the cybercrime arena, one way to identify suspects is to figure out the location of the perpetrator at the time of the crime, with increasing levels of granularity. What country was the perpetrator in, what region, what house, and what computer within the house. Some types of evidence provide leads about a suspect's physical location or prior geographical background.

- *IP addresses*. Cybercriminals need to get online to do their cybercrime, requiring use of an IP address. As we covered in Chapter 3, IP addresses are assigned to specific service providers who, in turn, assign them to customers. Successful cybercriminals will work to ensure that the IP addresses logged when they go online do not directly trace back to them. Nonetheless, IP addresses still may provide a clue. Some cybercriminals are not very sophisticated or are sloppy, and even the best make mistakes.
- *Cell site, GPS, and other location data*. Records from cellphone usage and certain other forms of electronic communication contain information about the cell sites through which a call or text was transmitted. Some devices are equipped with GPS tracking and similar applications, and this data also can be collected.
- *Services used*. Certain Internet services cater to users in specific geographical areas. The fact that a suspect, his associates, family, or friends have opted to use a company offering services to a particular region can be a strong indication of the suspect's location or place of origin.
- *Language usage*. In building a pedigree summary, the target's use of language in the subscriber information and content of communication is often a good initial sign of his origins and whereabouts. For example, the convention used to enter a street address or date (even if the information is false) and simple spelling or grammar mistakes can be revealing.

Data from devices. During the course of an investigation, investigators may have the rare opportunity to search a device used by a cybercriminal. If the opportunity arises, investigators may find a wealth of information that can connect the suspect to the crimes.

Eskalibur and Attribution

In the Western Express case, we learned that the cybercriminal "Eskalibur" did a lot of business by email, receiving and fulfilling orders for stolen credit cards. He also notified his customers by email regarding upcoming vacations. His email records showed that he did not do business during his vacations, and then resumed business after the vacation ended.

Through building a pedigree summary, the evidence eventually revealed that "Eskalibur" likely was the online persona of Egor Shevelev, a man living in Ukraine. Ultimately, we obtained evidence of Shevelev's international travel records and were able to match his international travel with email records describing his vacations on several occasions. We also matched his absence of email communications with the vacations, a short hospitalization, and his arrest in our cybercrime case. This correlation provided powerful circumstantial evidence that Egor Shevelev controlled the email account in question, and became one line of proof among many that proved identity.

By the time of his arrest, Eskalibur was a prolific and respected vendor of stolen credit card data. Other cybercriminals occasionally impersonated him in order to rip off unsuspecting identity thieves who would think they were buying from the real

"Eskalibur". During the criminal litigation, Shevelev's defense attorneys sought to portray those running these imposter accounts as the true culprits of the charged cybercrimes. But the proof anticipated and rebutted this defense. The evidence led, piece by piece, from the online criminal activity to the defendant, and it was clear that the imposter accounts were the work of amateurs.

16.4 WRITING AND ARTICULATION REVISITED: CLEAR AND EFFECTIVE CYBER IDENTIFICATION

In Chapter 11, we discussed writing for cybercrime investigations. Here, we discuss the specific writing requirements for cybercrime attribution.

Cybercrime investigators have many opportunities to write about or explain the identification process. These opportunities arise throughout the investigation, but especially within applications for search warrants or paperwork used for interstate or international arrests. The information gathered to compile an attribution summary of a suspect may be used in support of legal documents or for court exhibits, another reason that careful documentation is needed. Paying special attention to the words and style of this documentation is crucial to ensure that it successfully identifies a cybercriminal and explains the chain of evidence. The writing needs to be clear, accurate, and detailed, avoiding confusion or ambiguity. Moreover, the evidence should be articulated in a way that methodically narrows the search to the right person, while ruling out reasonable arguments that the cybercriminal could be someone else.

To recap and highlight the important concepts:

- *Write clearly and describe pedigree, Internet accounts, dates, and times fully.* Avoid pronouns. Writing should stand on its own and be understandable a year later.
- *Use full and accurate account names.*
- *Use diagrams where helpful.*
- *Use screenshots where helpful.* As we have said before, a picture is worth a thousand words.
- *Be clear about what pedigree information is directly connected to the crimes – and what is follow-on information (indirectly connected).*
- *Document sources.*
- *Distinguish facts from opinions and conclusions.* For example, it may be a fact that something was written or provided. It may be a conclusion as to the accuracy or relevance of what was written or provided.
- *Explain the basis for inferences, opinions, and conclusions so the reader can independently assess them.*
- *Beware of hyperlinks and automatic hyperlinking.* Turn off your auto-hyperlinking features in your email, document, and spreadsheet software, and also replace certain characters within cyber pedigree when you write them. The "@" sign in an email address becomes an "[at]" and the dots within websites names get brackets around them. For example:

StolenCards1234@gmail.com	becomes	StolenCards1234[at]gmail[.]com
StolenCards1234@gmail.com	becomes	StolenCards1234[.]com

16.5 EXAMINING ISSUES OF PROOF

In any cybercrime investigation, a key question should be, "Who did this?" Law enforcement is especially interested in identifying those committing these crimes in order to bring criminal charges. The private sector also should ask themselves who is behind the attack. But when working to uncover a cybercriminal's identity, an important related question also must be decided. What level of proof about the criminal's identity do the investigators need to provide? The answer will depend on how the identification will eventually be used.

If the identification will be needed to bring a criminal case, then investigators' attribution of cyber misconduct will be used to support the future arrest and charging of an individual. In Chapter 5, we learned that the burden of proof for arresting and charging someone is probable cause, while to convict at trial the government must offer proof beyond a reasonable doubt. Effectively, this means investigators should be confident that they have proof beyond a reasonable doubt before making an arrest. Given the complex process of identifying a cybercriminal and articulating that proof, and the likelihood that some form of interstate or international assistance will be involved in apprehending and extraditing the defendant, a rock-solid identification is required at every stage of any criminal litigation.

If the identification will be used to bring a civil lawsuit, investigators also will have to attribute the conduct to the civil defendant. In a civil case, the burdens are lower, generally a preponderance of the evidence.

Other cases may require differing proof levels. There might be an increased or decreased level of certainty needed if the results are for the court of public opinion, political or economic purposes, to impose sanctions, or to provide the legal justification for nation-state operations, including a response in kind, espionage, or even uses of force.

Investigators also may gather information that is not admissible in a legal proceeding, for whatever reason. Or, investigators may discover email accounts suggesting a suspect uses a second cyber nickname, but can only find demonstrable proof for the first. Ultimately, whoever will decide whether the identification is sufficiently supported by evidence needs to be apprised of all proof of attribution, as well as any contrary indicators. The decision-maker should view both admissible evidence and inadmissible evidence in making the final determination. Of course, inadmissible evidence might add to the certainty of proof or subtract from it.

16.6 APPREHENSION: CONFIRMING PEDIGREE THROUGH STATEMENTS AND FORENSICS

The ultimate apprehension of a cybercriminal offers the chance for investigators to confirm their identification. Confirmation can be made by speaking with the defendant and examining any items recovered from or with the defendant, including identification documents, devices, and receipts, which should be analyzed for clues that may support attribution.

Law enforcement may ask the defendant certain pedigree details as part of the booking procedure and, legally speaking, this questioning is not considered an "interrogation". If formal interrogation is permitted, asking for pedigree information can be a warm-up to further questioning that may reach to the heart of identification and the defendant's online criminal conduct. A defendant's self-description (like name, address, contact information), whether inculpatory or exculpatory, should be examined closely for clues and compared to other pedigree information developed during the investigation.

If a suspect is arrested with his devices, a forensic device search can provide strong evidence about pedigree details and criminal conduct. Areas of forensic analysis pertinent to identity evidence include:

- *Content.* Documents, emails, photos, video, and other content in the device. These may be direct evidence of identity of the user and friends, family, and associates.
- *Settings.* A user's choice of settings on the device can be a source of compelling evidence. The name it is registered under, the date and time settings, the default language, and email, payment, or other accounts set up on the device may be strong clues confirming the suspect's identity.
- *Websites visited.* A forensic search of the device's Internet browser history will reveal the websites recently visited by the user. These websites might create a direct lead to a real person and also can expose the suspect's location, interests, and identifiers.
- *Games, applications and other personalizing information* can provide identification leads.

If the investigation was thorough and thoughtful, the arrest evidence is likely to corroborate earlier identification evidence. But if the pedigree information, physical evidence, or statement evidence appears contrary to the investigative evidence, these discrepancies must be thoroughly explored to ensure the correct person has been accused of cybercrimes.

Putting It Together: Eskalibur Proof at Trial

It is an extraordinary challenge to prove the identity of a cybercriminal who committed his crimes from over 4,000 miles away. In the Western Express case, we did so for several defendants, including Eskalibur, who put us to our full burden of proof at trial, requiring us to prove his identity as the person who committed the cybercrimes alleged.

The attribution proof started from information related to the cybercrimes, and was tied to a mere five items of pedigree:

- Nickname ("Eskalibur")
- Instant messenger account
- Egold virtual currency account
- Webmoney virtual currency account
- Email account.

From these five items, we gathered numerous pieces of evidence and made logical connections ("links in a chain" of proof) that tied them to the original pedigree items, to other evidence, and ultimately to the defendant. Many of these "chains" formed the strands of the web that proved the defendant's identity.

Among the many strands of proof:

- Using the instant messenger account, the suspect once indicated his name was "Egor", he was in Kiev, Ukraine, and he was 19 years old.
- The Egold account was tied to an email account.

- The Webmoney account was tied to another email account, but importantly was registered in the name of Egor Shevelev, a lucky break with a fascinating backstory.
- The suspect once provided a phone number for an account, and while the phone was not subscribed to anyone (a "burner phone"), it had phone calls with Egor Shevelev's home phone and parents.
- The nickname "Eskalbur" was tied to Egor Shevelev in a variety of accounts going back several years.
- The email account directed that funds be sent to the Egold and Webmoney accounts, and also by Western Union to Kiev.
- Egor Shevelev's apartment had a notebook that had both his name and the Webmoney account number written inside.
- Egor Shevelev's apartment had computers containing evidence of some of the original items of pedigree, and other pedigree with indirect links.

This proof was developed over many years, and to ever increasing burdens of proof as the investigation progressed. Ultimately, this proof had to be legally admissible in court and was presented to a jury of laypeople, convincing them unanimously and beyond a reasonable doubt that these crimes were in fact committed by Egor Shevelev. After we had done so, they found him guilty of all counts.

16.7 CONCLUSION

Cybercriminals rarely operate under their true identities. They disguise their activity and practice anonymity using the Internet. One of a cyber investigator's most important jobs is attribution and identification, piercing through that anonymity with clear, articulable proof.

The identification and attribution process is about connecting online activity to a specific person. From the investigator's perspective, step one is defining the cybercrime – the online criminal activity. Next, the investigator needs to identify the cyber pedigree information connected directly to that crime, and then look for more pedigree details with follow-on connections. Each new piece of information might lead to more clues, which may eventually lead to a suspect. At that point, the investigation expands to further prove or disprove this suspect's involvement. In the end, it is a flesh-and-blood person who will be on the receiving end of any consequences for his cybercrimes and the investigator must prove, to the requisite level of certainty, that this real person was correctly identified.

17 Apprehending the Suspect and the Investigation that Follows

This chapter is for:

- Law enforcement, prosecutors, and anyone interested in how a cybercriminal is arrested and extradited.

17.1 INTRODUCTION

For law enforcement investigators, one of the peak achievements of a cybercrime investigation is the arrest of an identified suspect. Many successful apprehensions of cybercriminals are the result of collaborative work from investigators in the private and regulatory sectors.

In this chapter, we will discuss the arrest process of an identified cyber suspect. We begin with the underlying charging decisions, including determinations about what crimes have been committed and the method of bringing official charges. Because so many cybercriminals are apprehended outside the jurisdiction where the criminal charges are filed, we next look at the procedures for arresting and extraditing defendants located in other states and countries. In addition, this chapter focuses on the practical and strategic aspects of planning a cybercrime arrest, ensuring that evidence is gathered at the time the suspect is apprehended, as well as the continuing steps of the post-arrest investigation.

17.2 CHARGING DECISIONS

Once a cybercrime suspect is identified, and the proof and articulation of this identification can be established to the necessary degree (discussed in Chapter 16), law enforcement officials and prosecutors can begin the process of planning the suspect's arrest.

The first step is to evaluate the evidence the investigation has produced and decide upon the criminal charges that will be filed against the suspect. In deciding this complicated issue, prosecutors weigh many issues that will factor into the future arrest, extradition, and prosecution, such as:

- *Proof.* Has the investigation gathered sufficient evidence to prove the suspect committed each charged crime beyond a reasonable doubt? Charging decisions require a thorough review of the jurisdiction's criminal statutes, including every element of the crimes under consideration. Chapter 6 sets forth various charges that might be appropriate in cybercrime cases.

- *Strength of the evidence.* If there is evidence to support a charge, has its value been confirmed through verification and analysis? During a prosecution, evidence will be presented in several contexts – to judges, Grand Juries, defense attorneys, and trial juries. It will be challenged repeatedly by the defense during the discovery phase, pre-trial hearings and the trial itself. If there is any concern about the strength of a piece of evidence – such as its source, meaning, or authenticity – it should not be the sole basis of criminal charges.
- *Scope.* Do the charges adequately reflect the scope of the suspect's criminal conduct? Or, to look at the question another way, if a jury were ever to hear this case, would the selected charges impart the entire breadth of the suspect's criminal activity?
- *Aggregation.* Are there connected crimes (for example, crimes involving the same victim, or a pattern of criminal activity) that the law allows to be aggregated into a single, higher-level charge?
- *Criminal groups.* Was the suspect part of a group of criminals working together? If so, is a blanket charge covering the entirety of their criminal activity appropriate (like conspiracy or organized crime charges)?
- *International extradition.* If the suspect will be arrested and extradited from another country, will the charges be honored under that nation's treaties with the United States (covered later in this chapter)?

Charging decisions can be complicated, with a range of facts, evidence, potential charges, dates, times, and defendants. Having a consistent system to organize the case evidence, ideally from the beginning of the investigation, is tremendously helpful in determining what crimes ultimately can be charged (see Chapter 11 for more on organizing and analyzing leads and evidence within a complex cybercrime investigation). Using such a system, criminal offenses can be matched directly to the supporting evidence. In Western Express, we used spreadsheets, through which each suspect's acts were correlated with a potential criminal charge and the relevant evidence. As the case progressed, this spreadsheet evolved and served many uses, from charging, to discovery, through trial.

17.2.1 METHODS FOR CHARGING A SUSPECT

As covered in Chapter 5, an arrest, and the accompanying charging document, requires probable cause to believe the suspect committed the listed crime(s). The charging document is either:

- A complaint/arrest affidavit, sworn to by a law enforcement officer, or
- An indictment, voted by a grand jury.

Here, we focus on arrests in connection with ongoing long-term investigations.[1]

With most cybercrimes, charging is done before the suspect is arrested, typically through a presentation of a sworn affidavit to a judge or evidence to a Grand Jury. If the charges

---

[1] As we covered in Chapter 5, some lower-level cybercriminals may be charged by complaint/affidavit – typically people caught at banks or stores conducting fraudulent transactions. On rare occasions, a bigger cyber suspect is caught red-handed, sitting at his computer with stolen data or child pornography on the screen, and charged via arrest complaint/affidavit.

are authorized using either method, the presiding court can issue an arrest warrant for the defendant, a required step for other jurisdictions to make an arrest. Obtaining a warrant prior to arrest represents a judge's or Grand Jury's finding of probable cause. It also demonstrates the prosecution's readiness to proceed towards trial. There are some circumstances where law enforcement may make a summary arrest (without an arrest warrant) even after conducting a long-term investigation, such as if an opportunity presents itself to locate the defendant or if they believe the suspect is getting ready to flee or destroy evidence.

17.2.2 "Sealing" Charges versus Publicizing Them

When a defendant is officially charged with a crime, every jurisdiction has different rules about whether the charging documents are public records or are "sealed" from public view. Generally, after a person has been arrested and informed of the charges by a court (an "arraignment"), the charging information is publicly available. But if official charges are filed before the suspect is arrested, they remain sealed until the suspect is apprehended and arraigned.

Each jurisdiction's rules on sealing should be reviewed closely. When the law requires charges to remain sealed until a defendant is apprehended, revealing details about them (even by law enforcement officials) may be illegal. In situations where investigators or prosecutors believe there is an important reason to publicly discuss sealed charges – for example, if there is a public safety risk – they may need to obtain a court order authorizing the unsealing of the charging documents.

Investigators may have strategic reasons to keep indictments and charging orders from being publicized before a charged suspect is arrested. If criminals know they are being investigated or that they have been charged, they are likely to flee apprehension or destroy evidence. International cybercriminals facing charges in the United States, upon learning they are charged, will avoid travel to any country that would extradite them to the United States.

Sometimes, after unsuccessful efforts have been made to apprehend a suspect, prosecutors may ask a court to unseal a charging document under the theory that if the suspects learn of the charges against them, they might turn themselves in, or someone else might provide tips as to their whereabouts. Sometimes prosecutors may believe apprehension is impossible, and "name and shame" is the next best option, as discussed in Chapter 8. Decisions to go public with charges before an arrest must be made carefully and for sound investigative reasons. For example, publicizing charges solely for the purpose of generating positive press coverage for the prosecutor would not be an appropriate purpose for unsealing charges.

Law enforcement should be aware of the double-edges of the "name and shame" technique. It has deterrent and other value, but it also calls attention to a government's limited ability to apprehend.

17.3 INTERSTATE PROCEDURES FOR ARRESTING AND EXTRADITING DEFENDANTS

The United States is a fascinating combination of independent states under a federal government. From the nation's founding, cooperation among the states in arresting and handing over criminals was recognized as a crucial necessity. Without such a system, a person could commit a crime in one state, flee over the border into another, and escape justice. The authors of the U.S. Constitution included the Extradition Clause to prevent such circumstances, stating that:

> A person charged in any state with treason, felony or another crime, who shall flee from justice, and be found in another state, shall on demand of the executive authority of the state from which he fled, be delivered up, to be removed to the state having jurisdiction of the crime.[2]

This legal principle is codified in the United States Code, which states that the executive authority of any state (typically, the Governor) can demand another state return a fugitive from justice by providing an indictment or sworn affidavit to the courts of the other state. The other state then must arrest or secure the defendant and hand him over to agents of the state from which he fled.[3] The Uniform Criminal Extradition Act (UCEA) has been adopted in 48 states and expands upon the federal law, setting forth procedures for handling the arrest and extradition process when a wanted individual is located in another state.[4]

In modern practice, the process of notifying other states about wanted individuals in criminal matters usually happens electronically. When an individual is wanted on criminal charges, an arrest warrant from the court with jurisdiction over the case is issued. Law enforcement agents then enter the wanted individual's personal identifiers and details of the charges against him into national databases, such as the National Crime Information Center (NCIC). Once the arrest warrant is registered in NCIC, law enforcement in another state will be alerted to the open arrest warrant, and this NCIC alert can help convey the legal authority to detain or arrest the individual.

So, for example, should a police officer in Florida happen to pull over a defendant wanted on cybercrime charges in New York, the officer may learn of the New York arrest warrant when he runs the motorist's license, triggering an automatic NCIC search. The officer is required to contact New York authorities to confirm the accuracy of the NCIC alert, the existence of the valid warrant, desire to prosecute, and willingness to extradite. If confirmed, he can arrest the cybercriminal based upon the New York warrant, and the cybercriminal can be charged in Florida as a fugitive from justice. Then, the suspect will either contest his extradition or waive such proceedings and agree to be transported to New York to face the charges there.

More typically in a cybercrime investigation, authorities in one state learn their suspect is in another, and they coordinate with the other state's law enforcement to effect an arrest (and perhaps execute a search warrant) at the appropriate time. In these scenarios, each law enforcement agency must ensure that the arrest and search procedures comply with their respective state's laws and procedures.

Extradition proceedings are a legal process through which a defendant has the opportunity to contest removal to the state where the charges are pending. A court in the state where the defendant was arrested can hold hearings and examine documentation before deciding whether to order extradition. The court may consider whether the arrest warrant is valid, the suspect is the person named in the warrant, and the wanting jurisdiction will come to arrest and transport the defendant. In all cases, transporting defendants across state lines is expensive and time consuming, and agencies may evaluate whether resources permit extraditing a defendant charged with a low-level crime. The court usually will not weigh in on the strength or merits of the criminal charges.

Because this extradition process can take a long time, many defendants waive the hearing proceedings and consent to be extradited to the charging state. If the defendant consents, or if after the proceedings are held and the court finds all requirements are met, the court

---

[2] U.S. CONST., Article IV, Section 2.
[3] 18 U.S.C. § 3182.
[4] South Carolina and Missouri have not adopted the UCEA.

will sign an extradition order and the wanting agency will schedule a time to pick up the defendant.[5]

17.4   INTERNATIONAL PROCEDURES FOR ARRESTING AND EXTRADITING DEFENDANTS

Arresting and extraditing a person in a foreign country who is wanted on criminal charges in the United States is a considerable process. Whereas interstate extradition is governed by established procedures within our country, international extradition involves the laws and practices of a completely separate and independent sovereign nation. As a result, international extradition requires assistance from the Office of International Affairs (OIA) in the U.S. Department of Justice.

The entire international arrest and extradition process hinges on the fact that criminal charges are pending in the United States. To arrest an identified suspect within a foreign country, that person has to be the subject of an arrest warrant on charges in the U.S. for at least some of his criminal conduct. Just like the rules for international evidence we learned about in Chapter 7, the process for obtaining defendants from abroad falls under Mutual Legal Assistance Treaties (MLATs), other treaties with foreign governments, and principles of nation-to-nation diplomacy and comity (recognition of the judicial processes of other countries). Extradition using any of these methods is conducted through OIA.

There are over 75 countries that do not have an extradition treaty with the United States, including Russia and China. These foreign governments will not return wanted defendants to U.S. authorities, and so OIA will not seek arrests in those nations.

When finalizing the state or federal charging document that will be used to seek the defendant's arrest and extradition from another country, it is important to consult with OIA about charges that might qualify for extradition. MLAT treaties and the laws of the other nation may mean that only certain charges qualify for extradition. Some countries will extradite only for serious offenses that exist in their own criminal statutes. If the criminal charge is not listed in the MLAT, or has not been enacted by that country, extradition may be impossible. Newer offenses like computer crimes and identify theft might not qualify as a basis for extradition, but traditional offenses like larceny would. Consulting with OIA, and ensuring that the indictment contains appropriate charges may help improve the result.

Along with the indictment or other charging document, the extradition process may require a prosecutor's affidavit and an investigator's affidavit, laying out the legal and factual basis for the charges and extradition. Depending on the nation involved, there may be many other documents that must be supplied. One of the most scrutinized areas will be proof of the defendant's identity. For traditional crimes, identity may not be a difficult issue. If someone commits a murder in Florida and then flees to a country that will extradite, the defendant's identity may be easily demonstrated through his own admissions, eyewitness accounts, security video, fingerprints, DNA, or many other forms of proof. With cybercrime cases, as we know, proving identity can be more complicated. The investigative trail from Internet crimes and pseudonyms to a living, breathing person can be long and requires thorough documentation. Investigators should be aware of this hurdle when embarking on an international arrest.

There are typically two ways the U.S. (through OIA) can ask another country to make an arrest, with a provisional arrest request or with a full-blown extradition request. The

---

[5] Occasionally, a defendant may face multiple charges in multiple states, and there are methods to address this situation. One mechanism is the Interstate Agreement on Detainers, which is a legal mechanism to deliver defendants serving a prison sentence in one state to another state to face pending charges there.

provisional request is for situations where an arrest is needed promptly, and the greater details of the extradition request will be provided shortly thereafter.

Interpol, an organization of collaborating police agencies from around the world, can sometimes be useful for effecting arrests. An Interpol "Red Notice" is a notification to certain countries that a suspect is wanted, asking the country's law enforcement to arrest the suspect and hold him for a future extradition request. This Red Notice has similarities to the NCIC arrest alert we discussed earlier.

Ultimately, it will be law enforcement officials in the foreign country who make the arrest (and conduct any related searches) according to their country's laws. Establishing contact with the correct agency in the foreign country generally can improve the cooperation received. In countries with more strained diplomatic relations with the U.S., or internal conflict between their government officials and policing agencies, asking for cooperation or sharing any law enforcement information may require serious consideration.

Once an arrest is made, the defendant typically will be held in a jail facility in the foreign country pending extradition proceedings. The extradition process can take months or years. Each country's legal proceedings are different but a defendant usually has the opportunity to challenge his extradition, including through layers of appeals.

One factor that can change the timetable is whether the defendant is a citizen of the country in which he is arrested. There are often higher levels of legal protection for citizens versus non-citizens when it comes to extradition and, needless to say, it is harder to extradite a citizen from his own country to another country. No matter where apprehended, the defendant may seek assistance from his country of citizenship to prevent extradition to another country.

Extradition of Eskalibur from Greece

Western Express defendant Egor Shevelev (cybernickname "Eskalibur") was a Ukrainian national who lived in Kiev. After painstaking investigative work, the investigation was able to attribute the online activity of Eskalibur to Shevelev and he was indicted in Manhattan.

Under Ukraine law, the country could not extradite one of its citizens to the United States, so we did not consider asking. But Shevelev traveled frequently, and we were able to have him arrested in 2008 while he vacationed in Greece, a country from where we could extradite him. After this arrest, Ukraine assisted in the investigation by executing search warrants at his residence in Kiev. In this time period, he also was indicted separately by federal authorities in Florida, who also sought his extradition to the U.S. There were extensive Greek legal proceedings until the Greek courts ordered extradition, and in 2010, Shevelev was transported by the U.S. Marshall's service to New York. It took a while to reach the trial stage, and the trial itself lasted ten weeks, after which he was convicted of numerous crimes. He later was brought to Florida to face the federal charges and was convicted there, too.

17.5   ARREST STRATEGIES AND THE HUNT FOR EVIDENCE

When a cybercriminal (and maybe some of his accomplices) have been identified and charged, the investigation turns to the practical and strategic planning of the apprehension(s). The principal factors in developing a plan include:

- *Choosing a time and place.* Investigators must ascertain where and when they will be reasonably certain to find each charged suspect. Good timing means knowing a lot about the suspects and their activities, and that means having good identification and attribution knowledge (see Chapter 16). It also means maximizing legal tools to learn about, and track, the suspects, including pen registers, geolocation, wiretaps, and more (see Chapter 7).
- *Simultaneous arrests.* When several members of a criminal crew have been charged and must be apprehended, simultaneous arrests are important to prevent some suspects from fleeing or destroying evidence. Coming up with a feasible plan for a "take down" of a criminal group requires significant investigative knowledge, preparation, and resources.
- *Coordinating with other law enforcement agencies.* Developing good working relationships with other agencies (local, or in other states and countries) is essential to creating a strong arrest plan. In many cybercrime cases, investigators are dependent on officials in multiple, distant locations to execute the arrests. The better the professional relationship, the likelier the suspects will be successfully found and apprehended. Coordinating with other agencies can be a major effort when simultaneous arrests are planned in several jurisdictions.
- *Search warrants.* The time of arrest is also an excellent time to obtain additional evidence through a search warrant. Search warrants can be obtained to search the suspect's residence, workplace, vehicles, and person. Without a search warrant for the places the suspect actually inhabits, evidence will be overlooked, lost, or destroyed at the time he is caught.
- *Seizing devices.* By the time an arrest is planned, investigators may know much about what devices the suspect regularly uses (phones, computers, etc.). Many cybercriminals have "doomsday" plans for encrypting their devices if they are caught by law enforcement. By plotting out the technical steps of how devices will be seized and preserved for forensic examination at the time of arrest, investigators can greatly increase the likelihood of acquiring usable digital evidence.
- *Recording statements.* At the time of arrest, a suspect might make a number of statements. Some statements will be spontaneous, in response to the unfolding events. Some will be responses to pedigree questions about his name, address, and other personal information. In some cases, an interview (interrogation) will occur. Investigators who plan ahead for how these statements will be taken and memorialized – especially when translators or foreign agencies are involved – will have better results in obtaining useful statement evidence.
- *Asset forfeiture.* If seizure and forfeiture of any of the charged suspects' assets is desired, it is optimal to have the necessary paperwork in place prior to arrest. By having these documents prepared, investigators can quickly serve them on financial institutions immediately following the arrest, thereby preventing the suspect or his associates from moving funds. As covered in Chapter 9, this process may require a temporary restraining order (TRO) to be served upon the suspect's banks. A copy of any orders also must be served upon the suspect to provide notice of the pending civil forfeiture action, and to inform the suspect that he must comply with the order (e.g. a suspect cannot transfer funds without permission of the court).

17.6   A SUCCESSFUL ARREST DOES NOT MEAN "CASE CLOSED"

Law enforcement officers, detectives, and agents often believe that a case is "closed by arrest". This phrase is very commonly used in law enforcement reports and is a method by which cases are classified within agency management systems. However, the process of bringing a cybercrime defendant to justice is never closed by the arrest. The investigation continues until a plea or jury verdict is finalized, and a just sentence is imposed.

Following the arrest of a cybercriminal, an intensive period of investigation begins. The interview of defendants, seizure of evidence, and initial review of that evidence inevitably lead to more clues, more email accounts, websites, and phone numbers. Investigators learn of the existence of new devices, storage spaces, criminal associates, and other aspects of the suspect's activity. In other words, the cyclical investigative process we discussed in Chapter 11 continues after arrest, and is unburdened by the need to keep the existence of the investigation secret.

Evidence gleaned from the arrest and initial search warrant must be reviewed quickly for evidence and intelligence. Where new leads are identified, follow-on actions should be taken. If new financial accounts or email accounts are discovered, or substantial time has passed since known email accounts were searched, new letters of preservation, subpoenas, and search warrants should be considered.

As devices are seized during the arrest process, search warrants must be reviewed to determine whether the devices are covered within the list of authorized items to be searched. Where there is doubt, a new search warrant should be obtained that specifically identifies the new digital devices. Interstate and international searches may require special legal scrutiny. For example, if evidence is seized in State A pursuant to a warrant of that state, but then delivered to State B for use in the criminal proceeding, investigators and prosecutors may need to obtain another search warrant from State B to forensically examine the digital evidence. The same can be said for international evidence.

Some defendants may not be located and arrested pursuant to the initial arrest plan, and for them, the hunt continues. Moreover, additional suspects may be discovered and criminally charged based upon newfound evidence from the first phase of arrests.

In sum, the cyber investigation does not stop with the arrest of a defendant. Rather, the arrest sparks new rounds of investigation that continue to identify new suspects and information until the prosecutor has enough to present overwhelming evidence at trial. The choice of pleading guilty or proceeding to trial is always with the defendant. The stronger the case, the more likely the defendant will plead guilty or the prosecution will prevail at trial.

17.7 CONCLUSION

Arresting and apprehending a cybercrime defendant is a major milestone but not the end of the investigation. From the underlying charging decisions to the arrest process to the extradition of out-of-state or foreign suspects, the apprehension of a cybercriminal requires careful thought and planning. The arrest of a long-sought suspect can be a moment of intense relief and fulfillment for investigators. But in a cyber case, the arrest is often the end of one investigative phase and the beginning of another. As the investigation takes new paths, the search for more suspects and evidence continues into and through the litigation phase of the case.

Part IV

Litigation

18 Criminal Litigation

> This chapter is for:
>
> - Prosecutors
> - Investigators of all backgrounds whose work might be used in a criminal case.

18.1 INTRODUCTION

There are many reasons to conduct a cybercrime investigation, but often the ultimate goal is to identify the perpetrators and bring criminal charges against them. When a case reaches this point, every facet of the investigation will be used to support the criminal litigation. In this chapter, we will look at the stages of criminal litigation, and explore how a sound cybercrime investigation will result in a sound prosecution.

Put differently, the criminal prosecution incorporates the work of everyone involved in the investigation, and should not be thought of as a separate phase just for the lawyers. Litigation puts each piece of evidence gathered and every investigative step taken under a microscope, as defense attorneys search for legal avenues and factual arguments that could undermine the prosecution's case. Early chapters covered important information on crimes to charge, gathering evidence, and conducting the investigation. Now we examine the proceedings where this work will be challenged.

When investigators are familiar with how prosecutors present evidence, and how it is contested in court, they can make investigative decisions along the way that will strengthen the ultimate court case. This knowledge is especially critical in cybercrime cases, which often require layers of proof not used for traditional crimes. Just as the criminal litigation provides a look back in time to all that happened before, investigators should continually look forward to the future for how decisions might affect potential litigation.

When prosecutors decide to move forward with a criminal case, the litigation occurs over several stages – including charging, discovery, pre-trial proceedings, plea-negotiation or trial, sentencing, and possible appeals. In this chapter, we examine each stage and how the prior investigation plays a role.

18.2 GOALS OF THE LITIGATION

At the outset, it is important to remember that all criminal litigation depends upon the investigators' ability to assemble thorough and convincing evidence of a suspect's guilt. The filing of criminal charges indicates an intent and ability by prosecutors to see the litigation through to the end – to trial if needed, and through post-trial defense motions. An investigation that does not produce sufficient evidence, or that was accomplished using questionable procedures, will not meet these standards.

When prosecutors decide there is strong enough evidence to initiate criminal charges, they usually have several possible goals in mind. These overarching goals are useful to consider when an investigation is ongoing, as they might shape the focus and breadth of the evidence gathered.

- *Justice and Fairness.* The heart of any criminal litigation is the prosecutor's mandate to seek justice on behalf of individual victims, the defendant, and the community as a whole.
- *Deterring criminal conduct.* Showing the community and the world that cybercriminals can be caught and brought to justice works to deter some criminals from engaging in cybercrime activity.
- *Punishing criminal conduct.* Prosecutors who determine that cybercriminals have broken laws and inflicted serious harm will request appropriate punishments through a plea bargain or after a trial conviction, including restitution, fines, prison sentences, and deportation.
- *Rehabilitating those who commit crimes.* Along with punishment, the criminal justice system ideally works to rehabilitate criminals in an effort to put them on the right track to avoid future criminal conduct.
- *Addressing countries and groups who commit crimes against us.* Publicly identifying countries and groups committing cybercrimes, accompanied by other means of international pressure, may discourage such cybercrime conduct as well as educate the public about the nature of cyberthreats.

18.3   LITIGATION BEGINS: FILING OF AN ACCUSATORY INSTRUMENT

In our overview of the criminal justice process in Chapter 5, we learned that criminal litigation is commenced with the filing of criminal charges, and we discussed the two general ways criminal charges are initiated against a defendant. A prosecutor can file a criminal complaint or information with an appropriate court, or a Grand Jury can vote an indictment.

For the investigator, it is useful to know what factors a prosecutor weighs when considering filing charges or presenting them to a Grand Jury. Some of the key charging considerations are:

- *Is there evidence that supports each element of the crime?* For a charge to be filed, an investigation must produce evidence that sustains every element required under the criminal code defining that crime. As we covered in Chapter 5, these elements usually include a culpable mental state (usually intentionally or knowingly), certain specified actions (like stealing accessing or harming), and sometimes specified results (like financial loss).
- *Is there enough evidence to prove the charges at trial?* Although charging merely requires "probable cause" to believe a defendant committed a crime, prosecutors should consider whether they have, or will obtain, proof beyond a reasonable doubt for trial, and whether they are convinced of the defendant's guilt.
- *Is there jurisdiction over the case?* Jurisdiction over cybercrimes often is established because the criminal conduct occurs within a particular geographical area, or because it affects an individual or business there. In a cyber case, the investigation must produce evidence showing the geographical nexus between the crimes and the jurisdiction of the court and prosecutor's office.
- *Is identification provable?* In every type of crime, there must be evidence proving the identity of the perpetrator. As discussed in earlier chapters, identification in

cybercrime cases frequently is proven by connecting the dots of online activities back to an identifiable human being. Prosecutors must see evidence demonstrating the right person has been identified as the cybercriminal.

- *What type of accusatory instrument should be used?* Even when prosecutors find that an investigation has produced evidence showing a particular person has committed criminal acts, decisions must be made about the level of crime and how it will be charged. Based on the nature of the investigation and the whereabouts of the identified suspect, prosecutors must decide which instrument is appropriate – complaint, information, or indictment.
- *In which court should the case be filed?* Prosecutors also must determine where to file charges. Typically, cases are filed in the federal courts when federal agencies investigate, and state courts with state or local investigators. A factor in this decision is whether the case might be joined with existing cases.

The investigation results will be the major determinant in all of these decisions. Different law enforcement and prosecuting agencies may have very different views on where and how a defendant should be prosecuted.

18.4 THE DEFENDANT ENTERS THE LITIGATION: APPREHENSION, EXTRADITION, AND ARRAIGNMENT

As we learned in Chapters 5 and 17, after the decision is made to charge a defendant, the next step typically is to obtain an arrest warrant by filing an accusatory instrument that commences the litigation. Though an accusatory instrument can be filed before or after arrest, filing beforehand is more common in cybercrime prosecutions that stem from a longer investigation. Once a defendant is arrested or extradited, he is brought before the court to be arraigned on the criminal charges.

At the arraignment, a judge usually decides whether to set bail, which generally is based upon the potential risk that a defendant will flee to avoid the prosecution. A judge evaluates the facts of the case and the defendant's personal circumstances before deciding whether to set bail. Bail generally is set as either an amount of cash money the defendant must pay to leave custody, or as a bond which creates a promise to pay or a lien of a certain value against the defendant's property. Different court systems may use a variety of bond options. If the defendant can meet the bail conditions, he is allowed out of jail, but if he cannot make bail he must remain in jail during the pendency of the charges. If he meets the conditions and is released, the cash or bond is collateral to ensure he returns for future court appearances. In some cases, a judge might release a defendant on his own recognizance, finding that a bail or bond isn't necessary. In others, the court might order a defendant to be remanded, or held without bail – finding that the risk of flight is so high that no amount of bail could ensure the defendant will return to court.

The quality of the investigation is vital to a successful arrest, extradition, and arraignment.

- *Evidence supporting identification is used throughout the arrest warrant, apprehension, and extradition process.* When an investigation produces strong, easily understood evidence of identification, it strengthens the entire arrest, extradition, and arraignment process. Prosecutors want airtight evidence about identification, rather than face defense arguments about this lynchpin of a cyber case during these early stages of the litigation.

- *Investigative evidence is used to locate defendants and arrest them.* The investigation also guides the likelihood and speed with which a defendant can be located and arrested. If investigators have not been able to uncover hard evidence of a defendant's location, this fact may affect charging decisions and the subsequent issuance of an arrest warrant, particularly with interstate or international arrests.
- *Investigation results greatly influence bail requests and decisions.* When prosecutors believe a charged defendant presents a strong risk of flight, they submit evidence about the defendant's criminal activity, financial assets, connections to other jurisdictions, access to identity-hiding technology and skills, and other factors showing how and why a defendant might disappear, rather than face the charges. The more information about the defendant an investigation uncovers, the better prepared a prosecutor is to form a position on bail or remand, and to convince the judge of it.

18.5 GUILTY PLEAS: PLEA POSITION AND NEGOTIATION

Once a defendant has been formally charged at his arraignment, the litigation of the criminal charges is officially under way. At all stages, the possibility of a guilty plea is present and considered by both sides, and often the prosecutor and defense attorney discuss potential outcomes and sentences.

Guilty pleas happen in two general ways: either the defendant decides to plead guilty to the crime(s) with which he is charged and to accept a sentence within the discretion of the court, or the prosecution and defense reach a plea bargain.

The defendant always has the right to plead guilty to the charges without entering into any negotiations with the prosecutor. Then it is up to the court to sentence the defendant within the range of legal sentences. Here, both defense and prosecution attempt to persuade the judge as to what sentence is fair, as we discuss later in this chapter.

More often, the defendant will engage in plea negotiations with the prosecutor (sometimes called plea bargaining). A plea bargain is an agreement under which the defendant voluntarily pleads guilty to certain reduced charges and receives an agreed-upon sentence. The negotiation process varies greatly among various federal and state courthouses. If plea negotiations are unsuccessful, the defendant can either plead guilty to the charged crimes or go to trial. In some cases, the prosecution will not negotiate a plea bargain.

The idea of a plea bargain is to provide a better alternative to the defendant than what he would face if found guilty at trial. If the defendant takes responsibility for his criminal conduct at an early stage of litigation, the prosecution will offer a better plea with lesser punishment. The prosecution benefits by having a faster resolution of the case, by not having to prepare and conduct a trial, and in some cases, by gaining the cooperation of the defendant. The burden on witnesses and the entire court system also is reduced. The farther the litigation proceeds towards trial, prosecutors may make the terms less lenient, or take any offered plea bargains off the table. Plea bargain terms ultimately must be approved by the court.

Plea negotiations are influenced heavily by speculation about how the litigation might play out, how the judge might rule on future legal issues, the strength of the prosecution's evidence, the likelihood the defendant might be convicted, and the judge's sentencing decision if the defendant is convicted after trial.

Some factors that prosecutors often consider in forming a plea position are:

- Will the plea ensure that a cybercriminal who committed extensive crimes is pleading guilty to criminal counts that adequately describe his conduct?

- Should the plea be crafted to include restitution or other measures intended to compensate the victims of the defendant's crimes?
- In federal cases and some state jurisdictions, does the plea fit the policies of the prosecutor's office and its plea-bargaining guidelines?
- Can the defendant offer useful information to the investigation, or cooperate with investigators to target other cybercriminals – and is the defendant willing to do so?
- Is there a practical or logistical reason to achieve an early plea bargain, rather than push a case to trial (for example, the complexity of the case, the needs of the victims, or because the defendant played a small role in a large scheme)?
- Is the defendant's conduct so egregious that the prosecutor is not interested in pursuing any type of plea bargain, and will require the defendant to plead guilty to all charges and be sentenced by the court in its discretion?

Plea negotiations are often the first time the investigation and prosecution are tested by the defendant and his attorney. If the defense attorney and defendant have identified flaws in the prosecution's charging decisions or the evidence presented during early stages of litigation, the attorney will use these defects to the defendant's advantage in the negotiating process.

For these reasons, the weeks, months, and years of the investigation that produced the criminal case are critical to the plea negotiation stage of criminal litigation.

- *Strength of the evidence directly shapes the prosecutor's plea-bargaining stance.* The stronger the evidence from the investigation, the stronger the negotiating position a prosecutor can take with the defendant and his attorney. If the evidence is stronger as to some charges versus others, or the defense exposes holes in the proof that the investigation did not discover, the prosecutor's plea position is weakened.
- *Better investigations lead to stronger sentences within plea bargains.* Along with being able to effectively convince defendants to plead guilty, better investigations allow prosecutors to secure stronger sentences under negotiated plea deals. When a prosecutor is able to demonstrate to a defense attorney the breadth of the evidence in the case, the attorney is far more likely to persuade the defendant to plead guilty and accept a strong sentence – because the risk of going to trial and receiving a less lenient sentence is clearly high.

18.6   DISCOVERY: SHARING THE INVESTIGATION WITH THE DEFENSE

Discovery is the litigation stage when prosecutors provide information about the case to the defense. The timing of discovery disclosures, and the content of the discovery, is dictated by statutes and court rules (state or federal). Generally speaking, prosecutors are required to give the defendant copies of investigation reports, records acquired from private individuals or companies, statements made by witnesses, search warrants and their results, records of traditional identification procedures used, and most other pertinent evidence in the case. These records are turned over at various stages after arraignment and before trial, with the exact schedule varying according to laws of the jurisdiction and court rules. Some states incorporate the concept of "open file" discovery, meaning at a specified point in the litigation, the defense is given access to the prosecutor's entire case file.

The defendant's discovery obligations are limited. Depending on the jurisdiction, some affirmative defenses (like alibis) may require the defense to turn over evidence to the prosecution, as well as reports by expert witnesses that will be called at trial.

Protecting sensitive information. Discovery rules contain certain exceptions that are designed to protect sensitive or confidential information. For example, if disclosing information would jeopardize someone's safety or ongoing investigative activity, prosecutors may be allowed to withhold some discovery material, including that which identifies victims and witnesses or the cooperation of criminal participants. Prosecutors usually must apply to the court for permission to withhold information from the defense. Even when laws give prosecutors discretion over discovery disclosures, obtaining a court order regarding nondisclosure is a prudent step since it means the decision has been reviewed and authorized by the court.

Given the nature of cybercrime cases, prosecutors should consider seeking orders protecting some types of evidence from discovery – such as the personal identifying information of victims. These details, if provided to the defendant, could subject victims to further risk of identity theft and fraud. One remedy is for prosecutors to redact information in discovery disclosures; another is to require the defense attorney to inspect the unredacted evidence at the prosecutor's office, rather than providing copies of it to the defense. A court may allow the prosecution to withhold disclosure of certain investigative details, such as special technology used or information from cooperating accomplices, if that does not prevent the defendant from planning his defense. Generally, continuing investigations are afforded more protection by a court than those that are concluded.

The discovery phase directly focuses on the investigators' work, and highlights the importance of accuracy, completeness, and discipline from the earliest stages of an investigation. We covered the law enforcement investigation in Chapter 13, and general cybercrime investigation concepts in Chapter 11. Below, we briefly list some ways that the investigation impacts discovery, and which an investigator should be mindful of throughout the course of an investigation:

- *An orderly system of evidence-gathering and report-generating improves discovery in many ways.* As we discussed in Chapter 11, a consistent system of documenting and organizing evidence and reports greatly benefits the investigation. During the discovery phase, it also allows the prosecutor to find documents, organize them, provide what is required to the defense and the court, and identify sensitive information that should be protected.
- *Investigators' reports will be turned over to the defense.* The defense attorney and defendant will scrutinize every word of investigators' reports, looking for mistakes, exaggeration, omissions, and other details that might poke holes in the prosecution's case. Of course, mistakes happen, and it is important to be able to admit them, rather than compound the error by inventing a reason or excuse to explain them.
- *Missing reports and information need to be identified and obtained.* Prosecutors (and defense attorneys) should be on the lookout for items that appear to be missing. For example, if there is an investigator's report on three meetings with a witness, but no report about the fourth meeting, that report needs to be found, or its absence explained.
- *If there is a hearing or trial, investigators who testify will be questioned about reports and other materials turned over during discovery.* Should a case proceed to hearings or trial, the prosecution's main witnesses will be the individuals who investigated the crimes. The evidence and reports will be the subject of much testimony for the prosecution and cross-examination by the defense, who may try to paint them (and the investigators) as faulty, sloppy, or dishonest. Cases are won or lost on overcoming these defense portrayals of an investigation.

18.7 MOTION PRACTICE, HEARINGS, AND PRE-TRIAL DECISIONS: TESTING THE INVESTIGATION AND PROSECUTION

After arraignment, the prosecution or defense can submit motions to the court, typically on a schedule to keep the case progressing. Motions are requests that the court rule on a question of law or procedure pertaining to the case.

Most pre-trial motions come from the defense and seek to dismiss the case or specified counts, suppress evidence on legal grounds, or weaken how counts will be interpreted. Prosecutors also may file pre-trial motions to obtain certain information from the defendant, to preclude certain defenses, or to seek required approval to use certain evidence. Some of the common concerns litigated in motion practice are whether:

- The Grand Jury was conducted properly
- The accusatory instrument meets the necessary legal standards for each count or if counts should be dismissed prior to trial
- Evidence gathered during the investigation should be suppressed on constitutional grounds because it was illegally obtained
- The court has legal jurisdiction over the case
- The defendant will pursue certain defenses, such as mental impairment or alibi
- The defendant's case should be severed from those of any co-defendants
- Whether the prosecution can introduce evidence of the defendant's uncharged bad acts (criminal actions not alleged in the accusatory instrument).

The court's decisions on motions often affect plea negotiations, strengthening or weakening each side's position. If the prosecution's evidence and charges are approved, some defendants take a renewed interest in reaching a plea deal, rather than face the consequences if convicted at trial.

Many motions are litigated in writing, with both sides presenting their interpretations of the law. Usually, the court issues a written decision. If the court is unable to decide the issues raised based on the parties' written arguments, it may require a hearing so that the facts or issues can be developed further. At a hearing, both sides might present oral arguments, evidence, and witness testimony. When witness testimony is presented by the prosecution, the defense may cross-examine and the judge will assess the credibility of the witnesses and make factual findings. Based on all of the evidence presented and her application of the law, the judge will make her decision on the motions. The ruling can be significant for the future trial. Hearings are an opportunity for the defense to hear prosecution witnesses testify on the record and under oath, which may reveal more information about the case. Poorly prepared witnesses could misspeak or get confused and that could weaken the prosecutor's case.

Motions and hearings are strongly influenced by the investigation. Hearing decisions will turn upon the investigation's adherence to the laws for obtaining evidence (as outlined in Chapter 7), and the evidence underlying the criminal charges (as we discussed in Chapter 6). The investigation-related issues that commonly arise in the pre-trial motion and hearings phase are:

- *Does the evidence support the charges?* When the defense challenges the legal foundation of criminal charges – within either a criminal information or an indictment voted by the Grand Jury – the court will review the evidence used to support those charges, comparing it to the allegations. When the prosecutor can demonstrate the factual basis and legal theory for each charge, the counts will be upheld.
- *How was the evidence gathered and is it admissible at trial?* Every motion to suppress physical evidence, statements by the defendant, and other forms of evidence

essentially asks whether the investigative practices in the case were legally sound. Motions and hearings test whether investigators collected evidence lawfully or improperly. Cyber cases usually rely on evidence obtained through search warrants and other legal tools, and defense attorneys will challenge both the underlying affidavits and how the tools were used.

- *Can the investigative results help prosecutors counter defense motions?* Prosecutors use the information obtained during the investigation to prevail on defense motions and hearing requests. The more thorough and reliable the evidence and investigative practices, the likelier it is for the prosecution to prevail.
- *Can the investigators provide quality testimony at hearings?* Some hearings, particularly those to suppress evidence, require the prosecution to call witnesses to explain how the evidence was obtained, and to show that it was done lawfully. Investigators should be thinking about this possibility while they are gathering evidence. Knowing that someday you might have to describe your actions in detail, and be cross-examined about the steps you chose to take or not take, should be a guiding principle in all criminal investigative endeavors.

18.8   TRIAL: THE INVESTIGATION LAID BARE

Although most defendants plead guilty during the course of criminal litigation, some cases eventually come down to trial. A trial represents the defendant's right to have the prosecution present proof beyond a reasonable doubt of the defendant's commission of each element of every crime charged. A very small percentage of criminal cases reach the trial stage – in the federal system, less than 10% go to trial.[1] In state criminal justice systems, the numbers can be even smaller.[2]

When cybercrime cases go to trial, the methods and results of the investigation are the primary focus. The numerous pieces of evidence that collectively prove the defendant's guilt are introduced through a variety of witnesses – representatives of Internet service companies, analysts with different skills, and investigators who did the leg work and connected the dots. The prosecutor takes the jury through the investigation's detection of the trail of digital and real-world breadcrumbs that lead back to the defendant.

The parts of a trial include:

- Pretrial motions (for any final legal issues to be addressed with the court)
- Picking a jury
- Opening statements
- Prosecutor presents evidence
- Defense may present evidence
- Closing statements
- Judge's instructions to the jury
- Jury deliberations
- Verdict
- Sentencing.

Let us look at the important ways the investigation is integral to each step.

---

[1] United States Courts, www.uscourts.gov/about-federal-courts/types-cases/criminal-cases.

[2] In New York and California, the most recent statistics show that over 97% of felony arrests resulted in conviction by guilty plea, while approximately 3% of felony cases went to trial. New York State Division of Criminal Justice Services, www.criminaljustice.ny.gov/crimnet/ojsa/dar/DAR-2Q-2019-NewYorkState.pdf; Judicial Council of California, www.courts.ca.gov/documents/2017-Court-Statistics-Report.pdf.

18.8.1 PICKING A JURY

The process of jury selection is called *voir dire*, from the French words meaning "to see, to speak". A pool of potential jurors is assembled by the court, and attorneys for both sides of the litigation are given the opportunity to ask questions about the jurors' backgrounds and viewpoints. The goal of *voir dire* is to identify jurors who could successfully and fairly reach a verdict in the case on trial. Jury selection may give the attorneys a chance to voice the key factual and legal disputes within the case, testing the jurors for their reactions to the particular questions at issue.

Laws vary, but each side generally can reject a small number of prospective jurors without having to provide any reason (a peremptory challenge). Peremptory challenges cannot be used to block jurors for improper reasons (such as race or gender). Each side also can ask the court to remove a potential juror if the individual appears to be biased towards either side, or is unable to serve for physical, personal, or language reasons (challenge for cause). The court also can remove a potential juror for cause even if neither side raises a challenge.

A cybercrime jury should be selected like any other jury. The best jurors are people with common sense, who are able to make difficult decisions based upon facts and logic, and who are able to follow legal instructions from the judge. It is the prosecutor's job to present the facts clearly for a jury of laypersons, whatever their backgrounds.

Prosecutors should not fall prey to the fallacy that jurors need to be cybercrime or technical experts to hear a cybercrime case. By looking only for "techies", the prosecution will end up dismissing thoughtful, logical jurors from other backgrounds who would have been a great fit for the case. Further, having tech "experts" on a jury can lead to difficulties if these jurors try to impose their own opinions about the evidence upon other jurors (rather than each juror using his or her own judgment and following the legal instructions of the court). Explaining the case to people without technology experience actually helps the prosecutor organize and present the evidence in a persuasive and absorbing way.

To find the best jurors in a cybercrime case, a prosecutor might discuss the following subjects during jury selection:

- *Types of evidence.* Records of Internet activity and financial transactions, computer forensic analysis, and technological information may be the mainstays of proving a cybercrime. Prosecutors can test the jury pool on their comfort-level with these types of evidence and a connect-the-dot approach to proof, while letting them know what to expect.
- *Complexity of the case.* Many cybercrime cases that reach the trial stage are complex to prove. The case may be presented as something of a jigsaw puzzle, or a web with many circumstantial logical links to be built, with the prosecutor giving the jury one piece of evidence at a time that adds up to the big picture in the end. These concepts are important to use in vetting the common sense and attention span of potential jurors.
- *Missing pieces or investigative missteps.* Jury selection allows prosecutors to discuss any problems with the case early to gauge jurors' individual responses. No case is perfect. There may be inconsistencies, missing pieces of evidence, mistakes by the investigators, or unlikable witnesses that the jury will hear during the course of the trial.

18.8.2 OPENING STATEMENTS

Once a jury is selected and the judge gives preliminary instructions, the trial begins with opening statements. The prosecution gives its opening first, since it is the party with the burden of proving the case. The defense then can give an opening statement if it chooses, but has no obligation to do so, or to do anything at trial since the defense has no burden.

The prosecutor's opening statement is an opportunity to tell the jury what crimes the defendant is accused of committing, and how the evidence in the case will prove that he committed them. The opening statement is not used for making arguments or inferences, but rather to lay out what the jury will hear and the prosecution's theory of the case.

By using the opening to sketch out the big picture, a prosecutor can help the jury put the pieces of evidence into the larger puzzle when they later hear the witness testimony and see the evidence. In a cybercrime case, even more than others, the prosecutor must confidently provide an informative overview of the case that outlines the proof and evidence to come, encouraging the jury to take interest in the case. Some important points to guide the opening include:

- What the case is "really about" (e.g. typically theft)
- That real victims were harmed
- Holding the defendants accountable for their actions and choices; cybercrimes typically are carefully calculated and executed
- How the evidence will prove the crimes charged, including evidence of identity
- Getting the jury involved with solving the case for themselves using the key events of the investigation and the proof you will present.

18.8.3 PRESENTING THE EVIDENCE: LEGAL ADMISSIBILITY AND JURY COMPREHENSION

After the opening statements, the prosecution begins to call witnesses to the stand for "direct" examination. Witness testimony provides essential evidence in a trial, but witnesses also introduce other forms of evidence to the jury, such as records, physical items, and the results of scientific tests or analysis. Cybercrime cases present interesting challenges regarding the legal admissibility and presentation of evidence. Prosecutors must prepare carefully so the judge will admit each piece of evidence, and so the jury will understand what they are seeing and hearing.

In federal and state courts, there are procedural rules that attorneys must follow in order to have various forms of proof "admitted" as evidence in the case. There are many factors that go into a judge's determination on admissibility, based upon the rules and laws of the particular jurisdiction where the trial is held. Some of the common considerations are:

- *Relevance.* Is the evidence directly related to the factual determinations the jury will have to make?
- *Authentication.* Has the evidence been authenticated by witnesses, records, or other sources as being genuine and correct?
- *Fair and accurate representations.* Related to authentication, do certain forms of evidence (such as photographs, videos, or copies of documents) fairly and accurately portray the original scene or item?
- *Chain of custody.* Also related to authentication, if an item was seized by law enforcement, has it been secured in a manner that preserved its integrity, and prevented alteration or tampering?
- *Hearsay.* As we covered in Chapter 11, hearsay is an out-of-court statement offered in court for the truth of the matter asserted. In other words, when a witness discusses (or a document contains) an oral or written statement made by someone else, and that statement is being presented to the jury as evidence of its truth, that is "hearsay". There is a general rule against hearsay because of the concern that it will not be reliable. The law favors statements made by witnesses who are in court,

under oath, and subject to cross-examination. However, there are many exceptions to the hearsay rule, including for business records, and judges decide whether a particular statement is admissible. If the statement is not being offered for the truth of what it states, the hearsay rule would not apply.

The prosecution or defense can object to each other's evidence on any of these grounds, and the judge will make a ruling. When preparing a cybercrime trial (or any criminal case), the prosecutor cannot anticipate all of the defense objections or the judge's decisions on each of them. However, as discussed in earlier chapters, cyber cases tend to be heavily dependent on records related to Internet account usage, other online activity, and data of various kinds. By mastering the procedures for entering records and other forms of data into evidence, cyber prosecutors can forestall many defense objections.

With the complexity of the evidence in many cyber cases, it is essential that prosecutors build the case presentation – both the testimony and the exhibits – to be clear, transparent, and verifiable. If anyone from the prosecutor's team becomes confused by the evidence or facts, then confusion among the jury will be even greater. In the best scenario, the prosecution's witnesses can explain facts and findings, but the jury can verify the information for themselves using the exhibits admitted as evidence.

When creating trial exhibits and planning witness testimony, prosecutors should consider the approach described in the following section.

18.8.4   The "Baby Step Exhibit" Technique

With all of these presentation needs in mind, we developed the "baby step exhibit" technique for introducing evidence in the Western Express case. This technique solved the problems attorneys can face trying to get complex and interrelated evidence into evidence with a single exhibit.

This more traditional "all-in-one" method for introducing evidence works, but can cause problems, especially when trying to do too much, too fast. The "all-in-one" method refers to using one exhibit to encompass multiple components of related evidence that may take many witnesses to fully authenticate. Under this method, a series of witnesses testifies, each laying part of the exhibit's foundation, but the exhibit cannot be admitted into evidence until the judge hears all of their testimony. When the final witness testifies and the prosecutor asks to move the exhibit into evidence, the judge has to remember all the prior witness' testimony in order to make a ruling. Any confusion or ambiguity is resolved in the defendant's favor.

The baby step exhibit technique works differently. Instead of using one compound exhibit, related evidence is admitted using multiple, separate exhibits. Each witness admits an exhibit related to his or her testimony, and complicated exhibits are broken into component parts.

Let us look at two examples of how the baby step exhibit technique can be used to enter evidence commonly needed in cybercrime cases.

18.8.4.1   The "Baby Step" Technique and the Laptop Computer

In this example, a laptop computer was recovered from a suspect (or the suspect's residence), the laptop was forensically searched, and valuable information was recovered. The prosecutor needs to get that information into evidence and before the jury. Each case will be different in terms of the testimony certain witnesses can offer, but the point is to break the process up into individual steps (even if certain witnesses can cover multiple steps). In our example, a different witness is used for each step.

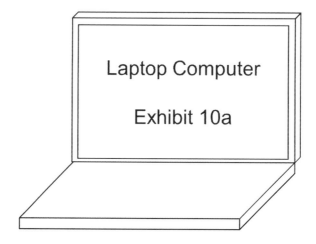

FIGURE 18.1 Laptop Computer: Exhibit 10A.

Using this method, the prosecutor first calls Witness A, the detective or agent who recovered the laptop, who testifies about those facts and confirms the laptop seems to be in the same (or substantially the same) physical condition as when it was recovered.

The prosecutor then moves to admit Exhibit 10a into evidence (the laptop). The defense attorney objects, but the issues are limited and clear. The judge admits Exhibit 10a (the laptop) into evidence as shown in Figure 18.1. However, this exhibit is of no help to the jury yet.

Then the prosecutor calls Witness B, the digital forensic examiner who created a digital forensic image of the laptop's hard drive. Witness B takes a look at Exhibit 10a (which is now in evidence) and confirms it is the same device she previously imaged. She describes that she created an exact, forensic copy of the data within the laptop and stored the copy on a new hard drive, and explains that this forensic copy is contained within Exhibit 10b. The prosecutor moves to admit Exhibit 10b (the hard drive containing the forensic image),

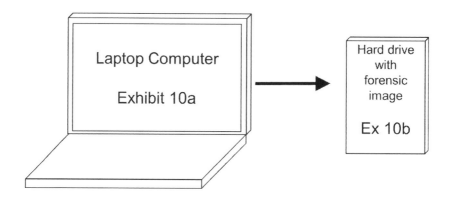

FIGURE 18.2 Forensic Image of Laptop Computer: Exhibit 10B.

FIGURE 18.3   Data Exported from Forensic Image of Laptop Computer: Exhibit 10C1 and Exhibit 10C2.

as depicted in Figure 18.2. The defense objects, but the forensic image comes into evidence. Exhibit 10b, too, is of no help to the jury yet.

Next, the prosecutor calls Witness C, a different forensic examiner who analyzed the forensic image of the laptop and exported relevant data. Witness C testifies that he has reviewed Exhibit 10b (the hard drive with a digital image of the laptop's data which is now in evidence), and that he previously conducted digital forensic analysis on this image and exported voluminous data from it – including stored content, email messages, Internet browser history, and photos. This exported data is Exhibit 10C1, a DVD with a lot of data in it, which the prosecutor moves to admit. This exhibit is just one small step forward, so the judge admits it into evidence. Then, the prosecutor moves to admit Exhibit 10C2, paper printouts of some of that data within Exhibit 10C1, which the judge also admits, and the prosecutor walks Witness C through some of those records, as summarized in Figure 18.3.

Now the prosecutor calls Witness D, an investigator assigned to the case who analyzed Exhibits 10C1 and 10C2, looking for evidence of the defendant's criminal activity, identity, or other pertinent subjects. Witness D created summaries of that evidence as trial exhibits. Witness D testifies about her review of Exhibit 10C1 and 2, and the creation of Exhibit 10D1, a fair and accurate summary of some of that data (e.g. a summary of certain email messages between two conspirators). The prosecutor moves to enter Exhibit 10D1, which the judge admits. Now Exhibit 10D1 can be displayed to the jury, and Witness D can walk them through the exhibit. This process is depicted in Figure 18.4.

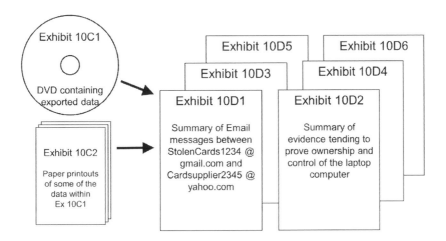

FIGURE 18.4   Summary of Relevant Information from DVD: Exhibit 10D(x).

Other exhibits can be admitted to summarize the data within the laptop in a helpful way for the jury and prove the crimes charged (such as Exhibit 10D2, which summarizes evidence that proves the defendant controlled the laptop).

Each of these exhibits "stands on its own", meaning it states on the face of it where it is from and what it means. The jury can get all the information it needs from the exhibit itself. The testimony of the authenticating witness contained no additional details that might have to be remembered, and so no read-back of that prior testimony will ever be required. Ultimately, the Exhibit 10Dx summary-type exhibits are what the prosecutor will highlight during her closing, and have the jury focus on during their deliberation.

The possibilities are limitless, the point is to create exhibits that will be helpful for the jury, and to get all of the evidence admitted in a logical sequence that takes small steps at a time, so that the judge's decisions when ruling on the admissibility of the evidence are simpler.

18.8.4.2   The "Baby Step" Technique and Financial Records

Now we consider another example. The prosecution has conducted a thorough investigation of the defendant's financial activities, and seeks to introduce evidence of them to prove the defendant committed cybercrimes, profited from them, and laundered the profits. The evidence is from many sources, the analysis was complex, but it needs to be simplified for the jury.

First, the prosecutor calls Witness A from Bank A, who testifies that Exhibit 11A is records from that bank kept in the ordinary course of business. The prosecutor moves Exhibit 11A into evidence (it comes in over the defense objection) and then asks Witness A about some important aspects of the records, including that the account is in the name of the defendant.

Next, the prosecutor calls Witness B from Money Transmitter B (e.g. Western Union), who testifies that Exhibit 11B is records of certain transactions kept in the ordinary course of business. Exhibit 11B eventually comes into evidence, and the prosecutor asks some questions about it.

Then, the prosecutor calls Witness C who testifies about Exhibit 11C, records pertaining to virtual currency transactions, such as Bitcoin, and gets Exhibit 11C admitted into evidence.

Finally, the prosecutor calls Witness D, who has previously analyzed Exhibits 11A, 11B, and 11C, and prepared a fair and accurate summary of relevant transactions from them, which is Exhibit 11D, as depicted in Figure 18.5. This example is simplified. Be aware there may be many issues about how to group various financial summaries in order to show both the relationship between various transactions and to prove the identity of the accountholder and other individuals making the transactions.

These are two examples, but the variations are endless. The key takeaways are:

- Create exhibits with an eye towards future usage in court, and for ease of witness preparation.
- Make the decision simple and straightforward for the judge about whether to admit each exhibit (doing too much in one exhibit might give the defense attorney room to attack, and may make the judge leery of admitting it).
- Make the path to the meaningful evidence as simple and straightforward as possible for the jury.
- Going step-by-step maximizes prosecutor flexibility, especially when some witnesses can authenticate or testify only about discrete pieces of evidence, or if judicial decisions are not favorable.

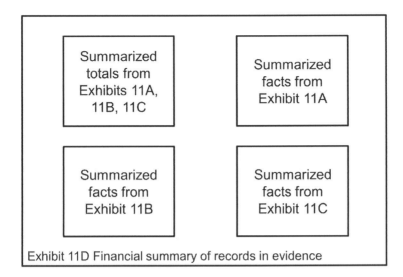

FIGURE 18.5   Financial Summary: Exhibit 11D.

• When all the evidence has been submitted, having discrete exhibits which are helpful for the jury avoids confusion as the trial unfolds and the jury reviews the exhibits during deliberations.

Western Express and the Baby-Step Exhibit Technique and Organization

In the Western Express trial, this "baby step exhibit" method allowed thousands of documents, photos, videos, and other items to be efficiently entered into evidence, while keeping them organized for the prosecution, court, and jury. We needed 54 witnesses and a massive body of exhibits to prove the case, but the "baby step exhibit" method made the process much easier for everyone.

We ended up organizing our evidence into the following categories:

• Records obtained by subpoena or other legal process from third party corporations (such as email providers, phone service providers, financial institutions, in the form provided by the organization)
• Evidence seized by law enforcement from defendants pursuant to search warrants (devices, paper documents, etc.)
• Digital forensic examination evidence (such as the data within a computer seized by law enforcement)
• Email records in viewable form, such as paper printout and electronic PDF (derived from records obtained from email providers above)
• Website records (from a variety of website preservation techniques)
• Reports that summarized the lengthy records evidence (derived from any of the above, often using multiple sources).

This organizational approach worked out wonderfully because it dovetailed with the "baby step exhibit" method to get these items admitted at trial.

First, we sought to admit evidence in a raw, sometimes unhelpful format. The representative from the bank, the email provider, or the phone company, would testify, and the raw records were admitted based upon the representative's authentication. With physical items, like seized computers, the special agent, or investigator who participated in the seizure provided the testimony to get the computer admitted, even though that witness had no personal knowledge of the helpful evidence subsequent forensic examination found within the device.

Then, later witnesses were able to testify and introduce exhibits summarizing and explaining the evidence they found within the raw exhibits. For example, later witnesses offered exhibits demonstrating the financial analysis performed, the forensic examination conducted, and the individual emails or patterns of communication identified.

Investigators and prosecutors can deploy the "baby step exhibit" method long before a trial is scheduled, which is another very helpful feature of this approach. In the months and years before trial, as records and data are obtained and analyzed, the team can begin to organize the evidence in categories that will help them become future exhibits – with an eye towards the charges that need to be proven and the jury who will be passing judgment. Using this proactive system in the Western Express case made the pre-trial preparation period far more manageable.

Whatever presentation method is used, there is one question that must remain front and center: will the exhibits help the jury understand these complex facts? Visualizing a jury sitting in an uncomfortable jury room, pondering dozens of counts in a complex cybercrime case, prosecutors and investigators can create a presentation of the evidence that makes the job of reaching a just verdict as simple as possible.

18.8.5   THE DEFENSE: CROSS-EXAMINATION AND COUNTERATTACKING WITH EVIDENCE

Defense Cross-Examination during the People's Case

Throughout the prosecution's presentation of witnesses and exhibits, the defense attorney has the opportunity to cross-examine and object. The overarching defense goal is to discredit the prosecution's evidence, thereby creating a reasonable doubt as to the defendant's guilt.

There are many strategies that defense attorneys use in this effort, and they vary with the type of witness and evidence. For an investigator or law enforcement officer, the defense might ask questions intended to show the witness was sloppy, unreliable, or harbored a prejudice against the defendant. For a technical examiner or analyst, the defense might attack the witness' training or competence, or whether the witness used the correct methodology at every step. For a representative from an Internet service company or financial institution who is testifying solely to introduce records, the defense might use the witness' lack of knowledge about the broader investigation to suggest the defendant did not commit any crimes.

- *Countering defense cross-examination.* Defense attorneys will cross-examine most prosecution witnesses hoping to find mistakes or uncertainties in their testimony, or simply to suggest defense arguments. The details of an investigation help combat these attacks, both in preparing a witness to testify, and while the testimony is under way. The defense attorney often is guided by the defendant, who arguably knows as much about the criminal activity in the case as anyone else. When an investigation has unearthed enough detail that the investigators and prosecutors are confident in their understanding of the criminal events, they can prepare for the defense attorney's efforts. After defense cross-examination, the prosecution is allowed to ask more questions of the witness. During this "re-direct" testimony, the witness can clarify information and sometimes add more facts that were not previously admissible.

The Defense Case (If Presented)

Once the prosecution has "rested" (meaning, finished its presentation of evidence), the defense can present a case if it chooses. The defense has no burden of any kind and many defendants choose not to call witnesses or offer exhibits. Instead, they seek an acquittal by attacking the prosecution's case, arguing the prosecution failed to prove the defendant's guilt beyond a reasonable doubt.

Sometimes, the defense does call witnesses and presents its own exhibits to the jury. Some defendants decide to testify on their own behalf, though that strategy is risky and exposes them to cross-examination by the prosecution. Other defense witnesses might include experts on scientific or technology topics (sometimes to counter experts called by the prosecution), character witnesses (within certain legal parameters), and even members of the investigative team if the defense believes will offer testimony that undercuts an important facet of the prosecution's case.

To counter defense attempts to discredit the prosecution's evidence, prosecutors rely upon a solid investigation, including facts discovered that were not used in the government's initial trial case:

- *Precluding irrelevant and prejudicial defense witnesses and exhibits.* The defense may seek to call a witness or introduce an exhibit that is irrelevant, inflammatory, or misleading. If so, prosecutors can request an offer of proof (a preview of the witness' testimony or exhibit outside of the jury's presence), so that the court can determine if it will be relevant to the trial. Prosecutors should consider the defendant's right to present evidence, potential appellate issues, and the prosecutor's ability to later comment and argue about defense evidence (but inability to comment if the defense does not present a case at all), when deciding whether to object to defense witnesses or evidence.
- *Cross-examining defense witnesses.* Cross-examination can be used to have defense witnesses confirm aspects of the People's case, including details related to cyber-crime activity, identification, and other evidence introduced by the People. This often is best done first, so that the confirmations are obtained before impeaching the witness' credibility on other matters, and the jury can hear right away how the defense witness corroborates the People's evidence. Because, defense witness testimony will generally not favor the prosecution, later questions can explore areas where the witness may lack knowledge or be shading testimony to benefit the defense, and credibility can be impeached.
- *Cross-examining the defendant, if he testifies.* As with other defense witnesses, an effective first step is to get the defendant to corroborate details he will be obliged to admit. This testimony also may resolve some issues relating to identity and commission of the crime. Prosecutors also can ask about prior witnesses' testimony and the exhibits that are in evidence, bringing them to the attention of the jury and seeing whether the defendant will corroborate or concede any of the facts within them. Cross-examination also is an opportunity to ask about facts or events not presented in the People's case.

- The defendant has two advantages as a witness – he is very familiar with the facts of the case, and he has the benefit of hearing all the witness testimony and seeing all of the exhibits before he testifies. On the other hand, the defendant does not know everything the prosecution and investigators have learned over the course of a long investigation, and probably has not pored over the records evidence in the case as closely as the prosecution. Further, if the defendant testifies deceitfully, sometimes these lies take more work to keep straight than the prosecution's evidence. The prosecution's informed questioning can get the defendant to confirm certain facts and exhibits are true, and work to establish where the defendant's testimony is untrustworthy.

18.8.6 CLOSING ARGUMENTS

At the conclusion of the prosecution's and defense's presentation of evidence, both parties can make a closing argument to the jury. In some state systems, the defense gives the first closing, and the prosecution – the party with the burden of proving the case – gives the second and last argument. In other states and in the federal courts, the prosecution gives a first closing statement, the defense offers its closing statement, and then the prosecution gives a rebuttal to the defense's arguments.

The closing arguments allow each party to sum up its own evidence, expose weaknesses in the other side's positions, and persuade the jury. In a cybercrime case, the prosecution closing takes all the pieces of evidence introduced throughout the trial, and shows the jury how they establish the defendant's guilt. Often this process involves highlighting disparate nuggets of information, and giving the jury the common sense explanation for how they all interconnect. Prosecutors might make these arguments by walking the jury through a trail of evidence they saw and heard during the trial, the testimony, and exhibits. Hopefully, the trial exhibits were created by looking forward to this closing argument and jury deliberation, so the argument presents a path through the exhibits and how jurors can review the evidence while deliberating.

In essence, the prosecution's closing is a summary of the proof uncovered by the investigation that ties the defendant to the crime. Many prosecutors write a draft of their closing long before the trial even begins, in order to consider all the points of evidence that will be needed to prove the case in the end. Thinking of the closing argument while preparing for trial makes the prosecutor consider different ways to explain the case to the jury and the trial exhibits that will be needed. As with the other phases of the trial, the more evidence and knowledge the investigation has produced, the more clearly the prosecution can make this final summation of the case to the jury.

18.8.7 JURY INSTRUCTIONS

When the closing arguments are concluded, the judge provides the jury with instructions on the law. The jury is instructed on the elements of each charged crime, and the legal definitions of many terms within those elements (such as intent, possession, or authorization). The judge also explains how the jury should consider the evidence, as well as the prosecution's burden to prove the case beyond a reasonable doubt.

Often, the prosecution and defense attorneys argue about the exact instructions the judge will read to the jury. There can be heated debate about whether certain instructions are required, or whether they will be prejudicial to one side or the other. While most judges encourage the parties to come to a mutual agreement, in some instances, the court will hear legal arguments and make the final decision.

It is good to know the jury instructions before making closing arguments, and even to consider these standardized jury instructions earlier in the case – when charges are being decided or when preparing a case for trial. The instructions' breakdown of each crime into its elements can be a helpful tool for prosecutors and investigators to ensure there is adequate and admissible proof of every charge.

18.8.8 Jury Deliberations and Verdict

After the court reads all of the legal instructions, the jury moves to a private jury room to start considering the evidence and deliberating about a verdict. Jurors are entitled to review exhibits that were admitted into evidence. This moment is the culmination of the investigation. The jury has heard and seen the investigation's results and sat through the prosecutorial efforts to provide the evidence in a clear, common-sense manner. Everyone connected with the investigation has worked to give the jury the exhibits and tools they need in order to view and decide the facts.

In the federal system and in all but one state (Oregon), the jury must review each criminal charge and reach a unanimous verdict to find a defendant guilty.[3] A jury may find a defendant guilty of some counts and not guilty of others. Or they may acquit the defendant entirely, finding him not guilty of all counts. If a jury cannot reach a verdict after an extended period of time (a "hung jury"), the court will declare a mistrial. In this situation, the case can be re-tried by another jury, or the parties can agree to a resolution of the case.

18.8.9 Sentencing

If a verdict of guilty is reached (or the defendant has pleaded guilty), the defendant will ultimately be sentenced. State and federal laws set forth the range of sentences available for each level of crime, and the court will determine the sentence within those ranges. Where prison is warranted, sentences might be imposed concurrently (running together at the same time) or consecutively (one after the other, resulting in a longer sentence).[4]

Since cybercrimes are often complex, a written sentencing memorandum is essential for the prosecution to communicate its recommendation to the court.[5] The prosecution can describe the facts of the case as presented at trial, the technological nature of the defendant's crimes, the effect on victims and the community, and other reasons why a certain sentence is appropriate. The defense also may provide a sentencing memorandum. In some courts, the parties also make oral statements in support of their sentencing positions. Victims often are allowed to make written or oral statements as well, describing how the defendant's actions impacted their lives.

This sentencing phase, like all the other litigation phases before it, relies upon a sound investigation:

- *Showing the broad impact of the defendant's cybercrimes.* In cybercrime cases, prosecutors may seek stronger sentences because of the profound ramifications of the

---

[3] Currently, there is one state (Oregon) that allows non-unanimous verdicts in some criminal cases. Until recently, Louisiana also allowed non-unanimous verdicts, but has now amended its state constitution to bar them. The United States Supreme Court will review the constitutionality of non-unanimous verdicts in 2019 in the case of *Ramos v. Louisiana*, appealing *State of Louisiana v. Ramos*, 2016-KA-1199, Louisiana Fourth Cir. Court of Appeal (Nov. 2017).

[4] In federal cases, sentencing decisions are based on detailed guidelines that encompass both the sentences available pursuant to the criminal code, as well as certain mitigating and exacerbating factors about the defendant and his conduct.

[5] This document also is helpful at later stages for departments of probation or parole, for appellate attorneys and appellate courts, and if the defendant is rearrested in the future.

crimes on specific victims, the security of the Internet, online commerce, financial institutions, and the community as a whole. These impacts can be described to the court when they are documented by the investigation.

*   *Allowing victims to add their voices.* People who are less familiar with cybercrime sometimes consider it a "victimless" crime – that big corporations might lose some money from it, but no great harm is done. To refute that misconception, the court should hear directly from victims of cybercrime at sentencing. If the trial allowed only some of the victims of a defendant's crimes to testify, the prosecution can supply letters or other statements from additional victims identified during the investigation to aid the court in sentencing.

18.9   APPEALS AND POST-CONVICTION LITIGATION

Defendants who are convicted at trial almost always appeal their convictions, alleging errors with the trial, evidence, and proof. State and federal laws allow for such appellate review. The prosecution must respond in writing to the defense motions or appeals, offering legal and factual arguments to show that no error occurred that legally requires the conviction to be overturned. A clear and concise record of the trial, the witnesses, exhibits, and proceedings allows the prosecution to refer easily to specific statements or events that support its positions. On the other hand, when the trial proceedings are confusing or ambiguous, the court may have doubts about whether aspects of the trial were handled correctly. As in all facets of the justice system, doubts are usually resolved in favor of the defendant.

Given the complexities of most cybercrime cases, appellate litigation is improved when prosecutors keep consistent written records of the evidence and procedural steps during the litigation.

18.10   CONCLUSION

During criminal litigation, prosecutors use the results of a cybercrime investigation to charge identified defendants with crimes. Throughout the litigation, the investigation is both the underpinning of the case and the source of ongoing information used to both strengthen the prosecution and rebut the defense. Becoming familiar with the stages of criminal litigation and the steps prosecutors must take to build and protect a case, enables investigators to take mindful steps. The investigative process, and the evidence it produces, are scrutinized and tested during litigation. Knowing how an investigation will be used and portrayed in court, including the importance of the prosecutor's closing argument, will help investigators create great prosecution cases throughout the investigation.

19 Civil Litigation

This chapter is for:

- Anyone who might sue, or might be sued, as a result of cybercrime
- Those unfamiliar with the civil litigation process.

19.1 INTRODUCTION

Cybercrimes occur incessantly and, in the aftermath of their damage, parties may contemplate civil lawsuits to obtain a remedy. When potential civil consequences are evaluated, the benefits of a prompt and effective cybercrime investigation are underscored. The evidence identified and preserved by investigators is essential for evaluating and litigating any subsequent civil action.

In this chapter, we provide a brief overview of potential civil lawsuits relating to a cybercrime investigation. We explore reasons for a suit, the basic outline of a suit's progression, and the role of a cybercrime investigation in the litigation's various stages. Each state and the federal system have their own procedures and laws, so this chapter covers the general litigation scenarios that might result following a cybercrime. Civil litigation surrounding cybercrime is on the rise, and the possibility of civil liability is a prominent factor driving changes in cybersecurity and technology.

Civil litigation surrounding cybercrime inherently arises from a criminal event, and so earlier chapters about criminal investigation and litigation serve as a basis for this chapter. As we round out the book, we also highlight comparisons in the civil and criminal litigation outcomes and the impact of a successful cybercrime investigation.

19.2 POTENTIAL LITIGATION SCENARIOS FOLLOWING A CYBERCRIME INVESTIGATION

Consider the scenarios that we covered in Chapters 5 and 9, where the events of a cybercrime might be litigated in a civil court case:

- Civil action to further the investigation or stop cybercrime activity
- Civil action against a cybercriminal for intentional tort
- Civil action under a specific provision of a cybercrime law such as the CFAA
- Civil action against another victim for negligent cybersecurity
- Civil action for breach of contract
- Civil action by regulator for inadequate cybersecurity
- Civil action by criminal prosecutor to freeze and seize assets.

We will outline each of these scenarios briefly.

19.2.1   CIVIL ACTION TO FURTHER THE INVESTIGATION OR STOP CYBERCRIME ACTIVITY

Cybercrime committed; the victim uses a civil lawsuit to issue subpoenas to identify the criminal or achieve preventive action.

In this scenario, someone is victimized by cybercrime but does not know who did it, and a third-party company will not voluntarily provide records that might yield clues to the perpetrator's identity. As we learned in Chapter 9, a civil lawsuit can be filed against "John Doe", an unidentified person known only by certain online identifiers, for the intentional torts comprising the cybercrime. By initiating such a lawsuit, the complainant can ask the court to issue subpoenas compelling third parties to produce needed records. For example, if threatening messages are being sent using social media or email, a John Doe lawsuit could be filed for an intentional tort (like infliction of emotional distress). The court then could issue a subpoena to the social media company or email provider for records that might yield clues about the harasser's identity.

There are other records maintained by third parties that might be helpful to identify the John Doe defendant, including IP address records, financial account or transaction records, and travel records.

Sometimes, a lawsuit against an unidentified defendant may involve actions to thwart ongoing cybercrimes being committed by that defendant. These actions might include court orders to seize domain names or servers, or requiring the cybercriminal and his preferred services to cease their activities. As we discussed in Chapter 9, Microsoft has pursued many lawsuits of this type, bringing the "John Doe" lawsuit to a new level by obtaining court orders to seize domains, disrupt botnets, and stop phishing activity.

19.2.2   CIVIL ACTION AGAINST CYBERCRIMINAL FOR INTENTIONAL TORT

Cybercrime committed; victim identifies the cybercriminal and sues that person for damages (intentional tort).

Here, investigation has revealed the identity of the person who intentionally committed the cybercrime, and the victim files a lawsuit against that person. Perhaps a rogue employee or business partner, a crooked civil investigator, or even a nation-state conducted an unauthorized intrusion into a computer system, broke into an email account, or otherwise illegally accessed a person's or company's systems. The victim could sue the criminal using causes of action for intentional torts under state or federal cybercrime laws like theft or trespass.

For example, in March 2019, the car company Tesla sued one of its former engineers for allegedly stealing the source code for the company's "Autopilot" self-driving car systems. The engineer brought the code with him to his new job at a rival Chinese car company. The suit alleges intentional torts for theft of trade secrets under federal and state laws, as well as a claim for breach of contract.[1]

19.2.3   CIVIL ACTION AGAINST CYBERCRIMINAL UNDER A CYBERCRIME STATUTORY CAUSE OF ACTION

Cybercrime committed; victim identifies the cybercriminal and sues that person under federal or state cybercrime statutes.

---

[1] *Tesla, Inc. v Guangzhi Cao*, Case 3:19-cv-01463-VC, N.D.CA (Mar. 2019), www.courtlistener.com/recap/gov. uscourts.cand.339740/gov.uscourts.cand.339740.1.0_1.pdf.

In this situation, a cybercrime victim sues the criminal under the provisions of a federal or state cybercrime statute. These civil causes of action give victims a method to recover losses resulting from specific cybercrimes, or to block ongoing cybercrime activity.

The Computer Fraud and Abuse Act (CFAA), for example, allows a victim to sue for an unauthorized computer or network intrusion. The CFAA's civil causes of actions have been used by employers to sue former employees who allegedly stole company data or damaged company computers. Many states have similar civil provisions, as well as causes of action to block the dissemination of malware, spam, and other harmful cyber actions.

19.2.4   CIVIL ACTION AGAINST ANOTHER VICTIM FOR NEGLIGENT CYBERSECURITY

Cybercriminal commits a cybercrime through or using Victim 1's systems; Victim 2 is also harmed and sues Victim 1 for negligence.

This chain of events is a likely scenario for a civil lawsuit. A cybercrime occurs through some compromise of Victim 1's network or data, leading to harm to Victim 2. Victim 2 sues Victim 1, alleging that Victim 1's cybersecurity negligence allowed the third-party cybercriminal to commit the crime.

For example, imagine Victim 1 is a company that stores the personal information of millions of customers. Victim 1's database is breached by unknown cybercriminals, resulting in the exposure of all of its customers' names, birth dates, social security numbers, and other identifiers. Some of the customers whose information was exposed band together and sue Victim 1, alleging negligent information security, violation of information security laws or regulations, and breach of contract for violation of the company's privacy rules.

In another instance, imagine Victim 1 is an attorney whose email account is compromised by a cybercriminal. The criminal reviews all the information within Victim 1's emails and then uses the email account to contact Victim 2 (a client), telling Victim 2 to wire a payment to an account controlled by a criminal associate. Victim 2, believing the email to be a legitimate communication from his attorney, wires the money as directed and it is stolen and unrecoverable. Victim 2 sues Victim 1, alleging that Victim 1's negligent cybersecurity allowed the cybercriminals to commit the crime.

In each of these circumstances, the facts of how the cybercrime occurred may be relevant to establish what security was in place and whether it was reasonable.

19.2.5   CIVIL ACTION FOR BREACH OF CONTRACT

Victim and Company have a contract (perhaps to provide technology services or to insure for certain harms). A cybercrime occurs, and Victim sues Company for breach of that contract.

Many technology services are available through contracts, perhaps between two businesses, or between a business and individual users. IT systems, cloud systems, email services, computer device maintenance, data entry and analysis, and security services are some of the common technologies that generally operate by creating contracts between businesses. These contracts typically include promises by the company to maintain certain levels of service and security. If a cybercrime occurs, services may be interrupted, data may be compromised and stolen, and customers may face financial loss (as well as a host of indirect consequences). The victims will look to the contract to see what promises were made about availability and security and examine whether there was a breach of the contractual terms.

For example, suppose Company A contracts to obtain cloud computing and storage services from Company B. An incident occurs resulting in a failure of these services for nearly a week, which causes Company A to lose millions of dollars. Company A blames Company B. Company

B claims that the fault lies with Company A, or that the contract does not provide for such damages.

Insurance policies are another form of contract and may lead to similar lawsuits, as we discussed in Chapter 9. The policy and the policy application must be examined closely for language that might include or exclude coverage of certain costs relating to the cybercrime. The facts revealed through the investigation may determine any litigated coverage issues by showing how the cybercrime occurred and whether certain security measures were in place.

19.2.6 CIVIL OR REGULATORY ACTION BY GOVERNMENT FOR INADEQUATE CYBERSECURITY

Company A is the victim of a data breach and reports it to the authorities (including regulators) as required. Law enforcement investigates the crime and the regulators investigate the level of security. The regulators ultimately allege that Company A had inadequate cybersecurity in violation of a regulation, and the dispute ends up being litigated in the regulatory forum or a civil court.

Businesses and organizations face increasing duties regarding information security and privacy under a growing range of regulations and laws at both the federal and state levels (discussed previously in Chapter 9). Organizations increasingly are required to report a data breach or other cybercrime, and then government regulatory-type agencies (State Attorney General, financial, or health regulators) may examine whether better security was required and might have prevented the incident, as well as whether it was detected and reported promptly. Critical factual issues may develop around how the cybercrime happened and whether the organization's security measures were reasonable, notwithstanding that they were ultimately circumvented.

Regulators and similar agencies may come to the conclusion that the organization was deficient in their cybersecurity, detection, reporting, notification, or investigation. They may believe that penalties and improvement are required. This determination may commence a process of negotiations between the agency and the entity to arrive at a mutually agreeable settlement. If these negotiations are not successful, a regulatory action or civil suit may be the result. All of these negotiations and potential actions may be informed by the findings of the entity's own investigation.

19.2.7 CIVIL ACTION BY CRIMINAL PROSECUTOR TO FREEZE AND SEIZE ASSETS

Criminal prosecutor brings a civil asset forfeiture action that is related to a criminal action.

We have learned in earlier chapters that prosecutors can seek to freeze or seize funds and assets that evidence indicates are the proceeds of criminal conduct. In some jurisdictions, the forfeiture portion of the case can be done within the same proceeding as the criminal case. In others, prosecutors must initiate a separate civil forfeiture case in the appropriate civil court. The purpose of these civil actions is to prevent the defendant from profiting from his or her crimes and they are especially important when criminal remedies alone cannot stop criminals from hiding or using illegally gained assets.

19.3 GOALS AND EXPECTATIONS

Before a party embarks upon any of the civil suits outlined above, it should take a hard, honest look at its litigation goals, the likely costs, and the potential outcomes.

19.3.1 GOVERNMENT AGENCIES

For government agencies, the decision to proceed with a lawsuit ideally reflects the objective enforcement of relevant laws, regulations, and agency policies and priorities. When government lawyers charged with bringing these cases consider whether to move forward with litigation or to settle, the primary goal is usually to ensure organizations are complying with laws and rules designed to protect the public. In the context of asset forfeiture procedures, the government's objective is to find and freeze criminal profits so that cybercriminals do not gain from their bad acts. Civil litigation by the government also is focused on careful allocation of scarce resources to achieve these goals.

19.3.2 PRIVATE LITIGANTS

With private entities and individuals, the calculus is quite different. The goals of private parties considering civil litigation over a cybercrime need not serve the public interest, but rather their own interests. These goals might include:

- Recovering compensation for financial damages (cybercrime-related losses or expenditures)
- Punitive measures (to punish another party for wrongful personal or business practices)
- Containment (to stop another party from engaging in harmful activity)
- Rehabilitating reputation (to publicly improve an entity's reputation after damage by another party's actions).

Organizations and individuals must weigh certain factors differently than government litigants.

Financial cost is a significant factor for a private party contemplating legal action, as the party may already have lost significant money from the cybercrime and civil litigation is expensive. The costs of a civil lawsuit usually include attorney's fees, court costs, payments to investigators and expert witnesses, as well as the costs associated with eDiscovery. In the cybercrime context, a potentially complex cybercrime investigation may add to the expenses. If a party is considering a lawsuit to recover money damages from another party, it must evaluate how much can be recovered, the chances of getting this recovery, and how much time and expense might be required in the process.

The human decision-making process is also an important factor when private parties consider a civil suit. Where government attorneys work on behalf of the public and make decisions based on legal and policy guidelines, a private party's choice to sue may be influenced more by human motivations, emotions, and individual personalities. A private attorney advises an organization or individual and recommends potential courses of action, but the ultimate decision is made by the client. Sometimes the decision is based on business, financial, and legal considerations, but sometimes it is based upon their human reaction to the situation at hand. An emotional decision may not be as sound as a dispassionate evaluation of the potential costs, benefits, risks, and potential outcomes.

Cybercrime investigations by private sector parties play a crucial role in assessing the viability of a civil suit. The evidence and conclusions derived from the investigation about the nature of the cybercrime, the methods used to bypass security measures, the harm caused, and criminal profits realized will serve as the primary basis for any civil action.

19.4 EXPERTS

Expert analysis and testimony are needed in many civil cases and are important elements of civil cybercrime litigation. Experts are able to summarize evidence and offer opinions about the cause of a cybercrime, information security measures, and damages.[2] Thus, in civil cases, experts can opine upon matters that are very close to the ultimate issues that will be decided by a jury.

Expert assistance may be needed before the litigation phase. For example, digital forensics or network security experts may participate in a cybercrime investigation from its initial stages, as a component of a private entity's cybercrime incident response plan. Experts who are involved in the investigation of the incident, and the information they uncover, may become key sources of evidence if litigation eventually is undertaken.

Once litigation has begun (or is contemplated), it is common practice for each side to retain experts who can review their own and the other party's evidence and form opinions. Of course, each side ultimately hires experts whose opinions support their side's position. If an expert who is hired to serve as a litigation witness appears in court, he or she must be approved by the judge as having the necessary qualifications to provide expert testimony on the subject in question. Expert witnesses, therefore, typically have a career background that establishes their expertise, including education, training, experience in the pertinent field, specialized knowledge regarding the topic in question, published writings, and a history of speaking engagements. Past approval as an expert in other courts is another factor a court will consider when qualifying an expert in subsequent proceedings.

19.5   SETTLEMENT NEGOTIATIONS

Settlement negotiations are an important method of resolving civil claims either before a lawsuit is filed, before trial, and even after a trial is completed.[3] Both parties to a civil suit are continually evaluating their positions and the potential of resolving it. Even when the case proceeds to trial and verdict, there are post-verdict motions and appeals that can take years, and the parties may still enter into a settlement even after a jury has heard the case.

Given that most cases eventually settle, an early settlement can save time, expense, and stress. A good cybercrime investigation can yield facts that help both sides evaluate the relative strengths and weaknesses of their cases and arrive at an appropriate settlement. Strong evidence for one party's position that clearly will be admissible in court creates leverage in the negotiating process, whereas evidence gleaned from questionable sources that cannot be authenticated will be less persuasive.

19.6   THE CIVIL LAWSUIT AND THE ROLE OF THE INVESTIGATION

In Chapter 5, we reviewed the steps of the civil litigation process, from pre-litigation investigation through post-trial appeals. As we have discussed already, the investigation performed by private sector parties or government agencies is a significant factor in the pre-litigation stages, as the parties determine whether to bring a civil action, what type of expert assistance will be needed, and whether to settle.

---

[2] Prosecutors in criminal cases have a more ready supply of witnesses who perform certain tasks as part of their daily duties and are available to testify about a whole host of specialized matters, including computer forensics, ballistics, DNA, and more. Sometimes these specialized witnesses are qualified as experts, sometimes not. Occasionally, prosecutors might need to hire an outside expert, but this approach is rare. In civil litigation, hiring an expert is much more common by both sides.

[3] Consider that in a criminal case the defendant retains the final choice of whether to plead guilty or proceed to trial, and that is a very personal decision with important personal consequences. In civil cases, the decision may have personal elements, but more heavily reflects financial considerations and a responsibility to the affected organization, its employees, shareholders, customers, and investors.

Now we will cover the phases of a civil lawsuit. If litigation actually begins, the role of the investigation can be even more significant.

- *Analyzing which court should hear the case: jurisdiction and venue.* With civil lawsuits, the plaintiff must evaluate which courts have jurisdiction over the case and might be the proper venue. A court must have "subject matter" jurisdiction over the dispute in question and "personal" jurisdiction over the defendants. Subject matter jurisdiction refers to the type of cases a court has authority to adjudicate, and many court systems are organized based on subject matter jurisdiction (civil, criminal, bankruptcy, probate, etc.). Personal jurisdiction typically is found in the state where the defendant resides, does business, or has some minimum contacts, and requires the defendant to be personally served with the summons and complaint. Venue refers to the court where the case will be heard, usually in a district that has a geographical connection to the parties or the disputed events. Both federal and state systems have laws and procedures for determining the proper jurisdiction and venue for a case. In a cybercrime-related suit, information from the investigation may help determine which courts have jurisdiction and venue by identifying responsible parties and locations where criminal events occurred.
- *Commencing the lawsuit: the complaint.* A lawsuit begins when a plaintiff files a civil complaint with the court and serves the defendant with a copy along with a summons to appear. The cybercrime-related claims the plaintiff chooses to outline in the complaint – whether for intentional torts, negligence, cybercrime causes of action, breach of contract, government regulatory sanctions or asset forfeiture – are dependent upon the information developed by a thorough cybercrime investigation.
- *Motion to dismiss.* The civil defendant usually responds to the summons and complaint with a motion to dismiss some or all of the plaintiff's claims, alleging they are legally or factually insufficient in some manner, or are legally barred. This motion rests on the defendant's cybercrime investigation, which may have revealed facts that negate the plaintiff's claims or frame the issue in a different light (for example, suggesting that another party's negligence was the cause of a data compromise). The plaintiff responds to the motion to dismiss, asserting facts and law as to why the causes of action are proper. The factual counterargument will rely on the plaintiff's investigative and expert findings.
- *Answer to the complaint.* The defendant must answer the complaint, admitting or denying each allegation made by the plaintiff. Though the answer is filed in response to the complaint, the deadline for the answer can be postponed pending decision on a motion to dismiss (since a dismissal eliminates the need to answer). The answer will contain factual counterarguments to the complaint that rely on the evidence gathered from any investigation conducted by the defendant.
- *Counterclaims, crossclaims, and joinder.* The defendant also may bring a counterclaim against the plaintiff (containing allegations about the plaintiff's civil wrongdoing), may bring a crossclaim against another defendant who is already part of the lawsuit, and may seek to join (implead) a third party as a new defendant in the case. For example, if Party 1 sues Party 2 for negligence over a data breach, and Party 2 believes its security software vendor was really the negligent actor, Party 2 might implead the software vendor (Party 3) as a new defendant.
- *Discovery (and E-Discovery).* If any of the causes of action survive a motion to dismiss, the case proceeds to the discovery phase, where each side demands documents, evidence, and deposition testimony from the other party (and from third parties). The discovery process is time consuming and expensive for each side, involving litigation over what should be disclosed and review of materials. The importance of systematically gathering, organizing, and storing evidence throughout

the investigative process is highlighted in this phase, as records and data evidence must be turned over. Expert analysis and opinions also are disclosed during discovery. In addition, legal privileges may be litigated. If an organization conducted its cybercrime investigation under the supervision of an attorney, attorney–client privilege or attorney work–product doctrine may be implicated. Whatever disclosure is had may expose the strengths and weaknesses of the investigation.

*   *Motion for summary judgment.* After discovery is completed, the parties may move for summary judgment on some or all counts, arguing there is no reasonable issue of fact that requires a jury to decide the matter. In other words, the judge can decide some or all of the issues before trial, using the pleadings, written motions, discovery, and sometimes a court hearing. The facts on which the court decides summary judgment may emanate directly from the parties' cybercrime investigations. A summary judgment decision dismissing a cause of action, however, may not end the case as to that claim, as a party might appeal the judge's decision.

*   *Trial.* In a civil trial the plaintiff generally has to prove its claims by a preponderance of evidence. Under this legal standard, the evidence must show there is over 50% chance the plaintiff's claims are true. If the jury (or judge in a judge-only trial) finds against a defendant, it may next decide the amount of damages caused to the plaintiff and the relative degree of fault of the defendant. Investigators and experts often will testify in a civil case involving cybercrime to explain the events and evidence to the jury. Presentation of evidence regarding the cybercrime and cybersecurity measures can be aided by summary exhibits that a jury of laypeople can understand. Thoughtful preparation from the beginning of an investigation culminates at the trial, where a clear chain of evidence can help the jury follow complicated technical facts and distinguish between dueling expert opinions.

*   *Post-trial activities, motions, and appeals.* Sometimes, additional damages need to be calculated after a trial verdict. If the trial verdict requires a party to pay damages, the Judge will assess the facts and issue a judgment and order payment of a specified amount. Often the amount of damages will be based upon investigative evidence showing the extent of a cybercrime, the harm it caused and the responsibility of the parties. A losing party may ask the court to set aside the verdict and order a new trial. It also might appeal to a higher court, alleging the verdict or damages judgment is inconsistent with the law or evidence, or that there were trial errors warranting a new trial. As always, the initial investigation forms the foundation for all litigation that follows.

19.7   ARBITRATION

Private parties also may consider arbitration to settle their dispute. Arbitration is a process where two sides agree (either by contract before a dispute arises, or after the dispute arises) to settle their disagreement not in a public court, but in a non-judicial proceeding. Arbitration is a confidential forum, with expedited discovery and a quasi-litigation process overseen by a neutral arbitrator, who rules on discovery matters and the ultimate issues of fact and damages. Arbitration is faster and less costly than litigation in the courts, and the dispute is kept private. For companies concerned about their reputations and negative exposure about a cybercrime incident, as well as litigation costs, arbitration is a litigation alternative to consider.

19.8 CONCLUSION

This chapter offered a brief overview of the civil litigation process for claims arising from cybercrime incidents, highlighting the role of a cybercrime investigation in the various litigation stages. The results of private sector investigations may become the lynchpin in determining whether to bring a lawsuit, reach a settlement, or walk away from the matter. These decisions are difficult and may depend upon the goals of the organization and the potential costs of litigation. The evidence produced during the investigation will serve to support the civil litigation at all stages, and the strength and organization of the evidence will significantly affect the likelihood of prevailing in court.

20 Conclusion

By now, we all have an appreciation for the broad impact of cybercrime, how it touches individuals, organizations, and governments everywhere, from small, local incidents all the way to international relations and conflict.

This reality points to a simple fact: we need more investigators who know how to investigate cybercrime and are ready, willing, and able to do it. As we have shown throughout this book, investigators of all backgrounds can learn how to conduct an effective cybercrime investigation. If nothing else, we hope this book has helped more people understand cybercrime's broad implications, and inspired more people in every sector to take on these cases.

We want to leave you with a few thoughts about what all of us are capable of doing to prevent and stop cybercrime.

We all can and must do more to secure ourselves from cybercrime as individuals and organizations. But we also must recognize that security alone will not stop the crushing cybercrime onslaught we face.

We all can and must get better at detecting, responding to, and investigating cybercrime, and reporting incidents to law enforcement and regulators.

All sectors can and must investigate cybercrime, separately and collaboratively, to ensure that malicious actors see justice and there is sufficient deterrence. We should assist government cybercrime investigations, remembering that only they have the ability to pursue justice on the public's behalf.

For *regulators* of all types, we *can and must* ensure that forthright reporting and investigation of cybercrime is encouraged and not unduly punished. The specter of reputational damage, regulatory action, and lawsuits can be negative influences on private sector organizations as they detect and investigate cybercrime, and yet we need them to do the right thing.

At all levels of *law enforcement*, cybercrimes *can and must* be investigated, because those not investigated never will be solved. To that end:

- Make it easier for cybercrime victims to report cybercrime
- Try to investigate *every* cybercrime, at least to some degree
- Investigate and prosecute identity theft. Identity thieves fuel cybercrime and much of the demand for stolen data, and these cases need resources
- Build cases, people, teams, and intelligence. Quick cases can be good, but looking to develop investigations and experience will benefit the agency and community two, five, and ten years out
- Share and collaborate to conserve precious law enforcement resources.

At our *highest levels of federal government*, we *can and must* focus domestic and international priorities and resources to combat cybercrime. We must motivate other nations to behave appropriately, so they refrain from, deter, and investigate malicious conduct that occurs within their own borders.

While this book is comprehensive and covers enormous ground, there is so much more to be said. Cybercrime will evolve, but the methods of good investigations will remain true as laid out here. With these foundations and the actions of competent, diligent, professional, and ethical investigators, we can wage the battle against cybercrime.

We created a website to include some additional resources at CybercrimeInvestigations Book.com. Please visit us there, and feel free to drop us a line about your experiences and any suggestions for improving the book in its next edition.

Index